Dancefloor-Driven Literature

Dancefloor-Driven Literature

The Rave Scene in Fiction

Simon A. Morrison

BLOOMSBURY ACADEMIC
NEW YORK • LONDON • OXFORD • NEW DELHI • SYDNEY

BLOOMSBURY ACADEMIC
Bloomsbury Publishing Inc
1385 Broadway, New York, NY 10018, USA
50 Bedford Square, London, WC1B 3DP, UK
29 Earlsfort Terrace, Dublin 2, Ireland

BLOOMSBURY, BLOOMSBURY ACADEMIC and the Diana logo are trademarks of
Bloomsbury Publishing Plc

First published in the United States of America 2020
This paperback edition published in 2022

Copyright © Simon A. Morrison, 2020

For legal purposes the Permissions on p. x constitute an extension of this
copyright page.

Cover design: Louise Dugdale
Cover image © Rachel McHaffie

All rights reserved. No part of this publication may be reproduced or transmitted
in any form or by any means, electronic or mechanical, including photocopying,
recording, or any information storage or retrieval system, without prior
permission in writing from the publishers.

Bloomsbury Publishing Inc does not have any control over, or responsibility for, any
third-party websites referred to or in this book. All internet addresses given in this
book were correct at the time of going to press. The author and publisher regret any
inconvenience caused if addresses have changed or sites have ceased to exist,
but can accept no responsibility for any such changes.

Whilst every effort has been made to locate copyright holders the publishers
would be grateful to hear from any person(s) not here acknowledged.

Library of Congress Cataloging-in-Publication Data
Names: Morrison, Simon Alexander, 1964- author.
Title: Dancefloor-driven literature: the rave scene in fiction / Simon A. Morrison.
Description: New York: Bloomsbury Academic, 2020. | Includes
bibliographical references and index. | Summary: "Considers club culture
via the prism of the fictions written about the subculture -
interrogating why, and how, authors write about electronic music
as text"– Provided by publisher.
Identifiers: LCCN 2019050911 | ISBN 9781501357671 (hardback) |
ISBN 9781501357688 (epub) | ISBN 9781501357695 (pdf)
Subjects: LCSH: Music in literature. | Electronic dance music in literature. |
Rave culture in literature. | English fiction–20th century–History and criticism. |
English fiction–21st century–History and criticism. Classification:
LCC PR888.M87 M67 2020 | DDC 823/.91409357–dc23
LC record available at https://lccn.loc.gov/2019050911

ISBN: HB: 978-1-5013-5767-1
      PB: 978-1-5013-8992-4
   ePDF: 978-1-5013-5769-5
  eBook: 978-1-5013-5768-8

Typeset by Deanta Global Publishing Services, Chennai, India

To find out more about our authors and books visit www.bloomsbury.com and
sign up for our newsletters.

All art constantly aspires towards the condition of music.
                          Walter Pater, 'The School of Giorgione', 1877

Contents

List of figures		viii
Preface		ix
Permissions		x
Acknowledgements		xi
1	Introduction: Writing the beat	1
2	Sub- versus supraterranean cultures	11
3	Revealing the scene: The global roots of subterranean club cultures	19
4	Re/presentations of EDMC in popular culture media	39
5	Defining Dancefloor-Driven Literature	61
6	Case study one: The figurative use of music in the work of Irvine Welsh	79
7	Case study two: Musical mechanics in the fiction of Jeff Noon	107
8	Case study three: Literary diegesis in the writing of Nicholas Blincoe	133
9	Conclusion: Towards subterranean systems theory	159
Glossary of terms and theories		175
Notes		181
Bibliography		222
Select EDMC discography		233
Select EDMC filmography		234
Appendix I: A Catalogue of Dancefloor-Driven Literature		235
Index		237

Figures

4.1 Marketing poster for *Ecstasy*, dir. Lux (Canada: Dolce Cielo, 2011) — 48
4.2 Marketing poster for *Irvine Welsh's Ecstasy*, dir. Rob Heydon (Canada: Silver Reel, 2012) — 49
5.1 Cover of Sarah Champion (ed.), *Disco Biscuits: New Fiction from the Chemical Generation* (London: Sceptre, 1997) — 64
5.2 The proposed twenty-fifth anniversary edition of Trevor Miller's *Trip City*. In this iteration, A Guy Called Gerald's soundtrack would be encoded onto a USB drive — 71
6.1 Cover of Irvine Welsh, *Ecstasy* (London: Jonathan Cape, 1996) — 91
7.1 Front covers of Jeff Noon, *Needle in the Groove* (London: Black Swan, 2001) and Jeff Noon and David Toop, *Needle in the Groove* (Sulphur Records, 2000) — 119
8.1 Front cover of Nicholas Blincoe, *Manchester Slingback* (London: Pan, 1998), with Blincoe featured on the cover — 154
8.2 Back cover of Nicholas Blincoe, *Manchester Slingback* (London: Pan, 1998), featuring Blincoe as model — 155

Preface

This book uses the 'rave' subculture as a route into an analysis of literary representations of a music scene. Almost as soon as this sonic subterranean culture took hold – during the Second Summer of Love in 1988 – and the sociopolitical impact of the nascent rave scene became clear, it quickly appeared on the radar of journalists, filmmakers and authors, all keen to use society's cultural preoccupations as source material for their output.

By first defining, and then expanding, the neologism re/presentation, this book questions why such cultural artefacts appear – secondary representations that orbit the culture itself – and what function they may serve. Further focusing on the medium of literature, the book then defines the genre of Dancefloor-Driven Literature – stories born of the dancefloor – using new primary input from three key case study authors to analyse three separate ways writers might draw on the pulse of electronic music in their fiction, interrogating that very particular intermedial intersection between the sonic and the linguistic. The book progresses to explore how such authors write about something so subterranean as the nightclub scene, considers how they write lucidly and fluidly about the rigid, metronomic beat of electronic music, and analyses what specifically literary techniques they deploy to accurately recount in fixed symbols the drifting, hallucinatory effects of a drug experience.

The book describes two key functions such a literature might serve: first, in terms of its enculturative potential within the contemporary society into which it is published and then, almost thirty years since the Second Summer of Love, the importance this collection of texts might have, archivally. Finally, the book concludes by proposing a theory by which all sonic subterranean cultures might be decoded; not through the music, but through these secondary literary artefacts. It is there that stories of that scene are locked, told to a silent beat.

Permissions

Aspects of this book have previously appeared in different forms in the following chapters and articles by the author: 'Dancefloor-Driven Literature: Subcultural Big Bangs and a New Center for the Aesthetic Universe', *Popular Music*, Volume 36.1 (The Critical Imperative), January 2017, 43–54; '"Surely People Who Go Clubbing Don't Read": Dispatches from the Dancefloor and Clubland in Print' in the @IASPM Journal, ed. C. Jacke, M. James & Ed Montano, 4.2, 2014; '"Clubs Aren't like that": Discos, Deviance and Diegetics in Club Culture Cinema', *Dancecult: Journal of Electronic Dance Music* Culture 4.2 (2012), 48–66; and 'DJ-Driven Literature: A Linguistic Remix', in Bernardo Alexander Attias, Anna Gavanas and Hillegonda C. Rietveld eds., *DJ Culture in the Mix: Power, Technology and Social Change in Electronic Dance Music* (London: Bloomsbury, 2013), pp. 219–314. The author extends thanks to those publishers who have allowed the author to rework and republish his work in this new form.

Thanks also go to the following writers and publishers for kindly granting permission to quote from both their new interviews with the author of this book and the short stories and novels used substantially in this analysis, centrally Trevor Miller, Sarah Champion, Irvine Welsh, Jeff Noon and Nicholas Blincoe.

From *Glue* by *Irvine Welsh.*, Published by *Jonathan Cape.*, Reprinted by permission of The Random House Group Limited. © 2001

From *Ecstasy* by *Irvine Welsh.*, Published by *Jonathan Cape.*, Reprinted by permission of The Random House Group Limited. © 1996

Thanks also to those who granted permission to reproduce images within this book, in order: Silver Reel, Dolce Cielo, Trevor Miller, Jonathan Cape, Black Swan/Penguin and Pan.

From *Ecstasy* by *Irvine Welsh* published by *Jonathan Cape.* Reproduced by permission of The Random House Group Ltd/. © 1996

Whilst every effort has been made to locate copyright holders, the publishers would be grateful to hear from any person(s) not here acknowledged, in order that acknowledgements might be included in future editions.

Acknowledgements

Many people have been kind enough to contribute their time and thoughts during the eight-year process of putting this book together. These include Rob Heydon and Adam Sinclair from *Irvine Welsh's Ecstasy*; and Elisa King and Nick Hussey from the Lux Ecstasy film. Thanks also to a figure who looms large in EDMC literature, Irvine Welsh, for sharing the bar of Molly Malone's, and then the back of a Glasgow cab. Thank you to the other case study authors, Jeff Noon and Nicholas Blincoe, for their generosity with their time. Thanks to Dr Adam Gargani for conversations around relevance theory and for inviting me to meet his family, for the story that would become my film screenplay *Zayna*. Thanks to Trafford Parsons, life artist, and to Professor Hillegonda Rietveld for the chance to write for her a Bloomsbury book and for her ongoing friendship and exchanges around the notion of re/presentation. Thanks go to Sarah Champion for reconnecting after all these years, and to friends from the dancefloor such as Graeme Park for talking in less frenetic circumstances than usual. I would also like to extend my appreciation to all my old friends and colleagues from the dance music media for contributions to Chapter 3. Thanks to Dr Mark Duffett, colleague and reader at the University of Chester for his very helpful input, as well as to other colleagues within the Department of Media at Chester, a university kind enough to offer me a home. I would also like to thank Dr Nikolina Nedeljkov for the many helpful conversations during a research trip to New York and during a visit to the British Library, and Professor Martin James, for his continued support.

For financial assistance in the trips that allowed me to visit New York, Chicago and Detroit for invaluable research that fed into Chapter 2, I would like to thank the University of Chester. For her financial assistance, and for everything else I owe beyond pounds and pence, I would like to thank my mother, who always bankrolled my studies. My family and friends have been endlessly supportive through the years in which I have been researching, and I would like to say a special thank you to the Ravers of Revesby, and to Daisy Cresswell, to whom this book is dedicated.

I would also like to end by thanking Professor Michael Allis and Dr Simon Warner. I thank the former for helping me get the initial manuscript over the finishing line and the latter for his valuable input in the early developmental years before his own retirement and for breaking the first rule of the supervisor/supervisee relationship and becoming a good and valued friend. I would like to say thank you to the creatives still committed to film and literary evocations of EDMC, and finally to those on the dancefloor who continue to make the scene such a fertile source of characters and stories.

This book, therefore, is also dedicated to the dancers from the dance.

1

Introduction

Writing the beat

A nightclub is a space beyond a liminal red rope – the threshold that guards the quotidian from the varied sonic and chemical pleasures contained within – for those allowed to step across, to transgress. Once within, the dancefloor is a further, sacred hermetic interiority. On the dancefloor, the combination of technological inputs and impulses on the human body creates a beatific, kinetic response: movement, pleasure, celebration. In his novel *Dancer from the Dance*, Andrew Holleran describes a 1970s incarnation of a New York dancefloor as 'That blonde rectangle of polished wood that had seemed to be at one point the aesthetic center of the universe',[1] while theorist Hakim Bey raises the notion of the 'Temporary Autonomous Zone',[2] a space beyond formal structures of control. A dancefloor might be considered such a temporary autonomous zone: both mutable and moveable, whether beach, field or burnt-out, broken-into warehouse. It may well be, in fact, the aesthetic centre of the universe.

This book will investigate the role of the nightclub as locus, but specifically, and uniquely, as a birthplace of stories; an entire genre of literature that I suggest is born of its multiple dancefloors. It will interrogate the way music is used within the resulting literary texts and also, taken together, will analyse what role such texts might have, in terms of both the society in which they were published and as an archive moving forwards. Several key studies have concerned themselves with the many decades of Electronic Dance Music Culture (hitherto EDMC) and the implications of, in particular, the reconstitution of EDMC as the 'rave' scene of the UK in the late 1980s.[3] However, there has been little consideration of the fiction that was also published at the time, which sought to tell the stories of this scene. This book therefore addresses that lacuna in EDMC scholarship by considering club culture – not directly but rather obliquely – via the secondary literature that reports upon it.

This introductory chapter identifies the central questions that drive the book, and outlines some of the key concepts and approaches integrated into its research, signposting some of the theories that will be used to unpack Dancefloor-Driven Literature, before the book ultimately builds towards proposing a new theoretical approach to decoding music-based scenes. It will also differentiate between some perhaps confusing and overlapping terms involving context (club scene, rave scene and EDMC, for instance), as well as text (Chemical Generation literature, club culture literature and what will be defined in this book as *Dancefloor-Driven Literature*).[4] The book is designed to be of use to both the cognoscent subcultural explorer and the newly interested, taking their first step onto this literary dancefloor. For the latter, the Glossary at the back of the book may help with an understanding of some of the terminology used in the book, and its lexicon of EDMC and intermedial scholarship, while it remains my intention to also hold the reader's hand, should they wish, and guide them into this magical and musical subterranean world.

Once upon a time on the dancefloor

The aim of this book is to question, and then ultimately answer, whether it is possible to understand a music-based culture by virtue of its specifically literary mediation. A number of supplementary lines of enquiry arise immediately from this central question: How might we characterize the different ways in which authors use music within electronic dance music-based fiction? Within this literature, what role does the sonic play in the sphere of the linguistic? Is it indeed possible to define an entire genre of Dancefloor-Driven Literature, and how might this be situated in relation to the literary outputs of other music-oriented cultural scenes, such as the Beat Generation of the 1950s and the 1960s counterculture? While these questions will all be addressed, they all orbit around one central conceit: that very precise, intermedial intersection of the musical and the literary as regards the UK club scene, principally of Manchester, in the late 1980s and 1990s.

To begin to outline the musical and literary territory covered in this book, I need first to establish my own motivation in considering a factual scene through its fictions. As I will detail here, the trajectory of my interest builds from that of a participant, initially in clubs of Manchester in the late 1980s and 1990s, then as a music journalist covering the global club scene and then – once it became apparent to everyone that I was too old to continue in that endeavour – as a popular music academic, based at the University of Chester. I wrote about clubs almost as soon as I went to clubs, always with an interest in what makes them tick (as though nightclubs were somehow clockwork, and could be deconstructed in order to be inspected, and reassembled). Further, I was intrigued in how to explain – whether as journalist, author or academic – my perception, and reaction, in words, and that interest extends to how, and why, other authors choose to write about, or locate their short stories in, nightclubs. In short, my career marks the slow retreat from Holleran's aesthetic centre of the dancefloor, as the progress of time inevitably takes the 'dancer from the dance', further from their youth and back towards the liminal periphery of the dancefloor, from where one can observe, and think, at a perhaps safer distance.

We are now far enough from the white heat of the initial big bang of this aesthetic universe for these stars to have cooled, enough to be touched, handled, explored. Now that I am also no longer at the epicentre of the dancefloor, my interest is less in describing the action and more in theorizing the very nature of the nightclub; in how you might make more objective sense of this scene, now that the subjectivity born of proximity has diminished. While there is much to mourn about the loss of youth, there is also much to celebrate in having the space, and time, to look back through a portal formed of pages, foregrounding the primacy of new research and interviews with key authors, to attempt to finally understand how you bring to life a horizontal dancefloor on a vertical cinema screen, or in the flat, silent, pages of a book.

Motivation

This musico-cultural terrain is marked out – largely in Chapter 3 – in order to establish the ethnographic context by which I found myself confronting the cultural phenomenon of the dancefloor head on, in any number of nightclubs around the world. The 'Second Summer of Love' of 1988 formed a cultural tsunami of effects that broke over the UK.[5] I was one of those many young people willingly taken in its wake. Finding myself in a position to bring an academic training in literature to reporting on this scene and its pulsing electronic soundtrack, I was able to forge a living by working within television, radio and the print media, given the keys to explore this electronic kingdom. As a music journalist for publications including *Muzik* and *Mixmag* and broadcasters including *Rapture TV*, *Club-A-Vision* and *Kiss Radio*, I was granted access to some of the key players in the dance music scene; I was given the chance to explore club culture as far afield as Beijing and Brazil; Moscow and Marrakech as well as two summers living in Ibiza, editing a magazine for London superclub the Ministry of Sound. All of this enabled invaluable experience and contacts that can now be utilized within this book in what will be defined as *retro-participant observation*.

Principally, my embedded reports from these subcultural trenches took the form of two long-running columns for the international magazine *DJ*. *Dispatches from the Wrong Side* (1998–2006) was an attempt to answer commentator Sarah Champion's claim that 'there should have been some kind of "Gonzo" journalism to capture the spirit but there wasn't',[6] a notion explored in greater depth in Chapter 5. These columns were collected together as the book *Discombobulated*,[7] while a second column, 'Around the World in 80 Clubs' (2006-8), allowed privileged access to the music scene in territories such as Antigua, Kosovo, Indonesia and the United States. *Discombobulated* ended its publishing journey on the shelves of a section of the Waterstones bookstore titled 'Club & Drug Literature'. In itself, the discovery of this tucked-away, almost hidden section of books seemed to provide keys to the subterranean – both access point and point of originality – into a possible new academic area of EDMC discourse that might consider this scene by reference not to the primary presentation of the culture itself, but secondary literary *re/presentations* of that culture, club fiction as cult fiction.[8]

Whether nightclub, rave or discothèque, academics (Thornton 1995, Malbon et al. 1999) describe how these spaces do indeed remain magical, secret places, devoted to the intensity – and perhaps the illusion – of the moment. How, then, do you make objective sense of that vibrant, visceral intoxicatory culture? What literary techniques might authors deploy to accurately recount in fixed symbols the drifting, hallucinatory effects of a drug experience? Are words even able to contain and describe the transformative effects of a rave? In terms of answering these questions, and outlining a methodological approach, this book deploys a blend of largely qualitative, ethnographic methods: participant observation/recollection, articulations derived from historically contingent subcultural approaches, textual analysis via literary techniques, and primary research with original input from key authors. This creates the most robust theoretical framework for decoding this scene, and the very particular issues of divergence that arise when reporting the hyperreal club culture experience in the rather more prosaic pages of a book.

Central to this approach is to focus critical attention in terms of both medium and time period. First, literature has been foregrounded as a re/presentative mechanism (over, for instance, cinema). Second in terms of a time-frame, the focus is for that literature to have been written and published, broadly speaking, between the years 1988 and 2000 – these edit points being the Second Summer of Love, and then the turning of the Millennium. In French language terms the period under examination is not, therefore, fin de siècle, but *fin de millennium*. Third, and finally, this quest for precision of attention also centres not only on the UK but also on the northern city of Manchester, as locus, particularly digging down to its subterranean strata, as many of the narratives investigated in this book are uniquely based in that city, just as many of the authors and editors are also connected to that location.[9]

There are, of course, other methodological approaches one might take when considering the intersection of electronic music culture and its literary fictions. As regards the necessary narrowing of methodology, this book is not intended to be a comprehensive or culturally historic overview of the rave scene, although Chapter 3 will set out that territory, in order to then identify the cultural artefacts that report upon it. I also build from a position that the dancefloor was a political leveller – egalitarian, with little consideration for ethnicity, gender, age or sexuality. This book will therefore not be drawn into these areas of discourse to any extended way, except where these issues impact on the literature under review. Much work has been conducted in this area,[10] and to further engage with the requisite depth of analysis would be detrimental to the focus of a book of this length. This was a scene characterized, certainly for me, not by notions of segregation but rather *miscegenation*, when such prejudices were largely removed by the levelling effect of the dancefloor. Further, I could have also been drawn to examine notions of audience, for instance in terms of readership and broader theories around reception. Theorists such as Claude Lévi-Strauss and Stuart Hall, among others, have argued that literary texts function because of their interest to a participant readership, but equally, for the function of this methodology, these texts must also be seen as a guide to the subterranean underground for non-cognoscent literary voyeurs.[11] Certainly, I want to understand how these literary works were received, in terms of critical, commercial, even academic reception but more fundamental to this book is not the reception but the conception, and production, of the texts. Ultimately, I find that this mediation between these words and the worlds they depict, between text and context, allows for a penetrative analysis that reveals, for instance, how music is referenced within these texts and how music itself is represented on the printed page.

Instead, this methodology has also been almost exclusively, and deliberately, qualitative, drawing upon scholarly approaches from principally literary techniques, such as naturalism and social realism, in order to deconstruct this literature. I am privileged to be able to draw upon my own experiences in clubland – what might be labelled as empirical findings drawn from retro-participant observation, or retro-auto-ethnography – to compare with the new input of the writers and editors concerned, some of whom I knew, and in one case bumped into, on the dancefloor. The book will therefore interrogate stories, scenes, even individual words: a micro textual analysis that might in turn reveal the macro, cultural and contextual reality.

Delineating the shelves of Dancefloor-Driven Literature

The list of Dancefloor-Driven Literature (Appendix I) is by no means intended as a canon, a word itself now loaded. It is instead intended as a starting point, a collection of Dancefloor-Driven Literature that contains a broad range of both themes and modes of production that might act as a starting point for a catalogue of such works. Thematically, club scene novels have intersected with football fiction,[12] and crime fiction, for example; in terms of production, they have ranged from commercially successful titles to self-published works. To detail the range of Dancefloor-Driven Literature that might be considered as primary sources, at one end there stands a buoyant market for self-published fiction. Novels such as *Kiss the Sky* by DC Gallin take clubland as locus,[13] as does *Club* by Pat W. Hendersen.[14] These novels, with admittedly limited readerships, are nevertheless important for their subjective, immured depictions of the clubland milieu, if not for their contribution to the enculturation of the scene, in a purely numeric metric of books sold. At the other end of the spectrum in terms of readership, club scenes can be found in novels by more commercial writers such as Nick Hornby, as in the following passage from the 2001 novel *How to Be Good*:

> 'I don't know what the secret is. That wasn't what I couldn't tell you.'
> 'So tell me what you couldn't tell me.'
> 'Drugs.'
> 'What do you mean, drugs? Drugs what?'
> 'That's how it started. E. That's what I think anyway. I was doing loads, and it was all that "I love you, you're my friend" stuff in clubs every Friday night, and … I'm one of those American comic-book guys. Spiderman and all them. It changed my molecular make-up. Gave me superpowers.'
> 'Ecstasy gave you superpowers.'
> 'I reckon.' He shrugs. 'Weird, innit? I mean, there's you at university and all that finding out about, like, your thigh-bone's connected to your knee-bone or whatever you do there. And there's me down the clubs dropping a few. And we've come out at the same place.'[15]

This Hornby novel, as well as *The Beach* by Alex Garland[16] and *The Black Album* by Hanif Kureshi[17] fall into this 1990s category of Dancefloor-Driven fiction; however, while the club scene features in these novels, it is not the main narrative driver for the project. Similarly, accounts such as *Clubland Confidential* by Frank Owen[18] and James St. James's *Disco Bloodbath*[19] consider the story of the Club Kids of 1980s New York, but from a non-fiction perspective that does not dovetail precisely with the theoretical orientation of this book. Douglas Rushkoff's 1997 novel *The Ecstasy Club*,[20] while eminently readable, is also less relevant to this study because of its similarly American locus.

However, a volume that is key in any consideration of dancefloor literature is Sarah Champion's 1997 collection of Chemical Generation fiction, *Disco Biscuits* (subtitled *New Fiction from the Chemical Generation*). This provides a useful starting point and will itself be analysed in Chapter 5.[21] This collection led, in turn, to longer fictional accounts by some of the writers included, notably, 1996's *Morvan Callar* by Alan Warner,[22] while Warner and several of the other principal progenitors of Dancefloor-Driven Literature are located in the shared space between Sarah Champion's collection and Steve Redhead's *Repetitive Beat Generation*.[23] In considering which authors to foreground for case studies, the three chosen authors certainly appear prominently in both of these volumes,[24] and this book might indeed be seen as building on Redhead's earlier work, in a process of scholarly constructivism. Primary research with the creators of short stories in that collection occupies Chapters 6, 7 and 8 of this book, foregrounding the work of Irvine Welsh, Nicholas Blincoe and Jeff Noon in the development of Dancefloor-Driven Literature. The process of this research therefore involved reaching out to, and securing new interviews with, each case study author, as well as key personalities such as author Trevor Miller and indeed Sarah Champion herself. Fresh primary input allows for an analysis of these club culture texts that introduces (while not exclusively relying on) the opinion of their creators. Their responses, allied with this close textual analysis, introduce new material and perspectives to intermedial discourse, notably when decoding how an author might capture and replicate, authentically, the essence of an electronic music culture.

Irvine Welsh deliberately sets out to tell stories of the dancefloor.[25] In my conversation with Welsh, further developed in Chapter 6, he explains that he only began to write as a means of keeping the spirit of the weekend alive.[26] In works such as *Glue*, *Ecstasy* and *The Acid House*,[27] notions of verisimilitude and naturalism come to the fore, as Welsh employs the argot of the dancefloor to keep the distance between character and reader at an absolute minimum, in order to better immerse the reader in the sensuous experience of the nightclub. Welsh is perfect, therefore, for exploring the figurative use of music in texts. Jeff Noon's collection of short stories, *Pixel Juice*, is examined, along with the novel *Needle in the Groove*.[28] *Pixel Juice* is important for the way that Noon plays with tropes of DJ culture and electronic music production in a linguistic context, and this author is therefore crucial to understanding the mechanical relationship of the sonic to the linguistic. The third author in this literary trinity is Nicholas Blincoe. Blincoe's first novel *Acid Casuals* overlaps Manchester's clubland with its criminal underworld – a thematic articulation also, interestingly, manipulated by Hendersen – and he is used to explore the naturalistic use of music in a text, through works such as this, as well as *Manchester Slingback* and *Jello Salad*.[29]

Intertextuality and intermediality

I have already used the term 'intermediality' and that in itself also needs some unpacking. Certainly, a key theoretical approach deployed in this book is that of a specifically *musico-literary intermediality*, and the attendant hope that my book both fits within and dialectically extends that particular discourse. At this juncture a clear distinction must be made between inter*textuality* and inter*mediality*, where 'text' refers to the objects compared – 'media' to the vessel for carrying and communicating that object. In other words, I am not so much interested in comparing two texts, such as two books or two songs, but analysing the intersection of two actual forms of media – these forms being music and literature – hence a musico-literary intermediality.

A scholarly focus on this cultural crossroads is not new. Calvin S. Brown's 1948 work *Music and Literature: A Comparison of the Arts* can be seen as an urtext for the evolving discipline of musico-literary intermediality.[30] Certainly, this work informed two later accounts: *The Musicalization of Fiction: A Study in the Theory and History of Intermediality* by Werner Wolf (1999)[31] and the Steven Paul Scher collection *Essays on Literature and Music (1967-2004)*, edited by Wolf and Walter Bernhart.[32] These, then, were the progenitors of musico-literary intermedial studies, and undoubtedly both works are integral to the evolution of the discipline, notably for outlining taxonomies for the ways music and literature interact, directly inspiring the creation of the original taxonomy within this book, and detailed in the section titled 'A taxonomy of uses of music in Dancefloor-Driven Literature' below. However, what is *new* is that this book now pushes such intermedial articulations into areas of musical and literary collaboration not previously interrogated in this detail. Centrally, none of these writers have considered *that* important relationship between words and music in the *digital, electronic sphere*. Wolf, for instance, writes of 'the theoretical fact that an actual "translation" of music into fiction is impossible',[33] without considering electronic music and attempts by the likes of Noon to remix and produce literature using digital technologies, or for Trevor Miller to publish the novel *Trip City* with a soundtrack. This research therefore builds upon these earlier articulations, using their theory when appropriate, introducing new ideas when necessary.

Known as 'Word and Music Studies' in the 1990s,[34] it is also striking to note how many intermedial volumes have arrived more recently, each adding to this evolving discipline, including *Write in Tune*, edited by Eric Hertz and Jeffrey Roessner, and published by Bloomsbury in 2014, certainly a key text in the writing of my book. Certain journals also became important for the groundwork of this analysis, including 2005's

'Literature and Music' special issue of the journal *Popular Music*. In the introduction to that edition, John Street remarks that

> the original proposal for this special issue began by noting the common elements between the study of music and literature. It suggested that the two areas often deployed the same theories and methods, but it also observed that this shared perspective had generated relatively little dialogue.[35]

This book is designed to articulate the necessary interdisciplinary language to develop that dialogue, to help draw together the twin worlds of music and literature.

A taxonomy of uses of music in Dancefloor-Driven Literature

The history of intermediality as an academic discipline has been defined by scholars keen to create taxonomies for the way music and literature have integrated. In 1982, for instance, Steven Paul Scher chose to analyse this fundamental relationship as (a) music *in* literature (where literature mimics the acoustic sound of music); (b) music *and* literature (the setting of text) and (c) literature *in* music (primarily musical narratives).[36] Elsewhere, Wolf chooses to focus primarily on 'the media involved': 'The formation of media "dominants"' and the 'quantity of intermedial parts' and whether 'total intermediality' or 'partial intermediality' is achieved.[37] (In terms of this book, the 'dominant' is literature, rather than music.) Building on Scher's taxonomy, meanwhile, Gerry Smyth cites the work of William E. Grim to divide his study into 'Music as Inspiration', 'Music as Metaphor' and 'Music as Form'.[38]

Despite these taxonomies, no theory is able to accommodate fully the parameters of this study: these prescriptive frameworks do not allow for either the very particular beat of electronic music or its influence on both literary form and theme, and beyond that, on the way that these authors *actually write*. As such, a fresh taxonomy for the uses of music in fiction is required. This can very simply be broken down into three separate uses of electronic music in Dancefloor-Driven Literature:

- Figurative
- Mechanical
- Diegetic

Although these three areas will be considered in varying ways with each case study author, one will be foregrounded in each chapter for more penetrative analysis, as follows:

- Figurative: Irvine Welsh
- Mechanical: Jeff Noon
- Diegetic: Nicholas Blincoe

The structure of Wolf's seminal account *The Musicalization of Fiction* is a useful template in the sense that Wolf progresses from outlining his theory, to the deployment of case studies to illustrate and illuminate that theory. He writes that the function of the latter part of his book is 'to provide space for the theoretical categories and typologies developed in part 1 to be applied to, and, as it were, tested in, the interpretation of specific literary texts',[39] and that is precisely the shape that this book will assume: outlining theory, then testing that theory with literary exemplar.

Book structure

Thirty years beyond the Second Summer of Love, we are now in a position to objectively analyse this particular 'rave' culture via the prism of its literary output. Using literary analytic tools, combined with personal retro-participant observation and new primary input from the relevant authors, this book stands as an objective consideration, and evaluation, of this particular generation's pulsing, electronic soundtrack and its literary evocations.

The following chapter will set out the terminology for this subterranean scene, before Chapter 3 considers (for reasons of ergonomic brevity) three simple, but central, questions: *What* was the club scene, *where* did it take place, and *why* did it have such a hold on society? Having established this musico-cultural terrain, Chapter 4 will progress to further outline the notion of re/presentation, building on examples of the representation of the club scene first in TV, then in cinema and finally in the media, and arguing for the important role of such artefacts in terms of contemporaneous enculturation. Chapter 5 will further narrow down to focus on one specific area of re/presentation – literature – first in further defining Dancefloor-Driven Literature and then considering two key texts, the Sarah Champion edited *Disco Biscuits*[40] and the novel this book proposes is the first example of Dancefloor-Driven Literature: Trevor Miller's 1989 novel *Trip City*.[41] The chapter will also make the argument for the role of these texts, taken together, as an archive, servicing historical preservation.

Having defined the scene, then the notion of its re/presentation and further, the specific re/presentation in literature, the book will follow Wolf's model in progressing to a more detailed analysis of three case studies in Chapters 6, 7 and 8. Each case study author is chosen, in part, to evidence a different use of music in literature, following the taxonomy outlined earlier. Finally, having considered each in detail, Chapter 9 forms a conclusion, drawing together the main points made, returning to the initial questions posed in this chapter, and then further advancing new theoretical frameworks incorporated into this analysis, proposing that we might access, decode and understand a subterranean culture through its stories. In other words, we can understand the music without any volume – without, in fact, listening to any music. No previous study has defined this literature in this way, analysed it in such depth or pursued an argument this far along the musico-literary trajectory, in an interrogation of a subterranean phenomenon. As such, the book breaks new scholarly ground while also adding to the important, welcome and ongoing discourse that centres on musico-literary intermediality.

2

Sub- versus supraterranean cultures

The last 'spectacular subculture'

Textual analysis will reveal a great deal about the tropes and modes of EDMC discourse. However, there are also challenges inherent in a purely textual approach, and in order to respond to the very particular issues raised in this analysis, I also need to pull back in order to hold up these texts against the cultural context in which they were published, comparing these fictional accounts against readings drawn from other theorists.

Here I am immediately drawn into the debate surrounding the use of the term 'subculture', which I must necessarily pause to outline, and address, before moving forwards. The Centre for Contemporary Cultural Studies (popularly known as the Birmingham School, or CCCS) was a research centre formed within the University of Birmingham in 1964, itself building on the work of the earlier Chicago school of urban gang sociology.[1] The CCCS provided a locus for many significant cultural theorists including Stuart Hall, Angela McRobbie and Dick Hebdige, the latter of whom is particularly useful to this account. More useful to my work, however, was the Manchester Institute of Popular Culture (MIPC), a hub based at what is now the Metropolitan University of Manchester, which ran through the 1990s under the management of Steve Redhead and Derek Wynne. The work produced by this hub has been fundamental for both its chronological and geographic proximity to the literature within this research: that being the 1990s and the city of Manchester. Now arguably less known than the CCCS, it is a central ambition of this research to foreground and celebrate the work of the MIPC, notably following the death of Steve Redhead in 2018, while also allowing space to critique its theories and positions. Indeed, this research and current book might be read dialogically as a contemporary extension of that work.

The somewhat eschatological contention that the nascent rave scene was the last 'spectacular subculture', not only of the twentieth century but perhaps – in this postmodern, digital age – of any time, will also feature as another original argument of this book. And this brings us to this contentious and ongoing argument, as it is also necessary to demonstrate that the rave scene was a true subculture – rather than a popular culture – and inherently political, counter to the position held by some academics and commentators.[2] If I find myself launching my own theoretical salvos, that is largely because I have the need to duck, and defend myself, against those that seem to be coming the other way. I do, of course, accept that 'subculture' is now a contested term. And I agree that a post-digital landscape does not allow for cultural formation of a mass significant enough to collect as a subculture, in the sense the CCCS or MIPC would understand it. Instead, we now see hyper-localized, digitally enabled microcultures connecting individuals around the globe, rather than physically in their local town, where they might once have felt safe with other young people of their tribe. Many commentators, notably those gathering around post-subculture theory, have written well on this development, although I do find some of these approaches reductive in their rush to seemingly re-write so much rich cultural history, although there is much on interest in the theoretical tussles between the like of Andy Bennett, David Hesmondhalgh, Tracy Shildrick and Robert MacDonald in the early years of this century.

First, it must be understood that this study is largely historical, focusing on a specific location in both time and space – largely Manchester in the 1990s – at a time when subcultures and 'subcultural studies' was a lively and rich area of enquiry, with Steve Redhead, among others, happy to use the word 'subculture' in the title of several books and articles,[3] and it is perhaps strange, then, that the term 'subculture' now almost seems toxic within the academy. This was a subculture, so subcultural discourse – notably that of the time – remains relevant. A key issue lies in the way that the CCCS saw subcultures in an overtly political, specifically Marxist context, as a form of resistance and 'push back' from, predominantly, the working class. In itself that can be challenged as an axiomatic position (there were, of course, middle-class punks, for instance, and punks interested in the music, but not the politics). In their chapter 'The Narrative Nightclub', Matthew Cheeseman and David Forrest track this cultural-linguistic evolution, stating that this is

> understood as the mobilisation of Bourdieu's (1984) framing on distinction in relation to subculture in conditions of postmodernity. Subcultures are no longer seen as resistant but as a smorgasbord of styles and identities that can be fluidly borrowed from at will. Sarah Thornton (1995) writes in such as fashion about club culture, following Redhead (1995) in suggesting that subcultures are not necessarily resistant but elastic and porous.[4]

The authors of that chapter further state that 'we recognise, then, that the debates in studies of subculture – between class and the individual, between ordinary life and spectacular style, worsened economic conditions and choice–are ongoing',[5] and indeed that is a position I have also accepted, and adopted in this book, necessarily drawn into this discourse and required to define, and defend, my own position.

Scenes, tribes and post-subcultural theory

However, as much as commentators have gathered to mark the demise of this particular term, they seem equally unable to settle what comes next, while none of their proposed positions also quite captures the essence of the culture at the heart of this book. Andy

Bennett suggests 'tribes' or 'neo-tribes',[6] while Will Straw and others suggest 'scenes',[7] which implicitly locate this music in a geographically fixed location, something I resist in this book (as we will see in the next chapter). David Hesmondhalgh successfully identifies issues with each proposed term in his paper 'Subcultures, Scenes or Tribes? None of the above', arguing that 'the concepts of scene and tribe are not, ultimately, useful ways to conceive of musical collectivities in modern societies, whether of "youth" or any other group'.[8] While his arguments are compelling – notably his call to create clear water between popular music studies and youth studies (where age is also largely irrelevant to my study) – his own settling on the term 'genre' is itself too connected to notions of consumption and distribution to work in the context of this book, where music is but one part of the picture.

This is very much a live, and indeed lively, discussion. In my own conversation with Matthew Worley of the appropriately named Subcultures Network, Worley reports that 'the term is at the centre of our own influential network. It's still being used and is still valuable in terms of a historical and theoretical framing because it's part of our lexicon. People know what you're talking about when discussing a shared understanding of taste, style and language.'[9] It is certainly interesting to see how frequently the term 'subculture' is cited in quotes from contributors within this book. In terms of a rearguard defence of subcultures, it is also illuminating to read how belligerent, even militant, Paul Hodkinson is, when defending his right to use the term 'subculture' in his analysis of the goth scene. Hodkinson shares my own journey from, as he terms it, 'Participant to Researcher', embedded in a scene that shares subcultural elements as the rave scene. Hodkinson takes subculture 'to imply a level of cultural *substance*, which might distinguish the goth scene, as a *subculture*, from more fleeting, ephemeral amalgams of young people, music and style'.[10]

Meanwhile, at the same time as Hesmondhalgh made his stake for 'genre', Tracy Shildrick and Robert MacDonald published 'In Defence of Subculture: Young People, Leisure and Social Divisions', useful for foregrounding the word 'defence'. They channel Blackman in commenting: 'Even in their consideration of dance/rave culture, for instance, the post-subculturalists forget the, at times, political, resistant, subcultural character of their subject.'[11] Their welcome use of the word 'political' will help support arguments I will make for the political framework of the rave scene in the next chapter. Indeed, it should also be acknowledged that following the attack on goth Sophie Lancaster, and her subsequent death, in Rossendale, Lancashire, in 2007, the Greater Manchester Police stated in 2013 that they would record attacks against alternative communities as hate crimes, allying subcultural affiliation with other possibly aggravating factors such as sexual orientation and race, again defining a clear political dynamic to subcultures.

Subterranean culture

My own position is that this book is a review of the literature from a pre-millennial, indeed pre-internet (for much of its lifespan) historic music scene, and the tenets of subcultural theory have therefore been, at times, useful to my own decoding of the rave scene and its attendant literature. However, notwithstanding Hodkinson's compelling call for the use of subculture in relation to goths, my position also holds that moving on – and certainly when dealing with more contemporary culture – we must accept Hesmondhalgh's statement that 'there is no possibility of a return to the concept of subculture in any adequate sociology of popular music'.[12]

So, if not subcultural, then how might we fix this musico-cultural scene? Indeed EDMC is not, in fact, really a *scene*, in the sense that 'scene theory' would posit, since (as my own journalism has identified) it was truly transnational and not necessarily geographically site specific (notwithstanding certain key locations, and the time/space location at the heart of this book). Equally, this is not a *deviant culture*, in any way participants would self-diagnose as deviant. And it is so much more than simply a *taste culture*, with a mass formed of distinct homological variants of fashion, politics and drug practices. The discourse of subcultural studies naturally progress into post-subcultural theory, yet as I have stated, when I read such studies I find they can, at times, become mired in pejorative barbs and reductive statements about what I consider still to be the important work undertaken before. Indeed, we are also now chronologically beyond the main thrust of post-subcultural studies.

Hodkinson remarks that 'the excessive number of different proposals as to how we conceptualise elective groupings creates a problem in itself'.[13] Where pre-existing terms fail, a new approach is called for; or rather – taking Hodkinson's point discussed earlier into consideration – an older one is salvaged, recycled, repurposed. This book seeks, at its core, to create dialogic links between cultures, where seeing them in a heuristic bubble is an anathema. Instead, such cultures seem to emerge consistently from a countercultural underground arranged in reaction to the dominance of a mainstream; still resistant, only now resisting boredom, conformity and the mundane. In any analysis of this binary dynamic, one can immediately locate opposition, and tension. In this reading, therefore, society can be critiqued as operating on (at least) two levels: the darker shadow of the subterranean and nocturnal world interrogated in this book, set against the reality of a more visible, mainstream society operating 'overground', and in daylight.[14] Here, I immediately run into semantic difficulties with the word 'mainstream'. Often used to denote the dominant societal overground, the word is less useful when interests are largely cultural rather than political, or fiscal (for instance, Antonio Gramsci's use of the term 'hegemonic' is also somewhat problematic in this sense).[15] To traverse such awkward semantics, therefore, and to avoid the theoretical baggage that comes with the deployment of the word 'subculture', I suggest the term 'supraterranean' to denote mainstream cultures operating 'overground', set against the operations of the 'subterranean' for these ostensibly underground and counterculturally oriented music-based style cultures, in keeping with Latin derivations and prefixes.

Although never proposed in precisely this way before, the notion of the cultural underground is, of course, not new. Indeed it was intriguing for me to read recently that Tracey Thorn – singer, songwriter and half of UK pop act Everything but the Girl – chose, as her holiday reading in the summer of 2019, a key text for this book: Andrew Holleran's *Dancer from the Dance*. In her *New Statesman* column detailing her reading of the Holleran text, Thorn herself recalls scenes in the book that 'capture the transcendental, transformative euphoria of the dance floor. At these moments, the writing becomes a love song to the spirit of the underground scene, the unifying passion for the right music in the right place at the right time.'[16] She adds a little later that 'there's also a sense of a wider world, set slightly apart; a conservative, straight world, from which the main characters are excluded, giving them a sense of perspective about its conventions and hypocrisies'.[17] The interest of theorists such as Jacques Lacan and Julia Kristeva in their articulation of the 'other' as a cultural construct is also immediately useful in the central positioning of this musical underworld as antithetical to supraterranean, hegemonic culture,[18] a nocturnal underground in opposition to the light of 9-to-5 daytime, an illicit underground network of repurposed spaces running alongside more legal club venues; indeed an architectural underground of nightclubs operating literally underground, in subterranean basements and cellars.

I am not necessarily suggesting the use of subterranean as a 'master-term' in Hesmondhalgh's words,[19] or a term that completely captures in one word everything it is required to do, but certainly one that will work within the parameters of this book. Of course much of this discussion of scene theory, or subcultural theory, in evocations of the rave scene – while compelling – is in any case something of a smoke screen because this book is not about a history of this culture, per se, but the fictions that surround it, and feed from it. Many fabulous histories of the rave scene have been published,[20] and in a sense, then, while I have been drawn into this discussion, and I am interested in progressing scholarship from purely subcultural articulations, I am equally aware that this book is not specifically about the 'thing' itself – whether scene or culture – but rather stories about 'the thing'. To focus on but one flowering of club culture, this book is not about the disco it is about the disco*texts*.

Subterranean life-cycle model/subterranean continuum

Building on Steve Redhead's ideas of 'the subcultural chain',[21] using the notion of subterranean cultures we can now start to trace how each generation evolves its own cultural forms, narratives and identities. Equally, each generation wrestles, tries to contain and is ultimately overwhelmed by a darker shadow: this subterranean id to the supraterranean ego. In aesthetic terms, subterranean culture acts as the creative engine that drives the varying modes of art upwards, and forwards; each generation is eager to define itself and its cultural forms as new, energetic and ultimately different from the one that bore it. As such, a generation can view its culture within a hermetic bubble, without consideration of what has gone before. This book instead counters that such roots are strong, traceable and desirable. Instead, one subterranean culture actually germinates from that which preceded, as though each subterranean emergence and life cycle might be tied to the seasons of birth, growth and decline – of spring, summer and autumn.

As an example, three important post-war cultural shifts can be located twenty years apart, loosely a generation.[22] Further, although defined by their seminal decades, all three actually have roots in the preceding years. Jack Kerouac's road trips, which form the basis of his novel *On the Road* (1957) and the broader Beat Generation, actually take place in the late 1940s. Of course it should be noted that Kerouac's third novel, published in 1958, was indeed titled *The Subterraneans* – his term for the way the Beat Generation practitioners lived out their lives, and indeed love lives, in underground bebop clubs, in the night-time hours. The Subterraneans are defined in the opening passages of the novel by the character Adam Moorad (the fictional representation of Beat poet Allen Ginsberg), who says:

> They are hip without being slick, they are intelligent without being corny, they are intellectual as hell and know all about Pound without being pretentious or talking too much about it, they are very quiet, they are very Christlike.[23]

Moving towards the rock music scene of the 1970s (described both electrically and eloquently by Lester Bangs in his writing for *Creem*, *The Village Voice* and *Rolling Stone* magazines), we can detect how this music has very clear roots in the late 1960s and the (First) Summer of Love in 1967 (where 'counter' might here overlap with 'sub' culture).[24] In reference to the San Francisco of the mid-1960s, for instance, author Hunter S. Thompson discusses a 'high water mark – that place where the wave finally broke, and rolled back' to mark the zenith and entropic collapse of that cultural movement. It is perhaps no surprise that this period is defined by 'Flower Power' and a connection to nature.[25]

It must follow, therefore, that under this twenty-year model the subterranean tectonic plates would shift once again in the late 1980s. And, indeed, the plates did move, the resulting cracks revealing once again the machinations of the cultural underground: acid house music, the drug Ecstasy and the Second Summer of Love, the very virulent sonic and pharmaceutical mix that I explore in this book. Tracking the same life-cycle trajectory of growth and decay, this next subterranean emergence of rave culture also eventually, and inevitably, died back.[26] I therefore argue for a subterranean continuum, for an almost horticultural, rather than subcultural, model of germination, growth and natural, entropic decay that more organic forms might follow. This theory articulates how subterranean life cannot exist in and of itself; rather, there is an essential subterranean lineage that runs between each form, continually subverting and influencing dominant culture as though in a perpetual helix. EDMC cannot, therefore, be considered to operate in a historical-cultural vacuum. Instead, one must necessarily and dialogically regard it in relation to the influences of other subterranean life, and this ongoing research stands as an objective consideration, and evaluation, of this generation – not rockers, but ravers – their pulsing, electronic soundtrack and its literary evocations.

In detecting these patterns, frameworks and – more broadly – subterranean systems, I am interested to note the presence of trinities: three cultural movements identified here across time, and then further, three homological components within each of those movements. I therefore propose another central argument that there exists an Unholy Trinity of cultural and pharmaceutical effects that coalesce to define a subterranean culture: this linking interplay of literature, music and intoxicants. Any scene must, then, be considered a reaction between forces,[27] the cultural formation necessarily the result of the collision of music with an accelerant formed of the chosen intoxicant of the day, subsequently reported, and recorded, in literature. These cultural ingredients have been explored before,[28] but never in this particular constitution. This book further contends that within each scene, one element of this Unholy Trinity is foregrounded. I argue that the Beat scene was defined primarily by its literature; with rock, it was music; and with rave it was the drug itself – Ecstasy, or 'E' – that defined the culture.[29] Perhaps (and as a consequence of the critical focus on the music, and then the drug within the rave scene in extant studies) there has, up until now, been a lacuna in the study of the third element of this Unholy Trinity: what is now defined as a Dancefloor-Driven Literature, which considers the scene from an apparently fictional perspective. This depth of literary analysis breaks new ground in musico-literary intermediality, and moves the conversation on from the purely subcultural positioning of EDMC taken by many previous theorists and commentators.

To conclude this chapter, then, the theoretical underpinning of the book is therefore formed of a methodology broad enough to incorporate elements of cultural theory with that of musico-literary intermediality and the literary approaches necessary to unpack these texts. If there seems to be a lacuna of any overt musicological interpretation in that typology, then that is deliberate, perhaps realizing concerns outlined by Richard Middleton in his introduction to *Reading Pop*.[30] The interest here is demonstrably not in the music as text, but dancefloor as *con*text, where music is foregrounded primarily in terms of its consumption. To counter this development in musicology, Middleton proposes the notion of a 'New musicology',[31] but American critic Lawrence Kramer comes closer with the term 'cultural musicology',[32] and that broadly holds true for this book, necessarily concerned more with the cultural resonance of music than its immanent tonality, with the way these writers write about music and use music rather than the music, in itself, as object. In forming this blended methodology, the approach is deliberately less concerned, then, with the quantitative methods associated with, for instance, digital data mining. Instead, it requires the authors to reveal their more analogue, personal data, while also drawing on the close and precise analysis of the texts themselves, alongside the contextual resources of literary and cultural knowledge and understanding that surround these texts. There is some consideration of modes of production, distribution, reception and readership, where it has relevance; however, this book remains focused on qualitative methods to address the central research question as to whether it is possible to decode a real-world musico-cultural scene, by reference to its fictional re/presentation.

3

Revealing the scene

The global roots of subterranean club cultures

The nightclub stands at a key location of social evolution, dancefloors forming political and cultural frontlines, where boundaries are tested, and sometimes breached. In order to understand the subterranean literature at the heart of this book – literature born of these dancefloors – it is important to offer an overview of the re-emergence of the dancefloor within the 'rave' or 'acid house' context, so as to contextualize the cultural space within which these texts were constructed and published. In effect, we need to find the beat, before we find out how people write about the beat.

In terms of my approach to analysing such spaces, as well as the retro-participant observation outlined in Chapter 1 from the time I spent living, working and partying in Manchester and Ibiza, fresh ethnographic research comes from one trip to New York, another to Ibiza and further one to Detroit and Chicago, central locations in this evolving story,[1] welcoming valuable input of music producers, academics and commentators. This chapter will introduce ideas from situationism, and theorists such as Theodor Adorno, Jacques Attali and Michel Foucault, and will build towards addressing critical questions raised by commentators such as Simon Reynolds and Rupa Huq, as they consider EDMC in a proposed non-political or apolitical context. To do so it will principally use Hakim Bey's theoretical construction of the temporary autonomous zone, resisting hegemony from a position of insurrection (here countercultural insurrection) rather than revolution.[2] It will also touch on Foucault's notion of a 'panopticon', a tower of observation based on Jeremy Bentham's prison design, where 'the gaze is alert everywhere'.[3] Whether one prefers the notion of the TAZ, or indeed Mikhail Bakhtin's sense of the carnivalesque, a key argument can be made that dancefloors have been fundamental in pushing a social agenda, spaces beyond formal control, and therefore inherently perceived as a threat: if dancefloors are subterranean, they are by definition beyond the gaze of society's panopticon.[4] Much cultural discourse is dedicated to topography and to the geographical locating of cultural intersections, in keeping with work done by 'scene' theorists such as Will Straw, Andy Bennett and Sara Cohen.[5] However, as outlined in Chapter 1 there are inherent limitations in an approach built on a rather specific fixing of time or space. Instead, my approach centres on a mutable locus: the dancefloor itself. An understanding of the mechanics of the psychogeographic space of the dancefloor unlocks the culture itself, and further suggests why filmmakers and authors chose it as site of the cultural mediations that will be explored in Chapter 4.

Building on notions of the subterranean outlined in Chapter 1, writer Sarah Thornton suggests nightclubs are 'like Alice's rabbit hole', in that they 'convey the participant from the mundane world to Wonderland'.[6] Certainly this book is my attempt to lead the reader down that rabbit hole and into the subterranean Wonderland of the club scene and its surreal dancefloors. Alice would have liked the club scene: she would recognize the need to escape, the wonder in finding an entirely different world mirroring that operating in the supraterranean realm, during the day, and the characters she would meet, in an environment where the bounds of time are similarly loosened. Indeed, this is also a conceit familiar from films such as John Badham's *Saturday Night Fever* (1977).[7] Detailing the story of one young Italian American, Tony Manero (played by actor John Travolta), the film positions the quotidian Monday-to-Friday reality of working in a hardware store against the subterranean riches to be found on the dancefloors of Saturday Night. The film was based on English journalist Nik Cohn's story 'Tribal Rites of the New Saturday Night', penned in 1976 for *New York* magazine.[8] In this text, Cohn relates stories of young Brooklyn men and women who devote their lives to the dancefloor, the beat of disco music and the pleasures of the weekend. Focusing particularly on a young man called Vincent, Cohn writes:

> Over the past few months, much of my time has been spent in watching this new generation. Moving from neighborhood to neighborhood, from disco to disco, an explorer out of my depth, I have tried to learn the patterns, the old/new tribal rites.

However, as late as 1994, Cohn told *The Guardian* newspaper:

> My story was a fraud, I'd only recently arrived in New York. Far from being steeped in Brooklyn street life, I hardly knew the place. As for Vincent, my story's hero, he was largely inspired by a Shepherd's Bush mod whom I'd known in the Sixties, a one-time king of Goldhawk Road.[9]

One of the most significant cultural evocations of the club scene was not about New York disco at all, then, but the UK mod subculture of a decade earlier. If Cohn was so effortlessly able to recall his perceptions of the UK mod scene, and transplant them upon a perceived New York dance scene (which then, in fact, did become reality) then, once again, the essential connectivity between such dance music worlds must be acknowledged. The roots are strong, and well founded.

I will now map this cultural terrain via three separate points of access. First, I will begin by analysing the organic, chemical and electronic technologies involved in the production and consumption of sound on the dancefloor. Then, in order to better understand the locations where these dancefloors reside, I will make a dialogic (and original) link between three separate nightclubs over three different decades, in order to follow these roots around the world and see how they connect. Finally, bringing these two elements together, the chapter will close by questioning why these 'dancers from the dance' went to such lengths, both transnational and transgressive, to engage with this culture, proposing that the answer lies in a physiological desire for pleasure and a political need for resistance. Providing a description of the music, the associated technologies and DJ techniques, the physical construct of the rave and associated Ecstasy consumption, this chapter will equip the reader with the knowledge to effectively navigate the Dancefloor-Driven Literature that will follow.

Technologies: Organic, electronic, pharmaceutical

Central to this book is the development and role of technology, and indeed the important interrelationship of organic, electronic and indeed pharmaceutical technologies. Technology contains within it an almost inevitable progressivism. Theodor Adorno strongly resisted the commodification and mass production of music in the twentieth century;[10] equally, as Gilbert and Pearson point out, while reggae producer Lee Scratch Perry might bemoan 'click track' culture, what would he make of Maezel's 1815 invention, the metronome? It, too, is technology.[11] In his overview of this sense of sonic progression, Simon Frith remarks:

> The history of popular music is obviously implicated in the history of technology (and vice versa) and technological history is almost always understood in terms of progress. We therefore take it for granted that each new device for carrying or mediating music is better than (and effectively replaces) that which has gone before. Phonography gave way to electrical recording which gave way to analogue recording which gave way to digital recording which will doubtless give way to something else in the years to come.[12]

Technological advancements have therefore been central in the development of club culture, where even the invention of the lightbulb and the illumination of the night-time environment provided new opportunities for urban leisure, for the first time bringing light to the chthonian realm: an artificial light, admittedly, but one nevertheless able to reveal the spectacular of the subterranean.

Much will be made in this chapter of the external impact of technology: sonic design, production and distribution, for instance, and the architectural spaces in which those relationships are played out. However, any discussion of technology also needs to encompass both the organic and electronic, internal and external. All such apparatus is necessary for the production and consumption of sound, when the impact of such technology is felt, and filtered, internally, within the human body. Further, our own physiological structure and desire for assisted transcendence also sits squarely at the centre of this interplay of effects, centring on what Aldous Huxley usefully describes as 'chemical technology',[13] and what Marcus Boon calls 'the technological discourse that surrounds stimulant use'.[14]

Here we must return our thoughts to notions of the liminal, as many thresholds are transgressed when decoding club culture. Physically, thresholds exist for the architecture of the dance: bolt cutters granting access to the decaying warehouses of urban centres, the liminal and legal boundary separating the underground from the hegemonic, supraterranean realm. Pharmaceutically, a pill needs to pass a raver's lips, the very boundary that separates the external from internal spheres, in order to be absorbed into the bloodstream. This chapter will therefore begin with a brief analysis of chemical and organic technologies which, like the electronic variant, develops through time. Indeed, it is impossible to view any dance scene without reference to a contemporaneous intoxicant, whether the cocaine that drove the 1920s jazz craze, the marijuana and Benzedrine that fuelled the bebop of the 1940s, LSD engendering the spiritual adventuring of the 1960s or the Ecstasy that sits at the heart of the 1980s rave culture and its associated literature. As Mike Jay points out, 'The patterns made by drugs in human cultures may be endlessly varied, but all are perhaps woven from the same fabric.'[15]

As outlined in Chapter 1, this research contends that in terms of the theoretical framework of the Unholy Trinity, it is the drug – rather than the literature or music – that defines the rave scene. Methylenedioxymethamphetamine (MDMA) was initially synthesized by pharmaceutical giant Merck as far back as 1912, as an appetite suppressant. Experimental American chemist Alexander Shulgin, the so-called Godfather of Ecstasy,[16] further synthesized the compound in his garden laboratory, and it was then used in therapy sessions in 1960s America. In the 1980s, opportunistic street marketers began to see the commercial potential in MDMA, or Ecstasy, as an empathogen that could bring down the walls between people. As MDMA also raises the heart rate and stimulates energy, it stands as the perfect pharmaceutical filter through which to discern the electronic beat that formed soundtrack to this music scene – the synthetic driving the kinetic – enabling people to hear music in different ways, and respond more positively to one another, while also bestowing the energy needed for their protracted response to repetitive music.

Moving on to the external technologies for producing and distributing sound, Jacques Attali discusses the industrialization and mechanization of sound in his seminal work *Noise*.[17] Attali recognizes that repetition is its own form of production, requiring new styles of performance, from musicians capable of controlling this new technology.[18] When we map this discourse onto electronic dance music, in particular, we find a music built entirely around repetitions, sequenced sections that build only to collapse in what are referred to as 'breakdowns' or 'drops'.[19] House music is built around a four-four beat, at a tempo of around 120 beats per minute. At the front of the production is the bass drum, with an off-beat hi-hat in support; the melody carried by a vocal, or perhaps vocal sample. Such a logical and mechanical approach to the ostensibly creative was enabled by two very important pieces of technology – the sampler and the sequencer – which, along with synthesizers and drum machines, characterize the early 'acid' house sound. American company EMU released the Emulator Sampler in 1981 as a new way to process and play sound. The initial lack of sample space necessitated short vocal stabs, perhaps simple phrases or acid-related aphorisms which actually suited the synthetic aesthetic of MDMA itself, with the attendant suggestion that there was no need to explore complex lyrical ideas. The development of the sequencer enabled the producer to separate lines of music and lay them out on a computer screen, so that they might be further manipulated. In this way, programmes such as Steinberg's Cubase Audio and Logic Audio, through to modern equivalents from Ableton to Apple's user-friendly Garage Band, have enabled producers to start tracks with relative ease, certainly compared to those earlier days of expensive studio technology.

Another key development was the introduction, in 1983, of MIDI technology (Musical Instrument Digital Interface) which, for the first time, allowed these digital components to be connected so as to be used together.[20] Two years later, Atari's ST computers were built with MIDI sockets as standard, further easing the music making process, much to the horror of more traditional music producers (this was a time of the 'Keep Music Live' campaign from the Musicians' Union, which I certainly recall from my early gig-going days). In *Discographies*, Ewan Pearson and Jeremy Gilbert speak to this very point: 'Some of the writers dismiss the computer-literate kids, DJs and others who have begun to make records by means of electronic technologies as not entitled to the term "musician".'[21] Such teleogical and technological philosophical conundrums provide ammunition for more prosaic, but pejorative perspectives on the scene. In response, Attias channels John Savage's 1993 comment: 'If there is one central idea in techno, it is of the harmony between man and machine.'[22] This chapter concurs with Savage that while the technology might be electronic, the device that ultimately pushes the buttons remains entirely organic – the DJ/producer – the facilitator, the manipulator and the bridge between man and machine. Cultural commentator Kodwo Eshun echoes those sentiments, suggesting 'machines *don't* distance you from your emotions, in fact quite the opposite. Sound machines make you feel *more* intensely' (emphasis in original). Or, as Ralf Hütter, of pioneering German techno group Kraftwerk, more succinctly puts it, 'It's in the nature of machines. Machines are funky.'[23]

Beyond the sampled vocal hooks and sequenced melodies, technology might further be seen as a very modern way of replicating, and connecting us to, something essentially primitive – the beat – in the form of the drum machine, specifically Roland's CR, TB and TR models. In 1982, Roland released the TB-303 (where TB stands for transistor bass), creating the squelching sounds familiar on early acid house records: centrally Phuture's 'Acid Tracks' through to Hardfloor's 'Acperience 1', Josh Wink's 'Higher State of Consciousness' and Fatboy Slim's praise poem 'Everybody Needs a 303'.[24] It is this arena of tracks that Irvine Welsh integrates into his prose, analysed further in Chapter 7. A year later, Roland released their TR-909, synonymous with the 'mentasm' or 'hoover' sound present in tracks like 1991's 'Mentasm' by Second Phase and 'Charly' by the Prodigy. However, neither of these machines are as iconic as the Roland TR808 (where TR stands for transistor rhythm), heard on tracks such as Afrika Bambaataa's 'Planet Rock', Cybotron's 'Clear' and even, in an admittedly different setting, Marvin Gaye's 'Sexual Healing'.

As Roland intended the 808 for musicians making demos, the sounds produced were never intended to sound like authentic drums, characterized instead by a sharp snare and rounded bass. When technology did move on, and drum machines were able to replicate more authentic sounds, the 808 was relegated to pawn shops, where it became affordable to young producers and pioneers of what would become the street DIY aesthetic of electro and hip hop in the 1980s, fulfilling the idea that 'innovative or important technological practice often stems from the "misuse" of "low" technology items'.[25] Graham Massey of Manchester electronic band 808 State (named after Roland's machine) explains: 'There's something so special about an 808 in terms of its feel. I know to a layman all these machines sound the same. But the history of music will prove otherwise.'[26] These technological developments culminated in the moment when DJ Frankie Knuckles played his blend of disco, rock and European electronica at the Warehouse club in Chicago in the early 1980s,[27] in so doing creating the sound that would (arguably) be named after the club: 'House' music, before going on to play records over a drum machine at the city's Power Plant nightclub.

Jacques Attali's *Noise* was published in 1977, exactly a century after Thomas Edison's first experiments in recording sound with his phonograph, and strangely synchronous with the apotheosis of the disco boom. In *Noise*, Attali refers to four distinct cultural stages in the history of music, each linked to a mode of production, or set of technologies. 'Sacrificing' refers to the oral tradition synonymous with earlier histories, while 'Representing' runs up to 1900 and refers to the commodification of music and its representation in the rarefied environs of the conservatoire. More pertinent to this book are the phases of 'Repeating' and 'Post-Repeating': the age of trapping and sealing sound in recorded form and the subsequent fidelity in the broadcast and dissemination of that sound, notably in a nightclub construct. From the outset, this was a highly contested, political area, with the magazine *New Society* leading a rear-guard action to such developments. In a 1966 editorial they argued that the gramophone had now become 'a system for distributing deviant sound to the disaffected cultural minorities',[28] suggesting an interesting moral response to, and fear of, recorded music that will be further explored later in this book. The technology that enabled the recording of sound did indeed have a severe impact on Attali's 'Repeating' stage, as society evolved to develop the spaces where people might instead enjoy the original recording, amplified to fill a room, in human company, instead of its reproduction by a band or orchestra. These early nightclub spaces were formed of a series of collaborative relationships. Vicky-Ann Cremona usefully distinguishes between ludic and paidian styles of cultural performance: where the former, if undirected, is nevertheless primarily an onstage activity, whereas the paidian is much more of an immersive, participatory event.[29] These emerging dancefloors were of a decidedly paidian, chaotic formation, formed of 'the buzz of energy which results from the interaction of records, DJs and crowd'.[30]

Recording and distributing music also set the scene for the function of the DJ, the Disc Jockey or, in the terminology of Holleran's 1978 novel 'discaires'. DJ culture can be seen as modern minstrelsy, fulfilling Attali's notion of breaking down the normal balance of the producer and consumer of music so that instead we find DJs as 'prosumers',[31] contributing much more fluidly to the structure of the music, even as it is played. In 1972, for instance, Japanese company Technics introduced the 1200 turntable. This model featured a particularly robust motor, so that DJs found if they moved the record against the natural pull of its revolution, then let go, it would bounce back to normal speed. Thus, a lucky quirk bestowed the technique of 'scratching', which will have important resonances in the analysis of the literary techniques of Jeff Noon in Chapter 7. In 1979, Technics released the follow up, the 1210 Mark 2, featuring a sliding pitch control so that a DJ could more easily 'beatmatch' two records produced at slightly different speeds and again, Noon makes linguistic simulacra of these DJ techniques. The Technics 1210 is the industry standard for vinyl-based DJs to this day: I myself have two 1210s set up in my apartment, with slipmats signed by DJs Paul Oakenfold and Seb Fontaine, although my DJing is – thankfully – now restricted to at-home events (building on my *DJ* magazine column, my DJ nom-de-plume is DJ Wrong, and that does also rather encapsulate my abilities). Long ago, I decided that the world had enough DJs, and that my endeavours might better be steered towards analysing and reporting on the music, rather than playing it.

Returning to Adorno's resistance to recorded music and the impact of such industrialized music on contemporary society and here, we find mass production reinforces the ongoing compartmentalizing of music into the serious and the popular, the prioritizing of performance and the site of the authentic.[32] Adorno, for instance, argues against those who fetishize sound as independent from what is being played, perhaps failing to appreciate a technological environment in which live performance can be captured, reproduced and broadcast at great fidelity. Walter Benjamin bemoans the lack of 'aura' in recorded music,[33] while Adorno 'detected Fordism in the standard 3-minute recorded hit number'.[34] Adorno was even disparaging of the standardized concept of four beats to the bar which means, as noted in the consideration of the construction of house music, he is likely to have found such music an anathema, or to have enjoyed any time on the dancefloors of Ibiza. Adorno may well have seen digital music as the absolute end of times: when CD systems for DJing were superseded by newer digital systems such as Traktor, Serato and Final Scratch, it negated the need for physical product completely. The vinyl product had given way to the MP3. As Frith comments,

> Digital technology has confused the relationship of taste and history. Popular music is no longer rooted in a particular time and place but continually revived, remixed and re-released and [sic] until it occupies a kind of virtual, history-less space.[35]

In the maelstrom of Frith's 'history-less space' there must also be further room for returning technologies, acknowledging a fetishization of older, often analogue forms of equipment. I once interviewed Graham Massey not about his work with 808 State, but a project called Sisters of Transistors, based entirely around the organ. He explains: 'I got into keyboards because of 808 and the synths and things but these are the obscure kind of keyboards, the outer rim for keyboard collectors.'[36] Vinyl has also made an incredible comeback; symptomatic, perhaps, of an irresistible, returning need for the authentic,[37] with the renewed popularity of Record Store Day, while a friend of mine also organizes the annual Cassette Store Day, breathing sonic life back to the humble compact cassette. Meanwhile, Greg Wilson – one of the first DJs at the Haçienda nightclub in Manchester – continues a successful career that often sees him DJ not with

Traktor, or Serato, but a Revox B77: a vintage reel-to-reel tape player. Wilson appeared at 2019's Camp Bestival festival, with both of us speaking in the Literary Tent. I was intrigued at that point to hear Wilson call for a recognition of the electro producers from the earlier 1980s, who often get missed in any analysis of EDMC, which often sees the Warehouse as Ground Zero.

Locations: The dancefloor as psychogeographic locus

This chapter has outlined how music technologies have enabled connections within the liminal borders of the dancefloor, and within the human body. However, each dancefloor also remains rooted to its broader physical and geographical locus. Here theoretical concepts such as *psychogeography* – which, in simple terms, considers the emotional effects of locations on the broader consciousness – function as a useful tool in terms of unpacking the impact of the nightclub.[38] More broadly, 'scene theory' also considers the homological gathering of cultural and geographic forces that might birth music 'scenes', with Andy Bennett being a particular commentator exploring a 'music scenes perspective'.[39] Developing on subculture theory – but as we have seen in the previous chapter, arguably improving on the perceived restrictive limitations of that approach – a scenes perspective seeks instead to localize subcultural formation. However, I will also look to link these local scenes, via a 'trans-local' mechanic (while of course links might now also be forged digitally or 'virtually'). Bennett argues that such theory refers 'to a particular local setting, usually a city or district, where a particular style of music has either originated, or has been appropriated and locally adapted',[40] foregrounding the cultural impact of a nightclub on its location, beyond what might be measured in purely financial terms. Bennett argues that in this sense 'a locally created music style becomes a metaphor for community, a means through which people articulate their sense of togetherness through a particular juxtaposition of music, identity and place'.[41] This certainly holds true for Manchester's dancefloors in the 1990s, in the literature that told its stories, in the psychogeographic impact of that time, and in my own memory.

Electronic dance music is produced globally but interpreted locally, and in order to contextualize all of that cultural history, the following analysis focuses on three significant nightclubs as geo-cultural case studies over three successive decades, considering the architecture of the clubs themselves, the broader locales in which they are situated and the fundamental deeply rooted connection between music, culture and place. It should be noted that of course that is not to dismiss the role of locations such as Detroit and Chicago, London and Berlin and many, many others, but more to tell one story, through three linked chapters. Recognizing, therefore, the tension that lies between physical space and the axis of time, my consideration of these clubs (the latter two which I often frequented) is also necessarily historical, and subjective. Building on Derrida's notion of 'hauntology', Mark Fisher further confirms that 'hauntology is the proper temporal mode for a history made up of gaps, erased names and sudden abductions',[42] and further that such temporal haunting 'signifies both the dwelling-place, the domestic scene and that which invades or disturbs it'.[43] It is within such a context of ghostly invasion and disturbance that I spoke to New York DJ Danny Krivit, the two of us sat in his parked car on the Lower East Side, Danny agreeing that records continue to connect us to such places,[44] as sonic spectral hauntings, commenting 'we all connect to what we remember about that time, and how that record made us feel'.[45]

1970s New York

It was in the 1970s that nightclubs first began to be popularly referred to as discotheques, the French word for 'record library', disco quickly becoming the name for both this particular scene and the music that formed its soundtrack. However, as already proposed in this book, the disco scene must be considered only one of many different variants of the sonic subterranean genus of dance music cultures because the actuality, of course, is that the story goes back much further.[46] In her *Vanity Fair* article 'Boogie Nights', Lisa Robinson situates the emergence of this dance-club scene in the preceding decade, highlighting 1960s discotheques such as 'Regine's, Le Club, Shepheard's, Cheetah, Ondine and Arthur'.[47] However, for exigency, the contingencies of the disco scene will be revealed by focusing on one such discothèque, Studio 54.

Opened in 1977 on West 54th Street, Anthony Haden-Guest argues that Studio 54 was a space beyond formal structures of control, housing a homology of effects that Robinson distils in her *Vanity Fair* article as 'open drug use, on-site sex, and ecstatic, all-night dancing'.[48] Barthes's decoding of a wrestling ring might also be mapped upon the Studio 54 dancefloor: a place to construct the ideal, spectacular version of one's self, where mythography trumps biography.[49] Haden-Guest reproduces one particular photograph, for example, where Beat Generation author William S. Burroughs is seen in the club with singer Madonna, two apparently incongruous characters who will, perhaps even more strangely, reappear in the analysis of the second nightclub in this overview. Other peculiar dialogic links can also be found. In the late 1970s Burroughs shared a New York apartment with Hakim Bey, and Bey suggests that 'the TAZ is the last and only means of creating an Outside or true space of resistance to the totality'.[50] He agrees such a space might be a nightclub, where dancing is 'the essence of the party',[51] and further marks 'music as an organizational principle'.[52] Whichever term one prefers, a further argument can be made that beyond society's gaze – as spaces beyond formal control – dancefloors have been fundamental in pushing a social agenda. The Studio 54 dancefloor lay beyond the gaze of the societal panopticon, and 'remained a vehicle for sensations'[53] for Haden-Guest, a portal to Bey's Temporary Autonomous Zone.[54] The dancefloor, then, might be considered more akin to Rimbaud's conception of 'free freedom', where Middleton argues, 'Disco might mark a key moment: when "slaves" in the all categories I have mentioned – Woman, Black, Low, the "living dead" rising from the grave of history – were summoned to the dance floor and took it over.'[55] In terms of scene theory and subcultural locality, 1970s Manhattan – with its homology of flared trousers, cocaine consumption and disco soundtrack – can certainly be seen as a 'scene' in Bennett's sense, notwithstanding the veracity of Cohn's early report. It is almost impossible to think of 1970s New York without the immediate cue of a disco beat to form diegetic soundtrack: musical-historical and hauntological connections that are worked out, in a naturalistic and Mancunian sense, in the fiction of Nicholas Blincoe.

The successful impact of any music might best be gauged by the massed opprobrium of its opponents. The 'Disco Sucks' movement gathered pace throughout the latter 1970s and perhaps burned brightest on 12 July 1979 during the Disco Demolition Night at Comiskey Park in Chicago, when radio DJ Steve Dahl encouraged rock fans – wrong-footed by these new dance styles, new club spaces, new drug practices and perhaps most importantly a new, gay clientele sharing the dancefloor – to burn disco records. For many years that event seemed utterly reactionary, with resonances of Nazi book burnings, and it is perhaps both therefore particular poignant, and significant, that the Chicago White Sox celebrated, rather than commemorated, the fortieth anniversary of that event by inviting Dahl to pitch the first ball in their game against the New York Yankees on 13 June 2019. Krivit is circumspect about the cultural life cycle of the music form, reporting: 'The Disco Sucks thing was kind of inevitable. Overnight it really was a bad word.'⁵⁶ Meanwhile, the real beginning of the end for Studio 54 might be traced to the moment owners Steve Rubell and Ian Shrager sold the building in 1981. The vainglorious 1970s were now over and the 1980s were to become something very different, the appearance of the 'Gay Cancer' marking the downward trajectory of this party's gravity's rainbow, a disease that would ultimately be diagnosed as AIDS, taking Rubell's own life in 1989.⁵⁷

However, this music would prove resistant even to these incendiary tactics. Haden-Guest remarks: 'Disco lived. It was just that now it was called Dance music. The disco bonfire in Chicago hadn't consumed disco after all.'⁵⁸ Only a few years after the Disco Sucks inferno, and only a few miles from Comiskey Park, the ashes of disco reassembled in the architectural space that would become the Warehouse nightclub.⁵⁹ In that space, DJ Frankie Knuckles helped reform the predominantly black, gay disco music into a new predominantly black, gay electronic music.⁶⁰ UK DJ Graeme Park agrees, in valued conversations we have shared, that 'when dance music started and really exploded in the late 80s, early 90s, it was like a new exciting genre. Some people would argue it's just disco music for the modern age.'⁶¹ The 16 December 1978 issue of British industry magazine *Music Week* reported:

> The disco revolution in America has not been equalled since rock exploded in the fifties – and it will happen here too ... the rock takeover, the disco takeover. ... We're in the midst of a British club boom. More discos have opened their doors in the past month, it seems, than during the rest of the year.⁶²

Bennett agrees that, although this scene might be considered local, the nature of travel and technology at the time meant that the music spread rapidly, in a process the next chapter will further define as 'enculturation', where 'trans-local scenes are also increasingly characterised by global flows of people – DJs, promoters and fans.'⁶³ The person who originally found the site for Studio 54, the German Uva Haden, wanted to open a nightclub that would 'outdo anything he had seen in Europe',[64] indicative of this trans-local, transatlantic process of collaboration, and appropriation. In these early years of a brand-new decade, the New York club scene was back as the centre of attention and did indeed have an impact on British music personalities, as the city began to exert a wider influence and the focus shifted back towards Europe.[65]

1980s Manchester

Manchester-based band New Order visited New York many times in this period and established a fundamental link between Manhattan and Manchester.[66] While in New York, the band indulged in the city's nightclub scene, as singer Bernard Sumner explained when I interviewed the band for UK magazine *Muzik*: 'Yeah we went out to a lot of clubs, like the Fun House, Paradise Garage, AMPM, Berlin, Peppermint Lounge, Hurrah.'[67] Certainly, these experiences proved formative for a band interested in pushing the electronic envelope, ultimately feeding back into a significant new nightclub experiment back in their northern hometown, the key locus for this book and the fictional renderings of the city that will be analysed more closely in the following chapters.

New Order's record label was Factory, its nomenclature partly drawn from Manchester's industrial past, partly from Andy Warhol's Factory (Warhol, of course, a mainstay at Studio 54). The label was operated by a number of people, one of whom was Granada TV presenter Anthony H. Wilson. At this time New Order were succeeding commercially, the label had money, and they decided they wanted to invest some of that back into their hometown. The argument was whether to spend the money on a synthesizer – the wish of Factory producer Martin Hannett – or in a nightclub (in itself that helps locate the relative value of technology and architecture at that time). Wilson, something of a cultural philosopher, had digested the Situationist International Manifesto,[68] and specifically Ivan Chtcheglov's 'Formulary for a New Urbanism' essay. Whether he truly understood situationism, or merely borrowed its ideas as an advance of subcultural capital in Thornton's terms, is still contested. However, he did settle on one passage that read: 'That's all over. You'll never see the hacienda. It doesn't exist. *The hacienda must be built.*'[69] And indeed the Haçienda nightclub was built, in an old yacht warehouse on Whitworth Street West. In various interviews I have conducted over the years with the people involved with this project, Wilson, New Order and their manager Rob Gretton all profess that the motivation was to give Manchester precisely the kind of nightclub they had experienced while in New York,[70] and the club's Factory catalogue number (a sequential code accorded to all Factory products) happened to be 51, intriguingly close to 54.[71]

At this time Manchester was still in the grips of a post-industrial malaise, very much in keeping with Chtcheglov's perception of the 'melancholic city'.[72] Ben Kelly's stripped-down industrial design for the nightclub therefore spoke to this sense of an industrial aesthetic, in keeping with the tenets of vernacular architecture. The club opened its doors on 21 May 1982, with the incongruous choice of risqué British comic Bernard Manning as host. More significantly, Beat author William Burroughs gave a reading at the Haçienda in October of that first year. Club culture author (and case study for this book) Nicholas Blincoe was there that evening, an intersection of beat and rave that will be further detailed in Chapter 8. Bringing together the two characters from the Studio 54 photo referenced previously, Madonna then gave her first UK appearance at the club, on 27 January 1984, performing the song 'Holiday'.

The Haçienda was a cavernous, high ceilinged – and often empty – venue that seemed to exist as a club without an agenda, without an audience, until ultimately it found its meaning with the emergence of the acid house soundtrack at the heart of this book, later in the decade. Within this scene, the stripped-down techno beat of tracks such as T-Coy's 'Carino' and 'Salsa House' by Richie Rich perfectly suited the industrial aesthetic of Kelly's design.[73] With such tracks playing, hands were held to the heavens – or at least a postmodern interpretation of what heaven might be – in a quasi-religious upward swell of Ecstasy-driven emotion and energy that was now easily able to fill the space. The Haçienda's dancefloor functioned as tabula rasa, with little concern for the reductive, denominative tags of race, gender or sexuality, fulfilling Thornton's suggestion that 'going out dancing crosses boundaries of class, race, ethnicity, gender and sexuality'.[74] DJ Mike Pickering recalls a dancefloor formed of 'black kids to working class kids from sink estates who rubbed shoulders with homosexuals and bohemians alike'.[75]

In *Distinction*, Pierre Bourdieu suggests that economic capital might denote cultural capital, in terms of hierarchies of taste.[76] In the Manchester of this time, that vector might also be reversed, so that cultural capital is, instead, exchanged back for economic capital, as the psychogeographic resonance of this nightclub space generated an inward flow of income to the city, and a genuinely regenerative impact on a desolate part of the city centre. The wider impact of the building, culturally, became fundamental to the city's explosion as 'MADchester' – very much a 'scene' in Bennett's terms – at the end of the 1980s.[77] Tabloid newspapers ran features about this scene, detecting a new homological grouping: baggy clothing, smiley face T-shirts, music that married both the indie and dance aesthetic, and the drug Ecstasy, all encapsulated in the Happy Monday's track 'Loose Fit'.[78] Manchester City Council certainly understood the cultural importance of the building, just as they understood the importance of other cultural landmarks such as Old Trafford, the home of the Manchester United football club. When the UK experienced its first death from Ecstasy on the dancefloor of the Haçienda on 14 July 1989 – sixteen-year-old Claire Leighton – the leader of the City Council Graham Stringer (later MP for Blackley and Broughton) had the vision to write to the inquiry arguing the club made a 'significant contribution to the active use of the city centre core'.[79] This was the city, and scene, that I myself moved to weeks after that death, in September 1989. Having spent the previous six months travelling around Australia (during which time I first read Kerouac's *On the Road*), I had to ask someone what 'Stone Roses' were, since everyone had T-shirts with those words emblazoned. My subsequent indoctrination into MADchester and its musics was swift and soon complete.

The Situationists wanted churches destroyed. Factory Records had – perhaps inadvertently – built clubland's own postmodern, industrial cathedral, Chtcheglov's 'Temple of the Sun'. Again, New York is key to this transnational, trans-temporal knowledge exchange. Wilson argues:

> It's necessary for any period to build its cathedrals, it's necessary for any youth culture to have a place, a sense of place, and Manchester never had one for two years. And we find ourselves in a financial situation where we can do something about it, and thirdly it's necessary for a city like Manchester, which is an important city and which has been important to music to have the facilities that New York and Paris have, and not to have the facilities that New York and Paris have for young people would be a disgrace.[80]

Chtcheglov remarks: 'All cities are geological. You can't take three steps without encountering ghosts bearing all the prestige of their legends',[81] a position linking once again with the subterranean, with Derrida's notion of hauntology, and very much supported in the experience of visiting New York.[82] One can only imagine what Situationists such as Durruti,[83] Debord and Chtcheglov might have made of the demolition of the Haçienda in 2000, and its almost immediate reconstruction as fabrication, in a warehouse in Manchester's Ancoats for the filming of the 2002 Michael Winterbottom film *24 Hour Party People*, with the club not only built but now also 're'-built, this time to re/present the nightclub in cinematic terms.[84] As an extra in the club scenes for that film (of which more will follow in the next chapter) I can attest that that this, in itself, was a 'situation'. In a sense the demolition of the Haçienda represented in architectural terms what Reynolds refers to as a 'post-rave fragment' – the dissolution of the homogenous and spectacular into the disjointed and postmodern – as the club was sold off, brick by brick.[85] It would be equally interesting to know what Anthony H. Wilson (who died in 2007) would make of 'Tony Wilson Place', an open area opposite the site of the Haçienda, or indeed the fact that the cultural centre there is called Home, the name of the club that once competed with the Haç. Another arts centre will open in Manchester in September 2020, on the site of Granada Studios where Wilson himself worked. This one is to be called the Factory. Haçienda parties, such as Graeme Park's Haçienda Classical performances, are ubiquitous and events will survive in perpetuity in the myth. That would almost certainly be Barthes's contention.

Situationist Guy Debord discusses a notion of the 'drift' (dérive), where direction is left not to design but something more akin to fate – letting, for example, the switching of the traffic lights direct your movement, as I like to do when walking the streets of Manhattan.[86] In the paidian construct of the dancefloor, the dancer drifts around a microspace defined by its parameters, drifting in and out, momentarily, of people's gaze – affect is generated by space and the position of bodies. More broadly, this new music also engendered a transnational drift which, touching on Lyotard but also Deleuze and Guattari, Bey terms 'psychic nomadism', or even 'rootless cosmopolitanism',[87] with Graham St John's preferring tribes of 'technomads'.[88] Bennett discusses how 'the relative ease of long-distance travel, combined with a desire to go clubbing in new and exotic locations, has engendered a growing culture of "dance tourism" among contemporary youth'.[89] This dance tourism is reflected in a third significant location that I will now outline.

1990s Ibiza

Brothers Mike and Andy McKay moved to Manchester from Lincolnshire in the 1990s (although Mike had also been living and modelling in New York, that city again forming a key source of inspiration). The influence of the Haçienda was now waning, and the brothers divined that there might be space for something more esoteric, and exotic, in the city's nocturnal landscape. The McKays located a basement club Equinox, just behind Manchester's Canal Street, the heart of the city's 'Gay Village', and in 1994 they opened their night, Manumission. The Latin word 'manumit' means 'freedom from slavery', and from these very beginnings that was the philosophy that underpinned the club. Playing on the sense of the spectacular so successfully harnessed by Studio 54, the brothers arranged for carnival processions to trail along the well-worn cobbles of Canal Street, bringing 'cabaret into clubland'.[90] The brothers ran the club in Manchester for sixteen weeks (14 January to 19 April 1994) with such spectacular success that they attracted the unwanted attention of Manchester's dark side: the gangs competing for the security and drug concessions at the city's clubs. MADchester was morphing into GUNchester,[91] gravity's rainbow tracing its entropic, downward trajectory.[92] After one incident in which both Andy and the club were doused in petrol and threatened with immolation, the brothers closed their doors on Manchester. The club's make-up woman suggested they take a holiday to recuperate, and indeed they 'drifted', to Ibiza. Andy McKay explains:

> We spent a week on the beach and in the second week we thought we'd go to a few clubs. We blagged our way in pretending we wanted to do a night and were gobsmacked by the difference – it was everything we ever wanted Manchester to be.[93]

Here Ibiza's island dimensions are crucial. As described earlier, a dancefloor might be considered a Temporary Autonomous Zone; however, Ibiza itself might further be an island-sized zone, the island perceived as a liberating locus for fantasy and escape.[94] On dimension, Bey writes: 'The TAZ must exist in geographical odorous tactile tasty physical space (ranging in size from, say, a double bed to a large city)',[95] while on matters temporal he adds: 'It can be truly temporary but also perhaps periodic, like the recurring autonomy of the holiday, the vacation, the summer camp.'[96] Ibiza fits both dimensions, an island where even such apparently fixed notions of both time and space are loosened.[97]

Later in 1994, the brothers started the Ibiza incarnation of Manumisson at the Ku (now Privilege) nightclub, estimated to be the largest nightclub on earth, with a capacity of around 10,000. Sitting atop a hill, besides the main Ibiza Town to San Antonio road,

Ku began as a collection of villas nestled around a swimming pool which, in a process of organic, architectural evolution, merged together to form one open-air arena.[98] Each summer Manumission's themed parties grew in scale and vision. Again, the myth helped to sell the party, rather than the more pragmatic fact of who happened to be DJing. The promotion pushed on other fronts – production, performance, theatrics – with Mike's sculpted beard and partner Claire's mane of red hair forming part of the island's iconography. As Andy McKay explains:

> People come to our parties … and people come to Ibiza beyond that … to free themselves from whatever they do in their ordinary lives. … At least for those hours while they are at Manumission they can free themselves to do whatever they want, to be whoever they want.[99]

Manumission became the island's site of modern bacchanalian excess, perhaps the culmination of everything Rubell and Shrager intended with their dancefloor on West 54 Street. Indeed Haden-Guest titles his study of Studio 54 'The Last Party', but in the scope of this book that assertion must, of course, be challenged. Instead, and in keeping with the processes of subterranean life-cycle modelling, this book argues in the conclusion that it is this 1990s rave scene that will ultimately be seen as the very last homogeneous subcultural formation, Haden-Guest's 'Last Party'. Further, the trail can be traced to a very distinct date: 31 December 1999. The club scene, once so bright and spectacular on the dancefloors of Studio 54, the Haçienda and Manumission now bloated, sponsored, expensive. However, during these years it is impossible to consider the evolution of EDMC without reference to the island of Ibiza, along with locations like Detroit, Chicago, New York, London and Manchester, among many others places, with their own stories and contributions to our central narrative. Together these locations also formed the foundations for the fictions that would be constructed by Welsh, Noon and Blincoe, fictional simulacra of very real music scenes.

The politics of dancing

Having identified various spaces in which this culture took hold, and the technology involved in the production and consumption of the music that filled those spaces like sonic gas, this chapter will now consider why this combination of place and activity should have such an enduring hold on humans and their wider society. Dancing intersects with all aspects of our lives: exercising, *exorcizing*, expression, communication, display, attraction and the consequence – or perhaps conversely, and more accurately, the driver of all these – pleasure. On the dancefloor, a 'dancer from the dance' might be carried away from their workaday reality to a carnival wonderland, a 'sensual pleasure landscape'.[100] Such rewards are, it would seem, highly prized, and in the purpose of their pursuit the rave scene would birth what Sheila Henderson refers to as 'a generation devoted to defining their identities through pleasure'.[101] However, the clubbers – or 'ravers' in their late 1980s incarnation – also accessed this scene for what it did to their feet, as well as their head. It is, after all, called 'dance music' and 'dance culture' – few other music forms are so precisely allied to a vernacular purpose, built to engender physical movement. To interrogate these contingencies, therefore, I will first analyse physical movement and physiological pleasure, before concluding with an analysis of the sociopolitical consequences of such human gatherings.[102]

Scientific methods can be deployed in order to decode what dynamics are here at play. Movement, even in and of itself, induces pleasurable feelings, and this is something we can empirically deduce from everyday behaviour, throughout our lives. From babies being rocked, to children on a swing, to the elderly in rocking chairs, something comforting is found in movement, an urstate that remains integral and essential, whether children dizzy with movement, or adults dixy with intoxicants. Alongside movement, the sensation of sound also stimulates the vestibular system and causes very similar sensations.[103] Vibrations caused by music in the ear can even trigger muscular reflexes, from tapping your foot in time to music to the need to dance. Loud sound, therefore, together with that consequent movement, triggers the pathway to the pleasure centre of the brain – the hypothalamus – found on its pre-frontal cortex. That pathway is patrolled by the neural transmitter serotonin, the transmitter also triggered (or, more correctly, 'tricked') into action by the drug MDMA. Further, the vestibular system is also affected by the visual system, for instance if your eyes are closed, or you are in a dark-adapted environment. As already noted, if merely listening to the music engenders pleasure, the vestibular system is working overtime when in a club. In essence, then, music causes movement causes pleasure.

In even more closely analysing the social science of dancing, it can be argued that we would not dance at all, and thereby derive this pleasure, unless there were an ontological driver for such activity. Here, just as with other species with dance rituals – even lower vertebrates – dance can be seen as a consequence of evolutionary tooling. In this reading, dancing forms a mechanic for ensuring people come together, for celebration, and that further, such celebration might statistically lead to the potential for procreation. In an interview I once conducted for *DJ* magazine with Dr Neil Todd, senior lecturer in Life Sciences at the University of Manchester (an early attempt to understand why everyone – including myself – had this innate need to move), he concurred that 'if one looks at it from an evolutionary angle, it clearly has to be advantageous from an adaptational point of view'.[104] Consider once again the Saturday ritual – the Saturday Night Fever – and dancing can certainly be seen to be built around modes of display and attraction, decoded via a psychosexual theory of simulated intercourse, where a talented DJ can also manipulate a dancefloor as though it has become one hyper-sensitized creature.[105] Added to this already heady mix, MDMA also releases oxytocin, which helps humans bond, and the drug therefore functions as an enabler for such connections. Electronic dance music must therefore be seen within this context: the necessary soundtrack by which men and women, and indeed men and men, and women and women, are drawn to the dancefloor – *in part* – for the potential it holds for this reproductive, evolutionary function.[106] I say 'in part' because it should also be added that for many the rave scene, powered by Ecstasy, actually reduced the role of sex as a driver to take to the dancefloor, in an environment where a humble hug was often the limit of anyone's innate physical desire or need. As Sutherland remarks to Anthony Malone in Holleran's *Dancer from the Dance*, 'That is all that's left when love has gone. Dancing.'[107]

Beyond this potential sexual imperative, another consequence of large gatherings of human beings is automatically political, which might best be proven by the fact it was ultimately rendered illegal in the UK. Commentators discuss the dance 'revolution' (or 'insurrection', in Bey's terms), and if the dominant hegemony launches a 'War' on drugs, then the context has necessarily been politically charged. This book therefore argues strongly against the reductive position that this new club culture had no political dynamic. In so doing, it pushes back against commentators such as Rupa Huq, who states that this 'early rave was seen as ideologically vacuous',[108] inherently implying that the scene was inauthentic, and Simon Reynolds, who pejoratively questions 'whether recreational drug use is any kind of adequate basis for a culture, let alone a counterculture'.[109] In response, this chapter contends that the rave scene was much more than a weekend pursuit, and cohered with enough mass to form a genuine subculture, and one with an imminent political dimension. As Irvine Welsh remarks on this point, 'It's become a bit of a kind of acid house cliché – punk had politics, rave didn't', adding that 'the biggest number of arrests in post-war Britain were in Blackburn',[110] referring to the illegal warehouse rave parties in that town. Further support for this resistance to Reynolds is provided by Harry Shapiro, who describes how 'Reynolds is still clutching the worry beads':

> The very fact of large numbers of young people gathered together to hear/dance to music and take drugs is seen almost as a political act in itself simply because it is an activity that society at large does not want to see happen.[111]

On 31 October 1987, only months before the Second Summer of Love, the UK's prime minister at the time, Margaret Thatcher, infamously claimed in a *Woman's Own* article that there was 'no such thing as society'.[112] While she may have been perceived that to be true within the UK's everyday life, on the dance fields and in the party warehouses and nightclubs of the UK, young adults found their sense of society, and they found it on the dancefloor. The irony, of course, is that amid this countercultural, and of course illegal insurrection, promoters such as Tony Colston-Hayter, of Sunrise, were actually proving themselves very capable business people and, in fact, just the kind of opportunistic, visionary entrepreneurs of whom Thatcher should have been justifiably proud.[113] Simon Frith also concurs that 'there is such a thing as society and it is through music more than any other cultural activity that people become part of it'.[114] In the February of the year that Thatcher made her comment, US hip-hop act the Beastie Boys released their anthem '(You Gotta) Fight for Your Right (to Party)'.[115] Although intended as something of a parody, the track seemed to herald a rallying cry, parental authority representing a simulacrum for hegemonic society itself. Bey concurs that '"fight for the right to party" is in fact not a parody of the radical struggle but a new manifestation of it',[116] Henderson adding 'fighting for the Right To Party has united many of the youth who never got political before'.[117]

It might indeed seem a peculiar policy strategy to legislate against what writer Stuart Walton demonstrably argues is an innate anthropological desire in people to have a good time. Yet the Pay Party unit was set up to police (or at least attempt to police) these raves in 1989 (the ravers quickly termed them the Acid House Squad), and then new laws indeed follow. One must therefore automatically question – if the rave scene had no political dynamic – why this need to legislate?[118] UK legislation against the misuse of controlled substances dates back only as far as 1916, the start of a government's attempt to manage the population at a time of unfathomable crisis. Yet through the 1990s, the UK witnessed a new and hyper-legislative response from the Conservative government to the rave scene. This included the 'Acid House [parties] Bill' or the Entertainments (Increased Penalties) Act of 1990 and then the Criminal Justice and Public Order Act of November 1994.[119] That latter act specifically (and infamously) defined this music as including 'sounds wholly or predominantly characterised by the emission of a succession of repetitive beats', a significant meeting of the musicological and the judicial. The bill must also be seen as a direct response to events that took place at Castlemorton in May 1992, a week-long rave that is seen as an apotheosis of the 'free party' scene, the dancefloor now formed of a succession of Worcestershire fields. For many young people – unwilling to give up any more cultural ground and determined to legislate their own lives and physiological systems – Castlemorton became the frontline. As Walton remarks, 'Your serotonin levels are after all your own to manage.'[120]

Beyond this macro-political landscape, an equally important consideration must be the micro-political implications of club culture and nightclub activity, where such culture also revolves around the *politics of the personal*. As detailed, nightclubs remain a place of pleasure. Throughout, the individual pursuit of such libertarian, hedonistic freedom clearly runs counter to other, wider hegemonic forces. To rave is therefore positioned as an inherently political act; a site of both affect and effect. Perhaps the club scene was perceived to be apolitical in the sense that ravers had little interest in conventional party politics, and yet it is squarely political in this transcendental sense that as a collection of individuals, the entire scene necessarily distrusted, and resisted, dominant culture. Reynolds describes, for example, a 'cult of acceleration without destination'.[121] Instead, the theoretical position of this book is to stand alongside Shapiro in contesting that *the party is the point*: Reynolds's 'destination' perfectly, and hermeneutically, sealed all along, within the confines of the dancefloor. This is something that as a writer and researcher I feel very keenly: I frequently read accounts of the club scene that claim it has no political ideology and find that hard to square with my own memories of going to events organized by Freedom to Party, set up wholly to push back against this government legislation. This scene was oppositional, with weekend pursuits spilling out into weekday societal changes.

Walton writes: 'Might we go further and argue drug use, as an accelerant of dance cultures, actually has positive social implications?'[122] This is contested, controversial territory, but certainly the Stonewall riots must be mentioned, assisting with the levelling of homophobic attitudes in both the United States and United Kingdom.[123] In 1990s Manchester, Chief Constable James Anderton, the city's so-called God's Cop,[124] railed against gay revellers 'swirling around in a human cesspit of their own making',[125] and Chapter 6 will expand on the way Anderton was parodied by case study author Nicholas Blincoe, in his 1998 novel *Manchester Slingback*.[126] Anderton was himself soon consumed by a rainbow revolution that bequeathed Manchester the new bars and nightclubs of the city's evolving Gay Village, as the area regenerated. Walton adds: 'Relations between the sexes, and between gay and straight, at last became as unrecognizably fluid as sixties youth culture had promised.'[127] An argument can therefore now be made that the promise of liberation encoded in the First Summer of Love was ultimately to be delivered in the Second.

This regeneration is wholly tied up with nightclubs stimulating a new night-time economy.[128] Research by the MIPC considers the role nightclubs have played in the regeneration of city centres and throughout the 1990s every UK city, it seemed, had its 'superclub', just as it had its football stadia: the Haçienda in Manchester, Cream in Liverpool, Gatecrasher in Sheffield, Back to Basics in Leeds and Ministry of Sound in London.[129] Entirely new phrases entered the local government lexicon: the 'nighttime economy', the '24-hour city'. Licensing laws changed for the first time since that 1916 bill, and this once little-known music scene entered what author Dom Phillips defines as the 'superclub' era,[130] with clubbers drawn from the subterranean realm and into the new light of 'highstreet clubbing', heavily sponsored festivals and alcopops featuring packaging drawn straight from a rave aesthetic.

The club as carnival

There was another, darker driver to these concessions. Soviet-era theorist Mikhail Bakhtin argues that in the face of carnival – real revolutionary threat – society will always seek to accommodate that threat; to manage, absorb and ultimately commoditize its spirit, the fringes subsumed into the dominant whole.[131] Bakhtin's ideas will be further developed in Chapter 5 but certainly within the locus of the dancefloor one can locate a place where ideological, and hegemonic, tension resides. Society creates practical solutions – it allows for licensed outlets where such behaviours might be accommodated, such freedoms granted – the better for them to be contained, and monitored, ravers now in plain sight on the high street, in plastic reconstructions of the rave ideal.[132] One argument proposes, for instance, that because of the preference for Ecstasy over alcohol, the big breweries had lost control of the intoxication market and licensing legislation was only loosened to accommodate their wishes. Where once ravers truly raved beyond the all-seeing eye of Foucault's panopticon, outside of society's view, they were now pushed, once again, into the temporal pen of the weekend, hiding in plain sight.

This is the politically and culturally charged terrain Bey seeks to evade; to disappear from the physical manifestation of Bakhtin's vision of a 'grotesque reality', with his vision of the TAZ: 'The TAZ is like an uprising which does not engage directly with the State, a guerilla operation which liberates an area (of land, of time, of imagination) and then dissolves itself to re-form elsewhere/elsewhen.'[133] Bey highlights 'the concept of music as revolutionary social change',[134] in a way that locks securely with Noon's anti-authoritarian perception of music if, admittedly, within the construct of a club/cyber fiction. It also links to the idea of subterranean life cycles, and the continuum helix: that alien sound defined by an 'emission of a succession of repetitive beats' assimilated, understood and reduced. As Henderson details, this once unsettling house music 'now soundtracks everything from football and other sports coverage and kids' TV programmes to holiday and travel programmes'.[135]

Within the rave scene real ground was won, then, in terms of a more relaxed approach to licensing, and a perhaps more liberal approach to these alternative personal choices. Some ravers escaped completely, for instance those within the free party movement such as Spiral Tribe who pursued alternative lifestyles 'elsewhere and elsewhen', out of the weekend and indeed out across Europe,[136] forming Bey's revolutionary nomads who 'refuse to engage in spectacular violence, to *withdraw* from the area of simulation, to disappear'.[137] Huq concedes that these clubbers 'stretched Saturday night into a whole weekend';[138] however, this chapter concludes that this scene was stretched further still, into an entire lifestyle,[139] a view supported by Henderson who argues rave provided for 'a greater democratisation of youth culture than we ever witnessed in mod, hippy, punk or soccer casual heaven or anything since'.[140] I, and many others, would not be in a position to think, research and write about music as a career, were it not for those first steps we took onto the dancefloor. Discovering life with a 'loose fit'.

In exploring the nature and function of the dancefloor, this chapter has demonstrated how the nightclub is site for physiological, ideological, sexual and social evolution, and a place where a charged, subterranean dancefloor might, in a transcendental sense, challenge the supraterranean, hegemonic order. In this construction, the chapter has revealed how the dancefloor forms a frontline for these cultural, political and social exchanges – these salvos between dominant and underground spheres. The power of the dancefloor, in Foucault's terms, is drawn from a shared knowledge of other lifestyles and choices. It is perhaps not surprising, then, that this rich context of social, sexual and political energy should provide inspiration for film, TV and media representations. I will now analyse such modes of cultural re/presentation in the next chapter, before focusing on literature as a tool of mediation.

4

Re/presentations of EDMC in popular culture media

The previous chapter mapped out the subterranean world that also underlies and underpins this text of this book, in order that cultural representations of that scene might now, in this chapter, be better understood. After defining the notion of 're/presentation', this chapter will consider three specific medial modes of re/presentation that reproduced, in cultural terms, the hitherto secret manifestations of this world: TV, film and the print media. Further, it will interrogate why this new music scene formed such a rich resource for writers, directors and journalists, at the same time revealing inherent inefficiencies with these chosen forms, in terms of accurately, and authentically, capturing the essence of a music culture. Accepting inherent flaws in these media representations, this chapter will conclude by focusing where, instead, the truths of this subterranean music scene might better be preserved, with the following chapter interrogating literature as one specific mode of representation robust enough to contain cultural knowledge within its archive.

In terms of a theoretical framework to address these issues, much research has been undertaken into the role of representation, and I acknowledge, again, that the term itself is contested and problematic. Stuart Hall's edited collection *Representation: Cultural Representations and Signifying Practice*,[1] for instance, is certainly a useful starting point, although Hall foregrounds the role of visual representation, suggesting the key signifier of late modern culture is image, which might itself be challenged. Hakim Bey also highlights inherent issues with a more synchronic view of representation, suggesting we need to work towards replacing 'representation with *presence*'.[2] Bey continues: 'Art in the World of Art has become a commodity; but deeper than that lies the problem of re-*representation* itself, and the refusal of all *mediation*.'[3] Building on this resistance, it was also interesting to detect further antipathy to Hall's understandably CCCS-oriented focus on representation, at the 2017 biannual conference for the International Association for the Study of Popular Music, at which I spoke, on these very issues.[4] Narrowing this analysis to musicological discourse, Werner Wolf writes of 'music and its "re-representation" in musicalized fiction',[5] and it is also interesting to note Mark Fisher commenting 'we had been used to the "re" of recording being repressed, recessed, as though it really were just a re-presentation of something that already existed in its own right'.[6]

I agree, then, that this does indeed remain a contested field, and a more elastic and contemporary theoretical approach is therefore required. This methodology therefore deploys the original tool of re/presentation to further decode the importance of such popular culture artefacts. This graphological neologism denotes the method by which a culture might be described and communicated, via its cultural artefacts. It also allows for a split analysis of the function of such texts into their role for a contemporaneous audience, in their *presentation*, and as an archive preserved for a future generation, in their *re/presentation*. This re/presentation therefore refers not only to music text but also to subcultural *context*, the slash denoting a certain modernity in terms of graphology and an 'and/or' situation, rather than a simple stress on the 're' of representation. In this way the films, for instance, or TV, can present a music culture, in creating and distributing stories to a contemporaneous audience, but it can also re/present that culture in terms of a broader communicative function, curating stories which might also encode a knowledge transfer to both a future and a contemporary readership.

This chapter looks at the first of these modes, analysing what role such texts had in presenting this subterranean world, and the contemporaneous enculturation of this music culture. At this juncture I should define how I am using the term 'enculturation'. Sarah Thornton describes the process of enculturation as the cultural mechanism by which an artefact, such as a music recording or indeed cultural intelligence itself, moves from 'the private to the public sphere'.[7] Similarly, club mediations reproduce the landscape of the nightclub, the habits of casual and recreational drug consumption and the hitherto secret, almost magical machinations of the DJ for the more causal cultural voyeur. As such, this term can be more broadly related to the mechanism by which Dancefloor-Driven Literature, for instance, enables the distribution of cultural knowledge, just as it describes how a niche, stripped-down, post-industrial sound from Detroit, New York and Chicago became the ubiquitous soundtrack of the late twentieth century.

In keeping with the overarching theoretical strategy of the book, the chapter will deploy a mixed methodological approach, starting from the primary analysis of the texts themselves – examples from UK television programmes *Inspector Morse*, *Men Behaving Badly* and *Spaced*; North American cinema productions *Irvine Welsh's Ecstasy*, and *Ecstasy*; and British print media products *DJ* and *Mixmag* – which have all attempted to represent and capture something of the essence of dance music culture in their varied medial forms.[8] While textual analysis of these mediations will reveal a great deal about EDMC discourse, this chapter also holds up these artefacts against the works of cultural theorists. Once again, the output of Steve Redhead and the MIPC proves useful in this decoding. For instance, in *Repetitive Beat Generation* Redhead cites *The Face* magazine's contentious assertion that 'films, TV and radio are all media that can express the transient nature of the nation's nightlife better than the ... ethos of the novel (Not to say that cinema's attempt to capture the clubbing moment have been uniformly successful)'.[9] As much as I admire Redhead's work, I do strongly reject this particular position, calling on the more supportive work of John Hollowell, John Hellman, Marc Weingarten and Stan Beeler in order, instead, to outline the gap Beeler defines as 'the dialectic relationship between the phenomenon and its artistic representations'.[10]

Although Beeler's *Dance, Drugs and Escape* is impacted by its descriptive approach, one of Beeler's arguments will be useful in establishing a theoretical position by which to defend the function of these cultural artefacts. Beeler argues:

> Club fictions have two important functions with regard to club culture and its aficionados; the first is to describe the subculture to the mainstream and the second is to allow the members of the subculture to celebrate their participation in ways other than clubbing.[11]

This book will refer to this distinction as Beeler's first and second functions, and it is the first of these that is the more pertinent in terms of enculturation. It is after all natural that cultural artefacts built around clubbing will be of interest to clubbers, involved as they are in the primary activity itself. But it is this mechanic of cultural dissemination that further contributes to the production of knowledge around EDMC – not only cinematic but also televisual and, above all, literary-focused – extending to those outside these inner circles of this subterranean life.

Indeed, as the sociopolitical impact of the nascent 'rave' scene became clear, it inevitably came onto the radar of writers, filmmakers and journalists, who were all keen to use contemporaneous cultural concerns as source material for their output. Beyond secondary readings, therefore, invaluable, fresh, primary input from these key journalists and filmmakers, immersed in this music culture, will be integrated into this argument. Such original input is fundamental to any new consideration of the processes of re/presentation, both strengthening its dialectic progress and advancing, once again, the discourse of musico-literary intermediality to which this book contributes original thought. In this chapter, therefore, I am not inherently concerned with any qualitative judgement of these artefacts, but more with registering the very fact that they exist, and exploring why that might be. For instance, I question whether such writers and filmmakers were hoping to ameliorate some of the sharper, subversive activities of DJs, and the machinations of the dancefloor, in their fictions, or rather to simply profit from this interest, commercially.

As described in the previous chapter, the dancefloor stands as a site of great energy and potential, certainly one significant enough to command the front pages of media as varied as tabloid newspapers and teen pop magazine *Smash Hits*; to feature in *Harpers & Queen*; to loom large enough to be lampooned by the 'News At 10' and in pantomime, to be raised in the House of Commons.[12] So ultimately ubiquitous was this culture that it is seen as suitable subject matter for mainstream comedic vehicles, including UK sitcom character Alan Partridge and the animated US sitcom *Family Guy*, in which the main character Peter Griffin, rather accurately, mimics the effects of Ecstasy.[13] Certainly, in terms of cultural exposition, products such as films, books and TV shows are a useful indicator of the societal penetration of any new music form, the machinations of the rave scene perhaps only entering the public consciousness via commercial films such as *It's All Gone Pete Tong*[14] and *24 Hour Party People*.[15] In this way we might judge the ultimate enculturation of the rave scene by its use as subject matter for the 2000 film *Kevin & Perry Go Large*.[16] For such a broad and commercially oriented parody to work, cinema audiences must be familiar with the subject of parody, and complicit in the joke, for the comedy to register.

Having outlined this theoretical field, my own analysis of the re/presentation of a subterranean music culture will now start with TV, before scaling up to a consideration of its presence in cinema, and then the mass and niche print media.

Re/presentation of EDMC – TV

The enculturative penetration of any music culture is confirmed the moment it forms viable subject matter for mainstream television, and the rave scene did indeed find itself broadcast in this way. Although a number of such TV mediations will be considered here, it is not within the methodological approach of this book to offer a quantitative overview of such material; instead, the most efficient approach is to consider specific scenes within certain televisual vehicles, in order to understand what they might then reveal of the culture they depict.[17]

The first case study is the 'Cherubim and Seraphim' episode of the sixth series of British TV series *Inspector Morse*.[18] Broadcast in 1992, this episode appeared at around the apotheosis of the rave scene (argued by some commentators to be 1991). At this time, knowledge of the scene was not widely disseminated beyond the moral panic of the mass media, which in itself was enough to present writer Julian Mitchell with the rich source material for his fictional mediation of EDMC. The dramatic incongruity within the piece is generated by placing the cultured titular inspector within the nefarious and illicit world of night-time raves, following the death of Morse's niece, Marilyn Garrett. One exchange perfectly captures the elision of these two worlds:

> Morse: What sort of party, birthday?
> Owner: They probably said so.
> Morse: What do you mean?
> Owner: Oh, dear. Youth culture's a bit of a mystery to you, is it officer?
> Morse: You could say so.
> Owner: Young people, when they say parties, what they mean is drugs. Now I don't allow drugs down here, I'd lose my entertainments license. Of course you can't stop it altogether. But this isn't London where anything goes, you people are always poking your noses in.
>   ….
> Lewis: Where was this party, someone's house?
> Owner: Someone's warehouse, more like. What you do is rent a space call it a private party. There's not much that people like you can do, without getting heavy.[19]

Beeler correctly identifies a diverse range of understanding from the characters in this episode, in terms of the way this subterranean activity is perceived. Morse anthropomorphizes the role of an incognate and dismissive society, whereas a drugs squad officer, demonstrably younger than those around him, explains the unknown rituals of drug use. Interestingly, like many intoxicants in Dancefloor-Driven texts (including the novels of Noon and Miller), the drug cited in the programme is invented – in this case a pharmaceutical called 'Seraphics', creating a genus of fictional drugs.

This polarizing function in the mediation of the subterranean and 'other' is further exemplified by two UK comedic TV programmes of the period. Series Five of *Men Behaving Badly* includes an episode titled 'Cardigan',[20] broadcast in 1996 and therefore at the centre of the period analysed in this book. In this episode the main character, Gary, realizes his life has become staid and mundane. Deciding to confront this outcome he declares: 'Right, we're going to a rave.'[21] This decision is also welcomed by fellow 'man behaving badly', Tony, currently competing with a student for the affections of Deborah, who lives upstairs. What follows is a representation of the club scene archetype, with the friends driving out into the countryside to find their rave idyll. What they arrive at, however, is a largely inauthentic, if amusing, simulacrum of a rave, complete with a pneumatic hard dance soundtrack. Explicit drug taking would be a narrative misstep for a mainstream comedy such as this (where such behaviour might be considered problematic in terms of the limited 'lad' construct of the comedy, and too 'bad'),[22] and alcohol is presented as the cause of the intoxicated behaviour of the characters, with Gary crawling across the dancefloor only to turn and vomit towards the lens of the camera. Safely back at home, the programme resolves its dramatic arc with the characters considering their options:

Gary: It's going to be a while before I go out again.
Tony: Yeah, I mean what's wrong with stopping in, popping on a record with a proper tune—
Gary: —a proper tune
Tony: —and resting up with a nice pot of tea?[23]

There follows a swift narrative reverse when the action then hard cuts to the two men raving again, this time in the more reassuring environment of their local pub, the Crown. The music is electronic and heavy, but again, the friends have pints of beer in their hands and therefore merely mimic the combined effects of music and drug explored in the previous chapter, without authenticity, a point reinforced by the fact that they are surrounded by old men, also dancing.

Roland Barthes argues that all narratives share structural similarities,[24] and certainly in reading works of Dancefloor-Driven Literature, and other medial re/presentations, a narrative structure emerges for many of these stories. This will be referenced throughout this book as their *Narrative Arc*. These discursive traits haunt many EDMC texts – a parabolic storyline arc that carves the same trajectory the author Thomas Pynchon famously described as 'Gravity's Rainbow' – in reference to V2 rockets.[25] This arc maps the genesis, zenith and nadir of the narrative: the anticipation, the actuality, the aftermath that orientates us through the story. In simple terms, the up and the down. This structure is also the journey of a night out: going out, coming up, coming down. Indeed, it is the story of club culture itself: the first flowering of the rave scene up to 1992, through the vainglorious commercial mutations of the 1990s, to a demise Dom Phillips very precisely pinpoints as 31 December 1999 – the commercial club scene now bloated, solipsistic, mired in money and violence.[26] Kembrew McLeod, as with other commentators, links this parabolic journey with that of the (first) Summer of Love as 'the subcultures of the rave scene (and their music) grew darker and more negative as the initial drug-enhanced utopianism wore off and the drugs and relations between ravers became more harsh'.[27] Every high, then, must be paid for by a subsequent low; every Summer of Love by a Winter of Discontent. As Mark Almond, singer with Soft Cell and early adopter of Ecstasy, reports to Matthew Collin,

> With all that group of us who first took Ecstasy, it all turned a bit sour in the end. Everybody fell out, it was too much too soon – friendships and bonds we had during that time all accelerated and happened too quickly, and then it became routine and everybody became pissed off with each other, and there was nothing really there to cement the friendship.[28]

If 'Cherubim and Seraphim' closely follows this Narrative Arc, and the 'Cardigan' episode of *Men Behaving Badly* teases it, the 'Epiphanies' episode of UK comedy *Spaced* entirely, and deliberately, subverts it.[29] Broadcast towards the very end of the time period under consideration, on 29 October 1999, the sitcom revolves around two friends sharing a north London flat. In this episode, a bicycle courier named Tyres stops by to invite the friends to a party. At this stage – only seven years after *Morse*, three beyond *Men Behaving Badly*, but far enough for such narratives to have matured – the audience is witness to a much more assured re/presentation of the club milieu. Tyres might himself be a dealer of drugs; certainly he is still under the effects of intoxicants when we first see him, finding beats and music in the ambient sounds of the flat.[30] Equally, it is evident that the drama is moving beyond an illegal rave phase to a depiction of the club scene more in key with the superclub concept explored in the Dom Phillips's work *Superstar DJs, Here We Go*. The nightclub scenes were filmed at the London nightclub the Cross, but equally are redolent of other London clubs of the time, such as Turnmills or Ministry of Sound.

In their assurance, these club scenes also immediately feel more authentic. The characters are clearly under the effects of Ecstasy, the narrative cleaving closer to the actuality of a nightclub experience, notwithstanding the fact that such tropes are played out for comedic effect. More authentic, still, is the overt way the writers – Simon Pegg and Jessica Hynes – deliberately choose to subvert the Narrative Arc. Initially, the rather strange artist who lives in the flat downstairs – Brian – does not wish to join them on their clubbing adventure. Many years previously, in 1983, he spilt someone's drink in a nightclub and was punched.[31] On being asked to join them, he responds, in tortured tones, 'I don't ... go ... clubbing'.[32] Persuaded otherwise, once in the club Brian subsequently spills someone's drink again, only this time receives a hug, not a punch.[33] This is a dancefloor fuelled by Ecstasy, not lager, and the conditions are therefore very different.

Although all characters have taken Ecstasy and partied through the night, there is apparently now no price to be paid for that indulgence that might pay off, in dramatic terms, the high they achieved. The episode ends, simply, with the characters back at their flat, feet tapping to music long silenced,[34] a moment that will feel familiar to the cognizant viewer, in keeping with Beeler's second function. Ironically more authentic than a drama like *Morse*, the veracity of this comedy derives from writer Simon Pegg's own involvement in the club scene, which evidently afforded him both inside knowledge of the scene and a philosophical standpoint that places him in opposition to the more reductive and reactionary examples explored here. Pegg explains: 'We wanted to play homage to the British clubbing scene, we wanted to show it in a truthful light.'[35] Key, then, is authenticity. In his article 'Authenticity as Authentication', Allan Moore argues that authenticity is 'interpreted by an engaged audience as investing authenticity in those acts and gestures'.[36] In essence, everyone's perceptions of the scene are always mediated in some way, whether through flyers and magazine adverts, or indeed through the prism of Beeler's 'secondary artistic phenomena',[37] a point picked up by Bey, who argues: 'If you make media the center of life then you will lead a mediated life.'[38] It is the engaged audience, not the text itself, that confers authenticity on the depiction of these 'acts and gestures', a mutable gift dependent on the cognizance of that audience, whether participant or voyeur.

The existence of these TV episodes is itself indicative of the cultural force of the rave scene in the 1990s, substantial enough to form viable material for televisual vehicles as varied as comedy and police dramas. Television must be seen as the most ubiquitous and penetrative medium, broad in terms of both its national reach and its presence in the domestic living room. These 1990s mainstream UK television texts therefore undoubtedly assisted the enculturation of this niche subterranean scene, bringing this underground culture out into the light of the supraterranean realm, even if that light were, at this stage, the cathode light of a TV screen, rather than the natural illumination of daylight.

Re/presentation of EDMC – cinema

The soundtrack to rock 'n' roll was first encoded, for many UK teenagers, in films such as 1956's *Rock around the Clock*.[39] It is also cinema that reveals more central thematic issues of EDMC, together with stylistic problems inherent with cultural, and specifically cinematic, re/presentations of the scene.[40] Like TV mediations, here we witness rave culture once again emerging from the dark corners of the underground, revealed by the bright, projected lights (in this instance) of the high street multiplex, where the tropes and modes of this culture become more widely translated.[41] In analysing such secondary artefacts, this chapter will now address what Sean Nye identifies in the EDMC journal *Dancecult* as 'a current lacuna in club culture scholarship – namely, the scarce critical-aesthetic engagement with filmic representations of EDM culture'.[42]

Cinema has always been preoccupied with contemporaneous concerns, seeking to project back to us our subconscious fears and desires, whether alien invasion narratives in the 1950s providing metaphors for fears of communist invasion, or the more internalized horror of director Alfred Hitchcock in the following decade, marking an altogether more personalized terror. Beyond these broader articulations of the sub*conscious*, however, cinema is also irresistibly drawn to telling stories of the societal sub*terranean*, perhaps better (as outlined in the conclusion to Chapter 3) to contain, and thereby understand it. Chapter 3 argued that while the rave insurrection may be perceived as a transcendental blending of the solipsistic and the hedonistic, it nevertheless contained an associated assembly of effects that we can now see formed a cohesive context for viable cinematic representation. Both fiction and non-fiction documentary filmmakers were keen, like their TV counterparts, to use society's preoccupations with EDMC as backdrop their work, ultimately forming a recognized subgenre, the 'EDMC films' listed in the Filmography, containing texts from both sides of the Atlantic, and from both the UK and continental Europe.

For any film to succeed in terms of authenticity for a participatory audience – Beeler's second function – it must render a particularly believable environment, notably in its key nightclub scenes. Conversely, any slight divergence will quickly leave the film unbelievable, and therefore a failure, in those terms. In conversation, the Haçienda DJ Graeme Park comments on the representation of Studio 54, in the film *54*,[43] as 'amongst the worst club scenes I've ever seen in my life. You watch it thinking, clubs aren't like that.'[44] In terms of these more axiomatic issues associated with rendering a clubbing scene in cinematic form, Michael Winterbottom's film *24 Hour Party People*, by contrast, proves more authentic, which I am in a privileged position to assert, having been to both the Haçienda and the film set simulacrum.[45] As noted in the previous chapter, as a consequence of the demolition of the Haçienda, the film's producers reconstructed the cavernous nightclub, almost immediately after that demolition, in a nearby warehouse in the Ancoats area of Manchester, rivets of architectural verisimilitude used to construct the set. Almost on a 1–1 scale, nearly everything was restored, and in the right place: the alcove seating, the balcony and the bar, which was serving alcohol and therefore almost certainly contributed to the naturalistic flow of the evening.[46] Directors bemoan the need for extras to populate these fictional dancefloors and thereby make those dancefloors realistic;[47] however, these scenes included a soundtrack supplied by actual Haçienda DJs Mike Pickering and Dave Haslam, to further engender this sense of verisimilitude.[48] As Park explains, 'TV and film, I think, are generally not very good at getting club scenes done and that's because people have to pretend they're dancing to music, whereas in those *24 Hour Party People* scenes everyone was dancing to music.'[49]

Two North American productions will now be analysed: *Ecstasy*[50] and *Irvine Welsh's Ecstasy*,[51] both of which use club culture, DJ scenes and drug use as context and content, and can therefore be usefully compared and contrasted. As both are similarly titled, for the sake of clarity each film will be identified by reference to its director: the film based on an Irvine Welsh story will therefore be referenced to as 'Heydon', for Rob Heydon,[52] the other as 'Lux'.[53] The fact that both *Ecstasy* films are Canadian-financed productions and either in part (Heydon) or entirely (Lux) filmed in Canada highlights the striking coincidence of their concurrent release,[54] and this connection is accentuated further in the similar URLs for the websites of the two films: http://www.ecstasymovie.com (Heydon) and http://www.ecstasyfilm.com (Lux). In my conversation with the director, Rob Heydon explains that copyright conflicts with the Lux project meant they ultimately had to change the name of their final project, to *Irvine Welsh's Ecstasy*.[55]

These connections reveal the ongoing penetration of club culture within more dominant media forms at this time, servicing what Redhead describes as 'a young, cinema-going audience's experience of the weekend'.[56] In narrative terms, both films also demonstrate the discursive traits that haunt many EDMC texts – the same parabolic Narrative Arc previously compared to Gravity's Rainbow. Although these films take place in an indistinct near-present they are certainly not focused, like the UK film *Weekender*,[57] on the scene's pre-1992 'genesis'.[58] However, even standing as narratives moored in a post-rave context and located in legal nightclubs rather than illegal warehouses, they are nevertheless mindful that, to function as subterranean narratives, they have to cohere to certain cultural signifiers. Middleton refers to such signifiers as the 'different elements making up a socio-cultural whole'[59] that can be quickly understood, and navigated, as semiotic signposts by both filmmaker and audience. Hebdige discusses 'subcultural stylistic ensembles' – homological clusters – formed of 'those empathetic combinations of dress, dance, argot, music, etc.'[60] that provide what Middleton refers to, somewhat reductively, as 'structural resonances'.[61] In semantic terms, even the titles of EDMC films detailed in the Filmography – *Groove, Sorted, Weekender* – are all phrases lifted directly from the dancefloor, utilizing the argot of the scene to allow for what Saussure describes as language that 'blends with the life of society',[62] or, for Thornton, 'cryptic shorthand, innuendo and careful omission'.[63] It must also be assumed that there is an agenda – at turns both provocative and promotional – behind the choice of the word 'ecstasy' as the title for a film, building bridges of experience and knowing understanding between creator and consumer. As described in Chapter 3, street-level marketers realized they required a more appealing name for methylenedioxymethamphetamine, and such is the ubiquity of EDMC that the potential audience for these two films, the so-called Chemical Generation,[64] would be well aware of this connotation of the word, beyond its dictionary definition. There is therefore a level of assumption that to even pay your money and enter the cinema the audience is 'in the know' in Thornton's terms, the title functioning as codified shorthand, a signifier of the film's subterranean content and intent.

However, the use of the word 'ecstasy' in the two films is, in fact, rather problematic. In the case of the Lux text, the red pills that form the focus for the film's drug consumption are pharmaceutical rather than recreational, and stolen from a mental hospital, and are therefore not MDMA. In the case of the Heydon film, the issue concerns the marketing of the film itself. The film is based on an Irvine Welsh short story entitled 'The Undefeated', and subtitled 'An Acid House Romance' – a text that I will return to in Chapter 6. The film therefore appropriates the title of the actual collection *Ecstasy*,[65] rather than the novella within one must presume for the greater marketing impact of the final product. This is only further reinforced by incorporating the name Irvine Welsh, an author Collin calls 'the most extraordinary literary phenomenon of Ecstasy culture'.[66] Welsh's novel *Trainspotting*,[67] and its subsequent film adaptation,[68] provided Welsh with immediate and substantial subcultural capital. His name, therefore, remains a guarantor of countercultural intent, in terms of content, soundtrack and cinematic style, and that cachet is transferable, as evidenced in the marketing poster for *Irvine Welsh's Ecstasy*, which echoes *Trainspotting*'s own poster. You will also note the promotional use of a comment from my own feature at the time, interviewing cast, crew and indeed Irvine Welsh, for UK EDMC magazine *Mixmag*[69] (Figure 4.1).

Both film texts subscribe to what film critic Mark Cousins refers to as 'Closed Romantic Realism',[70] where the fourth wall is very much in place and the drama is contained entirely within the construct of the film. Cousins references the word 'romance' as 'emotions in such films tend to be heightened', and realism because 'people in such movies are recognisably human and the societies depicted have problems similar to our own'.[71] However, within the realistic construct of the nightclub scenes, emotions are then further heightened when accelerated artificially by drug consumption and pushed beyond the boundaries of the real. It might be further argued that the most intriguing character in both narratives is indeed the drug itself – the most interesting relationship that which unfolds between character and intoxicant. In the Heydon film, a voiceover towards the beginning of the film recounts the various street names for MDMA: 'eccies, disco biscuits, super marios, white doves, the club drug, the love drug, the hug drug, X, E, MDMA, 100% pure

Figure 4.1 Marketing poster for *Ecstasy*, dir. Lux (Canada: Dolce Cielo, 2011).

ecstasy',[72] assembling argot like the mountain of white pills that forms the marketing poster for the Lux film, on top of which stands a girl in her school uniform. At one stage in the Heydon film, meanwhile, white pills also fall through the air, in slow motion, suggesting oversupply and overconsumption, and that the underlying driver of both films' narrative is excess (Figure 4.2).

Dick Hebdige is keen to stress the fundamental role of music to a subculture and when translated to the cinematic medium, modes of diegesis become particularly crucial.[73] Diegetic and non-diegetic music can broadly be defined as follows: diegetic music is that which occurs within the environment of the film – for instance, the music a DJ is playing in a nightclub, that which Gorbman describes as 'music originating from the narratively implied spatio temporal world of actions and characters'.[74] This is set against non-diegetic music, likely to be the underscore or incidental music to the piece, designed to be detected by the audience in the cinema but not the actors within the narrative. As films that fall within the EDMC genre, and that have music itself at their core, a close reading of particular scenes from these two films reveals structural issues particular to the representation of an EDMC scene in a cinematic medium.

In first considering the use of diegetic codes within the Lux film and in one of the early foundation scenes, the four principal female leads are in the nightclub where one of them works as a DJ. All consume the red pills that one girl, Dianna Meyer, has stolen from her mother Alison, a nurse at the aforementioned mental facility.

Figure 4.2 Marketing poster for *Irvine Welsh's Ecstasy*, dir. Rob Heydon (Canada: Silver Reel, 2012).

To convey the impression of the drug taking hold, the director makes sharp cuts in the edit to denote excitement and heightened sensation: eyes are dazed, sweat drips, heads are thrown back in a sexualized display of ecstatic rapture. However, perhaps even more important than the director's schema is how the transformative effect of the drug is conveyed acoustically. As Monaco remarks, our eyes choose what we see, while our ears have no such choice,[75] and in diegetic terms the music certainly bulks up and throbs, sounds melt, voices are distorted and there is a distinct ringing in the ears. Further, the ringing sound might be said to cross the diegetic divide – not only diegetic but *meta*diagetic – a bridge of shared, subjective experience that links the perception of audience with character, the better to construct this naturalistic setting. This is a key signifier of EDMC film texts: we, as viewer, share the auditory equipment of Dianna's sister, Chantel, hear the same muffled tones of the beat perceived subjectively, mediated first through a sound system and then further through the pharmaceutical filter of her drug consumption. Important in dramatic terms, the scene also reflects an essential and peculiar issue in EDMC films: how to convey the transformative effects of a powerful drug for a passive, sober, film audience. It is not simply a matter of mise en scène as geometrics: in the process of rotating a horizontal dancefloor onto a vertical cinema screen, the intensity of the experience dissipates heuristically, and an uneasy tension appears between the audience's desire for a good time, set against cinematic representations of other peoples' good time.

This dislocation is more precisely illustrated by the composer of the film's diegetic club soundtrack, the DJ and producer Nick Hussey, who provides invaluable primary input into this precise, and nuanced, area of discussion. In my conversation with Hussey, he reports he was given time-coded scenes from the film in isolation, without any postproduction sound, so had to imagine and then compose the music that might have been played in the club at that time. Hussey therefore needed to write to the rhythm of the movement in the club scenes (resulting in music ranging 126–140 beats per minute), and in effect fit his music to the tempo of the dancing and the movements of the DJ, retrospectively, to give the impression that her physical actions might have sonic consequences.[76] In the interview, Hussey explains:

> You have to make it fit – you have to find the certain tempo of the scene and work it out so there's no singing where there's any talking and vice versa. When you're writing a song that's easy – there's two verses, the chorus and outro, all in a set order. But when you're doing a film you can't. You've got to cram it in when you can – get the best bits from the scene, not necessarily the best bits from the song. It's challenging.[77]

These issues of authenticity and mise en scène also come to the fore in the Heydon film. In my conversation with the director at the Glasgow Film Festival at the time of the movie's release, Heydon agrees that for the action to translate 'you have to make it as authentic as possible'; in other words, the audience has to buy into the story, the situation and the soundtrack. [78]

Here, the clubbing scenes fall into two distinct categories. First, there are the principal club scenes portraying the Edinburgh nightclub at the centre of the piece, the Sanctuary, which were filmed on a set in Northern Ontario.[79] Actor Adam Sinclair, who plays the male lead Lloyd, notes how a film set can be an unnaturally artificial environment for such action, with long pauses between moments of high activity. He identifies an essential difficulty conveying the energy of the dancefloor, in being able to 'capture that club element'.[80] As Sinclair explains, 'I've danced for four hours before but it's very rarely that I've danced for 20 hours.'[81] This is a rather unnatural environment, then, where as an actor you have to find, very quickly, your way to 'the moment', while the director must at the same time bear in mind very practical issues, for instance the fact that the bass from a speaker may be enough to make the camera shake. Second, and as opposed to these more staged scenes, Heydon also employed guerrilla tactics, taking his actors undercover into the Liquid Rooms nightclub in Edinburgh,[82] and filming clandestinely with Canon 5DMKII cameras fitted with prime lenses. Essentially a hand-held camera and therefore relatively inconspicuous, Heydon describes such cameras as 'technology that would be able to capture the essence of that scene'.[83] These immersive scenes are undoubtedly more successful in terms of the more aggressive machinations of *cinéma vérité*, taking the dramatic action into a working nightclub, and overlaying fiction upon a genuine, and therefore automatically authentic, club experience.

Once again, the diegetic soundtrack is key if the audience is to be part of the party and feel its beat. Gorbman takes issue with the term 'incidental music', arguing: 'The moment we recognise to what degree film music shapes our perception of a narrative, we can no longer consider it incidental or innocent.'[84] With films that focus on the tropes of electronic dance music, the importance of the soundtrack is even less 'incidental'. For instance, in one of the set-based club scenes in the Heydon film, the two protagonists meet on the dancefloor and instantly fall in love. To convey this process, Heydon incorporates circular dolly shots as the dancefloor beyond the two dissipates.[85] The music throbs and pulses, then cuts out, as they approach one another, other dancers melting out of focus as we centre on their connection and the chemical reaction between them. Whether the effect of actual love, or merely the 'love drug' Ecstasy, Heydon must convey this intense experience in audiovisual terms. Here creativity and artistry can be reduced to numbers, where the commercial imperative is keenly felt. Heydon secured fifty-one tracks for the *Ecstasy* soundtrack for under $20,000 which, as he himself points out, compares rather favourably to a single episode of American TV series *CSI*, where the budget is more likely to be $30,000 per track. It took eight months to secure permissions for the music used and even then, some pieces that were used as dummy tracks for the club scenes were ultimately not secured causing, once again, slight discordance between diegetic soundtrack and the kinetic flow of the scene. Heydon explains that their solution to this issue lay, quite simply, in 'the magic of filmmaking – editing and lighting and having them dancing to a certain BPM and finding something with a similar BPM that we do have permission to use and just cutting so that it works'.[86]

The club scenes in the Heydon film detail a coherent homology of effects that the character Lloyd describes in the film as 'the clubs, the drugs, the music'.[87] It is for directors like Heydon to ultimately assemble the varied strands of this primary phenomenon into Beeler's commercially viable 'secondary artistic phenomena'. The fecund mind of Irvine Welsh, for instance, had to impose a structure in order to turn club myth into the origin story 'The Undefeated'. Director Rob Heydon then imposes further order, not only visually but also in terms of narrative – making the principal male character Lloyd an international drug dealer, for example – to create a more dynamic story in keeping with tropes of the crime genre, also explored by Nicholas Blincoe. At each stage, then, these texts evolve so that they become more coherent narratives, rather than initial impressionist renderings of a more organic, and chaotic, subterranean scene. In that process, however, it might be argued that Heydon's film suffers from being too ordered, the romantic realism too neatly 'closed off', in Cousins's terms. Once again, the energy is lost the further removed we are from the dancefloor itself. As Monaco remarks, 'The great thing about literature is you can imagine; the great thing about film is that you can't.'[88] When a primarily sonic scene is reconfigured in a visual medium, the results, while superficially engaging and entertaining, struggle to capture the charged excitement of the nightclub itself, the inspirational potency of its soundtrack and, ultimately, the genuine experience of the individual club goer on the dancefloor.

As Park suggests, screen representations of the rave scene present a mixed picture. Aside from the very practical issues in conveying the club culture experience to a movie viewer, there are also broader, moral issues to consider. Some theorists denounce the cultural colonialism that such films represent, where the cinema screen might be seen to represent the very height of superficiality. Beeler, for example, suggests that such cultural products represent a 'selling out to the established entertainment industry',[89] as the supraterranean world seeks to take ownership of (and thereby profit from) stories of its subterranean dark side. In such terms, 'the idea of deviance becomes just another marketing tool',[90] beset by 'the contaminating processes of commercialization, commodification and diffusion'.[91] And yet it must be assumed that both *Ecstasy* films, in their representation of recreational drug consumption, diegetic and non-diegetic music codes, reference to nightclubs, and especially in their provocative referencing of MDMA in their title, are indeed placing themselves centrally within an EDMC film corpus. Taken together (and aside from the coincidence of their title) the release of the two films in the early years of the second decade of the twenty-first century demonstrates the ongoing cultural penetration of club culture, its continued relevance as a subject matter, and enculturative potential for a twenty-first-century cinema audience. Perhaps it also mirrors the recent resurgence of dance music throughout the decade in both Canada and the United States as 'EDM', reinforcing McLeod's notion that 'the ongoing, accelerated process of genre naming speaks volumes about group identity formations'.[92]

In terms of verisimilitude, however, replicating the nuanced tropes of the dancefloor in film form is evidently problematic, further complicated by the fact that audiences are likely to be seated in a quiet, dark cinema, a complete anathema to the heightened emotions of the club experience outlined in the previous chapter. In one conversation with the author Irvine Welsh, he reports: 'You can show a nightclub scene on screen but it will never be as good going to a nightclub because the whole thing is about participation.'[93] If this process is so fraught, the question must be asked why directors such as Lux and Rob Heydon – and indeed the other directors mentioned here and in the Filmography – continue to make cinematic products from re/presentations of the club scene? While commercial imperatives provide one answer, a broader consideration of other mass media modes of re/presentation is needed.[94]

Re/presentation of EDMC: Print media

According to editor Sarah Champion,

> I don't know who said it now but someone had said 'surely people who go clubbing don't read'. I can't remember now where it came from but there was a general assumption and I think it's partly to do with the fact that electronic music doesn't have words and therefore it can't be 'intelligent'.[95]

Champion makes a further claim about genre-specific media and this subterranean scene, suggesting that 'there should have been some kind of "Gonzo" journalism to capture the spirit but there wasn't'.[96] In interrogating Champion's suggestion of a lacuna in auteur journalist voices, and addressing questions of musical genre, key magazine titles that focus on the musical tropes and modes of the dancefloor – *Mixmag, DJ* and *Ministry* – will now be explored.[97] Media commentators such as Marc Weingarten, John Hollowell and John Hellman will also be integrated, as regards their broader historical analysis of New Journalism,[98] of which gonzo journalism forms a subset. However, in considering a specific 'club culture' journalism, no one particular theory exists by which to decode this material. The approach will therefore necessarily be qualitative, although the chapter will draw on the primary, quantitative input of the embedded personnel – the editors and journalists from this period of music reportage – who responded to my questionnaire, as well as inviting Sarah Champion to revisit her remarks in the light of the passing of time, some seventeen years later.[99]

The fundamental role of the media in subcultural formation was arguably missed by the Birmingham School, as highlighted by Thornton, who writes how that school 'gave positive valuation to the culture of the people, but only at the cost of removing the media from their pictures of the cultural process',[100] and indeed Redhead, who argues: 'The media development of subcultures is as important as it has always been.'[101] My own access to this subterranean world was via my work with the media, and it always seemed to me that journalistic mediations on subcultural formation operate in two distinct ways, and on two very different levels.[102] These might best be described via reference to Stanley Cohen's famous societal consideration of 'moral panics' and 'folk devils',[103] which here can be mapped onto the responses of the mass, and then niche, media. As already noted in Chapter 3, the mass media exhibits its own rather regimented and predictable response to any new subterranean emergence, breaking the societal topsoil, especially one with an unrecognizable soundtrack of 'repetitive beats'.[104] In the summer of 1989, for instance, *The Sun* newspaper ran the headline 'Spaced Out', with an accompanying image of 'ravers', the subheading detailing how '11,000 youngsters go drug crazy at Britain's biggest-ever Acid party'.[105] The mass media fulfils a cyclical role, moral panic translating into effective PR: the louder the opprobrium, the more the party participants will feel that they have succeeded.

Second, the nature of the mass media dictates the necessity of moving on, to consider the next moral panic. What follows is an information vacuum. In a pre-digital age that prioritized, and valued, information much more highly than our own, niche, trade and fanzine publications were able to fill this void. This media formed a portal for information – an insider's guide to this new scene – offering readers knowledge, and therefore access, to this subterranean realm. Style press such as *i-D* and *The Face* were quick to pick up on this new sound.[106] As Thornton notes, 'Throughout the early months of 1988, *i-D* ran stories on aspects of what would come to be clustered under the rubric of acid house',[107] while trade publications found themselves caught up in the moment, their sales miraculously, and exponentially, improving.[108] Consequently, and in a predictable commercial life-cycle model, more corporate publishing houses began to divine a market for magazines that might describe this new cultural phenomenon and mediate responses. Tony Prince, a Radio Luxembourg DJ of the 1960s who established Disco Music Club (DMC) in the 1980s, explains:

> When I left radio after 18 years, to start DMC, I decided not only to provide the world's first mixes for DJ's ONLY but to provide them with a monthly newsletter which accompanied their recordings. That turned out to be Mixmag which I edited and published. [...] As success embraced us, so I brought in more writers and, eventually, a full-time editor. Dave Seaman became editor, my son Daniel became Clubs Editor.[109]

In the same decade, a trade magazine for mobile DJs titled *Jocks* enjoyed similar success, changing its name to *DJ*. As early editor Chris Mellor recalls,

> The beautiful thing was the publisher had no idea what we were on about. He thought the thing would fail but it kept growing and making money so he let us get on with it. Simple as that.[110]

Beyond these two key titles, London superclub Ministry of Sound published its brand extension, *Ministry*, IPC launched *Muzik*,[111] and Future Publishing offered *i-DJ* and as a freelancer I was keen to contribute to all of these. In terms of more independent publications, *Jockey Slut*, *Sleaze Nation*, *Wax*, *M8*, *7*, *Knowledge* and *One Week to Live* might also be highlighted. Many of these publications had their own offshoot publications in Ibiza – I myself edited Ministry of Sound's Ibiza publication, *Ministry in Ibiza*, in 1999 and 2000 – and fanzines such as *Boys Own* also enjoyed a relatively wide readership. At their height, both *Mixmag* and *Ministry* were selling towards 100,000 copies each month,[112] and even on a purely statistical basis, the notion of generational illiteracy on behalf of Champion's now forgotten 'someone' must already be questioned, reinforced by Tony Prince, who adds: 'Why would they say clubbers don't or can't read, that sounds very snobbish? Most people are clubbers. Some of the world's most intellectual people like getting down (and up!)',[113] while his son Dan concludes: 'Some of these people were lawyers, teachers, accountants and doctors. Case closed.'[114] Clubbers certainly were reading, and in their hundreds of thousands.

Before analysing the form of this club culture journalism, consideration must be given to the function that this very specific area of the media served. Centrally, these magazines, like cinema, enabled participants to connect to their culture away from the scene itself, in line with Beeler's second function. As Rupa Huq notes, 'These publications, implicitly aimed at men, contain lifestyle articles and personal profiles on "name" DJs in much the same way as girls' teen magazines',[115] outlining how this media provides the emotional and sartorial responses that bestow cultural significance, in the process articulating ideology and defining the scene in terms of its fashion, argot, drugs and politics. Certainly these publications distribute intelligence, arming these subterranean revellers with the linguistic, musical and fashion capital to see them through each and every weekend, playing on notions of authenticity, representation and belonging.

In addressing the role of the print media in re/presentations of the club scene, Redhead identifies how 'the glossy male monthlies, *Arena*, *GQ*, *FHM*, *Maxim* as well as *Loaded*, have helped to market the repetitive beat generation fiction to an eager, younger, male, consumer audience'.[116] However, there are fundamental issues with this position. The 1990s were a troubled time for the print media, facing for the first time the emergence of the digital sphere and its resulting commercial pressures. This was also a time when much of the personality that journalists had previously expressed in their writing was also challenged.[117] There was no sense that Dancefloor-Driven writers (beyond one or two instances) would see their fiction published in any of these titles, contrasting with the example of Hunter S. Thompson, whose most celebrated work of gonzo journalism, *Fear and Loathing in Las Vegas*, initially appeared in two parts within the pages of *Rolling Stone*.[118] Champion identifies this as a 'big missed opportunity'.[119] Instead she simply acknowledges that 'a magazine's job is to review the records',[120] and certainly these titles would typically feature reviews of music and events, interviews with DJs and producers and listings for where to go each weekend. These restrictions of function – and the ephemeral limitations of the magazine format – might begin to explain this lacuna in auteur voices.

Ferdinand de Saussure is important in this context, in terms of appreciating the culturally communicative aspect of media, and how the signs of, in this instance, a music culture are referenced and reformed in linguistic terms. Language and argot are, of course, used to drive narrative but more importantly, they are deployed naturalistically, in order to keep close to the object, in order to engender proximity for the reader. These contingencies are developed in subsequent chapters in the context of fiction but certainly, they are also useful when decoding EDMC magazine writing. Further, in resisting the scientific rigidity of structuralism, a more contemporary linguistic theory is useful, in suggesting that language, communication and meaning are actually negotiable. Relevance Theory, like all pragmatic linguistic theory, posits that hearers routinely rely upon contextual assumptions, which can include assumptions about language, and are either retrieved from memory or constructed in the process of utterance understanding, in deriving the intended meaning of speech.[121] Moving towards his post-structural position, Barthes is also helpful in outlining a 'cultural code', a context by which to examine the text, formed of 'the stock of social knowledge on which the work draws',[122] fundamental to the function of the text. Such communication is therefore determined by *a priori* associations and assumptions about language, allowing the knowing recipient to reassemble meaning at the point of reception.

Club culture journalists are writing for individual readers, yet also creating codes to be decoded and reformed in literary terms, by a cognizant-participant community. During her interview Champion foregrounds her own love of slang, as the argot of the dancefloor:

> It's about capturing a subculture, it's about capturing the dialect and the slang and street culture and the atmosphere and the vibe of the whole thing, in print. That's what I wanted to do. What defined it as a movement would be the use of dialect, the use of slang, the use of made up words, the use of street speech, the use of very experimental punctuation.[123]

This is central to club culture communication, with EDMC journalists using the tenets of synthetic personalization to reach out linguistic roots, and make readers feel as if they were being addressed personally, and casually. At times they also deploy this further level of connotative code in order to consciously obscure clarity and conceal meaning, to the bafflement of the casual cultural voyeur working at the denotative level, in Barthes analysis, but to the benefit of those who can understand, and decode, the communication. The same, of course, holds true for the 1960s counterculture and the Beat Generation that preceded, each forming its own language and codes in order to coalesce linguistically into a subterranean 'scene', linguistically 'other', and clearly delineated from the supraterranean realm and its more transparent communications. For the purposes of illustration, I can offer the following personal recollection. During my editorship of *Ministry in Ibiza* magazine, writers could never be explicit about drug consumption, although that was clearly implicit in the culture of the island. Various words were deployed as code, the main one of which was 'spangled'. I later wrote for *Mixmag* and was amused to see that their style guide banned the use of the word 'spangled', on the grounds that it 'is a *Ministry* word'.

At this juncture a more penetrative consideration of gonzo journalism will reveal a literary seam running through the three countercultural scenes mentioned in my introduction, linking Beat to rock, but also clearly running further through, to rave and it attendant Dancefloor-Driven Literature. As defined by Douglas Brinkley in *Fear and Loathing in America*, gonzo journalism 'requires virtually no rewriting: the reporter and his quest for information are central to the story, told via a fusion of bedrock reality and stark fantasy in a way that is meant to amuse both the author and the reader',[124] while Hollowell details the extremity of its tone, 'since it calls for the writer to provoke many of the incidents that he describes'.[125] Its greatest proponent was the American journalist Hunter S. Thompson, one of journalism's 'literary rock stars',[126] who placed himself at the epicentre of his stories, to become 'part of the action'.[127] Gonzo journalism is necessarily personality journalism: to reclaim a literary term lost to cinema, the author must truly be seen as 'auteur'. Like auteur directors such as Jean-Luc Godard and François Truffaut, their presence is felt in the way they direct the story from the very heart of the action, in every word. Here we can appreciate how, in terms of style, Thompson was himself accused of mimicking Jack Kerouac – writing immersively, and *musically* – in a way that might also be carried through to Irvine Welsh et al. Again, such an approach is immediately an anathema to the tenets of structuralism, where the only interest is the text. Here, we can link writers linguistically with the same subterranean, sonic root note.

As outlined in the opening section of this chapter, Thompson's incendiary style of gonzo journalism sits within the broader school of New Journalism, encompassing these writers who utilized a more participant-based subjective form of reporting and in our conversation, Champion confirms: 'I was interested in New Journalism. That's what inspired me to want to write because that was the first movement away from factual journalism towards the kind of gonzo thing'.[128] Scott Manson, ex-editor of *Ministry*,[129] notes the presence of this tradition and reports: 'Absolutely. Getting wasted and causing trouble was a big part of club writing',[130] although James 'Disco' Davis, his long-time club reviewer, adds 'with Gonzo the experience of the journalist was central with the story taking a back seat. In club journalism there was plenty of messed up stuff but the story usually came first.'[131] Duncan Dick, currently editor of the UK's leading EDMC magazine, *Mixmag*, carries on that thought:

> Drugs have been assimilated into the mainstream now. What's interesting about a chemical viewpoint at a club or a festival in 2013? Most people there are already wasted, what special insight does that chemical viewpoint give you? Too many aspiring journalists thought and still think that getting wasted and copying the cadence and hyperbole of *Fear And Loathing in Las Vegas* makes them special.[132]

DJ and writer Jonty Skrufff concurs: 'I am well aware of gonzo journalism and I am well aware of many journalists who've partied as hard as anyone. But few then write about it, wisely, in my view.'[133]

For centuries newspaper journalists have studied their particular craft and followed regimented rules by which to construct their copy. One-time editor of *The Independent* newspaper Amol Rajan funnelled the advice of the paper's founder in a *New Statesman* column, recalling Andreas Whittam Smith's advice that 'journalism is a street: we are on one side; the people we write about are on the other. It's our job not to cross the street.'[134] While I agree there is a long white line in the middle of the road, in my media career I felt that clubland, and the music journalism that reported upon it, seemed to be about just such transgression, and trespass. Returning to my motivation, when I began writing it was not only that I wanted us in the fourth estate to cross Whittam Smith's street but further, that there should be a street party as we did so. That line was *there to be crossed*. I found this culture vibrant and intoxicating, and felt strongly that it necessitated a new approach to writing, to deconstructing the disco. Such behaviour seemed possible, perhaps because of the muso-cultural territory, perhaps because of the ego and ambition of youth. Certainly, it required a leap of faith on behalf of editor, publisher and reader. I was lucky that my own editor at *DJ* was Chris Mellor. When the emergence of the internet led to Mellor pulling the listings pages that I edited, he offered to keep both the pages and my payment for those pages available to me. That formed the opportunity to mount a gonzo attack on the dancefloor, with the column 'Dispatches from the Wrong Side'. It was an overt, ideological decision to use the methods and mechanics of gonzo journalism to better decode the machinations of club and drug culture. New Journalism, or immersive reportage, implies the contemporaneous close presence of the journalist, perhaps too close when authentic rendering requires distance, time and reflexivity, a more controlled mechanic by which to detail events. Champion is therefore right in her claim that this scene necessitated a new approach to writing; or more accurately, a relatively old one repurposed. It was not enough to report on a party – the writer should be part of that party.[135] I feel that Forde is correct in his analysis that auteur spirit is now being removed from music journalism.[136]

Hellman channels Zavarzadeh in his assertion that 'nonfiction novelists are uniformly absurdists in their intention'.[137] I agree the dancefloor is absurd. Dancing is absurd, when considered pragmatically, if not anthropologically, as I have attempted to do in the previous chapter. It must logically be further absurd for a third party to then report on that process so that others, so far removed from the action they were not even there, might read about it. Hellman suggests that 'new journalistic works share a factual subject matter and an aesthetic form and purpose',[138] and certainly gonzo journalism must be seen as enjoying the most elastic of literary aesthetics, where object is always subservient to the course of language. Barthes knew this, recognizing in *Mythologies* 'the journalist who starts with a concept and seeks a form for it'.[139] Barthes's work on myth and the construction of persona is particularly important when one considers the subversive aesthetic of gonzo and its subscribers. Barthes continues, 'Since myth is a type of speech, everything can be a myth provided it is conveyed by a discourse.'[140] The path to meaning is therefore further obfuscated by the gonzo poeticism of the prose, the at times impregnable argot of the dancefloor and an essential negotiability of the facts.

In terms of a subterranean scene as rich in narratives as EDMC, there are therefore two methods by which you might report on the scene: fiction and non-fiction. This is abrasive, shifting territory – that essential friction between fact and fiction. As demonstrated, music journalism is a looser discipline than news reporting – club culture journalism even more so – but in seeking to discover whether Champion's lacuna lies with inauthentic media representations of EDMC or rather the scene itself, the inherent problem lies, once again, with the dancefloor. It is so vast in scope and vibrant in sensibility that in the ultimate reckoning, attempting to further bend it out of shape using the techniques of gonzo journalism is problematic. Again, this partly explains why these journalists resisted what might seem an obvious stylistic path or were dissuaded from attempting to do so by their editors.

The answer to the issues raised by Sarah Champion's anonymous literary critic is therefore multiple. Clearly clubbers did read, with EDMC magazines such as *DJ* and *Mixmag* still published today, and while the gonzo tradition was at times evident, in a shifting, postmodern environment perhaps entirely new terms are needed, where the twin worlds of fiction and non-fiction are too polarized to be useful, when so many non-binary grades exist in between.[141] We are now starting to move closer to the 'aesthetic center' of Dancefloor-Driven Literature.

The friction between fact and fiction

This chapter has considered the notion of enculturation and cultural presentation in relation to a subterranean music scene and its efflorescence into the supraterranean realm. In so doing, it has analysed how different modes of such re/presentation (whether TV, cinema or print media) have contributed to the popularization of EDMC within the contemporaneous society into which these varied texts were published, or broadcast. The limited commercial and critical success of such texts must be acknowledged, bearing in mind comments from the likes of Park and Welsh around cinematic representation. Equally, for many participants congregating around Beeler's second function, they may well also stand as unreliable narratives, now held up in a cultural-historic context. In a sense, however, the subjective, qualitative assessment of whether these texts are accurate and authentic as cultural artefacts is less interesting to my research than the central truth that they did, in fact, exist. For it is within these fictional ethnographies that the landscape of the nightclub was, perhaps for the first time, revealed for many non-cognate readers and viewers. At the same time the homological characteristics of this scene – such as casual and recreational drug consumption and the hitherto secret, almost magical machinations of the DJ – were also revealed, not merely for a restricted number of participant clubbers, but for a potentially infinite crowd of global cinema-goers, TV viewers or members of the public with the modest funds to buy a magazine.

UK rave culture began very much as a scene for a cognizant 1980s in-crowd, emerging – then quickly evolving – in key cities like London, Manchester and Nottingham, mediated at the time through style magazines such as *iD* and *The Face*. By the end of the twentieth century, the scene had penetrated deep enough into cultural consciousness to form a viable subject matter for mainstream UK TV series such as *Morse* and *Men Behaving Badly*, as well as comedic vehicles films including *Kevin & Perry Go Large*. 'We are DJs', says Kevin, early on in that film. 'And where do DJs go for the summer?' What once was the inside secret of an Ibizan TAZ had now become an in-joke: Perry knows the answer and by 2000, so did everyone in the audience. Once spectacular but essentially subterranean secrets such as the island of Ibiza had emerged from the darkness of the nocturnal rave underground through the cinema screen, the domestic TV screen and the pages of newspapers and magazines.

Any consideration of re/presentation must also introduce the element of time and further cultural-historic contingencies. It is the robustness of the medium, therefore, that now becomes key: the medium in which these subterranean words, and worlds, might be both contained and conveyed. The answer lies, perhaps surprisingly, with journalist Hunter S. Thompson who, drawing on American novelist William Faulkner, observes in a key aphorism for this book that 'the best fiction is far more *true* than any kind of journalism – and the best journalists have always known this'.[142] Redhead brings this slippery idea to club culture in asking novelist Alan Warner if fiction is 'a way of telling contemporary history better',[143] while Hollowell refers to New Journalists simply as non-fiction novelists. Further, American author and essayist Gore Vidal, in conversation with countercultural British journalist Mick Farren, agrees: 'You can be more truthful in fiction. Professional historians, by and large, have their prejudices, which condition everything they write'.[144] Vidal explains that it was an innate respect for history that drove him to write his historical novels *Burr*, *Lincoln* and *1876*, in his words to 'correct bad history'.[145] For the purposes of this research we might further bend Norman Mailer's subheading for his reportage novel *Armies of the Night*,[146] his account of the 1968 Democratic convention in Chicago. Mailer describes his work as 'History as a Novel / The Novel as History', which might be further adjusted here as Cultural History as Fiction / Fiction as Cultural History. In essence, fiction or non-fiction are both necessarily mediations of the truth and it is by no means evident – especially in current times – that the latter is any more secure, and trustworthy, than the former.

Returning to the physicality of the medium, the pages of a magazine appear flimsy when set against the studier stock of the bookshop novel, where journalism, traditionally, has a shelf life as long, indeed, as its life on the shelf.[147] Here we arrive at the very heart of this analysis, in appreciating why the re/presentation analysed in this chapter is primarily important for its role in contemporary enculturation. While journalism purports to be truthful, it is ephemeral, whereas fiction, apparently fabricated, endures. When music-oriented writers tackled the rave scene, the terrain was no longer suited to the kind of gonzo-guerrilla warfare that had been waged before, those tactics perhaps even outmoded when deployed to tackle the modern dancefloor. In terms of these literary and linguistic impulses, therefore, and in the analysis of this book, that friction defined earlier became so frantic in the 1990s that in fact, the spirit of gonzo flipped completely into the realms of fiction and a purely literary mediation. Instead, the response was to bring up the big literary guns of the past – naturalistic, realist fiction – to wrestle narrative order on what was always an unwieldy, shape-shifting dancefloor. My analysis now progresses, therefore, from the less important notion of whether clubbers read, but rather, *what* they read.

5

Defining Dancefloor-Driven Literature

That blonde rectangle of polished wood that had seemed to be at one point the aesthetic center of the universe.[1]

Andrew Holleran, *Dancer from the Dance*

Having broadly considered the notion of re/presentation, this chapter will now focus on a specifically literary mode of re/presentation, before offering a series of detailed case studies, from Chapter 6 onwards. While the previous chapter considered the notion of enculturation, and the more contemporaneous effects of such mediation, this chapter will concern itself more with the central, overarching theme of this book: the role that, taken together, this subterranean literature plays as a developing, cultural-historic literary corpus, in now focusing on the 're' from re/presentation. As we saw in the Introduction, novelist Andrew Holleran's manifestation of the dancefloor in 1970s gay New York is as a 'blonde rectangle of wood', and yet as evidenced in Chapter 3, the dancefloor is mutable: whether a beach, field or warehouse. This chapter will therefore consider the role of the dancefloor, in whatever incarnation, as a driver of stories, also interrogating the way the music of the dancefloor is then used within these literary texts – both specific references to music tracks and technologies, and the impressionistic rendering of the sonic architecture of the story.[2]

In decoding novelist Andrew Holleran's 'aesthetic center of the universe', we can return to the questions that have driven this book: How might authors write about something so otherworldly as a nightclub scene? How might they write lucidly and fluidly about the rigid, metronomic beat of electronic music? What literary techniques might they deploy to accurately recount in fixed symbols the drifting, hallucinatory effects of a drug experience? In responding to these questions, this chapter considers a range of writing available and specifically two key texts: Trevor Miller's 1989 novel *Trip City*[3] and the Sarah Champion edited collection of short stories, *Disco Biscuits*.[4] In the analysis of these texts, this chapter will define the Dancefloor-Driven Literature that sits at the very heart of this book, addressing notions of production and readership, and considering whether its authors sufficiently cohered in order to form a literary scene, further extending out dialogically to establish aesthetic connections with other literary movements.

The dancefloor is both modest and massive, witness to micro-moments and the birth of what this book will ultimately define as *subterranean systems*. Such systems are apparently hermetic, relying for their homological coherence on the three important root factors outlined in the Introduction: music, literature and intoxicants. However, this book has also drawn links between three such systems, twenty years apart: the late 1940s bebop beat captured by the Benzedrine-driven clatter of Jack Kerouac's typewriter keys and that of the broader Beat Generation; in the late 1960s, the distorted wail of the rock guitar solo replicated in the wild improvised New Journalism of writers such as Hunter S. Thompson; and the 4/4 pulse of electronic dance music in the 1980s and the words that tried to describe that euphoric, celebratory beat. The UK's 'style bible' magazine *The Face* contended 'you wouldn't think [...] that dance culture would be well suited to literature. While dance music may be fluid and ephemeral there's few things more solid than 200 pages of paperback'.[5] Despite this pessimistic outlook, this chapter will evidence how the grooves of these records were indeed replicated in the graphological groove of words, which then coalesced to form a Dancefloor-Driven Literature. Nightclubbers, now repurposed as 'ravers', engaged in semantic wordplay. 'Everything begins with an E' was a popular aphorism of the dancefloor and in terms of the linguistic determinism examined here, it is hard to argue.[6]

This academic melding of musical and literary approaches to decoding texts is not new and the antecedents of musico-literary intermediality must be acknowledged,[7] as well as the appearance of more recent accounts.[8] However, no precise theoretical tools or language has yet been developed to decode this particular drug-fuelled literary collection and the electronic soundtrack lying beneath its pages, and establishing this analysis is therefore not without its challenges. If the object of the dancefloor is chaotic, and paidian, then perhaps its decoding must necessarily also be so. An appropriate response, therefore, might be to reach for new methodological technologies, whether the fresh approaches to fieldwork explored in the EDMC journal *Dancecult*,[9] or the elasticity of a New Academicism called for previously.[10] In establishing a new methodology, this chapter will expand upon the original, three-way taxonomy outlined in the Introduction. This taxonomy, building on that of Scher[11] and Smyth,[12] now forms the theoretical underpinning of this book, distilling three-ways music is deployed in Dancefloor-Driven Literature. Each will be interrogated, in turn, in the next three chapters:

1. A figurative or metaphoric use of music in the Jungian role as symbol
2. A mechanical use in terms of the construction of the text
3. A contextual, perhaps *sub*textual, use of music naturalistically to provide a rich diegetic soundtrack for the narrative

Developing ideas outlined in Chapter 1, a lacuna in terms of any overt musicological interpretation in that taxonomy is deliberate. In his introduction to *Reading Pop*, Middleton outlines how 'the discussions of "dance music" in the 1990s—have gravitated towards forms of "consumptionism", which want to locate the textual moment'.[13] The driver of this book is indeed to continue, and build upon, the interdisciplinary bridges between musicology and other more sociologically driven interpretations of music, in reaching for Middleton's 'textual moment'. Where its ontological basis is essentially dialogic, the book integrates elements from musicology, cultural studies and linguistics in order to create a mixed methodological approach,[14] while accepting, as outlined in

Chapter 1, the parameters for defining this literary movement are rather more fixed: the 1990s and, broadly speaking, the Mancunian dancefloor diaspora.[15] This was a time when the homological influences of fashion, crime, drugs, clubs and music all aligned, a time when the literati infiltrated the dancefloor and mingled with the glitterati, using the tools of fiction to try to make sense of its colour and chaos.

Whether these writers were working alone, or might be seen as co-conspirators in this literary infiltration, is the subject of some contention. Certainly they were perceived from the outside as the 'Chemical Generation', in an overt reference to the Beat Generation, itself possibly a rebooting of the Lost Generation of the 1920s, both post-war scenes and with their own frantic jazz soundtrack.[16] Conversely, one might contend that the drawing together of such writers in the same Sarah Champion edited volume, *Disco Biscuits*, was a matter of commercial convenience rather than genuine cultural cohesion, and indeed in conversations with the three case study authors, each makes no demonstrative claim to be part of this particular literary 'scene', feeling somewhat artificially drawn together as such, even if they did indeed know one another. José Francisco Fernández agrees that 'Sarah Champion [...] believed that the porous quality of the new fiction was something natural; fiction could receive the influence of disco music just as the Beat Generation in the 1950s had been affected by jazz'.[17] However, in a culturally historic context the Beat Generation, for instance, might themselves be considered a very varied assemblage of writers, drawn together by a quirk of chronology and the world in which they operated, as much as any shared creative vision and intent. If Dancefloor-Driven writers were therefore, and justifiably, considered part of a 'generation', we must also allow for that fact that that was imposed externally, and somewhat forced.

In his conversation with Steve Redhead, for example, Blincoe recalls an Irvine Welsh text: 'As I was finishing *Acid Casuals* I noticed there was this book out, *The Acid House*. So I went out of my way to read some reviews of it'.[18] In my own conversation with Jeff Noon, Noon mentions both Irvine Welsh and 'Nick Blincoe',[19] and in my interview with Irvine Welsh, he reports: 'I've got so fucked up over the years with all these people so when you meet them it is like meeting family members. And getting together it's like, it's just great to see people. It's a community, a global community.'[20] However, the individual commercial successes of these authors became a very defined point of difference, with one writer performing much better financially. Blincoe reports: 'One of the interesting things about this, is that apart from Irvine, the rest of us have struggled a bit, in terms of becoming household names if you like.'[21] Artistically and geographically, however, these writers were united by a proximity to the locus of the dancefloor, drawing on its discourses for stories, and its beat for the stylistic energy of writing. Dancefloor-Driven Literature provides a conduit to the sonic scene and in that sense two of these literary artefacts are particularly significant, and require closer interrogation.

Disco Biscuits

The publisher Sceptre's 1997 collection *Disco Biscuits* represents the urtext for this analysis. An assembly of nineteen short stories, the collection is subtitled 'New

Fiction from the Chemical Generation' – in itself semantically interesting, for its use of the preposition 'from' (rather than 'for') suggesting a communal, collective sensibility on the part of the authors, as well as the readers. In my conversation with the editor of the collection, Sarah Champion, Champion recalls: 'We were a chemical generation. We all were taking everything we could possibly find for the experience, for the party, for the music.'[22] Working in the music media from the age of sixteen, Champion was able to operate from an insider perspective, astonished (as detailed in the previous chapter) that EDMC magazines such as *DJ* and *Mixmag* were unwilling to carry short stories, in the way *Rolling Stone* would publish Hunter S. Thompson, and that there was therefore no cult fiction chronicling the beat of her age. As Champion explains, '*Disco Biscuits* was an experiment really for me trying to find writers who I wanted to read, writing about the life I was living myself, something I could relate to'[23] (Figure 5.1).

It seems this inclusivity extends along boundaries of shared cultural and pharmaceutical interests, rather than, for instance, gender. All of the authors in *Disco Biscuits* are male, a point that should at the very least be acknowledged, if not

Figure 5.1 Cover of Sarah Champion (ed.), *Disco Biscuits: New Fiction from the Chemical Generation* (London: Sceptre, 1997).

explored at length within the limited scope of this book, although as the case studies are taken from *Disco Biscuits*, that does of course also affect its gender balance. In the course of researching this study of Dancefloor-Driven Literature many female writers have been identified, and listed in Appendix I, including A. D. Atkins, Toni Davidson, Nina de la Mer, D. C. Gallin, Lisa McInerney and Nicola Monaghan, with Geraldine Geraghty's novel *Raise Your Hands* one of the reading highlights of the eight-year process of researching and writing this book. The editor of *Disco Biscuits* is, of course, female, and the content of *Disco Biscuits* was ultimately her decision, a result not necessarily of design, but rather circumstance. Champion herself responds that her favourite writers were male, underlining connections with previous generations noted in this research, reporting 'when I was fourteen I started reading things like Jack Kerouac and Charles Bukowski.[24] I wanted my generation to have that put down as well, that moment captured.'[25] Certainly her collection stands as an overt attempt to meld music and literature, two worlds that orbited her own personal and professional life, in order to reflect her contemporary society back upon itself. A call went out to writers who were interested in stories that revolved around the dancefloor (simply requesting 'a celebration of acid house') and it quickly became apparent that non-fiction's loss would be short fiction's gain. These contributions represented some of the last words from the cultural underground in the dying days of the twentieth century.

As outlined in the Introduction, several of the principal progenitors of Dancefloor-Driven Literature – and certainly each of the case study authors in this account – are located within both *Disco Biscuits* and Steve Redhead's 2000 collection *Repetitive Beat Generation*. With the Redhead volume we find a title that itself plays on the Beat Generation literary scene of the 1950s, as well as the UK's Criminal Justice and Disorder Act of 1994, which in Section 63 (1b) describes music played at raves as 'sounds wholly or predominantly characterised by the emission of a succession of repetitive beats'.[26] If Redhead's *Repetitive Beat Generation* seems interchangeable with the Chemical Generation soubriquet, it is all the more incongruous that Redhead argues: 'The repetitive beat generation writers in general barely take any direct inspiration from the writings of Jack Kerouac, Allen Ginsberg and William Burroughs.'[27] Even from a micro, stylistic level I must take issue with this position, and indeed the case studies will certainly do so; but on a macro, systemic level, direct parallels can easily be drawn. Redhead does acknowledge, however, a causal link between writing and music in each scene, touching on the music-literature-intoxication compound identified in this book:

> In reality the 40s, 50s and 60s beat generation fiction and poetry was as much to do with incorporating other cultural forms into writing (Kerouac's free-form jazz writing) and the wide cultural influence of the writing on lifestyle (drugs, hitch-hiking, music) as its status as a post-war literary movement.[28]

Redhead also makes the claim that this 1990s reforming of musical and literary elements formed 'the sharpest counter cultural literary movement to emerge since the beat generation,'[29] although – as suggested in the construction of systems in this book –

the spirit of gonzo and New Journalism can also be integrated into that heady mix. This point is reinforced in Champion's own introduction to the *Disco Biscuits* collection:

> It was perhaps inevitable that this culture would finally influence literature too. In the fifties and sixties, jazz and psychedelia inspired writing from Jack Kerouac's *On The Road* to Allen Ginsberg's *Howl* and Tom Wolfe's *Electric Kool Aid Acid Test*. In the nineties, we have Irvine Welsh's *Trainspotting*, the book, the film and the attitude.[30]

Redhead asks Champion if she used 'fiction [...] as a version of contemporary history'.[31] Champion responds: 'The idea, the way it came about, was that it wasn't about the DJ or celebrity, it was the antibook of the "rock star" – it was much more about the people on the dance floor – they were the stars.'[32] Centrally, these were not stories of the DJ personalities behind the decks; rather, they pulled narrative focus round to the dancefloor itself. Building on contingencies outlined in the previous chapter, in her introduction Champion contends:

> How can you capture the madness of the last decade in facts and figures? For all the record reviews and attempts to turn DJs and promoters into celebrities, dance magazines have failed to document what really happened, as rock and punk journalists did. After all, the true history is not about obscure white labels or DJ techniques or pop stars. It's about personal stories of messiness, absurdity and excess – best captured in fiction.[33]

Champion argues that her collection was 'right bang on the moment. People wanted something. If that hadn't come out, and Irvine Welsh hadn't come out, that generation wouldn't have had any interesting books.'[34] These, then, were stories driven from this generation's dancefloors, all locked within the pages of this urtext.

As described earlier in this account, a subterranean system defines itself by its language and signs: the semiotic meaning behind the 'smiley face' and knowing wink of acid house culture, for instance, and equally the language of the culture encoded in its founding texts, both musical and literary. 'Disco Biscuits' is in itself slang for Ecstasy,[35] and in this way a scene can hide behind the arras of argot, a thin page of thinly veiled code behind which Champion exposed 'my punk, my psychedelia,'[36] the last 'spectacular subculture' of the twentieth century, in Hebdige's terms.[37] If the 'succession of repetitive beats' seemed culturally alien to the ears of supraterranean society, then its literature was similarly impregnable. Dancefloor-Driven authors reached for both the metre of the English language and the lexicon and rhythms of the dancefloor in a new blurring of musico-literary intermedial forms required to contain such an atmosphere within the pages of a book.

Memes of music run as sonic seams through this collection, fulfilling each of the uses in the taxonomy outlined earlier in this chapter. In figurative terms, in the Jonathan Brook story 'Sangria' we hear that 'the drug is like the music,'[38] a trope that will be dramatically reversed in the work on Jeff Noon explored in Chapter 7. In the story 'Inbetween' by Matthew de Abaitua, we hear a character report 'your conversation is like techno, one repetition after another'.[39] Within the story 'Electrovoodoo' fictional characters even question music's origins, in philosophical terms: 'Like, where does music come from, right? Out of the body. Heartbeat, breathing, stomach pumping food: they've all got their own bpm.'[40] The second use of music in literature relates to writing musically, and certainly we also find evidence of such approaches in the volume. Mike Benson writes impressionistically, dropping to the lower case in 'Room Full of Angels' in order to engender a stream-of-consciousness, melodic flow: 'I can hear thumping banging grooving pulsing sounds all around me. I can feel it feel me. i'm inside it as it enters me.'[41]

Close textual analysis reveals that the key approach of these authors, however, reflects the third use of music, in terms of its use as sonic diegetic backdrop, in building a subterranean, sub-page soundtrack from words. In the following examples the authors imply a degree of understanding, a knowledge transfer hinging on cultural relevance, where the reader of the text will, again, be expected to fill in the gaps using their own *a priori* understanding of the scene and its soundtracks. In 'Sangria', for instance, we are told 'The music's pure',[42] and later that 'the music has been stripped down so there is nothing but the beat, the first instrument of the world'.[43] Some authors choose to paint more precisely, with narrative detail that might include musical genres, or nuanced description of DJ technique. Nicholas Blincoe includes aspects of this musical process in his story 'Ardwick Green': 'The idea was to keep it ambient, maybe a little Balearic. But Jess only functioned in excess of 150 bpm's and the idea of a smooth cross-fade was the jump-cut, one-twenty to one-ninety bang.'[44] In Charlie Hall's story 'The Box' the narrator is untrusted, recounting events while himself under the influence of drugs, while the DJ reports: 'I play house. I keep it fat and funky. I want to convey that happy sexy vibe I got through funk, as well as the moody weird shit and the trippy frequencies of dub.'[45] Elsewhere, Ben Graham effectively transcribes the aural into the linguistic, and specifically onomatopoeic, in 'Weekday Service': 'Echoing, stygian dub and unholy blasts of klonking techno stream from the large, battered speakers that balance precariously at either end of the room. The soundtrack only heightens the sense that we've wandered into some self-contained, alien landscape, entirely detached from the outside world.'[46]

In the pursuit of naturalistic verisimilitude, some authors go further by including real DJs, real clubs and real music tracks in order to authentically render the architecture of the nightclub in fiction. Content analysis of such product placement within the collection reveals the following DJs: Andrew Weatherall, David Holmes, Kenny Ken, Fabio, Mickey Finn,[47] and parties: Clink Street raves, Shoom, Spectrum, Super Nature, Sunrise, Boy's Own, Joy, Taste and Full Circle.[48] There are also specific music references. In the Alan Warner story 'Bitter Salvage' we are also told:

> The DJ is only playing the 45s of Funkadelic, A sides and B sides in chronological order (implying the lucky bastard has two copies of each single): 'Better By The Pound', 'Stuffs & Things', 'Let's Take It To The Stage', 'Undisco Kid' etc.[49]

In the Puff story 'Two Fingers', we hear how

> Kenny Ken got back into the groove and dropped a crucial slab of reggae-fused breakbeat. I wasn't too sure if he was mixing Desmond Dekker's 'Israelites' into the track but it definitely sounded like it. I recognized the: 'So Thata Every Mouth Can Be Fed' refrain.[50]

Later in Puff's story we are told that 'Kenny Ken went on to finish his set with a storming junglist version of Eek-A-Mouse's "Ganja Smuggling", before throwing down the gauntlet to Fabio to keep it rocking "Inna Ruff Tuff Drum'n'Bass Stylee"'.[51] Puff's story is almost fan fiction, the positive portrayal of DJs and music described functioning as cultural shorthand, setting the scene. As well as the broader real-world heritage and aesthetic infrastructure of the rave scene – the importance of the summer of 1988, the origin of the drug Ecstasy, Ibiza as locale – music genres such as drum and bass, jungle and house are all used as details to establish, naturalistically, the veracity of the subterranean scene these stories uncover, and describe. Without this subcultural capital, in Thornton's terms, such stories might, instead, prove impregnable and inauthentic, in terms of both subject and style.

Beyond precise textual analysis of the stories within *Disco Biscuits*, it is also important to consider the impact, as a whole, of this Dancefloor-Driven urtext in a cultural, and indeed commercial, context. While the term is now much critiqued, in the original publication of *Sound Effects* Frith argues that rock music is not high art or low art but rather a '*mass* culture',[52] and in literary terms such methods of mass production might be applied to *Disco Biscuits*, which shares much of its cultural mass with cult – even pulp – fiction. *Disco Biscuits* was a publishing sensation. According to Champion,

> It sold 60,000 copies in a few weeks, which makes it the best-selling anthology of all time. The whole thing was the biggest phenomena in the publishing industry. No one in publishing could get their head around it at all.[53]

Champion recalls 'bookshops had a whole section of books with drugs in the title',[54] in reference, perhaps, to Waterstone's 'Club and Drug Literature' section, where my own book *Discombobulated* would also find its home, and moving musico-literary intermediality to an entirely commercial sphere, we also witness at this time the ingress of the literary into the otherwise solid preserve of the audiovisual. This book was sold not only in bookstores but – as highlighted by Nicholas Blincoe – also by more traditional music retailers such as HMV.[55]

The marketing of the book was also handled very differently, with adverts in EDMC media such as *Kiss Radio*. Champion comments: 'Reviews in *The Times* and *The Independent* didn't sell it, it was sold by being in *Mixmag* and *DJ*, and having club nights.'[56] Indeed, just as the books found their way into traditional music retailers, the subterranean rave milieu also became a unique literary locus. Redhead reports how book readings became 'gigs' – for example, Jeff Noon's 1995 novel *Pollen* was launched at the Haçienda, Manchester's signature nightclub at the time,[57] while the Arthrob parties featured readings by Irvine Welsh, combined with DJ sets by Andy Weatherall and Richard Fearless.[58] Champion worked the street-level PR for the book herself, promoting *Disco Biscuits* parties with key DJs such as LTJ Bukem, Marshall Jefferson and Derrick May, with Irvine Welsh reading. This intense relationship between the sonic and linguistic is redolent of the Beats, and events where Jack Kerouac and Allen Ginsberg would read over a bebop soundtrack. As Champion reports, 'For the publishing industry it was mind-blowing.'[59] In terms of reception, readership and audience, the result of such gonzo marketing also had an important impact. Champion recalls a conversation with one fan of the book:

> I had nightclub bouncers coming up to me and saying 'this is brilliant – I'd never read a book before but I loved this. And I'm going to go and get Irvine Welsh and I'm going to go and get some more books'. And that was quite exciting.[60]

Champion even reports a man in a Brixton pub attempting to sell stolen copies of *Disco Biscuits* as though it were illicit, literary contraband.

Without *Disco Biscuits* as an extant artefact, then, historical-cultural authenticity dissipates. According to Champion, 'not many people can go back and talk about it as vividly as people who were there at the time, writing at the time',[61] and that is very much the inherent importance of this literature, and its function, a point that will be expanded in the conclusion to this chapter and further developed in the book's conclusion. Like Harlem in the late 1940s, or San Francisco in the late 1960s, a literature accompanies a subterranean scene and tells its stories. We can understand the UK club scene because we can view it through this literary prism, this portal into the past provided by *Disco Biscuits*. The short story format seemed perfect for capturing these ephemeral highs; although *Disco Biscuits* authors did write novels, many found it harder to sustain that dramatic momentum across the longer form. Champion reports: 'Taking that to the level of writing a novel is so hard. I think that's possibly why it didn't become a wider genre, as well.'[62] Her assertion must be challenged however, as this book evidences there was, in fact, a literary output substantial enough to function as a genre. Indeed, one novel – Trevor Miller's *Trip City* (1989) – can be identified as forming the very first work of Dancefloor-Driven Literature, in its reformation as an ostensibly 'rave' narrative. Smyth suggests that 'Alan Warner's debut novel, *Morven Callar*, was one of the first novels to attempt to engage with the phenomenon of rave culture that swept through parts of Britain after the late 1980s'.[63] However, Warner's work dates from 1996 – seven years later than *Trip City* – and this claim must stand as an original contribution this book makes to ongoing musico-literary scholarship.

Trip City

Miller did not feature in the *Disco Biscuits* collection, an omission all the more remarkable given that he was born and bred in Manchester, like Champion, but actually in the same suburb, Chorlton-cum-Hardy. However, his work remains fundamental to this evolving exploration of a specifically electronic musico-literary intermediality and the genesis of Dancefloor-Driven Literature. *Trip City* also fulfils all points of the taxonomy of musico-literary intermedial functions, in terms of music being used mechanically within (and, crucially, *without*) the text, and its diegetic, and non-diegetic, soundtrack.

A cultural and causal root link has been identified between beat, rock and rave generations in this book, with subterranean systems exerting an influence across time. In their contemporaneous review of Miller's novel, the London *Evening Standard* described it as 'an *On The Road* for the post warehouse party generation',[64] and it is no accident that when the 'hero' of the novel – club promoter Valentine – travels in a coach from Manchester to London, the girl he meets and befriends is reading that key Beat Generation text. These links between the musical and the literary are found in the hypogean matter of this text, but also in the desire of the author to draw upon the musical in the creation of the literary, reaching for the rhythms of music as literary muse. As identified in Chapter 3, house music is characterized by a 'series of repetitive beats', a legal definition that can equally be considered musicological, and indeed linguistic, with Miller making the intriguing claim: 'Originally I wanted to write the whole thing with a 4/4 rhythm to mimic House beats'.[65] Certainly Miller's clipped language in this novel is used leanly, almost electronically, in an austere style reminiscent of Lost Generation author Ernest Hemingway, a writer Miller cites in our conversation.

Trip City opens with the line: 'It was a blue Monday. Grey light split the blinds. Traversed the wooden floor. Then it hit the bed. Cold and piercing and harsh. There was no gentleness left'.[66] Beyond the reference to 'Blue Monday', the most successful track by Manchester electronic band (and co-owners of The Haçienda) New Order,[67] we find linguistically precise, adjective-light prose that defines, in stylistic terms, the novel that will follow. One might even scan the lines as you would a line of poetry – or a sequencer such as Cubase might track a line of music – detecting the beat and the metre of the prose, in a simple act of scansion that reveals (as we shall later see, in Derridean terms) music beyond, or behind, the words. Elsewhere, the words 'safe in his pocket' echo across several pages,[68] just as a DJ might drop a hint of the track on the other turntable into the mix, as literary beat refrains. There is now resistance from Miller himself as to whether he was writing in 4/4 time, just as Beat scholar Jim Burns, in my conversation with the writer, argues against the common-held belief that Kerouac wrote to the rhythms of bebop jazz.[69] Of course structuralists would propose that the opinion of the author is, in any case, immaterial (a position I firmly resist), and certainly there are musico-literary references throughout both the form and function of this text, and connections that can be made between Kerouac's jazz evocations and the electronic soundtrack of Miller's world.

In terms of musical mechanics, *Trip City* is important in this intermedial interrogation for another central reason. Smyth contends that the novel is a 'legible form – one that is usually consumed alone and in silence',[70] adding that

> the novel does not produce any remarkable sound of itself, other than perhaps a rustle of pages as it is being read or a dull thud as it is set aside or replaced on a

shelf. In fact, silence appears to be built into the novel's historical, sociological and commercial heritage.[71]

However, *Trip City* runs entirely counter to that proposition. In 2015, *The Huffington Post* declared: 'The only way to write a story set in an EDM scene is to make a novel with a soundtrack' and yet a quarter of a century previously, that is precisely what happened.[72] In *Trip City*, Miller describes at one point how 'images crystallised. Like a poignant film with no soundtrack',[73] and yet includes an audio soundtrack within the paratextual matter of his own book, thereby turning up the volume on Smyth's silent novel.[74] When published, *Trip City* was packaged with a soundtrack produced by Manchester electronic music pioneer Gerald Simpson – more commonly known as 'A Guy Called Gerald' – covermounted as a cassette (the available technology of the time).[75] Gerald's music was even subtitled 'The Soundtrack of the Novel', encouraging the reader to combine Miller's words with the sonic backdrop of Gerald's beats. This hints of a 'prosumer' agenda,[76] in that providing such music implies a more proactive agency on behalf of the reader, constituting the remixed reality of the story in the process of combining its musical and linguistic elements. It also raises key questions as to the extent to which listening to the relevant music is important, when reading about it[77] (Figure 5.2).

Gerald's music is dark, urban, urbane: tension and menace build in the music, influencing the reading of the words.[78] 'Trip City Mambo', for instance, is an unsettling, jarring piece of nocturnal electronica, the sounds of the city melding with hi-hats, hand claps and a dark, rumbling bassline. 'Valentine's Theme' builds once again from

Figure 5.2 The proposed twenty-fifth anniversary edition of Trevor Miller's *Trip City*. In this iteration, A Guy Called Gerald's soundtrack would be encoded onto a USB drive.

an ominous bassline and haunting, almost Gregorian vocals that suggest a dark *dyscopia*. This idea of a 'literary soundtrack' was picked up by other publishers who provided soundtracks to accompany the publication of their texts. In this way *Disco Biscuits* itself and Champion's next edition, *Disco 2000*, were also published with an accompanying CD soundtrack (similarly designed as, although not packaged with, the book itself);[79] the US version of Simon Reynolds's *Generation Ecstasy*, titled *Energy Flash*, came with a covermounted CD soundtrack,[80] while Calcutt and Shephard note that 'in 1997 Welsh's *Ecstasy* was even tied in with a dance CD', in reference to an author who will soon be analysed more closely.[81]

This intermedial interrogation has previously touched on cinematic reference points in decoding these literary texts, notably in the previous chapter, where intermedial tendencies might naturally lead on to notions of interdisciplinarity. Indeed, such a hybrid approach to methodology often reveals useful and original approaches to decoding cultural artefacts, and many cinematic theories have been useful to this book. This includes a return of the term 'auteur', where a defined palette of stylistic and thematic tendencies bestows individual character to a literary work. In returning to another cinematic theory, this chapter will further repurpose the notion of 'diegesis' defined in Chapter 3,[82] making the case for a specifically *literary diegesis* in its function within fiction. The third musico-literary intermedial function, as defined by the methodological taxonomy of this book, is this very particular diegetic role of music within the text, as silent, naturalistic soundtrack, reinforcing the sonic architecture of this subterranean world. Beyond Gerald's non-diegetic underscore, content analysis of *Trip City* reveals references to specific music artists and songs embedded diegetically in the text: Kid Creole, Kylie Minogue, 'Car Wash', 'Superstition', 'Phuture', 'Superfly Guy' and Bill Withers,[83] as well as music genres such as acid house,[84] jazz,[85] hip hop,[86] house[87] and funk.[88] The choices for the soundtrack are, at times, surprising, where for literary effect the marvellous must at times be revealed as mundane: 'He shivered. Buttoned up his jacket. There was a tune in his head. "High Noon"? No. It was the Shake 'n' Vac commercial.'[89]

Using this notion of literary diegesis we find that Miller creates soundtracks for his club environments via the DJ protagonists that he ultimately, as author, controls, as though puppets manipulated from on high. Although the primacy of balance of intermedial forms in this novel is not the music (in terms of the Wolf/Scher taxonomy), music certainly forms this silent audio bed or underscore, upon which the drama unfolds. In this sense, the notion of literary diegesis might be taken further, in arguing that the diegetic music within the novel almost becomes almost *extra*diegetic, merging into a rolling, ongoing score behind the text; silent, triggered by context and suggestion, its volume turned up by the *a priori* cognizance of the reader. Indeed *Trip City* is compelling when the use of music is not specific, but implied, in this 'beyond' diegetic way (or even *meta*diegetic in terms defined in the previous chapter),[90] although I should be clear this is to bend the terms beyond an Aristotelian sense of narrative or their more common usage in literary analysis, and more specifically to my consideration of music in literature.

As an example, we are introduced to a DJ, Jay: 'Jay flicked the crossfader. A fresh mix stuttered in [...] the V.U. meters pulsed, peaking red out of green. The floor was rammed. A twelve inch static in his hand.'[91] Here Miller uses music diegetically in the nightclub construct, where it might be perceived by the reader as non-specific background, and an implied wash of sound designed to engender a more impressionistic atmosphere in the prose. We read, possibly hear or even see (dependent on one's synaesthetic reception) how 'discordant jazz dripped down the stairwell, uneasy bop',[92] while elsewhere, at the Tower nightclub, 'the music upstairs was hip-hop. House. There were no soulful grooves. The crowd danced predictably. One step wonders',[93] and later how 'the soundsystem pulsed from Hitman Records. A house track from Chicago. Machine gun samples cut the road.'[94] Such real-world music genres engender a sense of authenticity, aural signifiers that together, through their implication, create a naturalistic underscore that lies just beneath the words, sonic signposts by which the reader might orientate themselves through the text, and onto its dancefloor. Into this literary landscape Miller then blows a fabulist drug – the green chemical FX – further warping the soundtrack; indeed, so powerful and penetrative is this drug that, in an interesting typographic innovation, it even turns the print of the novel green.

Stephen Benson argues that 'fiction serves as an earwitness to the role of music in everyday life, a record of why, where and how music is made, heard and received',[95] appreciating the sonic in the semantic, identifying the beat that lies beneath the page. In terms of this theoretical approach to how we actively hear, or provide volume to music cited in fiction, we might further consider the role music plays, in these Derridean terms, as a realm beyond the words, in a kind of silent, sonic hauntology. Jacques Derrida once performed live in Paris with bebop saxophonist Ornette Coleman: a useful, if ultimately unsuccessful, attempt to actually physically unite music and words, bebop and philosophy,[96] with Derrida scholar Peter Dayan reporting that the linguist was booed throughout the performance. Derrida did not write a great deal about music and yet in *Glas*, he remarks that after language, 'what remains has the force of music'.[97] As Dayan suggests, 'Music, in Derrida's texts, stands first and foremost for that which remains beyond anything that we can call our own.'[98] Derrida, then, felt that music was somehow beyond language, which is the central attraction for the intermedial writers who attempt to reach for precisely that sonic space, behind words. Further, just as the rhythm of society changes, its writers find themselves compelled to write to the beat of their times, whether bebop, rock or rave. Dayan continues of Derrida that 'music's role [was] to speak for him, to make of him, as it were, a ventriloquist's dummy'.[99] Dancefloor-Driven authors write with contemporary rhythms in mind, in the ventriloquial sense that they can then speak through the music (presuming the ear of the reader is tuned appropriately).

Beyond the mechanical mimicking of electronic music rhythms, and the more impressionistic use of music as subterranean scene setting, Miller is most interesting when fulfilling the first use of music in the three-way taxonomy, in his figurative use of music. In my conversation with the author, Miller argues:

> You can't have been in and around as many discos as I was and not have it seep into you. It's like cigarette smoke, you know. I think when you go to fantastic discos that's what happens. It infects you. It gets on your clothes.[100]

We are told at one point in the novel, for instance, that 'Sarah said he loved the music more than her',[101] as though music might be invested with the qualities of emotion and attraction. Miller also ascribes music with the characteristics of intoxicants: 'Perhaps the music would stabilize reality. Sometimes it worked. The power of the bass could root you to the floor. It was the only safe stimulant he possessed.'[102] At another point, Miller describes how 'the needle sat in the groove', in itself foretelling Jeff Noon's Dancefloor-Driven novel *Needle in the Groove*. As with Noon, music is more meaningful when metaphorical.[103]

Now a screenplay writer and film director based in Los Angeles, Miller confirms a cinematic method to his creativity. He explains: 'My drug hallucinations, they would often feature Jesus, bits of films, Spaghetti Westerns, the assassination in *Day of the Jackal*',[104] and such a rich cerebral mise en scène must also be accompanied by a soundtrack. The process is an immersive tradition that can certainly be traced back to Thompson's gonzo instincts (indeed the words 'fear and loathing' appear in *Trip City*, beyond the reference to Kerouac identified earlier),[105] but Miller operates ostensibly from a fiction, rather than non-fiction, position. Miller discusses 'the idea that you immerse yourself in the culture that you're writing about and by that very immersion you become so part of it that the writing is part of it as well'.[106] The ambition was, therefore, to decode the disco from within, from the dancefloor itself. Miller also notes:

> Foolishly someone somewhere wrote *Trip City* is the acid house novel which if you read it, it bears no resemblance to that whatsoever. Nothing really to do with it. And if it had of been it would have been about ecstasy and it would have been about different things.[107]

Here we must take issue with Miller's own reading, reintroducing Roland Barthes in contending that the author's opinion, while important, is only one in a range that are available. Certainly, in *Trip City* Miller references an earlier age in London's nocturnal landscape, the proto-rave club scene of the earlier years of the 1980s, when he himself was studying in the city, at the Polytechnic of Central London. However, the publication of the novel in 1989 – the year after the famed Second Summer of Love that defined a high-water mark for the rave scene – would necessarily lead the reader to imagine the city's contemporaneous rave landscape when reading the text. This is reinforced by the fact that the principal nightclub in the novel, the Tower, is based on real-world club space the Limelight, while the Wag, equally famed in the early 1980s, is renamed Mambo in this text. Like an artist working from a life model, if an author is able to keep the architecture of the story real, it can render the presentation naturalistic, thus driving authenticity.

Trip City was therefore a novel driven from the dancefloor, rather than a novel with dancefloors within it. The dancefloor needed Miller to tell its stories just as the road needed Kerouac, like Vegas needed Thompson. Miller reports (erroneously, in the context of my research): 'As far as I'm concerned I don't think before or since, many people had written club-based things, for a number of reasons but I think mostly because club people – present company excluded – are never normally that literary.'[108] There had, of course, been nightclub books before (Colin MacInnes's *Absolute Beginners*, among others) but in this late-millennial rave reconstitution of music and words, Miller was an early pioneer of this intermedial space. He recalls: 'So many people wanted to write the club culture novel but none of them did! They didn't write anything serious.'[109] The name that immediately looms large is that of Irvine Welsh, who will shortly take the role of our first case study author. Like Kerouac with bebop prosody and Thompson with the soaring literary riff, Welsh also sought to write to this new electronic beat and it was his first novel – 1993's *Trainspotting* (set in the late 1980s) – that arguably dug down into this subterranean basement and revealed its machinations to a new audience.

However, before we progress to Welsh, this story of Dancefloor-Driven Literature now takes a possibly controversial turn, in terms of revealing new interesting contingencies in musico-literary and EDMC research. *Trip City* was launched in a nightclub, and like the *Disco Biscuits* PR campaign, Miller also toured the book around the club scene, which he admits was based on Spalding Gray's one-man show *Visit to Cambodia*, explaining, 'I thought, I'll do the disco version.'[110] This live experience something Irvine Welsh would himself go on to do, with the Arthrob events, leading Miller to report, perhaps factually loosely: 'Again, I'm the person who pioneered that, not him.'[111] In his interview, Miller claims seeing Welsh in the audience of the one-man show, based on *Trip City*, that he took to the Edinburgh Festival. This is controversial, as according to Miller, Welsh has since denied his influence, Miller admitting 'I don't know (and probably doubt) that Irvine would agree that I had ANY influence on him, or his work.'[112] Miller contends: 'This is what I'd say about Irvine Welsh. Although his wasn't ostensibly set in nightclubs I think I blazed the trail a little bit.'[113]

In the light of Miller's words, might *Trainspotting* remain as pioneering as first perceived, or rather, half a decade earlier do we find in *Trip City* the true founding text of this Chemical Generation, Repetitive Beat and Dancefloor-Driven Literature? Certainly Miller is adamant on this point, arguing that it would be hard to avoid *Trip City* when it was published: 'I was on The Other Side of Midnight with Tony Wilson, I was on fucking everything.'[114] In 1989 Miller was undeniably alone in exploring this intermedial terrain, several years before *i-D*'s claim that when Welsh 'blazed out of nowhere in 1993, he became the first writer to take up the challenge of defining this chemical generation'.[115] As Miller remarks, 'When in 1989 was there the confluence of discos and literature? I didn't know of one.'[116]

Subterranean philology

This research is not pioneering entirely new methodologies, but largely repurposing that of *philology* – defined by Jonathan Bate as 'the pursuit of wisdom through the study of written words' – for this cultural archivism.[117] This is the overarching strategic, conceptual framework of this research: that one can learn truths about a subterranean scene, even retrospectively, through its specifically literary re/presentation. We must therefore necessarily move the argument on from that of linguistics, or musicology, to a more holistic consideration of the impact of these books as cultural artefacts. The author Neil Gaiman – interested in stories both temporal and celestial – writes that

> the human lifespan seems incredibly short and frustrating, and for me, one of the best things about being a reader, let alone a writer, is being able to read ancient Greek stories, ancient Egyptian stories, Norse stories – to be able to feel like one is getting the long view. Stories are long-lived organisms. They're bigger and older than we are.[118]

These literary re/presentations are the ancient Greek scripts of their culture, literary cyphers to be deciphered in the process of their future consumption. To find out about bebop jazz, for example, I have detailed how you might turn to the pages of Kerouac, and find the music – silent, but afforded volume by his words. Haight-Ashbury and the hopes of San Francisco in the mid-1960s are preserved in the words of Hunter S. Thompson. And so it follows that to reveal the rave scene of the late 1980s and 1990s, we might find the answers locked in the pages of *Trip City* and *Disco Biscuits*, texts born of the sacred space of the dancefloor.

Beyond the finite totality of the page, beyond the liminality of the dancefloor, there lies a much bigger picture. The focus of this book is not wholly concerned with the arbitrary construction of signs within a text; it looks down not only to the page but also to a wider context that builds systems between – and beyond – those texts. Wolf, for instance, reports that a choice of music in text 'is obviously inspired by the Pythagorean connection between music and cosmic order',[119] and *Disco Biscuits* authors actually reference their subterranean culture in altogether extraterrestrial terms, linking the two realms. In the Martin Millar story 'How Sunshine Star-Traveller Lost His Girlfriend', people rave under the stars and Millar also references the famed Full Moon Parties, where we witness a character 'raise his arm to the full moon',[120] as though the processes of hedonism itself were locked to the lunar. Such a relationship is not always positive, as Sunshine Star-Traveller reports: 'I'm a victim of the stars. Possibly even a chaotic rip in the fabric of the universe.'[121] Intriguingly, in *Fatal Strategies*, Baudrillard progresses this, in writing: 'We can no longer observe the stars in the sky; we must now observe the subterranean deities that threaten a collapse into the void.'[122] Certainly an intriguing thought, I also contend that instead of looking up to unknowable stars, we might instead seek to chart, and connect, cultural systems by reference to these subterranean basements of the city, the underground warrens of interconnectivity. This theoretical reading of intertextuality forms a mechanic by which these buried words not only gather on the page but also build bridges of semantic meaning and understanding across cultural space.[123]

Oscar Wilde famously claimed we 'are all in the gutter, but some of us are looking at the stars', but perhaps the gaze may now shift, and the objective be to appreciate the gutter with the same poetic elegance as the heavens; to understand and hear the music in its words.[124] We may then start to appreciate these worlds that operate on a further level, even deeper below Wilde's gutter, perhaps even elevating the subterranean, the cult, the pulp, the Dancefloor-Driven Literature of the underground to the rarefied heights of a 'canon', ascending the artificial construct of a high/low axis of literature defined by literary critic F. R. Leavis et al. This elevation will form a part of the conclusion, although I must also concede that 'canon' is indeed a loaded concept.

The dancefloor, then, is a multi-authored text. Each dancer from the dance adds their memory, privileged witnesses to this driving of ideas, this organic creation of narrative fiction. However, one must appreciate that memory is also fragile, ephemeral. Novels, however, endure – their shelf life beyond that of a newspaper or magazine, of a song or even a human memory. The question then becomes why, after a quarter of a century, would readers want to re-experience these events, second-hand? While more space would have allowed further penetration into theories of audience and reception to unpack this area, I can here lean on Walter Benjamin and his reference to the notion of the 'saved night',[125] a conceit I repurpose to accommodate what Dancefloor-Driven Literature has provided: once the needle has left the record and Holleran's dancers have left their dance and made their way to the liminal edge of the dancefloor, we can still understand the events that took place at the very centre of the 'aesthetic center of the universe', on this 'blonde rectangle of polished wood'. Dancefloor-Driven Literature is the *archive*, robust enough to carry code – subterranean philology – in the words preserved within, for future generations to decode. The saved night: books as nocturnal backup.[126]

6

Case study one

The figurative use of music in the work of Irvine Welsh

I used to do loads of clubbing and that's what I wanted to capture – to get that perpetual movement into my writing, the beats and rhythms of the language.[1]

Irvine Welsh

Over the next three chapters, I will focus critical attention on three key authors as case studies, each deployed in order to test the theoretical arguments and positions established thus far. As noted in Chapter 5, several of the principal progenitors of Dancefloor-Driven Literature are located in the intersection of Sarah Champion's 1997 collection *Disco Biscuits*,[2] and Steve Redhead's 2000 title *Repetitive Beat Generation*,[3] and all three of the case studies chosen for this research share that locus in common, as though residing in the shared space of a literary Venn diagram. Each has been carefully selected, based on the form and function of their work, their relationship to the dancefloor (often specifically Mancunian dancefloors) and the way their work reveals varied ways electronic dance music is heard within a text, thereby illuminating a real-world, music-based scene. Irvine Welsh now forms the first such case study in this musico-literary intermedial investigation. A fundamental author to any study of Dancefloor-Driven Literature, Welsh has been described variously as 'the most extraordinary literary phenomenon of Ecstasy culture',[4] becoming 'its icon and its bard',[5] 'the most prominent writer of the Chemical Generation'[6] and the 'poet laureate of the chemical generation'.[7] Certainly his is the most commercially successful voice to emerge from the subterranean world analysed in this book.

Welsh is foregrounded in order to respond to key questions outlined in Chapter 1: How might an author use music – both mechanically and diegetically – within his work? Specifically, how might we analyse the rhythmic, and indeed graphological, use of language and what further connections might thereby be drawn between the linguistic and the sonic? This chapter will also explore whether lines can be drawn between the work of Welsh and that of other Dancefloor-Driven authors, and indeed to the works of other culturally historic subterranean scenes, in line with both Bakhtinian dialogics[8] and the processes of what will ultimately be determined, in the conclusion, as subterranean systems theory. Although the three uses of music in Dancefloor-

Driven Literature (as defined in Chapter 1's methodological taxonomy for decoding these texts) will be considered in the case study of all three authors, each is also foregrounded to explore one use in particular, in order to facilitate a more penetrative analysis. In this way, Welsh is analysed with particular consideration to the figurative and signifying use of music within his work, in line with the Jungian role of archetype. In determining what music means in the works of Welsh, its signifying purpose both within and beyond the text will be assessed.

Within *Repetitive Beat Generation*, Redhead argues his primary interest is with the authors rather than their texts,[9] and this is a position largely supported in my book, which firmly resists a structuralist position in order to very deliberately reattach text to *context*, underlining the importance of the author's individual voice and vision in the construction of his or her narrative. In designing a mixed methodological approach to pursuing these contingencies, this chapter will therefore introduce primary input from Irvine Welsh himself, further progressing intermedial discourse.[10] Secondary theoretical sources are also drawn upon in order to supplement the primary account, the most significant of which is the work of Soviet-era Russian theorist Mikhail Bakhtin. In investigating discursive articulations of musical and cultural setting in the literature which reports upon it, the texts are also held up against theoretical readings drawn from the Serbian academic Nikolina Nedeljkov, and key commentators including Sarah Thornton, Steve Redhead and Stan Beeler, supported by the work on subcultures by academic sociologists such as Dick Hebdige. Again, research has previously considered the melopoetic intersection where 'writing and popular music meet',[11] and yet this research reveals a marked and problematic lacuna, in considering the role of specifically electronic music in literature. That space will be, in part, addressed by this close consideration of Welsh's portrayal of DJ and club culture.

Beyond secondary supportive accounts, close textual analysis of Welsh's own fiction will form the most useful device for decoding these literary constructions of the dancefloor. I should acknowledge from the outset that while Welsh's 1993 debut novel *Trainspotting* was particularly influential and successful, it will not form a significant part of this analysis as it is tonally, thematically and chronologically different from much Dancefloor-Driven Literature. Instead, and in terms of the primary texts chosen instead, 'The State of the Party' is Welsh's contribution to *Disco Biscuits*. This will function as the basis for a broader interrogation of Welsh's work, where two larger texts will then be examined for the thematic and stylistic ways Welsh integrates music into his literature. Welsh's 1996 collection of three novellas, *Ecstasy: Three Tales of Chemical Romance*,[12] has already been introduced in Chapter 4, as the short story 'The Undefeated' was turned into the 2012 cinema production *Irvine Welsh's Ecstasy*.[13] The 2001 novel *Glue* falls slightly outside the 1988–2000 parameters of this collection of Dancefloor-Driven Literature (in terms, at least, of its publication rather than genesis) but is nevertheless important for the presentation of a DJ archetype within the narrative.[14] This chapter will therefore build from short story to novella to novel, deconstructing individual scenes in order to reveal Welsh's stylistic aesthetic and tracing how the author attempts to retell, in authentic terms, the story of the dancefloor.

A brief biographical survey of Welsh's life and career will site some developmental influences and help orientate this analysis. Welsh grew up in the Leith area of Edinburgh, its very particular vernacular infusing his prose from the very start. In *Repetitive Beat Generation*, Redhead makes the important point that beyond Manchester, Scotland also forms a very important locus for club fictions,[15] notwithstanding the fact that Welsh also had a very close relationship with Manchester,[16] basing himself there for a time. (Indeed, I first met Welsh on the dancefloor of the Haçienda at some stage in the 1990s.) After a period living in London between the late 1970s and late 1980s, Welsh returned to Edinburgh and held a variety of administrative jobs for the likes of the housing department. However, it was the weekend that dominated Welsh's life, complete with the nascent pulse of house music and the attendant parties and intoxication. In conversations I have had with Welsh over the years (principally around stories I wrote for the magazines *Muzik* and *Mixmag*), he reports that he began to write through the week to keep these rhythms of the weekend alive. Welsh recalls, 'I was jumping around in fields and clubs at weekends and then going back to the nine to five and it was a terrible come down. It was a way of keeping myself going, keeping things ticking over.'[17] The physical, kinetic energy the author had artificially and pharmaceutically engendered at the weekend would distil into the creative energy necessary for the construction of stories to contain that spirit: the beat of house music becoming the beat of the keyboard, the beat of the prose that Redhead describes as 'stimulant-based writing'.[18]

Calcutt and Shephard note that

> Welsh has said that his work is a fictionalised version of the impact of drugs such as Ecstasy on British society, and he maintains that 'Ecky-culture' provided one of the few avenues for behaving like co-operative human beings in a society dominated by the narrow individualism associated with Margaret Thatcher and successive Tory governments.[19]

As detailed in Chapter 2, EDMC commentators such as Simon Reynolds, David Muggleton and Rupa Huq contend there is no overt or overarching political dynamic to the rave scene, but that position must be seen as problematic in terms of the theoretical framework of this interrogation, and the continual appearance of political dynamics. Indeed, this is a position reinforced by Harry Shapiro, who in *Waiting for the Man* remarks such fictions represent 'a survival strategy to get a large section of Great British Youth through the Thatcher years and as Irvine Welsh puts it, "the long, dark night of late capitalism"'.[20]

Redhead is also helpful in detecting 'new counter cultures' in this period: 'As Irvine Welsh argues, house music and its dance derivatives emerging in the late 80s were the inspiration for a whole swathe of fiction.'[21] However, while welcoming the critical attention Redhead pays to Welsh, my analysis challenges his reading of Welsh as an author who 'says his inspiration for writing is not really drug culture at all but "working-class culture" in general'.[22] Instead, this chapter contends Welsh's inspiration can be rooted firmly within the parameters of the dancefloor. This brings his writing in line with the overarching methodological driver of this book to move away from a more overtly Marxist reading of subcultures, characterized by the Birmingham School referenced in Chapter 1. Beyond the macro-political environment, in this fictional context we can divine the political when we arrive, dialectically, at *the politics of the personal*. As Welsh himself argues in another of our conversations, 'The fact that people party is massively political in itself.'[23]

In *Generation Ecstasy*, Reynolds writes:

> These kinds of experiences, shared by millions, can't really be documented, although the post-Irvine Welsh mania for 'rave fiction' has made an attempt. Most of this writing consists of thinly disguised drug memoirs, and as everybody knows, other people's drug anecdotes are as boring as their dreams.[24]

Reynolds's pejorative dismissal of 'memoirs' of intoxication immediately, and rather glibly, discards the works of Thomas De Quincey, William S. Burroughs, Hunter S. Thompson, Jack Kerouac, Samuel Taylor Coleridge, Jean-Paul Sartre, Aldous Huxley and, in fact, all of the writers discussed in the 339 pages of Marcus Boon's fascinating study of the intersection of writers and intoxicants, *The Road of Excess: A History of Writers on Drugs*. Many fabulous stories can be found beyond the interiority of the imagination – many on the dancefloor itself. In this chapter I must therefore necessarily, and strongly, argue against Reynolds's assertion, since this speaks to the very ontology of Dancefloor-Driven Literature which, this chapter will evidence, provides much more.

As noted in Chapter 1, there is a marked absence of the beat of electronic dance music in much of musico-literary intermedial scholarship. There is also an associated absence of Irvine Welsh. In all of the recent musico-literary analyses I have myself read in researching my own study, Welsh only appears in the following endnote on page 216 of Gerry Smyth's *Music in Contemporary British Fiction: Listening to the Novel*:

> The tradition of transcribing Scots for literary purposes is at least as old as Burns, although the modern trend is most closely associated with writers such as James Kelman, whose novel *How Late It Was, How Late* won the Booker Prize in 1994, and Irvine Welsh, who published the enormously successful *Trainspotting* a year earlier. Both of these novels, interestingly, incorporate music as an integral thematic element.[25]

This chapter now allows for Welsh to be rightly promoted from the footnotes of intermedial discourse.

Beats, rhythms and the literary remix

This chapter will now outline more generic areas of interest with Welsh, before preceding to specific texts. In considering the approach to music of the writers in these case studies, it is significant that all three were themselves musicians. Nicholas Blincoe was a rapper, with a single released by Factory Records; Jeff Noon a bass player, and Welsh first sang and played guitar with punk bands in London – including Stairway 13 and the Pubic Lice – before working as a DJ. Redhead confirms that 'Welsh's own commitment to DJ culture has been long standing but fame allowed him to indulge his passion for the decks',[26] and during that DJ career Welsh played at prestigious clubs including Bugged Out! and Sankeys Soap in Manchester, Back to Basics in Leeds and Manumission in Ibiza (discussed in Chapter 2, Welsh describes playing Manumission as 'the biggest buzz I've ever had in my life').[27] Welsh also toured with Ernesto Leal's Arthrob parties that merged literature with music, with Welsh reading to music from DJs such as Andy Weatherall,[28] subterranean sonic life confronting, head on, the supraterranean literary realm. Clear links can be made here with Beat Generation writers reading to bebop jazz in what, once again, must be considered a determinedly musical literature.[29] Redhead also detects a certain cultural melding, with literature presented as a 'gig', itself an 'echo of […] beat generation readings'.[30] As I write, Welsh is currently working with – among others – the current editor of *DJ* magazine Carl Loben on new electronic music productions, now hiding behind the comedic persona of German DJ Klaus Blatter.[31]

Methodologically, I approach the texts from the perspective of cultural musicology rather than music theory, as this is the level at which Welsh himself deploys music within his text: used simply, and diegetically, as silent literary soundtrack. Although Welsh does describe music, its reception (as described in Chapter 3) at times further distorted by drug consumption, more often he simply names particular tracks, without a description of how that music sounds, where more nuanced explanations of that music might be seen to disturb the narrative flow. In *LitPop*, Rachel Carroll argues that 'a literary soundtrack can arguably only function on an intertextual level whereby the citation serves to activate meanings signified by the music'.[32] The reader thereby needs to come to the text equipped with a certain understanding of this subterranean culture and its musical and technological practices to enjoy a truly penetrative reading of the text. If Welsh mentions a track such as D-Mob's 'We Call It Acieed' in *Ecstasy*,[33] for example, it will be up to the reader's understanding of both the culture and its soundtrack to then unpack and reassemble that aural referent,[34] based on cultural relevance and adequate reserves of Thornton's subcultural capital. A further example can be found in *Glue*, where the DJ character reports the following range of repertoire:

> Ah'm straight oan the decks, spinnin a few tunes. Thir's a good selection here; maistly Eurotechno stuff ah've no heard ay, but one or Chicago House and even some old Donna Summer classics. Ah pit oan some Kraftwerk, a quirky track off Trans-Euro Express.[35]

In the best cases, writer and reader of the text can reach towards the same meaning, reactivating, in collaboration, the sound of the music. As Carroll suggests,

> The function of the citation is dependent not only on the reader's capacity to identify the music in question but also to decipher the complex signifying codes to do with performance, genre, period, lyrical and musical content by which a pop song generates meaning in a non-aural context.[36]

Just as Hertz and Roessner note, in relation to film music, that 'any regular moviegoer will recognize that a carefully chosen song is a filmic shortcut to evoking time and setting',[37] so track selection is equally significant for Welsh in his literature. Stylistically, therefore, there is a level of assumption on the part of Welsh that to have even opened his book the reader is to some extent 'in the know', and in the subterranean realm, in order that the author can then employ the shorthand argot of the dancefloor and its soundtracks.

We can further extend notions of relevance not only to the diegetic soundtrack within the text but to the very process of reading Welsh. Textual determinism argues that texts orientate their own meanings, regardless of who reads them; however, in terms of the impact of Dancefloor-Driven Literature, a much more elastic model for understanding reception is required. Mark Duffett begins this process within his fan studies research, arguing that 'the encoding-decoding idea broke audience research out of the reductive trap of textual determinism';[38] however, with Dancefloor-Driven Literature we can discern an even more mutable, fluid and contested relationship between author and audience. As there has been relatively little published academic consideration of this literature, my research took me to unpublished PhD theses of scholars with similar interests. In her PhD thesis Nedeljkov, for instance, describes 'Postfuturist literary DJs',[39] channelling Jeff Noon's aesthetic in her comments to me that the reader, too, has to be 'a bloody good DJ'.[40] In this sense, meaning might be seen to be negotiated or, in Nedeljkov's terms, 'remixed', in its passage from writer to reader. She comments (in relation to *Trainspotting*) that Welsh's approach 'resensitizes one to literary subtleties, thereby reanimating and reawakening one's DJ skills, i.e., reequipping one with reading-writing-remixing tools and inspiration'.[41] This negotiated consumption of the text by the 'creative reader' and their own interpretative layering of cognizance can also be extended to the prosumer agenda outlined in the previous chapter, in terms of a process that empowers the reader to constitute the totality of the story, as well as its embedded soundtrack, in the process of reading it. In this way, the holistic truth of the tale might ultimately only be completed in this author-audience 'mix', in the final process of a story's reception and consumption.

Redhead also appreciates the rhythmic dancefloor tendencies in Welsh's writing, citing 'Welsh's own "creative" use of house music in his stunning dialect prose'.[42] As well as finding thematic material in the paidian chaos of the dancefloor, therefore, Welsh also finds a stylistic mechanic for retelling those stories – the sense of mixing, overlaying, segueing – drawing on the rhythmic pulse of the music to transfer 'that perpetual movement into my writing', thereby bringing up to date precisely what Kerouac had attempted with the more organic rhythms of bebop. Smyth argues: 'The question of rhythm must feature strongly in any theoretical consideration of the role and representation of music in the novel',[43] and certainly a key musicological consideration in this chapter is this use of *rhythm* within narrative prose, a shared driver of both the musical and the literary. Welsh is conscious of that sonic imperative, arguing in our conversation: 'For me you have to get the pace in the style'.[44] To retain the beat of the writing, for example, Welsh abandons speech marks in order to keep dialogue flowing, instead using the stylistic device of dashes, imbuing rhythm to the prose (for the same reasons, Kerouac constructed dialogue in a similar way). Far from enabling a disconnection between the literal and the literary, this graphological approach smoothens the process of recognition and association on the part of a cognizant readership. For example, the following dialogue takes place in *Glue*:

> Sharon looked at Larry. – We'll no git intae a club if wir aw skagged up, Larry.
> – Starin at waws is the new niteclubbin. Sais so in *The Face*, eh grinned.[45]

Further, I connect this use of linguistic rhythm to the naturalistic presentation of scene, notably in Welsh's almost autochthonous use of the Leith vernacular. Smyth mentions Welsh in a lineage of Scottish writers 'clearly inspired by the tradition of progressive Scottish writers launched by Alasdair Gray's *Lanark*',[46] and Nedeljkov also highlights Welsh's 'hybrid vernacular combining local slang with standard English, clearly indicating idiosyncrasies of a specific subcultural milieu—an idiom of the outcasts'.[47] Certainly Welsh is conscious of this, and also demonstrably resistant to it, for instance when explaining to Redhead his relationship to fellow Scottish authors: 'I think I was writing against them as well. […] You're writing against, you're reacting against, what goes before.'[48] This is allied to a crucial comment Welsh made to me in one of our conversations:

> To me, acid house is in your fucking DNA. That's why I wrote in the Scottish vernacular – not because I wanted to make a point like James Kelman or Alasdair Gray – but because I just liked the beat, the 4/4 beat. The English language is weights and measures – controlling, imperialistic – and I don't want to be controlled.[49]

In comments redolent of Trevor Miller, Welsh's own musical resistance to the linguistic imperialism of the English language denotes an author very much in tune with Bakhtin's idea that 'speech and gesture are gradually freed from the pitifully serious tones of supplication, lament, humility, and piousness'.[50] Again, in terms of proximity, Welsh is more concerned with creating a connection between character and reader – resisting the notion that the English language might further interrupt that very pure process of communication via its various linguistic diversions and instead adopting the more *route one* approach born of synthetic personalization. For Welsh, this relationship between his characters and the reader seems like a private, unmediated conversation, bringing their lives to life. Welsh reports,

> I like the idea that the characters I create are talking to the reader – it's almost like you're in a room with them, and sometimes they're not the sort of person you want to be stuck in a room with. It's like being stuck in a chill-out room with someone spraffing in your ear. But at least you can put the book down. You can't shut those fuckers up.[51]

Such characters are, instead, let loose within the text, their language bound by no sense of censor or moral privation, free to indulge in Bakhtin's notion that 'abuses, curses, profanities, and improprieties are the unofficial elements of speech'.[52]

Bakhtin's notion of 'carnival' and 'marketplace'

Bakhtin is useful both for thematic and stylistic synergies with Welsh and for providing a precisely machined key for unlocking this author's work: located, improbably perhaps, in his seminal text *Rabelais and His World*, which examines the characters, behaviours, actions – and principally language – of the work of François Rabelais, a sixteenth-century French Renaissance author. Drawing on Bakhtin as the principle theorist in decoding Welsh, four concepts will be useful. First, Bakhtin provides a useful discourse on the carnival and the 'Language of the Marketplace'. In this current updating, we can map clubland onto Bakhtin's carnival, even within an altogether more chthonian strata, where the dancefloor might also take the role of the marketplace within that carnival, populated as it is by similarly ribald characters, their nu-folk stories unfolding within the words of Welsh. Bakhtin writes how such environments

> exercise a strong influence on the entire contents of speech, transferring it to another sphere beyond the limits of conventional language. Such speech forms, liberated from nouns, hierarchies and prohibitions of established idiom, become themselves a peculiar argot and create a special collectivity, a group of people initiated in familiar intercourse, who are frank and free in expressing themselves verbally. The marketplace crowd was such a collectivity, especially the festive, carnivalesque crowd at the fair.[53]

Bakhtin notes 'the superlative of grotesque realism: the wrong side,[54] or rather the right side of abuse',[55] and this provides a second theoretical thread, highlighting interesting dichotomies. José Francisco Fernández (although writing principally about Nicholas Blincoe) describes an almost literary punk aesthetic:

> Welsh's fluency and apparent carelessness in matters of style, his unashamed breaking down of genre barriers and his refusal to be dragged down by boredom or complacency created a powerful impact on younger artists: anything was possible, anyone could write, any story was valid.[56]

Far from breaking genre barriers, however, this research argues that Welsh, of all the writers considered here, is most in line with an overt literary tradition, with Jeff Noon arguably the most progressive of the three. Instead, Welsh exhibits the tendencies of a dark, neo-Dickensian *social realism* that stretches back to Boswell,[57] even if acknowledging that for Welsh, his is the society of the 1990s dancefloor. When I put this idea to Welsh, he agreed first that 'writing was making sense of that scene', and then further that 'I wanted to write about that. It's fucking important social history.'[58] Accuracy is key; as Welsh reports to Redhead,

> I still hold to the idea that it's pretentious not to write about drugs. To me they're just an unremarkable part of the scheme of things. When I see a novel that hasn't

got any drugs in it I think to myself 'well, what kind of social life is this supposed to be depicting?' It's a subculture they're writing about.[59]

Resisting the pejorative position put forward by Reynolds, and contrary to accusations of carelessness by Fernández, in precisely documenting the lower echelons of Edinburgh society, Welsh might therefore be considered more in the tradition of Charles Dickens, George Orwell and other chroniclers of life as it is lived at street level. Indeed, this might be further extended to below street-level terrain, to the *sub*terranean, the thematic drivers of Welsh linking semantically with notions not only of realism but also of *sur*realism. The focus, therefore, might be said to be what lies beneath, firmly located by Bakhtin as 'the relief of the grotesque body; or speaking in architectural terms, towers and subterranean passages'.[60] Welsh also focuses on space in-between: on the liminal, and transgression of the liminal – the foregrounding of bodily interior and exterior, the way society operates over and underground – all are counterpointed as Welsh evolves as a writer of Dancefloor-Driven Literature.

Bakhtin's notion of a 'grotesque realism' is central to this chapter in relation to Welsh's portrayal of this Edinburgh cultural underground, and links very much with Kristeva's notion of 'the abject', specifically around bodily fluids and functions.[61] The romantic poets looked for beauty and found only monsters. In the same way, Welsh also considers the abject, further adding the filter of intoxication so that his style becomes 'hyperreal', with flourishes more akin to a dark, South American magic realism.[62] Further, my reading of Welsh contends that his writing moves overtly, and demonstrably, towards the grotesque, towards the abject dancefloor and its grimy intoxicants, with the conscious, commercial awareness that there was a lacuna of such literature on the bookshelves.

Disco Biscuits: 'The State of the Party'

Hints of the interplay of these influences and expressive tendencies can be found within Welsh's contribution to *Disco Biscuits* – the short story 'The State of the Party' – which contains early glimmers of what would become a more defined 'dancefloor-driven' impetus to Welsh's fiction. The conclusion to this chapter will argue for a dialogic approach to Dancefloor-Driven Literature, perfectly defined by Sheila Whiteley in the 'Coda' to *LitPop* as a position where 'meaning is always both socially and historically situated, generally specific, and inextricably bound up in relationships of power'.[63] Certainly in a short story publication each text must be seen to be in a constant relation with other texts around it, the very concept suggesting a collection that shares certain ontological characteristics. And yet 'The State of the Party' is, at the same time, at odds with many of the stories in *Disco Biscuits* in that tonally it is rather dark and, like *Trainspotting*, involves heroin and heroin overdoses rather than a more positive presentation of recreational pharmaceuticals.

In this story we meet two friends out drinking – Crooky and Callum – who leave a pub to go to a house party, followed by an old acquaintance of one of them, Boaby, who is a user of heroin. At the party, Boaby overdoses and dies, and the friends are entrusted with the task of removing him from the premises. Leaving with two female party goers – Michelle and Gillian – the group are set upon by football casuals,[64] and they abandon Boaby, dead but further beaten, and retreat home where, after splitting into pairs for sexual intercourse (with varying degrees of success), the two friends are left to come down from their combined heroin and LSD intoxication with the light of the new day illuminating the severity of what has happened. If tonally different, and set largely within a house party rather than a nightclub, there is certainly a nascent, spectral sense of music within the text, with references to playing compilation cassette tapes (on this occasion simply 'a nice, trancey tape'),[65] and Scottish bands such as Finitribe.[66] Real Edinburgh clubs are cited, if not directly visited: 'The Citrus' and 'Sub Club',[67] as well as references to not only Ecstasy ('E', and 'eckies')[68] but also specific brands of Ecstasy such as 'doves' and 'Malcolm X's'.[69] As noted in Chapter 3, the subterranean defines itself by its semiotics – the smiley face, the knowing wink – and here the references to both drugs and music engender proximity between author and cognizant reader of the text, drawing the two parties closer together via Calum's 'secret mental language, this pre-speech thought'.[70] In fact, so linked are drugs and music that at one stage we find the character Chizzie 'rolling a joint on an album cover',[71] fundamentally demonstrating the symbiosis of the two.

In 'The State of the Party', the city of Edinburgh plays the role of Rabelais's Fontenay-la Comte, a town of 'marketplace spectacles', where 'Rabelais could observe the life of the fair and listen to its voices', a town that importantly also 'developed its own popular argot'.[72] In terms of the rhythms of the street, we can trace the origins of Welsh's vernacular to Bakhtin's 'Language of the Marketplace', where Bakhtin remarks: 'Exaggeration, hyperbolism, excessiveness are generally considered fundamental attributes of the grotesque style.'[73] For instance in reporting on his sexual performance, Crooky responds, 'Ah fuckin split hur right up the middle man. The Royal Bank'll not be able tae sit on a bicycle seat or eat a good meal fir a long time eftir that!'[74] As with all the counterpointed positions considered in this chapter, this language is sited as oppositional, and resistant to hegemonic form, Bakhtin commenting how 'in the marketplace a special kind of speech was heard, almost a language of its own, quite unlike the language of Church, palace, courts, and institutions'.[75] My reading of both Bakhtin and Welsh concurs with Smyth that language has collapsed into the gutter, although I go further in arguing that it remains entirely possible to appreciate how the gutter has its own elegant soundtrack, its own rhythms, cadence and grotesque poetry. The effects of LSD are, for instance, compellingly detailed:

> This sense of isolation was briefly comforting, but it quickly grew suffocating and oppressive. They became aware of their body rhythms, the pounding of their hearts, the circulating of their blood. They had a sense of themselves as machines. Calum, a plumber, thought himself as a plumbing system. This made him want to shit.[76]

This description is important in advancing the notion of system (an important word for this book, as we shall see in the conclusion, notably) and for the suggestion that psychedelic drugs might somehow plumb you into the inner rhythms of your own physiology and beyond that, to existence itself. In 'The State of the Party' we can therefore detect key thematic tropes of Welsh's fiction emerging, in terms of the placement of music within the text and the stylistic use of the rhythms of language. However, the impact of the combination of drugs and music is an intoxicated state that Welsh, at least in this stage in his writing career, chooses to render in naturalistic terms, without the figurative inventiveness or graphological perturbations we find in later texts.

Music as signifier of taste in *Ecstasy*

Musical beats and subterranean memes emerge more specifically in Welsh's collection of three novellas, *Ecstasy* (1996). Enjoying a near synchronous publication with *Disco Biscuits*, the themes and stylistic concerns of Dancefloor-Driven Literature are more evident in this title – in terms of the figurative importance of music, taste distinctions and subcultural capital – even, as we shall see, from a cursory glance at the cover. The three stories within the volume are titled 'Lorraine Goes to Livingston', 'Fortune's Always Hiding' and 'The Undefeated'. The collection is collectively subtitled 'Three Tales of Chemical Romance',[77] and each individual story is subtitled for a different kind of romance, respectively 'A Rave and Regency Romance', 'A Corporate Drug Romance' and 'An Acid House Romance', again making very pronounced connections both to the music and to the intoxicatory practices of EDMC outlined in Chapter 3. The first story concerns an ageing female romantic novelist, in the Barbara Cartland mould,[78] and the clubbing practices of the nurses who tend to her. Let loose within this world is a predatory necrophiliac TV celebrity, Freddy Royle, whose behaviour is disturbingly synonymous with the actions of disgraced TV personality Jimmy Savile.[79] 'Fortune's Always Hiding' takes as its subject a poorly tested pharmaceutical drug, which has similar side effects on unborn children as the morning sickness drug Thalidomide.[80] However, the most significant Dancefloor-Driven text in the collection is the last – 'The Undefeated' – which will be more closely analysed in this chapter.

Alongside the form and content of this collection, it is also important to consider the marketing of the title. Welsh is an author very aware of the importance of the paratextual material of the book (discussing with Redhead 'the title, the packaging' of his earlier collection *The Acid House*),[81] and the impact that these decisions have on 'drugsploitation' literature.[82] Even the choice of title is overt – a provocative, commercial move on the part of either author or publisher to connect with a readership 'scene' – a point noted by Marcus Boon who describes how 'neo-generic fictional works such as Irvine Welsh's *Ecstasy* (1996) and Douglas Rushkoff's *Ecstasy Club* (1997) have emerged to describe the evolving subcultures that have sprung up around these substances'.[83] Linking to themes identified in previous chapters, Calcutt and Shephard remark on the novel's publication with a CD soundtrack and write: 'Launched in a fashionable nightclub, *Ecstasy* (1997), a collection of three tales, sold 100,000 copies in three weeks.'[84] These deliberate creative and commercial decisions, I suggest, and the resulting sensationalism, were not a consequence of the publication of these works, but conversely because Welsh was writing *towards* a specified audience demographic: a participant, cognizant readership eager for what Beeler describes as 'artistic and commercial popularizations of the movement'.[85]

Beeler further remarks, 'Welsh is only interested in club culture as an alternative to what he calls straight-peg lifestyles, an alternative to the mainstream',[86] which dovetails neatly with Sarah Champion's assertion that

> it is kind of ironic that Irvine Welsh became so huge with the clubbers and the rave generation but I think it was because there was just such a vacuum of somebody writing about the chaotic world of drugs and going out.[87]

Such articulations extend our analysis further into audience and fan studies, and Stanley Fish's work on 'interpretive communities'.[88] In Mark Duffett's reading, 'people – here fans and media consumers – build up their interpretations in the act of reading, they do so in the context of being part of *communities of readers*',[89] and in this sense, we are now considering a generation of readers, as well as a generation of writers. One might logically argue that it is easier to become a generation's 'bard' if you know precisely the tune that the generation wants you to play. As Duffett remarks in relation to media theorist John Fiske, 'Mass culture could only become popular culture when it was appropriated by ordinary people',[90] much like the reader-bouncer who Champion references in the previous chapter.

It might be argued that Ecstasy and the dancefloor play a more peripheral role in the first two stories, and we can therefore deduce that the decision behind the choice of *Ecstasy* for the overall title of the collection would undoubtedly have commercial imperatives, as regards theories of audience and reception, in line with notions of readership communities identified by Fish. Redhead, too, reports on the book's 'chiming with the MDMA influenced times in the mid-nineties Britain which undoubtedly led to its commercial success'.[91] This was therefore literature driven not only from but also demonstrably towards the dancefloor. That notion of commercial intent leading the creative imperative can certainly be extended to the cover design of the edition I personally have,[92] where, in extremely bright colours, we see a man's head, in blue, with a luminous letter 'e' between his teeth, this alphabetic pill at the precise point of transgressing the physiological threshold between interior and exterior of the body, the gaping hole not dissimilar to Bakhtin's consideration of the 'entrance to the underworld'[93] (Figure 6.1).

In the *Ecstasy* collection we are, once again, firmly in the realms of Bakhtin's 'folk culture',[94] a carnivalesque 1990s Edinburgh populated by characters of the clubland marketplace. In 'The Undefeated' we can immediately note an oppositional structure to the story: light against dark; day against night; the subterranean versus the supraterranean and a man from one (Lloyd) and a woman from the other (Heather) journeying towards one another along what Bakhtin calls a 'condition of unfinished metamorphosis: the passing from night to morning'.[95] Beeler also highlights this journey, noting how 'Welsh's representation of club culture in this story is of a

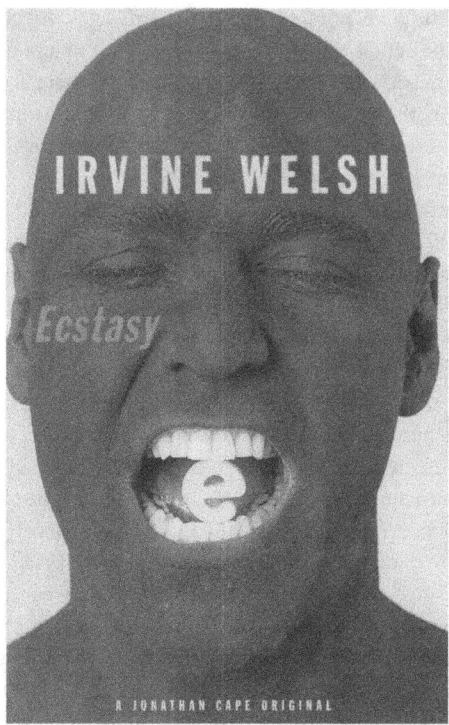

Figure 6.1 Cover of Irvine Welsh, *Ecstasy* (London: Jonathan Cape, 1996).

positive social force that enables people to break out of their restrictive patterns of behaviour and escape from the corruption of the dominant culture'.[96] Welsh delights in such oppositional paradigms: hegemonic culture versus countercultures; reality set against surreality; sobriety versus intoxication and the world that resides on each side of the rule of law. Such deconstructions create the necessary, if tense, space for narrative development and character evolution – the space that Lloyd and Heather must enter if they are to find one another – a journey further enabled by drugs and the dancefloor.

All of this is then set to an electronic soundtrack, the silently sonic beyond the linguistic. Smyth comments that 'music looms surprisingly large in the history of British fiction',[97] but of course there are distinctions in the way music is deployed. In *LitPop*, the editors channel W. H. Auden's suggestion that music is 'social', describing how an author can use a piece of music because it will also be recognized by the reader in their shared cultural – or indeed subcultural – experience, and therefore used to figuratively denote certain themes. Smyth suggests, for instance, that E. M. Forster used classical music 'as an index of a certain kind of cultural value that some characters [...] possessed'.[98] This polarity is entirely reversed with Welsh, where the author, instead, uses music to denote low cultural value. In our conversation, Welsh describes a fascinating technique incorporated within his writing – directly connecting music specifically in the production of literature – whereby he first considers the characters in his fiction, and then creates 'playlists' for those characters. He explains: 'When I'm writing I have this thing: Where they stay, who they lay, what they play.'[99] Welsh's central approach is therefore key: 'I think that if this character was in a film of their life, what would be the soundtrack?'[100]

In their introduction to *Write in Tune*, editors Hertz and Roessner agree that 'regardless of whether or not one actually likes the songs, they serve as the soundtrack of the time'.[101] Just as with film, the use of a song or a musical artist is a narrative 'shortcut to evoking time and setting',[102] particularly for Welsh, who places real music into his texts with a sonic precision to suit mood, circumstance or character identification and development. Even more intriguing is that this technique does not relate only to empathetic characters, and sympathetic music. More useful to this analysis is where music might be both diegetic and yet anempathetic, or unempathetic, within the text,[103] where Welsh might construct one of his playlists, for instance, for characters with whom he is entirely unsympathetic, giving them appropriately unlikeable music. In this intriguing approach to the relationship of words and music, to authentically represent character profile their music tastes must be rendered as accurately as the clothes that they wear, or their idiolect and idiosyncratic mannerisms that all combine to bring their personalities to life. When pressed on this, Welsh agrees such playlists are 'not necessarily a good thing', where he might decide characters like 'crap, shite music … stuff I would never listen to'.[104] Further, Welsh reports in conversation that he then physically plays the music he has playlisted for that character to himself, as he writes for their personality – whether he likes that music or not – so that music provides further aural inspiration to the creation of character, whether positive or negative. Indeed, Welsh confirms that through this self-imposed discomfort, he actually feels able to, and perhaps driven to, write a more authentically dislikeable character, as the experience of writing is itself rendered so unpleasant.

In *Ecstasy*, for example, we see bands widely perceived as rather bland used to denote something similarly deficient in the personality of the character who listens to those artists, much as Brett Easton Ellis used the music of Genesis and Huey Lewis and News contrapuntally in his novel *American Psycho*.[105] Here we can identify a key figurative use of music in Welsh's work, in terms of determining character based on their subcultural capital in Thornton's terms, or hierarchies of taste in those of Pierre Bourdieu, evidenced specifically by music.[106] Following a process of close textual analysis of this collection and dealing first with anempathetic music used diegetically within the text, we find ourselves at one point during 'The Undefeated' with lacklustre husband Hugh: deficient in every department including, it would seem to be implied, taste. Consider this passage, where Hugh greets his wife, the aforementioned and entrapped, Heather:

Good day? he smiles, briefly breaking off from whistling the Dire Straits song 'Money For Nothing'.[107]

The inference here is clear: Dire Straits are perceived to be safe and middle of the road, musically, and the playlist Welsh has drawn up for Hugh defines and determines him as just such a character. Of course, this cultural and literary exchange can only operate successfully if the readers themselves understand who that cited artist is, and their place in Bourdieu's now reversed cultural hierarchy of 'taste'.

Interestingly, then, it seems that for Welsh one actually ascends the taste hierarchy at the same rate one descends from supra to subterranean realms. After leaving Hugh, Heather experiences an epiphany and it, too, has its own soundtrack. Almost her first move is to visit music retailer HMV, reporting: 'I couldn't decide what to buy, so I ended up getting some house-music compilation CDs which were probably not that good but anything would be all right after Hugh's Dire Straits and U2 and Runrig.'[108] Her sexual and social emancipation is metaphorically denoted by these new music choices, mediated by the music press:

> I went for a coffee and thumbed through an *NME* which I hadn't brought for years and read an interview with a guy who used to be in Happy Mondays and had started a band called Black Grape. I then went back to HMV and brought their album, *It's Great When You're Straight ... Yeah!*, just because the guy said he had taken loads of drugs.[109]

Welsh figuratively works this process of experimentation and release by reference to both music and intoxication, here in a very physical battle of taste:

> Hugh's Dire Straits CD, *Brothers in Arms*, was lying on the coffee table. He always played that. I particularly hated the song Money For Nothing which is what he always sang. I stuck on my Black Grape CD and put *Brothers in Arms* in the microwave to prove that what people say about CDs being indestructible is a lot of rubbish. Just to make doubly sure though, I watched *Love Over Gold* obliterate in a similar manner.[110]

Beyond this MOR incineration (somewhat redolent of the Disco Demolition from Chapter 3) Heather's emancipation is also accompanied by a grammatical loosening of the prose. Welsh abandons commas where they might be expected in order to allow the words to flow with the rhythm of Heather's new-found freedom in intoxication, as compared to her previously and graphologically 'boxed in' life, when she quite literally saw things in boxes, whether that be her consideration of her past sexual partners, or her feelings towards Hugh:

> Name: Student Hugh.
> Committed to: the liberation of working people from the horrors of capitalism.

> Name: Jobless Graduate Hugh
> Committed to: fighting to maintain jobs for working people but to changing the system.[111]

Welsh conveys, graphologically, Heather's use of lists – even shopping lists – to exteriorize her thoughts. On the other side of this position, the narrative representation of Lloyd's interiority, in the Bakhtinian sense, is altogether more naturalistic, notably when further mutated by drug consumption, a narrative device further developed by Jeff Noon and more closely analysed in the following chapter. For instance, in reporting his decision to swallow three tabs of acid when confronted by a police officer, Lloyd describes how:

> Ah get the trips between my forefinger and thumb and ah swallow the lot, silly fuckin cunt; ah could have left them, the polis would never find them wouldnae search me anywey I've done nowt wrong but ah swallowed the fuckin lot when ah could've even fuckin flung them away. No thinkin straight ...
>
> > They called the child Lloyd Beattie
> > The cunt grew up a right wee sweetie
>
> Lloyd One calling Lloyd Two, can you hear me Lloyd Two? Can you hear me Lloyd Two? Can you hear
>
> > am I floating
>
> The beefy bastard is not amused. – These cunts robbed me! Ah'm struggling tae make this business pay n they fuckin wee toerags ... .[112]

On a macro, structural level, the novel is itself a musical composition, in terms of the dual consideration of form and content; however, we must also engage on a micro level, with the nuances of the text itself where, building on Nedeljkov's ideas around the meta 'object' levels of prose, melody might also be discerned.[113] This chapter has already noted that Welsh wrote to keep the rhythms of the weekend rolling, telling stories of the dancefloor to its now silenced beat (as Smyth reports, an author is perfectly justified in listening to music like a 'predator', stealing from its rhythms and cadences).[114] Here, then, we find an author writing to the electronic biorhythms of his subterranean milieu, with a naturalistic instinctiveness that is tangible in the prose highlighted earlier. However, beyond rhythm, Welsh also evokes subcultural shorthand to do so, where his approach to music is formed of broad strokes rather than precise musicological description, perhaps based only on the information of a track's name, or EDMC genre, which must then be further activated by the cognizant reader in its reception.

In their introduction to *Write in Tune*, the editors argue that 'pop music has come to serve as the foreground through which people filter the world or as the ubiquitous background of everyday life',[115] and close textual analysis of the story 'The Undefeated' reveals numerous references to many real-world artists, DJs, music tracks and indeed drugs (including brand names). Real-world DJs such as DJs Jon Digweed, Tony Humphries, Craig Smith and Roger Sanchez find their names 'dropped' into the narrative for the subterranean kudos they bestow,[116] although opinions about their music might be rather more prosaic: 'The chancing cunt telt me Digweed was shite', as an example.[117] In terms of a more positive and empathetic representation of music, the DJ (and colleague of Welsh) Andrew Weatherall is also cited. However, even then he only appears as 'Weatherall', as though reference to his surname alone is enough for the cognizant-participant reader, in possession of relevant reserves of subcultural capital, to complete the picture in relevance terms. Further, they may feel culturally enriched, and further rewarded, by their ability to do so, finding themselves on the inside of understanding. Heather, having replaced the family home with the dancefloor, seems emboldened by this new subterranean knowledge, her use of technical terms suggesting she is ascending the EDMC taste hierarchy. She reports,

> I was dancing away at The Pure, kicking like fuck because Weatherall's up from London and he's moved it up seamlessly from ambient to a hard-edged techno dance-beat.[118]

Pure is a real-world Edinburgh club and further content analysis reveals numerous other musical references throughout the collection, cultural shorthand for the intended audience, Welsh using real-world detail as cultural product placement, in order to naturalistically render the scene. Such sonic details include the band the Orb,[119] and implied 'good music' on compilations including one with 'Marvin, Al Green, The Tops, Bobby Womack, The Isleys, Smokey, The Temptations, Otis, Aretha, Dionne and Dusty',[120] where, again, the reader is expected to know the artist, though only part of their name may be revealed. We also find separate references to the bands Oasis, Blur, Primal Scream, Take That,[121] again to Bobby Womack,[122] and 'Piece of Clay' by Marvin Gaye.[123] Clubs and club nights are dispersed across the text to act as shortcuts to rendering verisimilitude.[124] On one page Lloyd bumps into clubland acquaintances and lists where he has seen them out: 'The Metro, the Forum, Rezurrection, The Pure, The Arches, The Slam Club ... big Slam punters, naw Terry n Jason ... Industria ... – Awright, boys!'[125] Elsewhere we find references to Solefusion, the Tunnel, Sub Club, City Café, Rezurrection, Tribal Funktion, Rectangle Club, Pure, Slam and Yip Yap.[126] Again, the effect is to bolster the realism of the setting within the fiction, and drama described.

Perhaps not surprisingly, references to Ecstasy are too ubiquitous to be listed here, but they also mentioned by specific brand names such as Supermarios, pink champagnes and Doves.[127] Also on offer in this pharmaceutical cornucopia are 'jellies', speed (and even rhyming slang that links music to that drug: Lou Reed), speedballs, acid or LSD, Ketamine, crystal methamphetamine and cocaine.[128] The effect, even in the process of textual analysis, is itself almost disorientating. In the pursuit of subterranean authenticity and constructing the context of this music scene, Welsh also mentions real-world EDMC magazine titles such as *Mixmag* and *DJ*,[129] and there is also – like the Alan Warner character Morvern Callar – a brief escape for Heather to the ultimate TAZ, Ibiza. These broad references to both music text and wider cultural context suggest that 'The Undefeated' is, as Beeler remarks, 'intended for a participant audience',[130] the references at times oblique, or codified, so that their linguistic relevance might only be unpacked by the culturally cognizant.

In line with Jacques Derrida, music almost dares the author to trap it linguistically; if we cannot be precise in that entrapment, we can at least, as Welsh does so effectively, write musically, and certainly, with the rhythms of the dancefloor in mind. In the following passage the use of music is ventriloquial, in the sense that Welsh uses music to set the scene and Lloyd speaks through the music so that the experience, itself, might also become audible:

> This operatic slab of synth seems to be 3 D and ah realise that I'm coming up in a big way as that invisible hand grabs a hud ay me and sticks me onto the roof because the music is in me around me and everywhere, it's just leaking from my body, this is the game this is the game ah look around and we're all going phoah and or eyes are just big black pools of love and energy and my guts are doing a big turn as the quease zooms through my body and we're up to the floor one by one and ah think I'm going tae need tae shit but ah hold on and it passes and I'm riding this rocket to Russia.[131]

This section, almost the very opening to 'The Undefeated', is interesting for the way the perception of music is internalized by the character, the soundtrack now metadiegetic in the sense that the reader further perceives it through the character's transformative drug consumption.[132] Certainly, in the synaesthetic rendering of the sonic into a physical three-dimensional shape, Welsh is close to the Ecstasy experience of the seventeen-year-old girl interviewed by Sheila Henderson, who said 'when you're on "E", it's like you're not dancing on the floor, you're dancing on the notes and the music is all around you'.[133] Also of interest is how the interplay of music and intoxicant is rendered in a way that is (or at least appears to be) linguistically loose: a punctuation-free stream of consciousness close to Kerouac's prose, and his own Benzedrine-fuelled responses to bebop, and linguistically idiomatic of the loose machinations of the dancefloor. Thematically, we also see a physical response from the character in his focus on what will later be considered Bakhtin's 'bodily lower stratum', in the physiological reaction to the experience (a further amusing link to Bakhtin is that the character cites Russia as the destination for this experience).

In that process, rhythm again is key. A stylistic genesis for this approach might be found in the rather older rhythms of oralcy – as found in the African vocal tradition – whereby we might feel close, and connected, to writers who write in a way that is itself close to how people speak. Consider Lloyd's comment again, and its inherent linguistic rhythm has the effect of engendering a proximity between writer and reader, where the character addresses the reader directly, as though a friend, in a process of synthetic personalization that is certainly found in Kerouac, whose novels seem like private conversations between writer and reader.¹³⁴ This style of writing pays no heed to literary conventions that might, instead, seek to build canyons of artifice between the two agents in this communication exchange. Where the text is written by, and for, participants of a subterranean culture (while also locking out the uninitiated), this proximity is of particular interest. Champion focuses on this notion when arguing in our interview for 'the rhythm of music and using the slang and using dialects that same way that Irvine Welsh was doing'.¹³⁵ In this way, the reader is therefore entirely with Lloyd on the dancefloor. By the end of the story, however, Lloyd has stepped up – like Welsh himself – to the DJ booth, although the representation of music remains opaque:

> Ah got up and started puttin on the tunes. At first ah wisnae really mixin, just sort ay playing the sounds like, but then ah started really gaun for it, trying oot one or two things. It was shite, but ah was so intae it, every cunt was getting intae it tae.¹³⁶

A central interest in 'The Undefeated' lies in how a writer renders the DJ process. In order to assist our understanding of the moment of a record's impact, it will be helpful to defer to a DJ – in this case Dave Haslam – who states that 'the important chemistry is the reaction between the music and the crowd; and the DJ is somewhere at the centre of it all, a catalyst'.¹³⁷ That production of sound in the printed word is something that occupies Welsh with Lloyd and, indeed in the following consideration of the later novel *Glue*, with the character Carl Ewart.

Music as metaphorical escape: *Glue*

The archetype of the DJ is a central feature of Welsh's 2001 novel, *Glue*, which builds on the uses of music within the novel explored in this chapter, in continuing to denote taste distinctions, while also introducing a fresh figurative use of music, in notions of escape. Having identified DJs (real and constructed) within the prose of Welsh, this chapter will continue to consider the interplay of music, drug consumption and behavioural patterns but will now push further, detaching the construct of the DJ from the broader context of the dancefloor, in order to divine what figurative role the DJ might play within this fictional environment. This chapter will therefore analyse what the DJ actually represents, and what the DJ contributes to these fictional dancefloors. For instance, does the DJ stand as a character of transformative significance or merely supplier of what has now been decoded as the diegetic soundtrack within the literary text? As outlined in Chapter 2, the DJ's work, after all, is about judicious track selection and the resulting 'mix'. However, where, in fact, does the DJ fit into this interplay of power relations?

Structurally, Welsh's novel is built around four Edinburgh friends, who the reader first meets as babies. In this way, these overlapping narratives are inherently musical in a formalist sense, linking linguistically to Bakhtin's conceptual work around polyphony and indeed to Werner Wolf's narrowing of that concept to his sense of 'fugal polyphony'.[138] This interplay of voices is immediately redolent, for instance, of Wolf's own musico-literary intermedial case study – the twentieth-century writer Aldous Huxley – and Huxley's concerns with musicalizing fiction in an 'attempt to portray the "multiplicity", the complexity and the instability of contemporary urban life from different points of view',[139] further linking to Bakhtin's ideas around multi-vocality, and indeed heteroglossia.[140] Through the passage of the novel, its narrative melody sees two characters slide downwards: one goes to prison and dies from AIDS, the other becomes a bloated caricature of his former self. The remaining two are awarded different degrees of escape, by virtue of their accumulation of subcultural capital: one, Billy Birrell, through success in boxing, and Carl, in DJing. Welsh supports this reading, explaining: 'Yeah he does it through music and Billy does it through sport and they are literal paths. It's the way that you can do it.'[141]

In a dialogic, thematic and metaphorizing sense, the glue that, for Welsh, binds a society, a subterranean scene or a friendship group is indeed its music and its drugs (as well as football and fashion affiliations) that denote a communality of shared experience. Carl argues in *Glue*: 'That's the thing aboot music, if yir really intae it, ye can go anywhere in the world and feel like you've goat long-lost mates.'[142] In this novel, while we can therefore trace the same entropic *Narrative Arc* defined earlier in this book and present in much of Dancefloor-Driven Literature, we can also note how that parabolic collapse is counterpointed, and melodically balanced in the musicological terms, in the process of the geographic escape of two characters. Here, to be a DJ is to enjoy economic, geographic and social escape, Thornton's ideas around subcultural capital enabling the character to rise up through Bourdieu's notions of taste and distinction following the accumulation of actual capital. If *Glue* stands as exemplum of the existence of such cultural and economic hierarchies, Carl stands as a figurative symbol of the transformative potential and upward progress in the carefully described arc of his transformation into a significant DJ, N-SIGN,[143] elevating this individual above the sociopolitical mire – important not for what he does, but for what he represents. Building on these ideas, it is therefore very interesting to my research that in Welsh's 2018 novel *Dead Men's Trousers* (an updating of the *Trainspotting* characters' lives), the character Renton is now a very successful manager of EDM DJs, including N-SIGN.

Early on in the novel *Glue*, it is the role music plays in the Ewart family home that provides both context and metaphor for a more loving, caring domestic environment than that experienced by the other friends, marking a point of immediate social and domestic differentiation with those households defined instead by poverty, abuse and alcoholism. Welsh's own reading supports this position: 'Music is a very inclusive thing. If you're playing a kind of music, and people are enjoying that music, it creates a warmth for them.'[144] Carl's father encourages his son's interest in music, once again setting him apart from the interests of his peers. Early on in the novel we see father and son at home, where 'Duncan Ewart has his young son, Carl, dancing on top of the sideboard to a Count Basie record',[145] and a little later we see the response in the son: 'Pit on Elvis, Dad, Carl urged.'[146] This closeness extends to paternal support for Carl's early forays into DJing, perhaps perceived by the father as the modern equivalent to his own rock and roll. Carl's early success is immediately detected by Billy, who observes:

He's got a wee bit too robotic, what's it he calls it, too techno-heided for me: ah liked it better when he was on that mair soulful trip. Still it's his tunes and he's daein awright. Getting noticed, getting respect. Goin roond the shoaps wi him, the clubs, n ye kin see it's no two schemies anymair, it's N-SIGN the DJ and Business Birrell, the boxer.[147]

We can therefore denote the figurative use of EDMC within the novel as a marker of high levels of subcultural capital, differentiation and of its potential for transformation and ultimately escape. Beeler remarks of this novel that 'although the DJs represented in the text are true enthusiasts, their interest is in purely aesthetic and professional matters',[148] a reading I dispute here, since music has played this much more fundamental, figurative role in Carl's life, Welsh himself agreeing that 'he's got that level of obsession that you have to have'.[149] Carl's interest in music in itself becomes a point of resistance. On a trip to Munich, the friends decide to shoplift some CDs and, even in these terms, Carl makes a value judgement when pejoratively describing the music that Gally, a character on the downward trajectory, chooses to steal:

It fuckin sickens ye what that cunt's loadin up oan; *Now That's What I Call Music Volume 10, 11, 12* and *13*, Phil Collins (*But Seriously*), Gloria Estefan (*Cuts Both Ways*), Tina Turner (*Foreign Affair*), Simply Red (*A New Flame*), Kathryn Joyner (*Sincere Love*), Jason Donovan (*Ten Good Reasons*), Eurhythmics (*We Too Are One*), loads ay Pavarotti eftir the World Cup, aw the shite ye wouldnae be seen deid wi and it fair pits me oaf.[150]

Taste, then, is important, even in terms of the music one steals. By contrast, Carl uses the experience to replace his favourite vinyl albums with CD equivalents: 'Ah backlist maist ay the Beatles, Stones, Zeppelin, Bowie and Pink Floyd. It's only that auld stuff ah ever listen to oan CD, and dance music, obviously, has tae be vinyl.'[151] Through the trip, Carl remains more interested in the interior of the city's record shops than its pubs, and this now begins to open up cultural differences with his existing friends, as well as fresh conversational possibilities with new ones, built on the basis of music:

The truth ay it is, and ah feel a bit guilty aboot it, but this is what ah like the maist now, crackin on wi some heads about sounds, checkin oot what cunts are listening tae, sussin oot what's gaun doon. Apart fae bein oan the decks, this is the highest form ay enjoyment for me.[152]

As he sheds the skin of his socio-economic upbringing, Welsh's 'self-mythologising process' builds for N-SIGN:[153]

They didnae like Carl Ewart, white-trash schemie. But they liked N-SIGN. N-SIGN's played at warehoose perties in London, raised funds for anti-racist groups, aw sorts ay deserving community organisations. They love N-SIGN. They'll never, ever get thir heads roond the fact that the only difference between

Carl Ewart and N-SIGN is that one worked liftin boxes in a warehoose for nae money while the other played records in one fir tons ay it.[154]

In his extensive reference notes at the end of *Subculture: The Meaning of Style*, Hebdige refers to Susan Sontag's concept of the 'métier of the adventurer as a spiritual vocation'.[155] It is precisely Carl's ability to play music that carves out this escape route, in the peripatetic possibilities inherent in the DJ lifestyle, fulfilling the belief of subcultural theorist Adam Brown that 'DJs have to some extent replaced the role of the band or the performer'.[156] As a writer and also travelling DJ, this is something that Welsh himself clearly saw in this lifestyle, stating,

> I do know some DJs that are millionaires and some that aren't but have been doing it for years and almost see it as a way of doing a bit of travelling. Whatever level you make it to, or whatever level you take it to, the ones that are really into it can make their life from music.[157]

Ben Malbon expands on this cultural and geographic distinction, in stating: 'The explosion in clubbing cultures over the last ten years has thus been accompanied by – and undoubtedly further fuelled through – the ever widening horizons of some of the clubbers themselves.'[158] The ability to DJ, therefore, affords Carl the opportunity to travel, to explore, to 'adventure', in Sontag's words. Like the Beat Generation hitting the road, to travel and tour is to escape the quicksand of the quotidian. Evolving success as a DJ then continues to signify separation – cultural, economic, geographic (and, it might be argued, moral) separation – as Carl moves away, first to London, then Paris, Berlin and ultimately Australia, in an apparent contravention of Reynolds's assertion that club culture is 'the cult of acceleration without destination',[159] or that the widely – and incorrectly – held view that this was a culture confined to the weekend. It is no accident that N-SIGN's album is called *Departures*.

In her essay 'Living the Dream', an early study of acid house parties and clubs in Manchester, Hillegonda Rietveld channelled Hakim Bey in arguing that 'the rave offered a release from day to day realities, a temporary escapist disappearance like the weekend or holiday'.[160] Although I strongly challenge the idea that such escape represents the totality of the EDMC experience, participants do indeed talk of 'living the dream' and elsewhere Simon Reynolds notes 'Rave's relentlessly utopian imagery – events/promoters called Living Dream, Fantazia, Rezerection, Utopia, even'.[161] A nightclub and rave dancefloor is itself a space of escape; equally a new identity, whether individual or group, might be constructed – and indeed is constructed within this book, from words. Nightclubs and raves are fabrications of both architectural and mythological form: the dancefloor is a dreamscape and the DJ, through sound, provides soundtrack to that dream. If this fits within a postmodern sense of re-invention and obfuscation then that also extends to the DJs themselves who, like N-SIGN, change their names to fabricate identities and conceal themselves behind banks of equipment, separating themselves from their audience and, arguably, from the usually prosaic ramifications of reality, preferring instead to play to specific notions of myth inherent in subterranean cultures. Barthes shows that the hegemonic production of myth is not a matter of a lie or confession but, rather, of inflection, a subtle change in the meaning of words. It is here, then, in this profane cultural mix of myth and mire that memories of the dancefloor are located, from which they are written, distorted, published and preserved. Further, through alternative mythmaking one might elevate oneself from this mire.[162]

A key interest of Theodor Adorno, meanwhile, was the relationship between art and society, and the need for writers to mediate their contemporary society (notwithstanding the fact that the Frankfurt School remained concerned, in a way in which I am demonstrably not, with the commodification of culture). In describing, very particularly, the lower echelons of urban Edinburgh society in its late-millennial context, Welsh must again be considered a social realist, concerned specifically with a kind of gutter-level realism that Tom Wolfe defined as *nostalgie de la boue*,[163] a longing for the mud, interests that similarly, and centrally, occupied Bakhtin. The third use of Bakhtinian theory for this account, therefore, details Rabelais's concern for this 'bodily lower stratum', what Bakhtin describes as 'the material body level, to the level of food, drink, sexual life, and the bodily phenomena linked with them'.[164] Certainly we can note a similarly physiologically oriented narrative obsession in Welsh and the characters he writes for. Bakhtin reports,

> All these convexities and orifices have a common characteristic; it is within them that the confines between bodies and between the body and the world are overcome: there is an interchange and an interiorientation. This is why the main events in the life of the grotesque body, the acts of the bodily drama, take place in this sphere. Eating drinking, defecation and other elimination (sweating, blowing of the nose, sneezing), as well as copulation, pregnancy, dismemberment, swallowing up by another body-all these acts are performed in the confines of the body and the outer world.[165]

Bakhtin argues that 'the soul's beatitude is deeply immersed in the body's lower stratum',[166] again touching on Beat concerns, particularly with Burroughs's interest in lower body functions. However, at the same time that Bakhtin discusses the trajectory of organic expulsion, I now build on this thinking when remembering that these orifices are the means by which a human might not only expel matter but also ingest material of an altogether inorganic, pharmaceutical nature, in terms of how intoxicants might enter the body. Lower bodily stratum orifices (such as Renton's anus that famously consumed suppositories in *Trainspotting*,[167] but also, for instance, nostrils) are the very flimsy, liminal boundary between the outside world and the interior of our own physiology; and of course veins, wherever they may be tapped, can be penetrated by the hypodermic needle. What might be considered subterranean, or subcultural, might also be read as subcutaneous. Within the space of a few pages of *Glue*, for instance, we find an inexperienced burglar defecating on the floor of a house he has broken into,[168] only for another burglar to then slip over it in a way that must be seen as both comedic and grotesque. This is soon followed by another character urinating into a friend's sports bag,[169] while elsewhere there is also a three-page discussion of the nature of a character's foreskin.[170] The presentation of such lower body themes speaks once again to Bakhtin's own conception of the grotesque, Bakhtin suggesting: 'We find at the basis of grotesque imagery a special concept of the body as a whole and the limits of this whole.'[171]

If the subject matter of *Glue* is therefore of figurative use in evidencing the transformative potential of the DJ in literature, then once again we find the style of presentation is equally key. Welsh is very deliberate in constructing his text in the syntax of the dancefloor, a master at the linguistic 'tell', the secret mythologizing code so beloved by Champion, that which Thornton refers to as 'cryptic shorthand, innuendo and careful omission'.[172] Hebdige addresses subcultural use of, and resistance to, the 'language of the Master', in a post-colonial context. Welsh deliberately subverts the 'language of the Master', in this case, once again, the English linguistic dominance of the British Isles, by choosing to write this novel – like his other works analysed in this chapter – not only in Scottish dialect but also in the particular vernacular of Leith, which in itself offers stylistic challenges. In a sense, Dancefloor-Driven writers directly fulfil Adorno's fears, outlined in *The Jargon of Authenticity*, that such argot 'gives itself over either to the market, to balderdash, or to the predominating vulgarity',[173] in itself a comment that aligns perfectly with Bakhtin's more positive consideration of the lexicon of the marketplace. Hebdige points out that 'any elision, truncation or convergence of prevailing linguistic and ideological categories can have profoundly disorienting effects',[174] and the following passage from *Glue* highlights the levels of understanding Welsh expects on the part of his reader:

> Ah head oaf back tae the decks tae check oot the sounds situ. Ah'm gled ah bought some records n eftir borrowin some fae Rolf ah've goat enough tae dea a good forty-five minutes quality mixin. Ah get ready tae hit the decks. The mixer looks a bit unfamiliar or maybe it's just the pills, but fuck it, jist git in thaire.[175]

As well as subverting the language of the master in a linguistic sense, Welsh also, and determinedly, subverts it in terms of graphology, in the placement of words and images on the page, further blurring the lines of subjectivity. Throughout his novels Welsh plays with the shape of text. In the 1998 novel *Filth*, for instance, the character of a tapeworm features prominently and graphologically in the text, representing something corrupt in the soul of the character with whom the worm has developed a symbiotic relationship. Naturally, it is useful to note Welsh's own reading of the genesis for that particular idea: 'That was 100% inspired by acid house.'[176] Welsh also uses graphology to provide a visual means to depict the affective characteristics of sonic gesture. Consider the following passage from *Glue*, which details N-SIGN's drug-affected state of mind as he gets ready to DJ:

> The bass begins to synchronise with my heartbeat and I feel my brain expand beyond the confines of skull and grey matter.
> wwwWOOOOOSSSSHHH[177]

Here, the literary soundtrack is once again diegetic, in the sense that N-SIGN's music is intended to be audible within the text as the character takes us through the narrative of the track. However, it is also once again metadiegetic when we, as reader, feel the bass perceived subjectively by the character, mediated through a sound system, and further through the pharmaceutical filter of drug consumption. This interiorizing of experience is evidently key to the construction of narrative in Welsh's novel, the author remarking:

> One of the things you can't do in film that you can do in fiction, is in the character's heads. You can work their internal narrative, which is a nice thing to do. People have their own anxieties, their own agendas and you can show that in a book.[178]

In order to convey the subjective sense of the transformative potential of the music, therefore, Welsh employs the syntax of the rave to engender a mutual level of understanding between author and interpreter of the words, as well as representing the transgressive impact of Ecstasy in the very graphological shape of the prose on the page, all in the course of a naturalistic representation of the experience, in terms of the linguistic parameters of a subterranean culture. To continue Hebdige's argument, Welsh chooses quite deliberating to truncate linguistic categories *precisely because* that choice engenders 'profoundly disorienting effects', naturistically providing the best literary context to re/present the social realistic environment of the dancefloor.

The transformative process that sees Carl Ewart become N-SIGN is a fascinating literary evocation of the heroic DJ archetype. In conversation with Redhead, Welsh remarks, 'in the early days you play such a part in this self-mythologising process – men do that anyway – you pick one aspect of yourself and you pump it up and push it and it promotes that side of you',[179] and the career trajectory of DJ N-SIGN demonstrates considerable mythmaking, in the sense that Barthes considers myth, in the construction of public image. Welsh again refers to actual British DJ trade magazines, such as *DJ* and *Mixmag*, to confirm that the media are complicit in the fabrication of reputation: 'N-SIGN cunts it up in Ibiza. N-SIGN top caner. Fuckin shite. All the dance press: fuckin mythologising shite.'[180] We even find Welsh fabricating a 9/10 review for the N-Sign track 'Gimme Love' in an unnamed 'music paper',[181] further constructing a mythological place for this DJ within the real dance music industry. The review reads: 'The new single finds the man in a more soulful mood, but it's an irresistible offering from the too-long-missing-assumed-fucked gadgie of the groove. Beyond wicked; follow your feet and your heart across that dancefloor.'[182] What is of interest here is that beyond a somewhat vague reference to 'soulful' and 'groove', there is little musicological unpacking of this track, or any true sense, in music journalism terms, of how it might actually sound. Elsewhere in the novel, Carl describes how one record 'just builds and builds then it levels oaf fir a bit, before kickin up a fuckin storm again',[183] which is undeniably descriptive, without actually truly decoding the track on any musicological level.

Form and function work in tandem – the theme of escape matched by a linguistic escape in its presentation – in the 'loose-fit' rhythms of the prose. For Wolf this is 'a means of creating aesthetic unity',[184] and that must also be extended to an accompanying narrative unity, to engender a meta-aesthetic function of the text. Writing in this way, the author asks more of the reader; in a sense, there is a kind of linguistic intoxicology at play. Welsh invites the reader to join him in the inner sanctum, with the cognoscent in-crowd luxuriating in the VIP room of our 'disco text',[185] the experience arguably more valuable as a consequence of the effort extended: if the reader can cut through the idiolect and dialect in order to fully decode the text, they might feel they are somehow closer to the scene, on the *inside* of Welsh's aesthetic. Language, then, can either support or subvert the reading process, depending on the cultural experience of the reader. With *Ecstasy* – and in response to questions posed at the opening of this chapter – it is apparent that Welsh presumes an *a priori* understanding of the mechanics of the DJ process and the music involved, rather than providing any educative agenda. At one stage, as Carl begins to DJ, his set list forms almost a club review: 'I'm mixing UK acid-house rave tracks like *Beat This* and *We Call It Acieed* in with old Chicago house anthems like *Love Can't Turn Around* and taking it right back up through Belgium hardcore, like this track *Inssomniak*.'[186] If the reader finds they are capable of turning up the volume to Welsh's sonic signification, they might feel rewarded, and emboldened, for possessing the cultural relevance to do so, and therefore very much part of Welsh's dancefloor, and subterranean scene.

Although of interest for the rolling rhythms of the prose, and the diegetic mediation of music within the novel, *Glue* remains primarily of interest for this key figurative use of music as an enabler of social and economic ascent. In this novel we track how life as a DJ might enable an eventual departure from the socio-economic mire to which a character such as Carl might be born, the 'schemes' of Welsh's own youth. As Beeler remarks,

> Welsh's image of club culture is a path to economic success for talented people from impoverished circumstances. Although Carl is very aware of the alternate social aspects of the culture, in the end, it is just a way to escape the restrictions imposed upon him by his social status.[187]

In thematic and figurative terms, 'E' might therefore, in this reading, stand for 'Escape'.

Cultural elevation and cult club fictions

In concluding this interrogation of Welsh's intermedial instincts and musico-literary experiments, the original questions that opened the chapter can now be revisited to map the findings against those inquiries. In terms of the triumvirate taxonomy of the uses of music in writing, this chapter has considered how Welsh uses music *rhythmically*, to inform his writing, and how the music of this very particular subterranean culture formed the literary diegetic soundtrack to his fiction. Principally, however, the chapter highlights music as metaphor: in the figurative role it plays in terms of taste hierarchies, in denoting subcultural standing and capital, and ultimate escape from a sociopolitical situation. An initial conclusion must therefore emphatically foreground Welsh's importance as a key proponent of musico-literary intermedial creativity.

Having explored these mechanical, diegetic and principally figurative uses of music in the work of Welsh, what then, beyond the page, is the broader role and relevance of these works? The answer returns us to the notions of marketing and audience penetration that opened the chapter. Welsh is a writer who operates on two levels. At the first, contemporaneous level, Welsh's fiction had an important enculturative function, in promoting this subterranean scene, within the pages of his books, to the supraterranean world, in line with Middleton's notion that music itself 'produces sense, or conveys meanings' in the social context of its consumption.[188] Electronic dance music has penetrative resonance because it stands as art form plus context: it is the beat of its society, with that attendant audience, in those particular spaces. Welsh's overt interest in the realms of Bakhtin's lower bodily stratum also enabled him to visit places as a novelist and chronicler of his age that many readers were not able, or willing, to visit themselves, demonstrating a deliberately constructed attraction to the abject in order to find glory, in both creative and commercial terms.

This almost fetishistic interest in the abject, in the 'other', is successful because it affords the cultural voyeur a look at – and perhaps even over – 'the edge'. As well as a core participant readership, already immersed in this earthly mud, Calcutt and Shephard further locate a non-participant readership 'enjoying the experience of extremes vicariously without having to leave [their] mundane mainstream experience'.[189] What we have with the works of Welsh, alongside Blincoe and Noon, is carnivalesque pulp literature of the lower bodily stratum, where for Bakhtin the 'carnival is opposed to official culture'.[190] Operating within a niche, subterranean culture should not, however, preclude the seriousness with which a text, whether literary or sonic, is treated, and certainly when reflected in the highest expression of literary art, the novel.

The second level on which we must consider Welsh's work is therefore the historical axis which, acknowledging the commercial success of this particular author, affords him particular status and importance. In *The Road of Excess*, Boon writes,

> For the foreseeable future, all novel recreational drugs appear likely to generate books about them that can be marketed as windows onto the world of contemporary youth or underworld culture – mostly using the now well tested approaches of De Quincey, Cocteau, and Burroughs – who now find themselves in the unlikely position of being originators of literary genres.[191]

It is important to note how Boon himself draws a link between writers such as Welsh and Rushkoff and the Beats, while also acknowledging the close links between art and society already identified by Adorno in works such as *Aesthetic Theory*. In this way, Welsh has added to the ongoing, broader understanding of DJ practices and EDMC, creating what Calcutt and Shephard describe, with reference to cult fiction, as 'an alternative and radical path to the recognized canon of high literature'.[192] He is also a writer who continues to enjoy considerable commercial success and whose

Dancefloor-Driven texts, as detailed in Chapter 4, continue to form source material for cinematic re/presentation.

The fourth and final use of Bakhtinian theory in decoding Welsh is his conception of dialogics, in opening out Welsh's work and creating links to other texts. Certainly, this can be seen as a broader strand of interest for this book, especially in its stated intent to link thematically and stylistically the texts defined as Dancefloor-Driven Literature both intertextually with other similar works and more broadly with the literary texts of other music-based scenes, in a wider subterranean system, or network. Again, while structuralists argue that language is composed of fixed signs, for Bakhtin the truth is more fluid, as language is always dependent on its social context, relevance and reception. The signs are visible, but they are mutable. In reading Bakhtin, then, it is entirely possible to see synergies between the world of the Rabelais's carnival and the world of the Welsh rave. Bakhtin details how:

> Rabelais himself studied all these aspects of popular life. Let us stress that popular spectacles and popular medicine, herbalists and druggists, hawkers of magic unguents and quacks, could be seen side by side. There was an ancient connection between the forms of medicine and folk art.[193]

Here we can detect the homology of the dancefloor, and in it, the mechanics of an essentially popular folk culture. In the marketplace, Bakhtin remarks, we might find 'the hawker of miracle drugs, and the bookseller',[194] precisely aligning the worlds of literature and intoxication that I am concerned with here and sighting them in the same space. Bakhtin might initially be seen to slightly contradict himself in remarking that 'the grotesque tradition peculiar to the marketplace and the academic literary tradition have parted ways and can no longer be brought together',[195] given that he later suggests that this might just be possible: 'Rabelais recreates that special marketplace atmosphere in which the exalted and lowly, the sacred and the profane are levelled and all are drawn into the same dance.'[196] That is also my central ambition with this book.

In returning to this idea of time, subterranean ideology can be seen as code, preserved through a journey along the horizontal axis of history, to be dug up and discovered at a future time. I contend that such ideology can be locked in music, and in literature, but it is even more securely stored when protected within a double helix formed of the two. These ideas will be further developed in the conclusion, but they mirror Steve Redhead's key conceit for this research, when he writes in *Repetitive Beat Generation* of 'fiction [...] as a version of contemporary history'.[197] Fredric Jameson discusses how culture can form 'archaeologies of the future, not forecasts of the past',[198] and in this way, Welsh and the broader Dancefloor-Driven Literature movement did indeed pen cultural archaeologies for the future, while linking back to previous texts from the Beat and rock scenes in a way that must be seen as essentially dialogic. In his novels – as well as those of the other Dancefloor-Driven authors under consideration – Welsh is preserving future history, linguistic grooves carved into the roots of his writing.

7

Case study two

Musical mechanics in the fiction of Jeff Noon

A second key author located within both Champion's 1997 edition *Disco Biscuits*[1] and Redhead's 2000 collection *Repetitive Beat Generation*[2] is Jeff Noon. Noon is now foregrounded in order to answer key questions, notably – as defined in the musico-literary taxonomy of this book – the mechanical way in which music is used in literature: in essence, how the techniques of music *production* might be mapped onto literary construction. Further, how might Dancefloor-Driven Literature form a laboratory for avant-garde stylistic and linguistic aesthetics? Is it possible to bring techniques from specifically electronic music to the literary sphere? Might an author be able to 'mash up' the genre of Dancefloor-Driven Literature with another genre, in line with the sonic mashups typical of electronic dance music?[3] And finally, with such a focus on adventurous technical and stylistic vision, is it still possible for themes to emerge and take hold? While each of these individual questions will be addressed, I will also refer to the overarching questions that drive this book as regards the ontological role of electronic music in literary texts, and the impact of those texts on a popular music culture.[4]

In designing an appropriate methodological approach to respond to these questions, this chapter incorporates new material taken from personal interviews with Noon himself. Noon's comments will be contextualized via secondary interrogations of his work in extant scholarly literature (again, largely unpublished PhD theses and conference papers), as well as complementary resources that consider intermediality more broadly, and the genre of cyberfiction more specifically. Usefully, Noon's progressive literary strategies are clearly laid out within his own manifestos, principally 'On the B-Side',[5] a guide to Noon's literary approach to remixing text, and within *The Guardian* article 'Jeff Noon's Literary Manifesto'.[6] Like William Burroughs's essay on cutup[7] and Jack Kerouac's 'Essentials of Spontaneous Prose',[8] these represent literary style guides from writers overtly concerned with form.

In terms of the primary texts chosen, the short story 'DJNA' from *Disco Biscuits* will, like the Welsh analysis, act as a starting point for a broader interrogation of Noon's work.[9] The 2000 novel *Needle in the Groove*,[10] and then the 1998 short story collection *Pixel Juice*,[11] will subsequently be explored. Both of these works fall within the time period book-ended in the Introduction of this book and are useful for the way in which they reveal Noon's stylistic aesthetic when exploring themes born of the dancefloors of that time. Just as demonstrably, some works will be acknowledged but not explored in the same depth. Noon's earlier novels, for example, do not carry the same technical interest as the particular works chosen. At the other end of the spectrum, later pieces such as his most stylistically adventurous project, 2001's *Cobralingus*, do not have the same thematic relevance and, in comparison to the works cited, have also been more widely considered in academic terms.[12]

Developmental influences can be located in the key biographical detail that Noon, like Blincoe, grew up on the periphery of Manchester (Droylsdon, Greater Manchester), which even in terms of psychogeography brings to mind notions of the liminal. This fact leads me naturally to consider whether these case study novelists work as participants in, or rather *observers of*, the city's club scene. Rather like an analysis that pairs the relationship of Kerouac as writer/observer to Neal Cassady as insider/instigator, or cartoonist Ralph Steadman trying to keep up with, and illustrate, the incendiary tendencies of gonzo author Hunter S. Thompson, we can immediately locate this particular author on both the outer edge of the city and on the periphery of the sacred space of the dancefloor: an observer looking in. Noon himself reinforces this assertion in our conversation – his intriguing use of language highlighting an ambiguity around his association with the Chemical Generation of novelists:

> I've always been outside of scenes, basically. I think I used to write quite a lot about the figure who stands on the edge of the dancefloor, which is this lonely figure, basically. And I think that's where I positioned myself when it comes to club culture. I've never taken ecstasy, for instance. I could never indulge in that central way, that visceral way.[13]

As Noon self-consciously writes in his own 'Pixel Dub Juice' (subtitled 'sublimerix remix'):

> More DJs go 'groove'
> What's Noon trying to prove?
> He's not been to a club in ten years.[14]

Whether at the periphery of the dancefloor or at the periphery of the city, we must again acknowledge the impact of Manchester's music scene, in reaching from city centre to suburbs with a sonic siren song.[15] Like Blincoe and Welsh, Noon found an early creative outlet in Manchester music, fascinated by the emerging punk scene, playing in bands and writing lyrics, which Noon describes as 'my first expression in words'.[16] Recalling his early writing experiences, Noon reports: 'I didn't really know what I was doing but looking back you can see that I was trying to capture a certain feeling in Manchester at the time, namely the rave era. I wanted to record what was going on around me.'[17] This is reinforced in Noon's conversation with Steve Redhead for *Repetitive Beat Generation*, in which (echoing comments of Irvine Welsh) he explains the need to represent the local club scene on the grounds of not only verisimilitude but also exigency:

> I was looking round Manchester and thinking what have we got here, we've got these young people on the streets, we've got the drugs, we've got the music, we've got the guns … I was writing a book about Manchester and it had to have that in it. […] What I noticed is that there are certain correlations between what say the cyberpunk of William Gibson introduced into science fiction with what the record producers and DJs were doing with the equipment.[18]

A thoughtful and introspective personality, Noon found work in the Waterstones bookshop on Manchester's Deansgate (the same location where I discovered the shelves labelled Club & Drug Literature). Indeed, he might perhaps be considered more comfortable within this daytime literary milieu, rather than the nocturnal nightclub landscape, notwithstanding the fact that this was a time, as described in Chapter 5, when these two worlds were colliding. Noon's background as an artist and playwright might also reveal useful links to the visual as well as the aural, in terms of abstract and impressionistic art, where nevertheless the central creative driver remains composition.[19] After initial success with the play *Woundings*,[20] friend Steve Powell suggested that Noon might write a novel for his new imprint, Ringpull. The result was Noon's fantastical debut *Vurt*, published in the same year as Irvine Welsh's *Trainspotting*, 1993, where, in an idiosyncratic Noon trope, hallucinatory dream-inducing drugs are represented by different-coloured feathers,[21] Baudrillard's hyperreality set against what academic and Noon theorist Nikolina Nedeljkov calls 'vurtuality'.[22] The novels *Pollen* (1995)[23] and *Automated Alice* (1996) followed[24] and established Noon as a key author for editor Sarah Champion. As recounted by Noon,

> This woman, Sarah Champion, who was quite an important figure on the Manchester alternative dance scene at the time, got in touch with me and said she was editing a book of short stories all based on rave culture and would I be interested. And of course I was, at the time, very interested in that.[25]

Reinforcing the potential incongruity of a cyber-oriented author appearing within that volume, Champion agrees that 'he may feel that it's a bit of a mistake putting him in *Disco Biscuits* because it put him in a certain category that he wasn't really in'.[26] However, in my own opinion, the resulting story, 'DJNA', is one of the strongest in the *Disco Biscuits* collection.

As evidenced in Chapter 5, Champion was deliberate in her design of the marketing campaign for *Disco Biscuits*, determined that it would launch in nightclubs rather than bookshops, using street-distributed flyers rather than *Bookseller* advertisements. Noon therefore found himself grouped with a 'generation', an amalgam of writers confirmed by their place on the contents page of this collection, linked by virtue of chemistry as well as literature. As we have seen, it also took him – at least to the periphery – of the dancefloor. Noon states,

> What's really important about that book, for me, personally, is what happened afterwards. We went on tour with the book. I think there was about six of us going round and they put us in clubs, nightclubs, which was a really strange thing to do because we weren't particularly at home there as writers, even though that was our subject matter. And the audience very often didn't really know why we were there. The last thing you want to see when you go to a club is a bloke nattering on from his latest book.[27]

Intriguingly, such incongruities and discomforts began to reveal inherent stylistic possibilities. In one club space, in the northern city of Leeds, Noon recalls finding himself standing next to Champion in the 'chill-out' room, waiting for his turn to read, noticing the ambient sounds of the reading disturbed by the sounds crashing in from the main room. Noon continues,

> The music from the other room started to mingle in with what they were saying, in my mind. And I turned to Sarah, who was standing next to me and said … I wonder if you could do a dub version of a story? And she looked at me as if I was a bit mad and said I wouldn't understand what that is. And I said … neither do I.[28]

At the time, Noon was working on the novel *Nymphomation*,[29] and such intermedial mashups lead him to re-imagine the text, recalling, 'I started to remix – that's the only word you could use for it – certain sections of that novel.'[30] This notion of binary forces at play, and of an author fascinated with fluid movement between the two, will become more important as this chapter progresses. However, even at this early stage we can locate the bookish Noon in the nightclub environment and yet inspired by the edgy newness of that experience to conceive of this experimental approach to blending techniques from the musical and the literary. Immediately, the notion of bricolage – the intertextual sense of appropriating different materials to create something new – provides a model for the way we might reposition styles and images.[31] In taking authors out of bookshops and placing them in nightclubs, we find such a melding of two worlds: the arguably more stable nature of the printed word upon the page, set against the fluid movement of the dancefloor. Noon's project, then, was to flatten reality (and even *sur*reality), rendering the three and even four dimensional into 2D, asking the reader to then play their part, using *a priori* cognizance and imagination to retransform his code into their own 'pop-up' conceived reality.

Influences: Cyberfiction and the Beat Generation

Smyth is almost alone in more recent intermedial authors in recognizing how 'music and British science fiction encounter each other in spectacular fashion in the work of the Manchester-based writer Jeff Noon,'[32] and certainly any consideration of Noon's work needs to acknowledge the role of science fiction, principally cyberpunk and its resultant cyberfiction. Where EDM producers create mashups by colliding two different sonic sources into one new musical creation, Noon performs a *literary mashup*, combining club culture and cyber culture to render future fantasy landscapes into which his characters are allowed to dance and DJ. As Sarah Champion comments, 'The way I saw it myself, was that because the whole experience of clubbing was so crazy and so fantastical, it was natural for there to be an element of sci-fi to it.'[33]

The phrase 'cyberpunk' was coined by Bruce Berthke in a 1983 story of the same name to define a darker, dystopian vision of a part-mechanized future, a dichotomous environment that Hannah Priest characterizes as 'high tech/low life'.[34] Moving closer to Noon's vision, Priest cites Lawrence Pearson in capturing the essence of Noon's narrative sensibility:

> Classic cyberpunk characters were marginalized, alienated loners who lived on the edge of society in generally dystopic futures where daily life was impacted by rapid technological change, a ubiquitous datasphere of computerized information, and invasive modification of the human body.[35]

In the journal *Popular Music*, Karen Collins progresses this discourse to an important consideration of the relationship between cyberpunk and music. In an article that considers the themes, techniques, moods and imagery of cyberpunk, Collins remarks: 'Cyberpunks are associated with technophilia, computer and hacker culture, smart drugs, and dark futuristic narratives.'[36] Although her study ostensibly considers industrial music, in epistemological terms we can map the same thinking onto Noon's focus on electronic music, especially as the two genres share ontological resonances. Cyberpunk author Bruce Sterling recognizes the trace lines of intermediality running between music and literature at this stage, identifying how 'the work of cyberpunk is paralleled throughout 1980s pop culture: in rock video, in the hacker underground; in the street-jarring tech of hip-hop and scratch music; in the synthesizer rock of London and Tokyo'.[37] This links usefully to Middleton's suggestion that 'the record groove, connecting to connotations of industrialised reproduction, spins us into the heart of the mechanical or cybernetic apparatus'.[38]

Ideologically, then, we find within cyberpunk the core genetics of Noon's interest in music, popular culture and street – indeed below-street – life. In our conversation, Noon reports 'science fiction can be seen as a remix in itself, of the present day',[39] and certainly we see him channelling this spirit, with its genesis in American cyberpunk writers such as William Gibson and Bruce Sterling, into his own more parochially English stories. As previously noted, at this stage very few writers were concerned with this subversive, subterranean and peculiarly British club scene and Noon found that, with this additional cyberpunk twist, he was sufficiently able to distort reality – often the grey haze of a Mancunian near future – to construct the architecture of his dark *dysco-pia*, to unsettle narrative. Noon argues:

> Cyberpunk viewed information as something that could fuse with the body, rather than something we just access, it's something that seemed to infect us. And I thought music was a kind of information so why don't I treat music in the same

way Gibson treats computer graphics or data? So that was another influence – let the music fuse with the body and remix the body.[40]

Noon's style has been described as 'anti-naturalistic'.[41] Certainly he is anti-tradition and anti-authoritarian, in terms of any suggestion he might be constrained by the logical determinism of chronology or even biology, as interested in obeying the laws of mathematics as Leavisite literary tradition. In Noon's work we feel the overt hand of the author-creator, intent not only on blending but also on bending influences – for instance sci-fi into lo-fi – and determined to warp social reality rather than realistically represent it, as Welsh or Blincoe might.

In a dialogic process of connecting Noon with a wider literary landscape, the Beat Generation authors must also be reintroduced, writers methodologically allied to the creativity of Dancefloor-Driven Literature. According to Andrew Wenaus, for example,[42] Noon chooses Jack Kerouac as one of the authors supplying the raw literary materials he 'remixes' within his 2002 novel *Falling Out of Cars*,[43] where even such cultural influences themselves become literary 'samples' to be reshaped, in line with electronic music production techniques described in Chapter 3. Stylistically, this is also an author exploring avant-garde literary techniques on a level with Beat author William Burroughs and his artist collaborator Brion Gysin, who together developed the 'cut-up' technique of slicing and splicing text.[44] Further, it returns to Bakhtin's ideas highlighted in the previous chapter, reinforced by Wolf in 'the imitation of polyphony through the technique of "cutting and splicing" […] the use of recurrent motifs and word music'.[45] Moving beyond the technology inherent in a pair of scissors, Wenaus is useful in highlighting how Noon builds further on the cut-up idea by using technology to subvert the notion of language as a fixed, linear series of signs or symbols. With Noon we are in a world where words themselves become linguistic breaks: sampled and sequenced, fractured and reconfigured. Concerned with the figurative use of language and yet content to concede some degree of meaning to technological fate in order to drive style, Noon plays to his teleological impulses to conceive of a theological, yet godless, technological environment for his fiction. Wenaus writes: 'Ultimately, Noon is confronting the ramifications of linguistic determinism in the age of information.'[46] With Burroughs, language and meaning is, in one sense, under attack; with Noon, language is also under construction.

More important to this book, however, is the way Noon strategically deploys the mechanics of electronic music production to the literary form. Wenaus argues that 'music – particularly the compositional techniques of contemporary electronic music – plays an essential role in Noon's writing',[47] and we therefore now find, directly linked, our two cultural spheres in singly the most innovative development of Dancefloor-Driven Literature.

Disco Biscuits: 'DJNA'

We witness the interplay of these influences and expressive tendencies within Noon's *Disco Biscuits* contribution, 'DJNA', an early example of the literary mashup of cyberpunk with this emerging tradition of Dancefloor-Driven Literature. Within cyberpunk fiction, argot is deployed to resist, linguistically, dominant power structures – street slang, neologisms – all arranged against the hegemonic machine.[48] Certainly we see that political and linguistic power struggle within Noon's work as, in fact, we have seen in the previous chapter with the use of dialect in Irvine Welsh's fiction. Gibson calls the heroes of cyberpunk the 'cognitive dissident',[49] and such dissidence runs through Noon's story, where hero DJ Helix is a fictional outlaw DJ, within a near future dance music culture.

In the opening sentence Helix is presented as '*persona non data*',[50] as he attempts to gain entry to a nightclub. The club bouncers become 'the St Peters',[51] preventing progress even when 'this close to paradise'.[52] In Noon's world, we find DJs presented as part of a cultural and political underclass, radicals pursued by authorities keen to mechanize the music process. In this world, DJ now stands for 'Dirty Judas',[53] clearly ranged against the hegemonic holy forces keen to see this culture extinguished through a combination of legislation and genocide, where 'new laws' mean 'dancing alone became an evil act, punishable by fire'.[54] Resistant ravers are 'sinners',[55] where raving, by its very expression, denotes freedom. One of my overriding arguments in this book is for fiction's right to represent reality's story and indeed, although rendered grotesque and caricatured, this representation in 'DJNA' is very much aligned with life at the time of the story's publication, which pitted subterranean clubbers against the supraterranean sociopolitical hegemony. In this instance, we can see that to DJ is in itself a political act: these sinners playing the role of Freedom to Party dance activists ranged against the creators and enforcers of the law, where the Criminal Justice Bill formed the crux of the original antagonism.[56] In itself, then, 'DJNA' is a literary response to those theorists who contend this was a scene without political intent or resonance, neither subculture nor subversion.[57]

'DJNA' is intriguing for this early confluence of the musical and literary in Noon's work, with very clear signposts for what will shortly follow. However, although there are cyberpunk refrains to the narrative environment, we are clearly told we are in 'Manchester after all. The city of forever rhythm, where Jesus danced in the rain.'[58] The presentation of music itself is also naturalistic: Noon describes the mechanics of the DJ process, for instance, but although he hints of the journey music will take in his imagination, at this stage it is rendered in physical terms:

> *Boom!* Music is a whirling shape that flies all around the dancefloor, something unseen but all mighty. *Shackalacka!* If you have the right equipment, the wine and the biscuit. *Boom!* Music can be heard! *Shackalacka!* The big bass goes boom and the treble goes shackalacka. *Boom shackalacka! Boom shakalacka!* Music is a force, a riot of information, a collective explosion, fed by all the DJs who ever lived and died. *Boom!*[59]

Also of early interest is Noon's description of how, in order to gain access to these 'legit clubs',[60] DJ Helix needs to render himself invisible, to disappear. In order to do this we are told he must 'fold his body into a dubmix'.[61] This is a key moment of Noon's *détournement*, borrowing from the lexicon of the dancefloor and repurposing it for original, linguistic means.[62] Noon's interest in dub and electronic production techniques would have yet more innovative and powerful consequences but here at least, there is the sense of the potential with which music might be used. The character Fig feels 'the music enter her system, like a blood-rush',[63] but the key word is 'like'; linguistically, Noon's prose remains rooted in the realms of similes rather than metaphors. For instance, in 'DJNA', the reader witnesses the 'needle spinning the groove'.[64] It will take another creative leap for the needle to truly penetrate, to find its way 'into' the groove.

Needle in the Groove: Genealogy, technology and metaphorphiction

Although chronologically later than *Pixel Juice*,[65] I will first consider the novel *Needle in the Groove*, for what its pages might reveal of Noon's thematic, rather than stylistic, interest in music. The novel concerns a bass player, Elliot Hill, who joins singer Donna, DJ Jody and drummer 2Spot in the band Glam Damage. Building from the naturalistic narrative of a band forming, recording and then playing live, the novel soon opens up into more of an experimental exploration of the very nature of music, and how it might be manipulated and ultimately misused.

As outlined in Chapter 1, for Scher musico-literary intermediality is distinguished broadly as verbal music, word music and via structural analogies that link the two. Building on Scher, Wolf also divines a three-way taxonomy, where literature might imitate music via the words themselves chiming musically ('Word Music'); texts imitating musical composition techniques ('Structural Analogies'); and via references or suggestions to real pieces of music ('Imaginary content analogies to music').[66] Although this present reading of Noon might find some use with the second of Wolf's categories, and while Scher's taxonomy also remains useful as a starting point, both theoretical positions are unable to provide a robust framework for the analysis of these texts. First, music in what has now been defined as Dancefloor-Driven Literature is of much more penetrative use: a literature wholly influenced by, and even set to, the metronomic beat of a specifically electronic dance music. Further, this particular novel also reveals much about the contextual culture beyond the beat, building on the notion of reconnecting text to both *sub*text and *con*text, in reaction to the structuralist experiment resisted in this book. Instead, in *Needle in the Groove*, music acts as both the essential sonic underpinning of the novel and the stylistic driver within the text. Music is ubiquitous and fulfils to different degrees all of the intermedial functions outlined in this book. First, music provides a diegetic soundtrack for the narrative, Noon going so far as to integrate imagined songs within the text, such as 'Scorched Out for Love', in the pursuit of verisimilitude – like Welsh – but in a markedly different way. In this sense, music engenders a naturalistic mood that might approximate this particular subterranean world: the beat of the nightclub hovering continually behind and beneath the page. Second, we see music used figuratively: as simulacrum for narcotics, and thematically, as genetic coding material. Third, we find music used stylistically, in a formalist sense operating within the very mechanics of the novel, as a way to influence, and build the text.

As regards context, the beat of the novel was the beat Noon felt resonating from the city centre of Manchester, out across the liminal periphery of the M60 orbital motorway. As Noon reports, 'I was very, very bound up with Manchester and the history of Manchester, at the time. And I really loved Manchester. I just loved it. Dark side and all.'[67] After a historical period without nightclubs,[68] venues began to open again in Manchester through the 1970s and when the punk scene erupted, Noon reports he 'suddenly felt very proud and patriotic about Manchester'.[69] The architecture of the novel is certainly built solidly from the nightclubs of Manchester which, if not specifically named, have echoes of clubs that existed in the city, notably Noon's fictional club creation, Zuum. In response to questions about the veracity of the club spaces within the book – built into the book in the same way as Blincoe, as we shall see in the next chapter – Noon comments: 'I probably had things in mind when I wrote them, visually, because you always get a visual picture when you write, but not specifically.'[70] The passage of time must allow for a certain disconnection between author and his text, because the real-world nightclub the Electric Circus certainly appears as 'The Circus' in the novel, with specific reference to the last night at the venue, which Elliot is able to recall in detail,[71] impressing Donna with his subterranean knowledge:

> I've heard of these / they played the last night of the circus / october 77
> that's right, says donna / I'm impressed / they never get mentioned.[72]

In keeping with much cyberfiction, Noon very deliberately populates his text with popular culture references (a cursory list includes Manchester acts such as Buzzcocks, the Fall, John Cooper Clarke, John the Postman, Frank Sidebottom, Simply Red, Joy Division, Magazine, Biting Tongues) that in themselves resonate as code – mooring the reader to a partly recognizable reality. When we first meet Elliot, in fact, he is 'standing alone on ian curtis boulevard',[73] and we immediately find ourselves in late-night Manchester, a subterranean world of cellar recording studios and nefarious nightclubs moving to 'midnight's vibration'.[74]

Elliot and 2Spot become friends by virtue of their interest in music, and in following the root note of that music back through subterranean timelines. In a thesis that specifically considers the notion of the remix in literature, Nedeljkov recognizes that 'they learn by learning the history of music',[75] and within *Needle in the Groove*, Noon constructs a generational background story to explain how music might mutate, shifts in time and culture that both unite and separate family and music styles. 2Spot's grandfather, Danny, was part of the skiffle act, the 4 Glamorous Men, which morphed into 1960s pop act the Glamourboys and then into early 1970s glam rock act the Glamour. 2Spot's father, George, was part of the punk band the Figs. And as detailed, 2Spot himself is part of electronic act Glam Damage which, even in terms of nomenclature, roots its heritage firmly in the grandfather's band. Noon clearly maps this out in a 'Glamography' in the front pages of the novel and in this way one can note, even within the bloodline of one family, how music is passed down through time – that the music of Glam Damage did not appear as from a void, but rather as the result of influencing forces, here exemplified in terms of sonic genealogy.

This three-generational model is also adopted by music writer Charles Shaar Murray in his only novel, *The Hellhound Sample* (2011).[76] Again the music 'gene' is present and it also mutates across time, although here it chooses a different musical pathway. Transferring the narrative to the United States, Shaar's novel tells the story of the Moon family. The youngest member of the family, Calvin, is a successful hip-hop mogul, in the mode of Puff Daddy.[77] His mother Venetia is a soul singer of the 1960s and 1970s. In turn, Venetia's father is Moon himself, an accomplished blues guitarist who, as a child, drew his own inspiration from witnessing blues guitarist Robert Johnson busking on the street. For Noon, as with Murray, the blues forms the root – the 'blue note' – from which all other forms of African American music arise, a point 2Spot makes himself: 'That's where it all comes from, he says / from out of the blues'.[78] Thematically this encapsulates – again in fictional terms – a concern of this research in mapping the subterranean system of late 1980s rave directly back to late 1960s rock, and further to late 1940s bebop. These two companion novels also encapsulate the essential interplay of music and intoxicants set to literature, using the fulcrum of fiction to convey the intersection of musico-intoxication as a generational activity,[79] in accordance with the tenets of what has been defined as the Unholy Trinity inherent in subterranean systems.

Another key theme of the novel is, therefore, intoxication, and music as drug. Initially, Noon's novel presents the fabulous conceit that music can become liquid, this liquid music then localized, in an essentialist sense, within a globe that can be shaken in order to be 'remixed'. In transmogrifying the sonic into liquid form, Noon creates the most powerful image in the entirety of this survey of Dancefloor-Driven Literature. Further, in the most avant-garde reconfiguring yet discussed within this book, Noon progresses from simile to metaphor – what the author himself calls metamorphiction – in discovering that music is not like a drug but *is* a drug. In a series of step changes familiar within narcotics narratives, the band find ways to misappropriate this globe of music so as to become intoxicated, tapping it for its liquid contents: the 'music' is first smoked then 'chased' before ultimately being injected – the final violation of the sanctity of the body – the ultimate threshold broken. The needle is now not only in the groove of the record but also through the skin itself and again the subterranean is mirrored in this subcutaneous invasion. This narrative trope is fundamental in destabilizing notions of the liminal threshold of the body, and music's constructed relation to the body:

> and I can't believe what I'm seeing / 2spot, with his jacket off / jacket off, and shirt off / his sweat-covered chest, stomach and arms, all on view / and criss-crossing all the flesh …
> marks of the knife
> cuts and splices / grooves and slices / scabbed and fresh / opened / and closed / and reopened / in a map of pain / all scratched out / in blood recorded / remixed
> and then
> broken[80]

Noon is very precise in clarifying in our conversation that the novel 'is very specifically about music: music as a drug and music infecting people. There you can see the literary conceit would work very well; the remix idea'.[81] The notion of the remix, in itself, will provide a useful segue between subject and style.

It remains a challenge for authors to be original when discussing the transformative affect of both music and intoxicants, but in changing the physical state of music to liquid form, *Needle in the Groove* ultimately stands as a successfully original attempt to consider notions of the sonic in pursuit of the literary. Here it is also worth pausing to consider the novel's critical reception. The 2001 Black Swan edition I used in my own reading is useful for containing reviews in the front section. *Maxim* magazine, for instance, describes how

> Noon has invented a strange new kind of language: text mixed and sampled like a dance record. Chapters repeat themselves – scratched and distorted, remixed and remastered – and there's a beat underneath it all … as fresh and compulsive as anything you'll read this year. As exciting as drugs and music.[82]

What is of direct use here is the way *Maxim*'s unnamed literary reviewer has drawn together literature, music and drugs – the Unholy Trinity that underpins this book – as though the three were equitable. Meanwhile the culture title *Sleaze Nation* takes this even further, remarking in their review that Noon's writing 'could almost have you dancing to this book'.[83] Perhaps the critic has answered the famous aphorism: writing about music is not like dancing to architecture but to literature itself.

I must now define a space between novelists who attempt to write to the way music sounds and is consumed (Kerouac through Thompson to Welsh and Miller) from those concerned with the way music is *produced* (Noon). Stephen Benson, for instance, details how Bakhtin transposes musical concepts – notably polyphony and counterpoint – into his literary critical discourse *Problems of Dostoyevsky's Poetics*,[84] but Noon further brings this conceit to contemporary EDM production. This author creates linguistic effects not so much with analogue musicological devices and consumption technologies, but with the techniques and effects of digital sound production, with electronic studio kit repurposed for literary creation. Smyth identifies how, in *Needle in the Groove*, Noon 'disdains traditional novelistic structure; instead, the narrative is organised in terms of various techniques (most clearly, sampling and remixing) associated with certain modern musical trends'.[85] Chapters are indeed remixed: at one point a chapter might segue into the next, at another we find dub versions of earlier chapters, stripped down to their linguistic root notes.

In first considering rhythm, there is certainly commonality with Kerouac's 'bop prosody'.[86] In typographic terms, Noon abandons the finality of the 'full stop' for the more persuasive 'forward slash', and exchanges speech marks for the more fluid dashes (beloved of Kerouac, Welsh and others) to allow for a rhythmic beat of consciousness to flow across the page, in some ways similar to the clipped 4/4 rhythms in Trevor Miller's

Trip City. Thus, unencumbered by restrictions of grammar, Noon's prose carries with it the intoxicating rhythms of both music and drug, as in the following passage:

> and did yer ever get so danced, like yer couldn't feel any more / like where you ended, and the floor began / and the crowd / did yer get some crowd / did yer get some serious bootleg-type crowd right up inside your skull?
> I did / got me some crowd like I couldn't feel any more
> where the ending of the skin began
> and where the crowd dissolved.[87]

Again, within this passage the rhythm is dictated by these forward slashes, separating text into linguistic 'breaks', or musical bars. The suggestion here is of liminal breach and physiological disintegration reinforced by both the beat of the prose and its grammatical collapse. If we return to the *Maxim* review we can, however, always trace 'the beat beneath it all' where, like Kerouac's best work, freestyle literary riffs always return to the consistent, narrative beat beneath – the road, the root note, the sequenced electronic pulse – all containing and sustaining the essence of the narrative.

Needle in the album

Music and literature have played off against one another throughout historic countercultural scenes, for instance on *Nothing Here Now but the Recordings*, an audio release of Burroughs's cutups,[88] and Chapter 5 has already noted how the novel *Trip City*, among others, came with an accompanying soundtrack. *Needle in the Groove* also became a site for an intriguing musico-literary collaboration, between the author Noon and music producer (and academic) David Toop, across the fourteen tracks that formed the *Needle in the Groove* album[89] (Figure 7.1).

Even as a process, such an intermedial collaboration provided further inspiration. Noon watched Toop work with sequencing software, for the first time aware of the potential of this technology, subsequently inventing twenty different effects, or filters – such as 'explode' and 'find story' – which he would ultimately use to filter the text of *Cobralingus*:[90]

> I was fascinated by the process he was going through and I was fascinated by the ease with which he could manipulate music compared with the struggle I had to manipulate text. The makers of sound equipment understand that musicians want to manipulate music in a certain way; that they want to put certain effects on it: turn it upside down or reverb it or echo etc., whereas the makers of wordprocessors don't think at all that writers want to do anything like that. So I always had to do it myself. And that's where I got the idea that I would replicate what David was doing.[91]

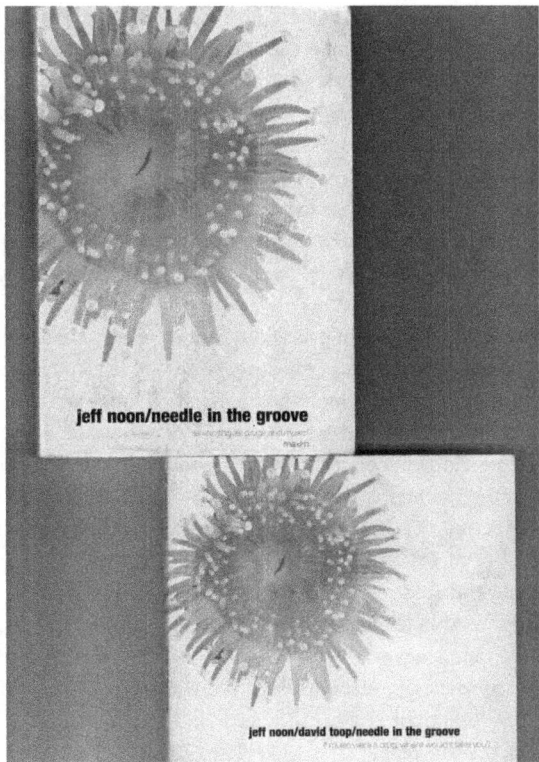

Figure 7.1 Front covers of Jeff Noon, *Needle in the Groove* (London: Black Swan, 2001) and Jeff Noon and David Toop, *Needle in the Groove* (Sulphur Records, 2000).

I contacted Toop during the research and writing of this book, to allow him to comment on this collaboration. His new, primary input (now many years after the project itself) is useful in creating a synchronous, comparative analysis of the way author and composer might each approach the same source material. It is therefore worth reproducing Toop's valuable input to this process in its entirety, in order to now understand the collaboration from the *musical* perspective:

> As I recall, Jeff Noon contacted me to record a few tracks for the publication of Needle in the Groove. I think the publisher might have suggested it as a publicity device. I felt that would be a wasted opportunity and instead proposed a complete album, a kind of audio counterpoint to complement the written novel. At the time, my friend Robin Rimbaud (Scanner) was running a label for sound and word – Robin has always had a strong interest in literature – so that was the perfect place for it. Jeff was very enthusiastic so I read the novel and picked out scenes that I felt

could be sonified. Is that the right word? Maybe not, but we talk about visualisation without having an exact equivalent for listening. Audiolisation, maybe!

But there were very atmospheric scenes in the book, and some scenes in which words struggled to convey the power of what can happen when you hear music, particularly in a club setting under the influence of drugs, alcohol, even just a heightened or suggestible mood. As a writer I'm very familiar with that particular struggle of translating a listening experience into verbal approximation. As a musician and composer I often begin from literary texts or film so it felt very natural to reverse engineer the scenes described by Jeff, to take them fully into the intangible.

The problem, of course, is that everybody will have a particular sound in their head when they read a description of music that doesn't exist. You risk contradicting that mental image or fantasy, though the book gave a lot of latitude in that sense. You felt that powerful experiences of sound were intensely subjective, almost as if everybody were hearing their own version of the music (which is more or less what happens anyway). What he was describing was informed by all the club music that had happened since punk and dub, so it was an invitation to make a kind of hybrid, which is exactly what I do anyway. There were also other histories: psychedelic music; electronic music designed to affect consciousness in some way; trance music and sound used in shamanistic ceremonies, a sub-text that music could be psychotropic without drugs.

In a way these projects connect to work I did with a sound poet – Bob Cobbing – in the early 1970s and an interest in poetry and jazz by Langston Hughes and Charles Mingus, the sonic landscapes of William Burroughs and the British poetry and jazz concerts of the 1960s, but they also grew out of my book on hip hop,[92] the research into the deep history of African-American oral culture and music out of which hip hop had grown. For me there has always been a strong relationship between all these forms because they address the gap between verbalisation – the word and thought – and sensation, the complex physiological, sensual, instinctive and intellectual response we have to sound. In our cultural setting the word is deemed law but experiences of inchoate and inexpressible feelings can be far more powerful. That's the contradiction.

It is hard to write about music. That's something with which I struggle every day. At the moment I'm writing a book on improvised music so there aren't even the usual elements of musical form to fall back on. How to describe a sound and how a sound changes, interacts with other sounds? But writers have always described intangible phenomena such as emotion, light, the weather, so of course it's possible. Sometimes I find myself picking at a single sentence for a day, rejecting each word, each analogy, as being reductive or misleading. You end up with an approximation, lost in translation, but words are central to how we communicate so it's a struggle that has to continue.[93]

In much the same way that Kerouac paired with both composer David Amram and TV presenter and pianist Steve Allen, Ginsberg with guitarist Steven Taylor,[94] or Welsh with DJ Andy Weatherall, Toop provides the sonic bed – disjointed, jarring music – over which Noon reads, and sometimes softly sings, sections of the book. There is no direct musical creation of the imagined 'Scorched Out for Love' track (although Noon sings its lyrics on track two) or any parallel soundtrack to the existing fictional music within the book. Instead, the collaboration forms an original soundscape for this dark *dysco-pia* – an unnerving aural landscape upon which is built the narrative architecture that Noon constructs with words. In furthering this innovative musico-literary collaboration, Noon and Toop then toured this concept, completing four events which Noon characterizes as 'two good, two difficult'.[95] Again, tracing such an activity back to the original *Disco Biscuits* launch events, Noon remains a somewhat reluctant live contributor,[96] especially as the years progress, commenting: 'You do start to look a bit weird. Until you get really old, like Burroughs, and suddenly … you can do what you want.'[97] Indeed, age can confer gravitas and Burroughs will appear again in this book, notably in the next case study.

Pixel Juice: Cyborg machines and the mechanics of music

Beyond thematic constructions, Noon's 1998 short story collection *Pixel Juice* is important in revealing his more stylistic ambitions. As opposed to the novel format of *Needle in the Groove*, *Pixel Juice* is formed of fifty short stories, in itself an expression of Noon's hyper-creativity in the later 1990s, the key period for this study. Within its pages we immediately find, once again, that music is the prime driver behind almost all of the stylistic innovations and avant-garde tendencies in this volume. As Noon explains, 'I'm very interested in English culture and what it means to be English. And the way that English people have made music has always fascinated me: Where that spirit comes from that enables us to do this amazing thing.'[98]

Pixel Juice is subtitled 'Stories from the Avant Pulp' and that synchronous concern for both high and low culture impulses lies behind much of the creative tension, energy and dynamism within this collection, while also directly linked to the aesthetic ambitions of Nicholas Blincoe. As noted in Chapter 5, Dancefloor-Driven Literature itself offers a melding of two worlds: the fluid movement of the dancefloor (further destabilized by the introduction of intoxicants) ultimately fixed by words. Although literature has previously infiltrated and addressed subterranean arenas, Dancefloor-Driven Literature deliberately sets out to appropriate this murky underworld as its context, and to wrestle narrative order upon this muddy milieu in order to stabilize it long enough to form text. In terms of this overlaying of high technique and high art upon the sleazy underground aesthetic of the street, and below-street, we find ourselves returning to a dada aesthetic,[99] to a fetishized concern for 'low-culture' that, like Bakhtin's lower bodily stratum, also informs the words and worlds of Irvine Welsh. Such a divergence serves as an indicator of Noon's polarized interest in high style and low morals, in organic dada and digital data.

Again, Noon is innovative in his literary exploration, and exploitation, of the DJ archetype, reconfigured as cyborg and in giving science fiction a *groove* (which in itself takes us back to the suggestion from Ralf Hütter of Kraftwerk that the 'Machines are funky', introduced in Chapter 3). This notion is firmly outlined in two stories – 'Orgmentations' and 'Hands of the DJ' – within this collection. Within these narratives, Noon posits that the ability to DJ is, first, a cultural weapon that can be wielded against dominant forces, in a Gramscian sense,[100] and second, that DJing is also a dark art, a magical gift that can be coveted; that it therefore signifies both power and mystery. Titular character Pixel Juice is an especially striking example of the DJ archetype, not least because she represents a rare female appearance in what can seem an otherwise male-dominated occupation, an issue of gender expanded upon in Rebekah Farrugia's important study of DJs and gender politics.[101] Also touching on Umberto Eco's notion of 'media squared',[102] and the nebulous role of the media in constructing versions of reality, Noon makes a very deliberate point, within the text, about the PR management of her reputation:

> The thing about the DJ, she was never one for hanging out. She didn't give interviews. Never turned up to accept awards. No known vices, which pissed off the marketing boys no end.[103]

An extremely skilled DJ (we are told how 'her hands moved around at sonic boom, making ghosts of themselves in the stage lights'),[104] Pixel Juice is also gay, and in a patriarchal context therefore does not stand out as feminine threat or as visual object of desire. As such, there is still no attraction for the media: 'No fucking story! Sniff, sniff.'[105] Noon then provides the reader with their own tickets to his fictional Magnetic Field Weekender festival, and makes it clear they should feel privileged as 'Half the known universe got turned away'.[106] At this festival, Noon deconstructs the DJ process – a useful guide to the reader, as literary tourist in this strange sonic world:

> She turned up the volume a touch, and then, slowly, lingering, let her left hand rest exactly one millimetre above the spinning vinyl. She was waiting, poised like a cat for the beat. Now! She brought the hand down, added some black bass of her own.[107]

Continuing this broader overview of the thematic resonance of music within the prose, Noon also deploys the vernacular of the music industry to explain his ideology. For instance, in his interview with Steve Redhead, Noon refers to the short story 'Metaphorazine' as one of his 'greatest hits' and to 'Homo Karaoke' as 'a kind of weird DJ story', before discussing creating a 'dub' of it, stripping it to its essential beats, which he does with several stories within this collection.[108] Elsewhere in this volume, 'Homo Karaoke' is built around the DJ sound clash, a sound system battle made popular in the reggae scene.[109] In this narrative, DJs do battle from trenches formed of sound systems, using records as their missiles. Here, music is literally a weapon, and DJ ability equates to the better skill to wield that weapon. The environment is therefore identifiable – the DJ's desire to build reputation, to produce myth, is understandable – but Noon then takes the DJ battle to its ultimate end, with DJs Perfume Sword and Skinvader strapped *into* machines. Perfume Sword tells us: 'It's dark in the booth, and the world closes in',[110] as he proceeds to actually get inside the music. There are details of his set, the 'wavelength',[111] for instance, that breaks across the floor as Perfume Sword explains his moves: 'Now I become the Lizard Ninja Tongue; antique Led Zep drum loop, hip hop scatter-shot maniac.'[112]

The conclusion of 'Hands of the DJ' introduces a sixteen-year-old aspiring DJ intrigued by the rock 'n' roll myths that surround the supposed dark art of DJing, and notably the gloves Pixel Juice always wears. We subsequently discover that one of Pixel Juice's hands is robotic, the other made of butterflies – a very deliberate counterpointing of the cyber and whimsically surreal, of William Gibson and Lewis Carroll, when, as identified in Chapter 3, a DJ's hands do indeed mark the interface between human and machine – organic flesh and electronic circuit board.[113] Certainly as we have seen previously in this chapter, the tenets of cyberpunk seek to consider, in a liminal sense, when the agency of man and woman becomes that of machine. Donna Haraway reports that 'in the tradition of "Western" science and politics … the relation between organism and machines has been a border war. The stakes in the border war have been the territories of production, reproduction and imagination',[114] while in terms of the machinations of DJ performance, Jonathan Yu adds that

> a DJ performance is constituted by not only the relationship between DJ and clubbers but also the combination of non-human actors such as the devices used to perform (turntables, mixer, headphones, cables, speakers and so on) and the materials of the setting (such as those that make up the nightclub).[115]

In one of many deconstructions, 'Hands of the DJ' contains the attendant suggestion that when it comes to electronic music production and performance, one requires machines to make the music, but also organic vision in its intelligent design. Noon focuses on this sense of a negotiable threshold between man and machine as a thematic concern; however, such a balance also forms a driver for his creative philosophy. For Noon's 'dub fiction', the creative process itself is partly down to his human, organic agency and yet partly also to automatic fate – the hands of machines. In effect, these cyberpunks are now *digital*punks. Leaving the creation of fiction to mechanical fate links in some ways to Deleuze's notion of 'machining the voice',[116] while also dovetailing – as indeed Middleton has remarked – with Derrida's outline of 'automatic writing; machine writing',[117] which traces its lineage through the spontaneous, typewriter-born prose of Jack Kerouac to the gonzo spirit of Hunter S. Thompson, as discussed in Chapter 4. Introducing electronics into this overtly avant-garde aesthetic reveals much about the analytic processes of Noon's imagination. As he explains,

> I have quite a split mind, I guess. I absolutely love mathematics and I love to work things out in that way. Against that, at other times and sometimes in combination with it, I will just pour out without thinking whatever is in my head and then try to fit it into the scheme.[118]

Tony Mitchell suggests that analysing or overthinking art disrupts the flow of inspiration;[119] however, conversely, Noon has demonstrated how an overt foregrounding of technique can actually unlock new possibilities and fresh innovation, revealing new strategies and truths.

DJ techniques in *Pixel Juice*

This chapter will now consider the intermedial way in which Noon deploys specific techniques of electronic music production and performance and maps them onto the literary, within (and sometimes between) the short stories that make up the *Pixel Juice* collection. Fulfilling Pater's aphorism that opened this book, for Noon music is

> without doubt my favourite art form, and the one that saturates my waking life from morning till night. So, I always try to use techniques invented by musicians in my novels and stories, simply because musicians seem to get there first these days, in terms of an avant–pulp interface.[120]

In his own intermedial overview, Wolf detects how,

> as a possible common denominator of most of these functions, one can point to a discontent with established conventions, especially with mimetic storytelling, so that music, owing to its 'otherness', becomes a valuable alternative model for organizing narratives. The musicalization of fiction could also frequently be seen as a means of exploring, and experimenting with, the medial boundaries of fiction in aesthetic contexts where these boundaries have become questionable.[121]

This analysis has already clarified how Noon pushed such ideas beyond the notions of the cut-up technique ascribed to Burroughs and Gysin. Noon reinforces this difference in our conversation, reporting that although superficially one might draw parallels, he was only obliquely influenced by his Beat predecessor:

> I read a tiny bit of Burroughs. I wouldn't call myself a fan in any way.[122] I understand what he's doing and I love the fact he did do it but it's not personally for me, it doesn't give me pleasure.[123]

Specifically, Noon is concerned not only with the avant-garde notion of introducing random abstraction to fiction but also, and specifically, with the techniques of electronic music production. If you 'cut up' and rearrange bars of music, for instance, the resulting disruption would fracture the melody beyond comprehension. However, conversely Noon considers how electronic sequencing techniques, for instance, might instead have powerful, constructive effects on the literary page. Noon reports: 'I'm a very practical, physical writer. I'm the kind of guy who experiments in the laboratory of language. [...] *Pixel Juice* was a good idea of the laboratory, if you like.'[124]

Smyth discusses the sense in which music novels might attempt to obliterate the division between form and content, and questions, 'Is it possible that fiction about music always has a tendency towards musicalised fiction – that is, a kind of writing that attempts to recreate some aspect of the musical material that has been invoked at a thematic level?'[125] In his (one imagines, self-penned) biography in *Disco Biscuits*, Noon agrees with Smyth that, rather like Welsh and Kerouac, he 'is writing to music: blues or dub or jazz or country or drum 'n' bass',[126] and while to a large degree this musicality lies in authorial intent, as a reader we also have agency to read music into the novel ourselves, and find the beat of the words. Smyth also notes how 'Derrida's scepticism towards the ontological (rather than the mere semantic) status of language resonates deeply within traditional debates regarding the status of music in relation to language', where 'musicology and deconstruction haunt each other (to use a resonant Derridean metaphor)'.[127] Derrida's notion of hauntology is in itself a play on the French pronunciation of ontology, where the haunting might indeed be of another spiritual realm, a spectre perhaps linguistic, or more broadly cultural, haunting a text.[128] Certainly, whether conscious or indeed from another spectral plane entirely, music runs through these Noon texts, lies constantly behind their words and helps bring them to life, in creative terms. Noon explains: 'When I started to manipulate text like music, I identified about five techniques that DJs use with music and one was dub, one was remix, one was a segue, one was scratching ... and what was the other one?'[129] Here we can reintroduce Ismo Santala's research to fill in that gap and suggest 'glitch electronica' as the technique Noon is missing.

No previous study has used Noon's own taxonomy to analyse his musico-literary techniques and develop this intermedial discourse. Although the sonic techniques overlap in many ways, they can be examined separately to consider whether, lifted directly from electronic music production and applied to Noon's literary products, they might apply a comparable linguistic effect.

The remix

The remix was specifically a product of dance culture and the desire of the dancefloor for ever-longer, extended versions of tracks in order to sustain the heightened excitement of the dance.[130] This must also be understood in relation to music technology and the evolution of the 12-inch vinyl format which, spun at 45rpm, allowed more space for the producer of the remix, and the DJ, to manipulate sound of the grooves. Initially, in an environment of vinyl 12-inch releases the remixes would occupy the second, or 'B-side', of the record and this is something Noon clearly aimed to introduce, and replicate, in his fiction: 'I very specifically wanted to do the B-side. The B-side of a dance single reflects on the A-side. A different view. A mirror image or whatever it is.'[131]

As noted in the opening section to this chapter, to further clarify his creative philosophy Noon published his manifesto – interestingly, in this context – named 'The Ghost on the B-Side'. Subtitled 'A Technique for Remixing Narrative', this document lays out Noon's technique and strategies for his 'dub fiction'. As exemplum, Noon chooses a random piece of his prose and melds that with a passage from the David Bowie track 'Starman',[132] 'pushing' the result through randomizing filters until we see a new narrative truth revealed. Noon announces chapters as 'remixes' in both in *Needle in the Groove* and *Pixel Juice*, and Santala's work is useful in identifying the specific remixes in *Pixel Juice* as 'Homo Karaoke' and then 'Dub Karaoke'; 'Blurbs' and 'Dub Blurbs'; 'Call of the Weird' and 'Dub Weird'; and 'Spaceache and Heartships' and 'Dubships'.[133] These prose remixes reshape the source text, rearranging and replaying fragments. For instance, the short story 'Blurbs' builds around a typical Noon theme in which an organism, the 'blurb', is introduced into a rather prescient narrative where, in a pre-socially mediated age, citizens of a warped Manchester are interested only in celebrity and broadcasting their news, the 'Golden Age of Appearances'™'.[134] In the main story we have the line:

> Save the family's brand identity! Save the logo!'
> Mummy met her deadline. So sad.[135]

If we then turn to the subsequent story, subtitled '(Press Release Twister Remix)' we find that many of the memes and linguistic fragments of the source text are rearranged and replayed, creating ripples of resonance that re-emerge in the dub remix: 'Logo bio death. Falling media slogans secreted zero-media. A nobody image.'[136] In a sensibility reminiscent of his stylistic and thematically fluid approach to music in *Needle in the Groove*, Noon reports: 'My main insight was to realize that words, whilst seemingly fixed in meaning, are in fact a liquid medium. They flow. The writer digs channels, steers the course.'[137]

Dub

A musical style created by Caribbean reggae producers,[138] a dub track is stripped down to its bare, bass elements. Like his fictional creation Elliot Hill, Noon was himself a bass player, which makes his prioritizing of the root notes all the more understandable. In linguistic terms, the dub 'effect' therefore denotes the stripping down of a story to its base, rather than bass, elements, Noon himself agreeing: 'It's where you take a finished piece and then you remove things from it, to reveal the bones, the skeleton of the piece.'[139] The author therefore foregrounds the low frequencies within his fiction, the sub bass rumblings of text that resonate at the visceral level of language, so as to really affect the reader. In this particular mapping of musical devices upon the linguistic, we find that Noon will often use the very next story in the collection to construct a linguistic 'dub' of the previous, stripping away the grammatical baggage. After 'Homo Karaoke', for instance, Noon next places 'Dub Karaoke', subtitled 'Electric Haiku Remix'. In the source text there is the line: 'The blast hits my building dead centre; elemental. Expressway to the skull. Headburst.'[140] Then in the subsequent dub, the entire story is stripped down to nine haikus,[141] the fifth of which reads:

> needleburst skullfire
> mutating beats-per-minute
> operating heartache.[142]

In the last haiku, meanwhile, we find that 'kisses of the remix' are able to dissolve 'all ghosts unknown'.[143]

Scratching

As outlined in Chapter 3, in 1972, Japanese electronics company Technics introduced the 1200 turntable. This model featured a particularly robust motor, so that DJs were able to pull, and push, a record against the natural revolution of the motor, to create a 'scratching' sound with the music.[144] Scratching quickly became part of hip-hop music culture, and here Noon creates a linguistic simulacrum of the sonic scratch, which he calls a 'fractal scratch', where typographical interpretations of a vinyl scratch replicate the iconic slashing sound with the forward and backward slash: '/' and '\'. As an example, Noon's story 'Orgmentations' ends as follows:

> (Hands of the DJ move around.) Oh, dear sweet reader, you really should have been there!
>
> \\\\\\\\\ FRACTAL SCRATCH //////////
> \\\\\\\\\\///////////
> \\\\\//////
> \\//[145]

The backward and forward pull of the slashes physically replicate the movement of the fingers backwards and forwards on the vinyl record, on the paper page, manipulating music as Noon manipulates text.

Segue

DJing must be understood as a musical craft, where 'jocks' have now become 'turntablists',[146] where all DJs owe something to the progenitors of the scene. Club culture historians Bill Brewster and Frank Broughton cite Francis Grasso as 'the granddaddy of modern club jocks',[147] blending and 'beatmatching' records in 1960s New York in a way 'we would recognize as doing the same thing as DJs do today'.[148] A DJ's skill is thus marked by the way they are able to effortlessly elide one record with another – a DJ technique known as the segue in EDMC terms – so as to appear seamless. This is another musicological technique attempted by Noon within *Pixel Juice*, beatmatching words to allow one story to blend into the following, forming a *linguistic* segue.

If we return to the story 'Orgmentations (in the mix)', words slide equally smoothly on the page under Noon's expert manipulation, as music in the grooves of a vinyl record might beneath the most expert DJ touch. DJs use the crossfader to cut between a sonic phrase in two records to create a linking bridge between tracks. If we now focus and hold on the line 'oh, dear sweet reader, you really should have been there!' in the first story,[149] we can then see how the story segues into the very next, 'Hands of the DJ' where, over the page and only a few lines down, Noon manages the same sonic effect, by teasing with the line: 'Vinyl went wet to the traces, held sway in time to the rapid-fire fingertronics; etch-plate aesthetics, fractal scratches (really should've been there) out on the limits of the human edit.'[150] In effect, this reappearance of the phrase is a linguistic ghost-echo, with Noon working the literary crossfader to create a refrain linking these two chapters, just as a sonic segue would link two 12-inch records.

Glitch

Although no scholarly work has yet considered the totality of these varied electronic music techniques deployed by Noon, Nedeljkov proves useful in her specific consideration of the remix in her research, alongside Santala, who foregrounds the dub remix and glitch electronica. As Santala highlights, 'glitch' is the notion that randomness and chance might be, in fact, appropriated in the quest of creating something new,[151] even if the initial chance might, in Noon's case, be born of a purely technological mistake. Again, we find this avant-garde idea (if now repositioned in a wholly digital arena) has an organic, analogue precursor with the Beat Generation, and Kerouac's prioritizing of the accidental. In 'The History of Bop' Kerouac reports:

> Bop began with jazz. But one afternoon somewhere on a sidewalk maybe 1939, 1940 Dizzy Gillespie or Charlie Parker or Thelonious Monk was walking down past a men's clothing store on 42nd street or South Main in L.A. when from a loudspeaker they heard a wild and possible mistake in jazz that could have only been heard inside their own imaginary head and that is a new art. Bop. The name derives from an accident.[152]

If we map such 'accidents' onto the electronic sphere, we arrive at 'glitch electronica', which Noon describes 'the music of machines with diseases',[153] the same impulse, perhaps, that leads to the current fetishization of vinyl technology, even with its attendant bumps and scratches. For Noon's dub fiction, this is a case of replicating fate in the automatic hands of machines, and here we find Noon truly pushing towards avant-garde abstraction. Although Noon's interest in dub reggae reveals stylistic innovations, for the purposes of this research it is here, within the more experimental realm of 1990s electronic music, that we find the author's interest in 'computers as a creative tool' for linguistic creation.[154] Here, Noon's interest is possibly more akin to electro-acoustic music's interest in working with the random abstraction of 'found sound',[155] rich source material for electronic, and sometimes accidental, sound sculpture. Noon is dealing with what Santala refers to as the sonification of modern life itself,[156] but also its further abstraction, traced once again onto literary form. For instance, Noon releases short digital 'spores' through the social medium Twitter, and one consists of only two words, one possibly mistyped:

> Destroyed?
> Destoryed!

When I ask him about this specific spore, Noon replies that his interest in this 'glitch' is in how 'one tiny change (transposing two letters) totally changes the meaning of the first word'.[157]

The avant-garde laboratory

Drawing this interrogation of Noon's creativity to a close, it will now be apposite to make some final remarks before very specifically revisiting our opening research questions. Middleton details how an author might be held by 'the relations between man, animal and machine',[158] and in this context the story 'Hands of the DJ' remains the key text. In devising a character with one mechanical hand, the other made of butterflies, Noon reveals once again an almost bipolar creativity, implicitly suggesting one needs both fantasy and technology, ultimately, to operate. In fact, we may need to make one last leap and appreciate the electronic *as organic*, if we are to agree with Ralf Hütter that machines are themselves inherently funky.[159] Perhaps the funkiest machine, after all, is the novel itself, a remarkable piece of technology that, in the context of my research, and this book, becomes a device for recording and monitoring subterranean genesis and germination, storing both organic voices and the beat of electronic music, for future generations of readers to hear.

A central focus must therefore be to emphatically celebrate Noon's ability to deploy arch, avant-garde techniques of electronic music production in the creation of ostensibly pulp stories driven from the dancefloor. This clearly progresses intermedial discourse and it is impossible, in fact, to conceive of these dazzling literary evocations without this author's overt interest in the synchronous sonic experiments taking place in Manchester's nightclubs. Noon reflects on this very point:

> Because I very specifically applied myself to this task of transforming language in metaphorical ways, for drugs and music, I think that task just allowed me to go down a certain pathway and I enjoyed that pathway and I applied myself to it.[160]

In terms, first, of how Dancefloor-Driven Literature might form a laboratory for avant-garde stylistics and linguistic techniques, we find that Noon himself uses the word 'laboratory' to describe his experiments in melding the musical with the literary. Such a critique also forms a useful model for exploring the many ways Noon has developed his binary, digital instinct and impetus in creating literary and stylistic 'mashups' between two forms. As outlined in Chapter 2, while a postmodernist position argues much of modern life is fluid and mutable, that movement nevertheless takes place between two fixed positions, certainly in a digital environment formed entirely of 1 and 0:

> To talk about street themes and music and DJing and so on, and apply some avant-garde techniques to it in some way always fascinated me. Then you can fuse those two things. All my work is fed from popular culture and the avant-garde and I mix those things together in different relationships. [...] The middle brow novel

has never meant anything to me. [...] In my life I think what I've done is that I've tended to reject the middle.'[161]

Centrally, in considering whether it might be possible to bring electronic music production to the literary sphere, this chapter must also conclude that Noon demonstrably achieves this fusion with powerful results, using the techniques of modern electronic music production to drive the progressive linguistic mechanics of his stories. In our interview, Noon remarks 'form equals content is what I was really looking at',[162] and further expands on this point:

> I was never, like, writing about music as such, it was almost like, words as music was what I was really going for in those days. So the words and the music are mixed up together, the subject matter feeds into that as well.[163]

Noon is much more of a natural *observer* among the three case studies of this book – comfortable at the 'edge of the dancefloor', at the liminal tipping point between passive observation and active engagement, unwilling to follow Irvine Welsh, for instance, onto the 'blonde rectangle of polished wood' and 'towards the aesthetic center of the universe'.[164] Such distance, however, allows space for the creative philosophy that underpins his literary project, and allows for the themes of his work to emerge.

Returning once again to the tenets of reception theory to test how Noon's avant-garde instincts might have impacted in commercial terms, one interesting aspect of this analysis is the impact of Noon on the book market. Certainly, Noon's writing analysed in this chapter brings it within the time period of my research (broadly 1988–2000) and certainly synchronous with the height of EDMC itself, which had a positive correlation on sales. Noon reports in conversation that 'I just thought that I'd found a subject that not many other writers were doing so I might be able to get an audience because of that',[165] and as we have seen in Chapter 4, the audience for that literature was, at that point, certainly present.

However, as George Melly describes through *Revolt into Style*, time's arrow has a perniciously wounding effect on the life cycle of a popular music culture.[166] Noon recognizes this impact: 'One of the interesting things about this is that apart from Irvine [Welsh], the rest of us have struggled a bit, in terms of becoming household names if you like.'[167] My research certainly reveals of a relative lack of recent commercial resonance for Noon's works (although he is certainly productive, and remains important) and questions why a writer of such invention and creativity might find generating sales so problematic. In personal communication, for instance, Noon indicates his 2012 novel *Channel SK1N* was published in digital format because of a lack of interest in a print edition,[168] bringing his output more in line with the self-published Dancefloor-Driven authors listed in the collection that forms Appendix I. Andrew Wenaus reinforces this point in stating: 'Exciting as these experiments are, for nearly two decades, Noon has expressed an increasing degree of impatience regarding the disinterest and dismissal of experimental literature by the contemporary British literary scene as he sees it.'[169] This analysis concurs that Noon's work is deliberately esoteric but in a pre-emptive response to critics of this overt stylization, Noon himself comments: 'I fully understand that some people just won't get this at all, and that's fine. We all move to different drummers.'[170] On its own, that is not enough to explain this commercial infecundity, and has driven Noon towards more noir, detective-based fiction in more recent years.

Wenaus contends that 'Noon's metamorphiction is fascinating in its investment in spectrality. The way Noon posits print culture in a kind of non-opposition with info-culture is a Derridean enterprise.'[171] Indeed any analysis that places 'music' on one side of the 'musico-literary' en dash, and 'literature' on the other, is also in itself an ostensibly Derridean conceit, and certainly there are ghosts in Noon's machine: from Noon's more precise 'spectral beat' that underpins the musicological linguistics of the entire enterprise,[172] to the overarching hauntology that links to the next case study. Wenaus also touches on this Derridean notion of 'hauntology' in reporting:

> For Noon, there is an intimate link between chronology, ghosts, and remix. [...] One remarkable aspect of Noon's writing is his ability to exhaust any variety of semantic connotations to a given word or phrase. Ghosts, in *Falling out of Cars*, stand variously for a loss of culture, a loss of a literary history, the gradual disappearance of print culture, and the more immediate loss of family.[173]

Certainly, the ontological driver within Noon's work might connect us with this notion of haunting, particularly the sense of previous generations, previous lives, previous music styles. Certainly these spectres hover over the pages of *Needle in the Groove*, where the reader specifically witnesses 'sticky ghosts of young desperate sex';[174] and in *Pixel Juice*, where the reader bumps into a 'media ghost',[175] that becomes a 'sucked ghost' only three pages later.[176] Wenaus writes: 'These are the ghosts with which Noon is concerned, those of human memory and of self-generating, rapidly updating information technologies.'[177] For Noon, however, ghosts not only haunt the narrative content but also infiltrate the form of his work, in the ghost echoes of, for instance, the linguistic scratch, and segue, sonic near memories. Considered together these are ghost texts, forming not only Adorno's 'archive of subjectivity' (which of course they do, as though crowdsourcing memories in fiction) but spectres of subterranean history, collectively haunting the future from the underground, from the subtext. Whether ghosts of the A-side or the B-side, these phantoms share their spectrality with Derrida's own ghosts; locked, but only temporarily contained, in the vault labelled by Benjamin as the 'saved night'.[178] Wenaus continues that 'ghosts are part of the future',[179] and the works of Noon – along with those of Welsh and Blincoe – gather together and then rise up in a process of celestial, linguistic spectrality, these novels carrying their ghost echoes, like scratches in the vinyl of cultural history.

An interesting moment in the interview between myself and Noon arrives when he traces his finger down the list of authors on the contents page of my copy of the *Disco Biscuits* collection, realizing he has forgotten many of the names. Then his finger stops: 'Nicholas Blincoe I remember. Because Blincoe was in Manchester of course, so I met him a few times.'[180] Many months after Noon's innocuous recollection, this research leads back to Noon's 2001 manifesto in *The Guardian*,[181] considered earlier in this chapter. Somewhat startlingly, this manifesto reveals what must stand (and in an age of digital archival preservation, it does stand) as a literary attack on his fellow writer.[182] Following Blincoe's 2000 publication of his own 'New Puritan' manifesto, Noon responds in *The Guardian*:

> The New Puritans have nailed their colours to the mast, and what a drab, lifeless banner it is. These are the dry, deft, slightly engaging tales that so many of our writers produce already, without any rules other than fixed tradition. The small thing, done well; a fearsome denial of the imagination.[183]

In a seminal moment in the course of my research for this book, Noon's manifesto reveals what he, himself, must now have now forgotten, this literary contretemps never escalating to the rivalry between, for instance, Tolstoy and Turgenev.[184] Suddenly, two of the chosen case studies for this book – up to that point not linked beyond their appearance in *Disco Biscuits* – have become creative counterpoints, literary rivals positioning themselves against one another. Noon calls the Blincoe co-edited short story collection *All Hail the New Puritans* 'a peculiar document',[185] adding 'fifteen fairly young writers have decided to remove all traces of formal density from their work',[186] before asking, 'Where does this fixation with the linear narrative come from?'[187] Most interestingly for the purposes of this book, in his own hauntological call for a 'post-future fiction' Noon remarks: 'Anybody who has enjoyed a good DJ set in a nightclub will attest to this sense of a story being unfolded through the music.'[188] We now find that these two authors – linked by virtue of postcode and literary proximity (keeping them 10 miles apart geographically, 150 pages in the *Disco Biscuits* collection) – poles apart in terms of their relationship to music and the written word.

8

Case study three

Literary diegesis in the writing of Nicholas Blincoe

In dancefloor terms, a successful sonic mix would segue from the end of the outgoing 'text' smoothly into the beginning of the next. If that process might now be mapped onto writing, a similar trope – or theoretical beat – can be introduced, to provide a bridge between the previous analysis of Jeff Noon and this consideration of Nicholas Blincoe. That bridge is the contents page of the 1997 *Disco Biscuits* collection.[1] During my meeting with Nicholas Blincoe, the author scans the list of contributors in much the same way that Noon did, for biographical traces of its names,[2] reporting: 'Jeff Noon I knew better, because we were both living in Manchester at the same time. But I haven't seen him in the last few years.'[3] Once again, the passage of time would seem to have ameliorated any lasting damage incurred by Noon's combative stance against Blincoe's New Puritan Project. However, it is nevertheless important to register the differences between these case study authors, as well as what brought them together – for reasons of fate and circumstance, as much as design – within the pages of Sarah Champion's collection. There is, for instance, resistance to the 'Chemical Generation' soubriquet, Blincoe noting: 'I can't remember who came up with that because it wasn't something we ever used amongst ourselves.'[4]

It is the epistemological drive of this book that Dancefloor-Driven Literature contributed hugely to the permeation of EDMC into the broader, contemporary cultural consciousness, and second, to the retrospective historic decoding of EDMC, where the notion of DJ, drug and dancefloor become literary meme. However, each of these authors demonstrates very different relationships with, and to, the spectacle of the dancefloor and the broader context of the club scene beyond, although running through Blincoe's early fiction, as with all case studies, is indeed the persistent beat of electronic music. This chapter will analyse the role music plays as soundtrack to his stories, and how that essentially silent beat contributes to the *naturalistic* totality of the piece, and to the production and transfer of subterranean knowledge. Responding to comments about such representations of Manchester's club scene, Sarah Champion agrees: 'I don't think there's been a Manchester book that really captures that. I think Nicholas Blincoe's the closest, with *Manchester Slingback* and *Acid Casuals*.'[5] Blincoe is therefore individually important to this book in terms of his own embedded experience in Manchester's clubland, his musical interests and productions and the influence of this electronic muse on his literary output and his specific interest in melding the overlapping nocturnal worlds of clubs and crime, while also bringing wider intellectual and philosophical interests to his fiction, including writers such as Jacques Derrida.

This chapter, like the previous case studies, will initially build from Blincoe's contribution to Champion's *Disco Biscuits*, in this case the story 'Ardwick Green', before preceding to an analysis of these two key Blincoe texts – *Manchester Slingback* and *Acid Casuals* – alongside *Jello Salad* (1997),[6] which is particularly important for its depiction of a rave scene. While Blincoe brings different thematic and stylistic elements to his Dancefloor-Driven fiction, in striving for consistency, my approach for decoding these texts will follow that of the other case study writers: namely, extensive primary input from the author,[7] reinforced by secondary theoretical readings and close textual analysis of the works themselves. In terms of this secondary literature used in order to decode Blincoe's writing, Jean-Jacques Lecercle's 1985 title *Philosophy through the Looking Glass: Language, Nonsense, Desire* is of particular interest, as Lecercle was Blincoe's PhD examiner at Warwick University,[8] his thesis – interestingly for the scope of this book – concerned with Jacques Derrida.

Methodologically, Blincoe is principally foregrounded in this chapter as a literary exponent of the third approach to musico-literary intermediality defined in the taxonomy within this book, where music is used diegetically to render a specifically *naturalistic* context. Blincoe's fiction therefore provides the perfect context for a discursive analysis of verisimilitude and further, how these naturalistic constructs might affect, or deflect, authenticity. In decoding Blincoe's naturalistic impulses this chapter will incorporate two key theories. It will focus more closely on the notion of *literary diegesis*, where electronic music is suggested by the author, or DJ within the club text, as a sweep of sound that forms a soundtrack to the prose. That soundtrack is consequently heard across the page; or, more accurately, as a beat behind, even beyond, the text, in Derridean terms. This chapter also introduces the new concept of *narrative pointillism*, an interdisciplinary notion that on this occasion borrows from art criticism. Narrative pointillism enables this chapter to prove how Blincoe achieves this naturalism through the precision use of detail, in order to engender a naturalistic and authentic rendering of the nightclub construct. Finally, this final case study is used to work towards a central concern of this research, namely the question of whether Dancefloor-Driven novels identified in this book sit within a broader sphere of 'cult' fiction. At the same time, it will examine whether, while ostensibly ephemeral, pulp fictions are robust enough to support Blincoe's grander philosophical thoughts.

New Puritan generation

Before exploring the Blincoe texts, the New Puritan project needs to be acknowledged. Blincoe's *All Hail the New Puritans* (2000) is a collection of fifteen short stories by writers such as Alex Garland, Toby Litt and Daren King,[9] as well as by the co-authors Nicholas Blincoe and Matt Thorne.[10] The fictions contained within this volume were all designed to conform to the New Puritan Manifesto, written by the editors and occupying the front page of the volume. In our conversation Blincoe contends that, in his opinion, the New Puritan writers actually cohered as a literary group more naturally than the writers grouped together as first Chemical Generation, and here as Dancefloor-Driven, although that is not a position I myself support in this book. Contemporaneous critical response to the collection was unfavourable, including reviews in the *New York Times*,[11] *The Guardian*[12] and the *London Review of Books*,[13] alongside the abrasive, iconoclastic rebuttal by Jeff Noon explored in the previous chapter. That critical discourse continued in Fernández's edited volume of writing on Blincoe's collection, *The New Puritan Generation*.[14] For instance, in his response to Blincoe's project, David Owen reacts strongly to the suggestion that one might be able to write to rules, citing literary critics F. R. Leavis and Harold Bloom in arguing for the essential anti-creativeness of such an endeavour. Owen argues:

> What these two editors appear to reject, then, is – in the absence of a better term – 'literary' writing, by which I mean writing that is unashamedly conscious of itself as a form of artistic expression, fully open to using the rhetorical means available to this end, including formal, stylistic and linguistic unorthodoxy.[15]

Located in Owen's sentence is the very frontline of the cultural entanglement between Blincoe and Noon. Clause Six of the New Puritan manifesto reads: 'We believe in grammatical purity and avoid any elaborate punctuation', which in itself sets the Puritan agenda immediately against that of the typographically innovative Noon, and indeed Welsh. Blincoe explains: 'I'm definitely a realist. I actually have a problem with things like science fiction, allegory, satirical writing. I have quite strong objections to it.'[16] Once again, the battle lines are clear when considering the avant-garde, cyber-experimentation of Noon. The New Puritan collection was published at the millennial nadir of the rave scene – and the temporal end-point of my own study – and it is clear from Blincoe's own publishing, and creative manifesto, that he had by this point moved beyond the club fictions that had defined his early publishing career.[17] In addition, as Jeff Noon so demonstrably makes clear, the ethos of New Puritanism is in itself formal and stylistic, rather than thematic, or driven from a particular place, such as the dancefloor. For these reasons, while acknowledging the New Puritan project, it will not form a major aspect of this chapter.

Blincoe's biography in *Disco Biscuits* reads:

> Born in Rochdale, but he usually claims it was Manchester',[18] and in conversation the author adds, 'Coming from Rochdale, I didn't really fit in. I was a punk and then a mod and then a kind of proto-goth, so I just didn't go out in Rochdale, I went out in Manchester, and that was like from being about 15, 16.[19]

Here we start to see how the city centre, and the gravitational pull of its varied dancefloors, became TAZ playground, transformative portal and locus for escape; all of which will, in turn, become a central theme for Blincoe. In this post-industrial setting, and in a process of cultural and architectural appropriation, Manchester's grand Victorian warehouses are now repositioned as rave spaces, economic recession and decay providing new leisure opportunities and, for authors like Blincoe, context for his own burgeoning creativity. Like Noon, Blincoe's cultural interests included fine art,[20] and his musical proclivities encompassed music production. He reports: 'I'd always been in bands. I was in kind of punk style bands in the 80s.'[21] Following the Beastie Boys' first single, Blincoe developed an interest in hip-hop culture, ultimately releasing a single on Manchester's influential Factory Records – co-owners, as discussed in Chapter 3 – of the Haçienda nightclub.[22]

Both Noon and Blincoe would, in a sense, 'outgrow' this dancefloor playground, moving on to other creative projects in other geographic locations but at this stage, at least, we can locate them both on the edge of the very same dancefloor although perhaps at opposite sides. In very evident counterpoint to Noon, for instance, Blincoe is less experimental, arguing that 'fiction writing should be very involved in the real'.[23] Although the narrative drama may be warped in his novels by the filters of electronic music and drug consumption, it is nevertheless warped from an initial base position of an understood reality, where the light of the spectacular is both harsh and true. Here is an author, then, not overtly concerned in the determinism of technique, or the progression of the avant-garde, Blincoe agreeing: 'I can't say that there's specific techniques. I wasn't experimental in my writing to really capture that.'[24] This positions the reader immediately in very different literary terrain to that of Noon, and perhaps closer to Welsh. Instead, in its concern with the simple reflection of things as they are, Blincoe's writing can be situated in terms of *naturalism*.

In literary terms, naturalism is an approach that replicates landscapes, people, even ways of speaking, as they might appear in the real world, with little to no artifice in that construction, piling up detail to present a deterministic vision of the world. Closely allied to the social realism of Welsh,[25] the characteristics of naturalism are defined by Margaret Drabble as 'the authenticity and accuracy of detail, thus investing the novel with the value of social history',[26] which will have important ramifications when moving on to a consideration of subterranean philology, as discussed later in this chapter. To achieve a successful level of naturalism in their presentation, many of the Dancefloor-Driven writers addressed in this book strive for that most loaded, problematic and elastic of concepts: authenticity. With Blincoe, these strands of naturalism and authenticity are entirely, and necessarily, linked and interdependent. Although a point strongly resisted by Adorno, authenticity can be seen to be dictated by specific constructions of meaning.[27] As we have seen, the subterranean world is full of semiotic inference – clothes, musics, drugs, even words themselves – these are all clues by which we can decode a popular culture, engendering a physical connection between writer and reader across the page. Through the verisimilitude of detail, through the articulation of, for instance, DJ technique and interaction, Blincoe is able to sketch what seems an authentic, yet also fantastic and almost mythological, representation of the DJ, clubber and their broader dancefloor milieu. In so doing, he builds a believable fictional environment within which, and against which, the DJ might play their music, and his characters might dance.

This book has often invoked the notion of the liminal – the way that the dancefloor marks a symbolic frontline between our understood experience of reality and something entirely 'other' – but it can also denote a legal liminality. As noted in Chapter 3, the early rave scene was, in itself, illegal and in consuming Ecstasy as part of the rave process, every individual was undertaking an essentially criminal enterprise. Beeler includes Blincoe within *Dance, Drugs, Escape* in a chapter titled 'Crime and Clublife', recognizing this natural overlap between worlds that are both nocturnal and marginal, and suggests: 'Club culture fiction is characterized by a profound disregard for the traditional political structures and rules of mainstream society and the subcultural participants seem ever ready to forge their own rules'.[28] Blincoe first steps down into this subterranean realm, but then takes this reality one step further in pursuing this trail of chemical breadcrumbs almost as an embedded reporter, asking that if there are drugs on the dancefloor where do they come from? Blincoe's brother was a crime correspondent for a magazine in the crime-blighted Moss Side area of Manchester and, at the time of writing his novels, he recalls: 'The bouncer wars were getting quite big',[29] with the infamous cover of the EDMC magazine *Mixmag* already referenced in Chapter 3 christening the city that was once MADchester 'GUNchester'.[30] If Welsh accessed the dancefloor via its interface with drugs and abjection, and Noon through the portal of cyber fiction, Blincoe very clearly does the same with crime.[31] Clubland and crime stand as nefarious, nocturnal bedfellows, environments that together share the axes of night and day, of underground and mainstream society, and thus provide a useful counterpoint for literary analysis. In detailing the shared night of clubbers and criminals, Blincoe recognizes this impulse of violence in its natural context: 'Absolutely. It never crossed my mind. You couldn't write about Manchester without writing about clubs. And you couldn't write about the clubs without writing about drugs. Or crime.'[32]

Disco Biscuits: 'Ardwick Green'

If you look back at the cover of *Disco Biscuits* (Figure 5.1), you will see that the authors listed on the cover of the first edition – presumably for their marketing impact – are Welsh, Noon and Blincoe, with Alan Warner breaking up the latter two. Martin Millar then forms the only further addition, the remaining fourteen gathered together under the catch-all 'many others'. This in itself indicates the influence that Blincoe had at this point, reinforced by the fact that his contribution, 'Ardwick Green', was chosen to start the collection. Beeler writes: 'In "Ardwick Green" it is clear that the violent social structures of the criminal element is [*sic*] in ascendancy and the clubbers have to accommodate'[33] within a plot where naive, nascent club promoter Andy approaches Jackie Pye, proprietor of a venue in the Ardwick Green area of Manchester, with a view to promoting a Sunday club event.[34] Andy has one leg in plaster and although explained in narrative terms (as a skateboarding accident), Blincoe renders no metaphorical resonance for that injury, which mirrors David Owen's criticisms of certain New Puritan tropes.[35] Although the party is a commercial success, Jackie Pye is an altogether unsavoury character and the reappearance of the character Conrad – after a period in prison – also darkens the narrative, now threatening the initial optimism that carried the enterprise.

Blincoe recalls that 'somebody pointed that out at the time that the stories in *Disco Biscuits* all tend to have bad endings. There's a kind of puritanism running them all – you're going to pay for your pleasures.'[36] Of course the resonance of the word 'puritanism' has semantic connotations when considering the project Blincoe would go on to co-curate; however, the preference for the tragic denouement is not an anomaly. As we have seen across club fictions, as well as crime fictions, in moral terms pleasure must be seen to be punished by pain, in keeping with the notion of the Narrative Arc identified in Chapter 4. Beeler agrees that 'in many of these works the "happy end" is not to be found, as the ultimate futility of club culture's ideals when confronted by the "real world" is apparent';[37] however, he reductively limits the scope of such fictions by imposing top-down theoretical frameworks, rather than appreciating the natural realism inherent in that representation. In terms of this criminal context, this research therefore progresses from Beeler's rather narrow interrogation of clubs and crime. Instead, the polarity must be reversed in arguing that if there was a crossover between clubland and crime in the work of Blincoe, it was not the consequence of a downward imposition of a rigid crime genre, or indeed any artificial construct, but rather a naturalistic representation of *how things were* in Manchester's nightclubs at that time. This is, of course, my own critical reading of Blincoe's narrative interest, but it is also the reading of someone who lived in Manchester at this time, in fact in the Moss Side area, and inhabited many of the same city dancefloors. Blincoe's story, in all its natural realism, builds upwardly, therefore, from the levelness of the street, of the dancefloor. Blincoe expands on this very point:

> I was self-consciously glamourising the situation. And for doing that I'm glamourising something that's morally dubious to glamourise – like heavy drug use. But I think the readers are intelligent enough. People take drugs because they're pleasurable so you need to give that upside as well as the downside.[38]

In terms of the methods by which Blincoe uses naturalism to draw the reader closer to his narrative, the fiction contains precise locations and real cultural references,[39] whether it is Andy temporally rooted by 'the end of the football scores and the beginning of *Blind Date*',[40] or references to real-world clubs such as Wigan Casino and Twisted Wheel,[41] as well as 'the Hacienda and over Blackburn at the raves and that'.[42] There is also music in the text, and within its words we hear the rhythms of the street, the rhythms of Manchester and the rhythms of the subterranean dancefloor. Crucially, Blincoe provides a realistic representation of promoting a club event, and the art of DJing at that event:

> Sitting sideways to the decks, he had to twist round as he practised on the cross-fader but he got a rhythm going, juggling the same three old school tracks until his first-night nerves settled: *Marshall Jefferson, Adonis, Frankie Knuckles*.[43]

Blincoe's stylistic driver renders the environment recognizable for the cognizant-participant reader, if the action perhaps remains remote for the more casual voyeur, for instance in the following exchange between Andy and his friend Jess. Centrally, the tone of his writing deploys the argot of the dancefloor in accurately depicting that milieu:

> He waved Jess over, shouting: 'All right?'
> Jess came up screaming, 'Double fucking top. What you reckon, you up for it?'
> Andy nodded, he was in synch. He said, 'How was last night?'
> 'Fucking large, mate. We went to Fonzo Buller's place then up to Blackburn.'[44]

In our conversation, Blincoe suggests dialogue is not a strong part of his writing and therefore, in terms of constructing a naturalistic fictional environment, he keeps close to what he knows, explaining: 'My main characters are often northerners. It's easier to have that voice in your head',[45] marking another distinct tonal shift from Noon's avant-garde experimentalism. This also holds true of the narrative itself, which spends a large part of the story not only in this Ardwick Green establishment, but even more particularly in its toilets, where Conrad takes Ecstasy, amphetamines, amyl nitrate (termed 'poppers' in the story) and heroin, before attempting, and ultimately failing at, a bout of onanism. 'I fucking love taking drugs in a lavvy',[46] Conrad exclaims, to no one in particular, but in a manner that resonates with Welsh's toilet grotesque, an indicator of the abject. This naturalistic rendering of the urban environment as it is lived (grotesque or otherwise) – this proximity to nature, even at its base level – also has an attendant impact on the authenticity of the story. These rotating forces of naturalism, social (perhaps anti-social) realism and authenticity all exert a gravitational pull over the text, a stylistic and thematic ebb and flow.

In terms of the commercial impact of the *Disco Biscuits* collection, Blincoe makes an extremely astute observation, which in itself conflates our medial spheres of music and literature, recalling (of the book's success) that 'this wasn't selling in Waterstones, it was selling in HMV'.[47] This Dancefloor-Driven Literature was now establishing itself as the paper simulacrum of its sonic, subterranean root culture, 'selling hand over fist' according to Blincoe.[48] Even in terms of commercial retail stacking, we see the literary infiltrating the musical realm just as, conversely, music productions were beginning to occupy the covers of Dancefloor-Driven works like Trevor Miller's *Trip City* and Irvine Welsh's *Ecstasy*. Blincoe continues: 'That was exciting. We did feel there was something new happening',[49] adding (with reference to the club tour that followed): 'We did do readings in nightclubs.[50] And we toured. I don't know how great it was or if anyone could hear it. But it was exciting.'[51] This repetition of the word 'exciting' expresses the energy and enthusiasm that surrounded the creative experimentation of 1990s Dancefloor-Driven Literature. Something new was starting to form, from *la boue de la discothèque*.

Acid Casuals

Clause Seven of the New Puritan Manifesto reads: 'All products, places, artists and objects named are real.' In this sense, music itself – the beats and breaks of real-world electronic dance music – become the diegetic soundtrack within Blincoe's prose. Key areas for this interrogation of *Acid Casuals*, therefore, will be verisimilitude and the use of music in text, the contextual environment of the dancefloor and how, taken together, these might provide a platform for a discussion of the themes of identity and escape, and drive what this book defines as subterranean philology. It will be useful to offer a brief synopsis of *Acid Casuals*, before proceeding to interrogate the rich role music plays within its narrative. The novel is a club/crime story which tracks the return to Manchester of Paul Sorel, newly reconstructed – following surgery in Brazil – as Estella: a transgender hitman assigned to murder club owner John Burgess. Although published in 1995, in conversation Blincoe explains that the novel focusses on the Haçienda nightclub of 1991–2, melding 'Acid Teds' and 'Football Casuals' within the murky milieu of Manchester's clubland to create the portmanteau title.[52] This creates an environment for colourful characters, these 'acid casuals and ravers' who form the corpus of the dancefloor,[53] itself a springboard for escape, whether physical or physiological, for this transgender hitman/woman who now stalks the clubs of Manchester. It will be fascinating to see how this pioneering transgender story translates to the small screen, if the current adaptation comes to fruition.

French connections run through Blincoe's literary output.[54] As noted earlier, Blincoe's PhD thesis centred on Jacques Derrida, and his supervisor in that project, Jean-Jacques Lecercle, writes in *Philosophy through the Looking Glass* of his 'discovery of a frontier between philosophy and literature, and its exploration. [...] *Délire* is the name for this frontier.'[55] Intellectual and philosophical, Blincoe incorporates Lecercle's grand interdisciplinary ideas within what will be shortly divined as an overtly pulp fiction. Lecercle writes how '*Délire* embodies the contradiction between the mastery of the subject and the re-emergence of chaos, of the original disruptive rejection',[56] and this chaos might be mapped onto the paidian dancefloor, chaos theory made manifest in what Lecercle calls 'the *délire* of hyper-normality'.[57] Lecercle centres *délire* against previous French concepts, arguing for its 'disaffection with the all powerful structural linguistics',[58] more in line with Barthes's thoughts on 'plaisir' and 'jouissance'.[59] Further, in an ongoing resistance to the structuralist idea that the literary text speaks in its own immanency, I also strongly argue that the intentions, motivations and preoccupations of the author are fundamental to a rich and complete 'writerly' understanding of their work, in Barthes's terms, beyond what the black-and-white limitations the text might itself discursively produce.

Blincoe's own input is therefore invaluable. In our conversation he remarks: 'I do like stream of consciousness, it's interesting',[60] indicating at least some openness to more impressionistic, musical writing. Blincoe certainly brings this focus to the dancefloor, reporting that 'there's some attempt to write "deliriously" in one chapter of *Acid Casuals*',[61] a rare stream-of-consciousness sequence from an otherwise stylistically controlled author, which I identify as Chapter Thirty, in a second reading of the novel. For instance, we find an almost rap prosody in the passage:

> Synapses splice this scene. Fuck this shutter down, steel bases. The Junkmeister at the controls, in the house, in the place to be. Shredding these walls like they weren't copacetic, crushing this hall without the aid of anaesthetic.[62]

In contrast to Noon, here we find music in the actual metre of the writing, but beyond this particular passage, Blincoe more often uses music in terms of its in-text consumption, rather than production, necessarily concerned more with the cultural resonance of music than its immanent tonality, with context more than text.[63] Understandably, Gerry Smyth questions: 'To what extent does a reader's knowledge of a musical text (or oeuvre, or figure, or event) bear upon the engagement with and understanding of developments within the fictional narrative?'[64] and Blincoe is helpful in this sense, as a sonic guide, his suggestive descriptions of the music easing the reader into the text. As an example, the first scene of the novel sees hitman Estella and club character Yen travelling back to Estella's rented apartment in Manchester. As Estella fixes drinks, Yen immediately turns on the 'Boss stereo',[65] bathing the novel in diegetic music: 'It was some kind of electronic synthesiser music, with no kind of rhythm track at all.'[66] Further decoded in Yen's narrative interiority as 'Ambient sounds' which dovetail nicely with 'a bit of spliff',[67] Estella's own take on the music interestingly reinforces Yen's reading: 'It was kind of dance music, but without a beat – just splashes of repetitive noise like the soundtrack to a lost disco.'[68]

In examining whether Blincoe successfully holds to the third point in the taxonomy of uses for music in literature, this novel demonstrates how – in constructing a naturalistic environment – the author keeps the reader close to the narrative, and to the dancefloor, in terms of both lexicon and diegetic musical selection. In working that connection in order to keep it seemingly fluid and direct, a writer allows for what Ferdinand de Saussure describes as a language that blends with the life of society.[69] With Blincoe, there exists a bridge of experience – between the creator and reader of words – constructed from bricks of cultural similitude, rendered naturalistically, without the artifice of an obvious literary construct. This is the sonic material that defines a popular music culture, building on Cornel Sandvoss's notion of the 'knowing field'[70] that links writer and reader in the production, and reception, of this literature. Once again relevance theory can be requisitioned from linguistics, in arguing that if that real-world music is *implied* by the author, it is for the reader, at the other end of the communication exchange, to use their a priori knowledge of the club scene and its soundtracks in order to unpack and reassemble that information. In other words, in Blincoe's writing there is often less interest in specifically naming tracks, as Welsh does, but rather in the broader suggestion of genre, tempo and mood of music that might be enough for the reader – using their own understanding of how the record, genre or even pace of a piece of music might sound – to complete the subterranean knowledge transfer, and turn up the volume.

Beyond the melopoetic interplay of words and music in describing the mellow, and indeed poetic, beat of this apartment soundtrack, *Acid Casuals* is at its heart a novel of the nightclub, a Dancefloor-Driven narrative. In progressing, therefore, to a fuller analysis of how Blincoe deploys music within his texts, the notion of *literary diegesis* will now form focus for this musico-literary intermedial discourse, which I will use in reference, as with cinematic scores, to denote specifically the use of *music in text*. Chapter 5 considered how Jacques Derrida argued that we remain determined to describe music in words because it is so tantalisingly beyond, and certainly behind, language. In his k-punk post of 23 January 2006, Mark Fisher offers his own 'Conjecture'. Fisher argues:

> Hauntology has an intrinsically sonic dimension.
> The pun – hauntology, ontology – works in spoken French, after all. In terms of sound, hauntology is a question of hearing what is not here, the recorded voice, the voice no longer the guarantor of presence.[71]

Fisher references Ian Penman's teasing of 'sonic hauntology' in his discussion of UK trip hop artist Tricky,[72] a notion that might be further repurposed here for 'hearing' a literary soundtrack that is neither sonically realized nor fully described. With Blincoe – and as opposed to Welsh's naming of real-world music and indeed Noon's fabrication of entirely new tracks – there is less focus on melody playing along the linguistic line of prose, or playing counterpoint to the words. Instead, Derrida's own positioning of music lying just 'beyond' writing links with my concept of literary diegesis, where music is implied, and lies *behind*, not within, the prose. With Blincoe in particular, the music is not necessarily in the forefront of the writing, therefore, but resides as the beat beneath the lines, haunting the text from beyond the page, in a way that must still be considered diegetic, as the music is still perceived by the characters in the narrative nightclub. In this way, the music forms a diegetic wash behind the prose, rather than the precision of detail Blincoe saves for other descriptions.

As an example of this literary diegetic soundtrack, later in the novel we find ourselves in the Passenger club, playing the role of the real-world club space PSV, in the Hulme area of Manchester.[73] Here, details of soundtrack again assist the reader in feeling the slower beat of the club's West Indian soundtrack: 'The DJ stood at its summit, the lower edges were filled with people dancing, throwing poses – some of them simply talking. The music was lover's rock, perhaps some jazz-tinged hip-hop loops every now and again.'[74] A short while later, Blincoe opens out into more of a contextual extemporization on how the city's soundtrack had recently fractured:

> The city had begun to redivide, like an amoeba that can't flow in two directions without splitting its heart open. Techno and its derivatives, musical and chemical, had got paler. Her friends, acid casuals and ravers, had begun to shun hip hop. It was a question of space; other-worlds against the inner-city. When raga re-ignited the dance halls, they left that alone too. It was too, too heavy. Let its bass heavy lines work on the asphalt, techno's electronic bleeps were communicating with the solar system: black holes and white space.[75]

This passage contains important points – notwithstanding its fictional construct – about the segregation of the beat along the lines of not only genre but also ethnicity. This deconstruction of the dancefloor would be familiar to participant readers at the time of the novel's publication, where 'down on the dance floor, the dancers leant back at impossible angles, thrusting out their hips, hard and low'.[76] It is also interesting to note that beyond the name of the novel's principal nightclub, Gravity, Blincoe also delivers an extended astronomical metaphor, as this book also moves towards a definition of its own systems theory.

At another point in the novel, Estella – assuming a useful vantage point (for both the contemporaneous reader and later EDMC archivists) on the upper balcony of a nightclub – is able to provide a naturalistic overview of the sights and sounds of a 1990s club space. Content to inhabit the liminal periphery of the action, she nevertheless describes its diegetic music as follows:

> Now she was upstairs again, she skirted around the edges of the dance floor and watched the crowds opening and folding around the solid beams of light and sonic bursts of discotic techno. She found the stairs and climbed to the balcony, looking for a panoramic grip on the excitement below.
>
> The dance floor was solid with luminous bodies. On the podiums that punctured the mass of dancers, figures reared above the crowd, waving high above the floor. Along the front of the stage, dancers were grandstanding to the music, throwing gestures out into the viscous mix of sweat and sound.
>
> The music descended to a low throb. Dry ice was blasted into the dance floor, propelled by the giant fans attached to the underside of the balcony. Rumbling white clouds, stained by coloured lights, inflated until they filled the club. For a moment the dancers were obliterated. Then the music began to climb again and a figure burst through the clouds, dead centre, his arms outstretched in a crucifix, his long hair covered by a yellow sou'wester. The music reached 125bpm and the crowd let off aerosol-powered car horns, blowing whistles as they thumped their bodies. A resonant thrill of dense electricity charged the club. Estella felt it squeeze the breath right out of her body. She could use a drink.[77]

This passage is in keeping with *délire*, Lecercle writing how '*délire* pervades the text, dissolves the subject, threatens to engulf the reader in its disaster, yet saves him – and the text – at the last moment, by preserving an appearance of order, a semblance of linguistic organization'.[78] We can see from Blincoe's evocative description how this dancefloor can indeed be chaos theory made manifest, but for Blincoe there remains the need to affirm – and 'preserve' in Lecercle's terms – naturalistic narrative order. In this way, he renders that chaos linguistically understandable, as opposed, for instance, to Noon's willingness to disturb the natural order in works such as the non-linear *Cobralingus*, or indeed Welsh's preference for product-placing references to real-world music tracks. The music is grandiose but non-specific, but whether described or implied, it is interesting to note the passage resolving, solidly, with the character's continued need for intoxication.

Bricks-and-mortar pointillism

Beyond the beat, music is also built into the physical architecture constructed in this novel, with two key locales: the nightclub Gravity, and the bar Warp, based, according to Blincoe, on the Haçienda nightclub and its offshoot bar project, Dry.[79] Interestingly, Blincoe himself can no longer recall which was which, only agreeing in conversation that 'one was the Dry Bar, the other was the Haçienda'.[80] Blincoe's recollection can here ally with my own retro-participant observation in order to piece together the reality. For even if the names have changed, a cognizant reader can certainly recognize real Mancunian club spaces within the novel, and it is indeed Gravity that mirrors the Haçienda, and Warp that plays the part of Dry. For instance, with Gravity we are taken into 'a room the size of an aircraft hangar',[81] which broadly reflects the dimensions of the Manchester nightclub, the space described in Chapter 3 that was formerly a yacht showroom. Further, we are then taken 'to a dim bar below the dance floor',[82] which would certainly be the Gay Traitor, a separate bar area of the nightclub. In comparison, we find that 'the WARP was a converted furniture shop, around three times as deep as it was broad. The granite bartop to her left ran along the whole length of the whole building. The style of the bar was what they termed post-industrial.'[83] Again, this description would be familiar to patrons of Dry.[84]

Such details form what this book will now define as *narrative pointillism*. In terms of its use in fine art, the term 'pointillism' denotes a form of impressionism where the whole image is constructed by the accumulated layering of single dots of paint. Progressing to fiction, it is this level of precise and considered detail that is evoked in the work of Blincoe, a kind of accumulative verisimilitude achieved by placing dots of descriptive detail upon the canvas of the page; those dots combining in order to construct the transcendental whole. This notion of verisimilitude also dovetails with Blincoe's concern for naturalism, in cleaving close to the truth of the scene, even if at times that admittedly necessitates more of an *acid naturalism*. Lecercle cites Julia Kristeva's work on verisimilitude and also channels French writer Raymond Roussel's 'fascination with technical descriptions, with details, and particularly with cliches'.[85] Here we see how an author might deploy such real-world details in order to engender verisimilitude and render the natural, urban environment within the text. Lecercle agrees verisimilitude and naturalism are linked, suggesting: 'The literary discourse of verisimilitude, then, lies beyond the opposition between truth and falsehood: it has the appearance of truth, is more "natural" than truth.'[86] One can therefore trace this essentially natural effect, created by the deployment of narrative pointillism, *allegedly* truthful detail (such as the names of clubs) set in the foreground against the broader diegetic wash of music in the background of the text.

Again, it is important to reinforce these ideas with examples, especially where such specific use of detail also extends from broader nightclub architecture, to drugs and drug practices. In terms of narrative pointillism, we are told by the character Cozy that 'a girl died in the Gravity. She had an allergic reaction to Ecstasy'.[87] As identified in Chapter 3, Blincoe here refers to the 1989 death of Clare Leighton in the Haçienda, the UK's first recorded Ecstasy-related death. However, as Lecercle points out, such verisimilitude does necessarily always hold true, or indeed need to hold true, to reality. The key villain in the novel, and target for assassination by Estella, is club owner John Burgess. We are told that in Warp, 'John Burgess had placed his own picture high on the wall where he could smile beatifically down on his punters'.[88] In this reading

Burgess would be playing the fictional role of co-owner of both Dry and the Haçienda – Anthony H. Wilson – and again, retro-participant observation would remove this photo from Warp and place it, instead, in Gravity.[89] (Of course it would take the most analytic of cultural pedants to find his or her reading of the novel disrupted by such erroneous detail.)

In essence, why construct fictional club spaces when you can describe real-world venues, from memory? The subsequent sketches of detail on the page can then construct, in three dimensions, the architecture of believable club spaces and further, fill those spaces with a real, if opaque, diegetic soundtrack: narrative pointillism contributing to the overall truthful, and naturalistic, rendering of the novel's nightclub infrastructure. This process further reinforces subterranean knowledge for the reader of the text, and ultimately enables authenticity. The venues come across as real world because they *are* real world.

Identity and escape: Hauntology and the spectral return of the author

Through his looking glass, Lecercle sees that 'a spectre is haunting structuralism, the spectre of the subject'.[90] Beyond the subject we might also be able to discern another spirit haunting the abandoned house of structuralism, that of the author and the cultural context in which they work, influencing the construction of their texts. In his seminal essay 'The Death of the Author', Barthes argues that the focus in the linguistic/ knowledge exchange must be re-balanced towards the reader of texts, rather than writer. Barthes suggests: 'To give a text an Author is to impose a limit on that text, to furnish it with a final signified, to close the writing.'[91] I challenge that dialectically, aiming instead to reconnect text to context and, in a sense, using a theoretical defribillator on the author in order to bring them back from the death.

Blincoe's own construction of context, for instance, adds greatly to a reading of his texts, specifically revealing the role EDMC played in his intermedial creativity:

> It was virtually my entire life. My then girlfriend had a boring office job so we were living for the weekend, talking about nightclubs and just being aware in the late 80s into the 90s there was a very strong feeling that Manchester was the most exciting place to be. It didn't cross my mind not to write about nightclubs.[92]

This concern with naturalism is strikingly similar to comments Welsh makes to Redhead, reported in Chapter 6,[93] and also to Hanif Kureshi's novel *The Buddha of Suburbia*,[94] where Kureshi uses 'rock and pop performance as metaphors for the complexity and ambiguity of gender and sexuality identities'.[95] A naturalistic approach does not necessarily suggest reflecting nature, per se, in terms of the trees and fields of the countryside but rather, reality as it is lived at that time, and the soundtrack to that reality. Certainly, in line with the analysis of the Kureshi novel, any analysis of *Acid*

Casuals needs to recognize the role identity plays within the text, especially as it forms such a focal point for the novel's principal protagonist. Of part Surinamese descent, Paul Sorel already contains a rich genetic heritage, which he further subverts by his gender reassignment surgery. This overt toying with notions of identity contributes to the narrative tension, as previous friends and indeed lovers fail to recognize Estella, née Paul, such has been the success of her operation. Evidently Blincoe's primary concern is the fluid spectrum of both ethnicity and sexuality and in the character of Estella; for instance, we have someone who is able to disguise both, now heterosexual in this newly configured gender assignment. Chapter 3 of this book considered the notion of the dancefloor as tabula rasa, a great leveller in terms of gender and ethnicity. *Acid Casuals* features principal characters from white, black and Asian backgrounds and the interplay of these characters within the novel stands as a naturalistic simulacrum of the interrelation of such ethnicities in the city of Manchester at this *fin de millennium* period. In telling the stories of the black community of Moss Side, or the Asian community in Rochdale (with which Blincoe would obviously be very familiar), the novel stands as a firmly naturalistic representation, in fictional terms, of a recognizable northern environment. Therefore, Blincoe is again not imposing an overt theoretical concern for ethnicity or gender on the text with any rigid or conscious authorial pressure but is once again representing in a naturalistic context the actuality of the city's dancefloors at that time, with all the attendant rich mix of sexualities and ethnicities. This was the society that Blincoe wanted to reflect, forming the real-world context he describes in fiction.

That is not to say, however, that these acid casuals are entirely happy within their identities: the theme of escape also looms large. The New Puritan Manifesto holds that 'the truth is not that fiction can be escapist, but that fiction embodies a desire for freedom',[96] and Chapter 3 of this book discerned how the dancefloor itself formed the locus for weekend escape, and that escape was further enabled by intoxication. As elegant and esoteric a plot device as this might be, again it merely stands as a naturalistic reflection of the diversity and identity anarchy of the dancefloor, as experienced by Blincoe at that time. Estella 'escaped' her hometown, and ultimately her assigned gender; characters such as Yen, Junk (who also appears in *Manchester Slingback*) and Theresa simply find personal escape from the pernicious clutches of the quotidian in the vibrant community formed on the dancefloor. Many readers will be readily able to identify themselves and their fellow clubbers in these dancefloor characters and their varied escapes, only reinforcing the sense of enlightenment they themselves gleaned – the moment they first stepped past designer Ben Kelly's industrial bollards and onto the dancefloor of the Haçienda.[97] Indeed beyond the parameters of the weekend, these subterranean Dancefloor-Driven novels must in themselves be seen as literary escape routes from the supraterranean life as it is lived, for most people, Monday-to-Friday.

Acid delirium and Blincoe's casual style aesthetic

Lecercle makes an apposite point about the relationship of language and identity in stating how 'meddling with language, risking *délire* and madness, means accepting disintegration and struggling to restore the unity of the self'.[98] Although interested in the disruption of identity, and rendering club scenes in a discordant, delirious way, Blincoe seems less interested in disrupting language, beyond the experimental chapter that Blincoe indicates was written *déliriously*. By his own admission, Blincoe would agree that a naturalistic approach requires, by definition, less artifice in the writing, with no sense that the author might interrupt the reading experience, reveal himself in any overt way or disrupt his own writing for effect – as Noon, and indeed Welsh, frequently do – in the construction of a cohesive narrative structure. In other words, the reading process should be smooth and the writer should keep clear of their story. There is no typographic innovation for instance, and no attempt to mimic the techniques of musical production, although there is some sense that, like Jack Kerouac, Blincoe writes with a certain rhythmic cadence – again reinforcing the Derridean sense of music behind the writing. For instance, in *Acid Casuals* Blincoe writes: 'Ragga boomed out of a monster sound-system, the walls were sweating in time to the music.'[99] If the beat itself has become electronic, the Beat resonance remains, with Blincoe affirming of that sentence: 'I knew when I wrote it that it was something that I'd written like 14 years earlier, when I was going through more of a Kerouac period.'[100]

Kerouac was described as a typist rather than a writer by Truman Capote,[101] and similar criticism was interestingly levelled at Blincoe, as he mentions in his interview with Redhead: 'People keep describing me as a journalist, but I am not a journalist. [...] I want to write what the immediate, contemporary history is but through fiction',[102] his comments redolent of Hunter S. Thompson's aphorism about the slippery relationship between historical truth, fiction and non-fiction. This ebb and flow between fiction and non-fiction, and indeed between high art and pulp, is a key focus of my research and something that I will explore in the conclusions of both this chapter and the overall book. Even fielding such similar criticisms serves to draw Blincoe closer to the likes of Thompson and Kerouac, linking Beat, and Chemical, Generations.[103] Blincoe is certainly explicit about his interest in the Beat Generation, both in his discussions with Redhead and in our own conversation, remarking:

> It did interest me. I didn't actually try it. It wasn't that I wanted to do things like Burroughs but I was more aware that ... Kerouac was very, very romantic and directly a very romantic writer, with spontaneous outpourings of powerful feelings and he wanted to write from a place that was beyond his consciousness.[104]

Blincoe's Beat connections also take a direct, and more intimate, turn. In Chapter 3, this book located William S. Burroughs at the Haçienda in October 1982.[105] We can also place Blincoe in the same space. Blincoe reports to Redhead: 'One of the big things in my life was seeing Burroughs read in 1982 at the Haçienda',[106] and following our interview we can locate the two authors even more precisely: on the same staircase in the venue, before Burroughs spoke, a literal near collision of musico-literary scenes, of Beat and rave. Blincoe reinforces Noon's comments from the end of the last chapter in recalling: 'It was very cool. He was quite an old man and rather frail but he had an incredible stage presence.'[107]

Acid Casuals stands as fictional ethnography, then, but also as a novel very much rooted in real places, populated by real people, listening to real music. Keeping close to such lived experiences – on the part of the author and their own embedded experience – creates a literary intimacy, and legitimacy, which further engenders authenticity in terms of cultural formation. Describing an essentially urban tale, this approach is nevertheless very much rooted in nature, even if that is reconstructed as an urban, perhaps even acid, naturalism. The robust nature of the crime plot at the heart of this novel allows for these further flights of narrative fancy, yet throughout Blincoe is concerned with truthfully reflecting the people and environment of his contemporaneous culture, and the soundtrack that lies beneath it all, rather than warping such contingencies beyond the natural. If the reader witnesses the transformative potential of pharmaceutical drugs, therefore, it starts from, and returns to, a fixed point in Blincoe's perceived reality. There is nothing that happens in this novel, therefore, which might not be imagined possible, in real terms, by its readership. Colourful characters inhabit this novel because there were colourful characters on Manchester's dancefloors at the time. Plot and character can therefore be exaggerated, so long as the actual texture, and architecture, of the novel's environment – its narrative foundations – is robust and represented authentically in terms of the sights and sounds and mis en scène (in cinematic terms) of the piece.

This chapter has now tested how Blincoe uses music diegetically and what effects might be created by such a deployment. For Blincoe, electronic dance music is used as a musico-literary tool as though he were an author DJ, providing a soundtrack, spinning sonic shorthand for a participant, cognizant readership. The associated drug consumption that accompanies that music and the buildings in which these practices take place are the narrative bricks and mortar used by Blincoe to render, authentically, the infrastructure of the novel. However, the play of music within and beneath the text of *Acid Casuals* is fundamentally more fluid and hypogean; textual and indeed *sub*textual. In this novel it stands as a naturalistic device to engender proximity between author and reader, as subterranean soundtrack. In this way Blincoe creates a 'writerly text', in Barthes terms, or one where the reader is afforded more agency in its consumption, by virtue of participant engagement in the story and its diegetic music, and in full control of the volume.

Manchester Slingback and *Jello Salad*

Gerry Smyth reports that 'novelists from every generation, working within every genre, have responded to the power of music by incorporating it into their narratives, by trying to harness its techniques and effects, and by attempting to recreate the emotions that come to be associated with particular musical styles, forms or texts'.[108] This is certainly pertinent with two Blincoe novels where use of a background soundtrack is strategic, in order to evoke a sense of a time and place. In *Manchester Slingback* the reader is taken to Manchester's Gay Village,[109] across two time zones: a period roughly equating to the latter 1990s when Blincoe wrote the novel, and a flashback to the Village in 1981.[110] The flashback period therefore falls slightly earlier than most of the Dancefloor-Driven Literature under consideration, although a form of EDMC is certainly evoked in order, once again, to construct this literary soundscape. Equally, passages from *Jello Salad* will be explored as the club scenes are demonstrably 'rave' events, but this novel is less useful as it marks the beginning of a geographic turn in Blincoe's work, the focus moving away from Manchester and away from the club scene. Again, this chapter uses these novels in order to register the role of detail, and now sonic detail, in the construction of a naturalistic environment within Blincoe's fiction, one with which the reader will feel empathetic, bringing to the page their empirical experience of the landscape described.

When detailing a popular culture, Blincoe reveals a homological web of cultural connections – the mixed interplay of music, fashion, drug consumption and behavioural patterns – that contributes to the clubbers' social practices and the naturalistic context of the dancefloor. Building on the Shakespearian notion of naturalism – that the aim of art must be to keep close to reality – to 'hold a mirror up to nature',[111] Blincoe instead constructs a mirrored wall, next to the dancefloor. The context might be fictional, but this is vivid, ethnographic fiction, this auteur once again embedded within the subterranean realm, establishing a better vantage point from which to subjectively, and reflexively, report. In a semantic reading to cultural studies, Matthew Collin identifies his sense of 'sub' cultures where behaviour is 'sur'-real within a 'mythologized underground',[112] which Hebdige distinguishes from the superficiality of surfaces.[113] Blincoe writes new club characters into this, metaphorically speaking, darkened cultural underground, where such subterranean shadows might inculcate hegemonic mythmaking. This is undoubtedly bolstered by establishing scenes where DJs ply their art within real-world club environments, some thinly concealed behind assumed names, some spaces simply given their real names, for example Manchester venues Rotters, and Pips. This strategy may be understood, in the same way as Welsh's literary product placement, in allowing an informed, participant readership a shortcut to the psyche of the characters through *a priori* understanding gleaned from, for instance, media representations of such clubs.

Within these spaces Blincoe then places a linguistic needle upon revolving, real-world music, sometimes specific: 'The last bars of Sammy Davis Junior's "Rhythm of Life"',[114] sometimes incongruous: James Last, Average White Band, Van Morrison.[115] More often with Blincoe, such aural articulations are, again, expressed via literary diegesis: 'Boy's Town, Hi-NRG disco stripped to its essentials', 'lumpy chunks of melody, bite-sized pieces. [...] The sound of a needle dragged across its groove and bunny-hopping into another beat', or simply 'The deafening fucking music'.[116] This music is spun out to a crowd often under the influence of real-world intoxicants, in a homological sense 'mixing the hardest sounds with the more profitable drugs',[117] where in *Jello Salad* Ecstasy-fuelled 'dancers had the same look: mad staring eyes, the gallons of sweat running off their faces and washing their heads away to grinning skulls'.[118] This pharmaceutical cornucopia might be revealed even within one line, for instance in *Jello Salad* where the reader is told it was 'Mannie's plan to keep smoking the dope. Once the munchies had cancelled the effects of the amphetamine, they'd be able to eat the cake.'[119] In this sense, Blincoe works Hebdige's 'invisible seam between language, experience and reality',[120] to once again create a naturalistic presentation of the dancefloor milieu and its intoxicatory practices.

Smyth writes that 'certain methodological parameters are essential before any meaningful analysis may commence: we need a subject, a period, as debate, a critical language and so on',[121] and that certainly holds true for the tight parameters of *Manchester Slingback*, its key narrative concern, as Blincoe remarks, the policing of Manchester in the pre-rave scene of the early 1980s.[122] The narrative unravels, like *Acid Casuals*, in the immured locus of nightclubs, principally the gay cabaret club Good-Days, based once again on very real Village venue Napoleons, a stage upon which Blincoe places his characters, co-conspirators in a weekend revolution.[123] Principal character Jake Powell appears in both chronological periods within the novel: in the latter when he has to return to Manchester to confront his demons, a trope of escape and return that recurs in the works of Noon, Blincoe and, indeed, Welsh, as well as in the lives of the authors themselves, who all moved away from the place where they grew up. In the chronologically earlier story, a teenage Jake Powell and his friends inhabit the haunts of the Village, at turns sleazy and fabulous, devoted equally to the needs of the moment (in itself a Beat concern) and the pursuit of the party. Oppositional forces can here be located between hegemonic, heterosexual daylight and that of the homosexual night-time world – the linguistic and literal frontline between the apparently boring and straight, and the bent or kinky – the argot of the dancefloor used to obfuscate the subterranean from the dominant power structures operating in the supraterranean realm. Key to both periods is the need for this marginalized community to party, perpetually oppositional and able to 'push back' against the character John Pascal: police inspector, religious zealot and frontman for the city's chief constable. In contrast to characters with invented names, this chief constable is actually identified within the novel as the very real 'Chief Constable James Anderton, spokesman for God in Greater Manchester',[124] the city's controversial 'God's Cop', who genuinely felt he was channelling God in his policing of the city.[125] This would evidently resonate with any reader with a connection to Manchester in this period, with James Anderton also immortalized in the 1990 Happy Mondays song 'God's Cop'.

While to a certain extent the beat endures, when Jake returns he finds the Gay Village much changed, now a plastic theme park to homosexuality.[126] Again, it is the level of detail within the physical architecture of the story that is evoked, in the precision of this narrative pointillism, with Blincoe writing of Jake's earlier time in the Village that 'these streets, this rigid Village grid like a down-sized New York, he knew every grate, every manhole cover, even the distance in high-heeled feet from block to block',[127] the author's eye for detail supported by my own retro-participant observation.[128] Blincoe assembles references to bands, brands and popular culture icons to populate the canvas of the text: everything from TV soap opera *Coronation Street* to Iggy Pop to more illicit contraband. When reading the novel it is, at times, as though Blincoe were operating a product placement service for the counterculture – the credit on his side of that exchange being a certain engendering of verisimilitude, in creating a novel that feels authentic in the hands of a participant reader. This stretches once again to intoxicants, in a novel where drug consumption is conspicuous in its ubiquity. The drugs are many and varied. For instance, we are told: 'Jake watched as Johnny rolled a something-denomination Deutschmark note into a tube, took a breath, and whooshed the speed down: it took him just two smooth goes. He finished by wiping the side of his Pips card down his tongue, grinning while he did it.'[129] The narrative is rooted in such specifics, moored by detail, reassuring the reader in the almost musical restatement of leitmotif to reinforce the legitimacy and authenticity of the world described.

In music terms, this is once again a drama with a more ambient (in terms of positioning rather than specific genre) literary diegetic soundtrack, as music leaks silently from the linguistic speakers wired into the fictionally rendered nightclubs of the Gay Village. Smyth argues that 'music offers the narrator a "home" – an absolute centre of value and meaning that remains stable – to which he believes he can always (re)turn, no matter the changes overtaking his country, his city, or himself'.[130] If non-specific, the music is indeed stable, and hard-wired into the prose, integrated into the text and integral to the rooting of the characters. Further, the reader hears the beat of the novel channelled through the characters' own auditory equipment: 'Jake passed through a low arch and, for a moment, two different songs blended together … Bowie singing "Golden Years" and, beneath it, the bass-heavy hum of a darker track.'[131] Further still, as with other examples I have referenced throughout this book, at times we also perceive the music metadiegetically through the filter of Jake's drug consumption, sharing his subjective experience and once again drawing the reader closer to the naturalistic reality constructed by the words: 'Jake crossed from the carpet to the wood-parquet floor and started feeling for a time signature, knowing it would be much, much slower than he expected … the speed was blowing through his body, gale-force five.'[132]

Moving on to *Jello Sallad*, and we find Blincoe beginning to move his narrative away from both Manchester and the dancefloor, in a career that will ultimately see the author move entirely away from fiction, and to a more politically oriented non-fiction. Most of the action in this novel takes place in London, and revolves around not the pulse of the dancefloor, but the heat of the restaurant kitchen, an evolution even noted in the text, where 'the idea of a nightclub was scaled down to a restaurant-it was just a case of being practical'.[133] However, Blincoe cannot help but design his principal characters as Mancunians, and to top and tail the narrative with nightclub scenes. Indeed, as with *Acid Casuals*, the denouement of the novel takes place in a rave. Therefore, although overall the novel has less resonance for this study, these nightclub scenes are worth examining, as they are chronologically much more part of the 'rave' incarnation of EDMC, in a story where one of the principal characters – like Carl Ewart in the Irvine Welsh novel *Glue* – is himself a club DJ. Sarah Thornton identifies 'the figure of the DJ with his finger on the pulse of the crowd',[134] adding 'the DJ became a guarantor of subcultural authenticity'.[135] These are both Dancefloor-Driven and emotive connections, here rendered in literary form, where for Blincoe the DJ is now a literary construct, spinning this silent diegetic soundtrack within the novel. We also witness how subcultural capital can enable the accumulation of actual economic capital, as shown by Phillips and his account of the rise of the 'superstar DJ' through the 1990s.[136] Again, and in an electronic context, this adds new layers to the analysis of music in literature, where at its heart resides this dancefloor DJ deity, eulogized in this scene in *Jello Salad*, where

> at the very centre of the arch, there was the DJ standing at his decks. The guy should have been dwarfed but the arch gave him a kind of grandeur: like Caesar or Stalin. Except this crowd was no disciplined mob-it was a giant insect culture brought out of a microscope, an alien swarm on wings.[137]

Once again, the soundtrack is evoked via suggestion, in this process of literary diegesis that might, for instance, describe music by reference to what it is not: 'This was something else entirely. It wasn't even house music. This was, according to a word he'd heard but never quite believed, the Jungle.'[138] In another scene Blincoe describes how 'the acid house tape in his Walkman was definitely making his head pound,'[139] using music to engender empathy with the character Hogie. However, although, like Welsh, Blincoe uses music to denote different taste hierarchies, here there is often only the implication of sound rather than the precise device of naming specific tracks, as narrative shorthand. In semiotic terms, Blincoe sites good music on the side of the nocturnal world – the 'Jungle' of the *Jello Salad* rave,[140] and the glamorous pulse of the infamous Roxy Room at Pips nightclub – as irresistible when compared to the blandness of, for instance, Pascal's Methodist hymns in *Manchester Slingback*. Notions of verisimilitude again come to the fore. In presuming *a priori* knowledge of (and therefore confident in describing) the techniques and musical ammunition of the DJ, Blincoe strives for an authentic experience, in the process establishing a joint account of subcultural capital to which both author and audience have equal access.

Especially useful is the way we can compare Blincoe's representation of the same real-world Mancunian club space, Pips, in these two novels, a further example of architectural narrative pointillism. In *Manchester Slingback*, for instance, the space appears as the 1980s iteration of Pips, where 'each of the separate dance-floors was set into a grotto, their walls painted in course white stucco.'[141] In the 1990s world of *Jello Salad*, meanwhile, we are told that 'the place was scooped out of the building's Victorian foundations and styled along some kind of crypt theme with a maze of roughcast fiberglass corridors. Manie stood with his back to plastic grotto wall, waiting.'[142] If the beat has progressed from Bowie and Roxy Music to 'slow, deep, House veined through with trippy beeps,'[143] the environment remains structurally much the same,[144] centred, once again, around the sacred, safe space of the dancefloor and the hedonistic practices of those who dance upon it: 'Fuck, Hogie thought. I fucking love this. Woo Woo. He propelled himself backwards, into the pulp core of dancers hoping the crush of bodies would form a protective circle.'[145] As this book will demonstrate, the adjectival use of the word 'pulp' in itself has deep resonances.

Smyth usefully critiques the relationship between music and the novel as equivalent to the relationship between the body and the head.[146] This chapter further extends this notion to a broader consideration of the urban lower stratum, which usefully segues with Blincoe's Dada-esque concern for a pulp 'low-culture' where, in these undignified realms of popular culture so removed from the heady heights of the conservatoire, we find grotesque intoxication, the lowering of language to the argot of the gutter and the mass-produced music that so troubled Theodor Adorno.[147]

Genre melding: Northern noir and pulp fiction

British broadsheet newspaper *The Observer* refers to Blincoe as 'British noir',[148] concerned, like the Beats, with Kerouac's 'myth of the rainy night',[149] with romancing the nocturnal. *Jello Salad* was published as part of Serpent's Tail 'Mask Noir' series and Blincoe adds that 'by the mid 80s all the interesting novels I was reading were American crime novels',[150] citing the likes of authors Elmore Leonard and James Ellroy. However, it is French theory that continues to hover over this writing. At the 2012 Avanca Cinema Conference, Dennis Broe presented a paper which convincingly argued (certainly in cinematic terms) that noir was not born of 1950s Hollywood but 1930s France.[151] Extending this further, there are also commonalities between Blincoe's novels and what has ironically been called the 'clubland' fiction of the interwar period, which would, in turn, influence authors such as James Bond creator Ian Fleming.[152] In this homological mix of late nights and seediness, clublife and crime, we can further define Blincoe's writing as a very particular *northern noir*,[153] where Saddleworth Moor might replace, for instance, New York's Lower East Side, where the music is not frenetic jazz but dark, *dysco-pic* electronica.

This thinking now takes a further step in judging whether, as northern noir, these novels can be classified as 'pulp fiction'.[154] In terms of a definition, Blincoe himself helps here, commenting that 'pulp fiction would describe any kind of cheap popular literature. In praising that, I would say that the things – like the girls, the vicarious pleasures, the contrariness, the eroticism – they're not bad things in literature and it's wrong to exclude them'.[155] Literature, then, should be inclusive, from its pop cultural references to its inherent soundtrack. Blincoe argues in our meeting that

> I was writing crime fiction rather than literary fiction because I was bored of the English literary fiction of the 1980s. I would have said I was in opposition to it, and happy to identify with strains that were kind of counterculture, like Irvine ... those drug and nightclubbing things of the 1990s.[156]

One might start this argument with the paratextual matter of *Manchester Slingback*.[157] In her *Independent* newspaper interview with Blincoe, Katy Guest indicates that it is Nicholas Blincoe himself who features on the cover of the 1998 edition of the novel,[158] in T-shirt and jeans on the front; fishnets and cheap dress on the reverse.[159] Certainly this might be seen as keeping in line with certain 'trashier' tenets of the pulp, and dada, aesthetic, if intriguingly oppositional to Blincoe's own foregrounding of the word 'puritan'.[160] In the paratextual matter of *Acid Casuals*, the author biography describes Blincoe as the 'High Priest of the New Pulp Literature', while on the back cover, *The Observer* pull quote adds that his work is 'British noir for the *Pulp Fiction* generation',[161] referring to the 1994 Quentin Tarrantino film of the same name. Certainly, in a literary sense Blincoe shares aesthetic traits – in terms of evoking eulogies to the B-Movie – with that contemporary cinema auteur, Blincoe remarking he is 'aware of him on your shoulder'.[162] (Figures 8.1 and 8.2).

In positively embracing the pulp, Blincoe certainly stands counter to the literary sense of canon, perhaps to the academy itself, arguments will be further developed in the conclusion. In terms of his countercultural impulses, that position would seem to be demonstrably held, Blincoe argues: 'I also had an intellectual snobbery that if you only thought that literature was the stuff sanctioned by traditions and universities, then you really weren't all that clever.'[163] However, with Blincoe's intellectual processing of culture, and his integration of principally French philosophy, and arguably French noir impulses, we might turn this argument around, in divining an inherently intellectual experiment in this drive down towards Oscar Wilde's 'gutter'.[164]

Whether, in fact, high or low brow, in now concluding this admittedly limited overview of Blincoe's first three novels, I should restate that the purpose of this chapter was never, in any case, to rank the literary position of the work of Nicholas Blincoe,

Figure 8.1 Front cover of Nicholas Blincoe, *Manchester Slingback* (London: Pan, 1998), with Blincoe featured on the cover.

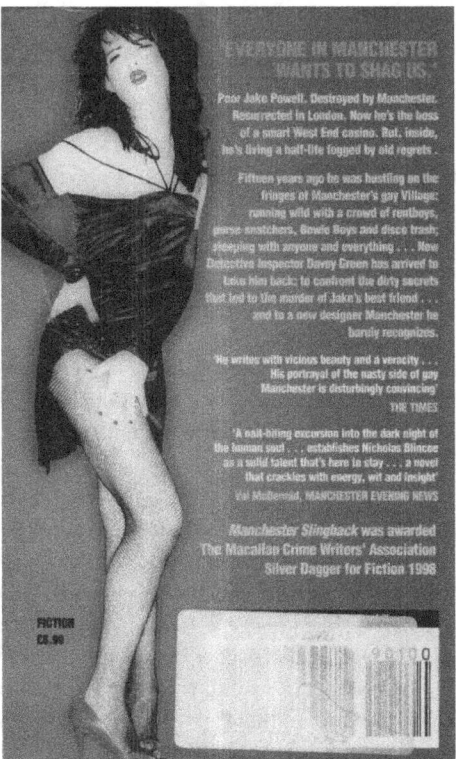

Figure 8.2 Back cover of Nicholas Blincoe, *Manchester Slingback* (London: Pan, 1998), featuring Blincoe as model.

per se. Instead, it set out to identify the existence of a diegetic EDMC soundtrack within his literature and to analyse what the narrative impact of such a soundtrack might be, in terms of naturalistic use of sonic impulses in the rendering of an authentic subterranean environment within his fiction.

While Smyth decodes music as inspiration, metaphor and formal influence in what he calls the 'music-novel',[165] Blincoe does not use music so much figuratively in terms of its semiotic referent, or mechanically, in terms of the construction of the text. Rather the use of music is contextual, perhaps *sub*textual, in that it provides a diegetic soundtrack in the subcutaneous matter of the narrative: driven into the hypogean level of the text with a narrative needle, deployed as the beat beneath the page to naturalistically reinforce the subterranean landscape. Blincoe's aesthetic project certainly shares the creative impulses of Dancefloor-Driven Literature but it is more overtly determined to represent things as they are: a proximate form of naturalism as opposed, for instance to the grotesque hyperrealism of Welsh or the fabulist cyber fantasy of Noon. Such naturalism is constructed from points of detail – a comprehensive narrative pointillism that includes, in the foreground of the narrative, the drugs the characters imbibe and the dancefloors they step upon – set against which is this deep sweep of diegetic music.

Already raised as idea in Chapter 5, although philology itself is arguably an antiquated theory in this digital world, it can have relevance when repurposed for such subcultural archivism, for subterranean cultural archaeology. Here we return to a key concept of this book: that one can learn truths about a popular music culture through its literary re/presentation. In terms of subcultural philology, therefore, this book contends that society might actually be better viewed, and understood, from the street level – and indeed below-street level – perspective of this pulp fiction. In this reading, the enculturation and exchange of knowledge is driven upward rather than down, the beat rising inelegantly up from the gutter rather than drifting effortlessly down from the conservatoire, in what Blincoe defines in our conversation as 'this idea that the most exciting things reach from below and achieve critical mass amongst people before they break out'.[166] In itself this is an entirely Derridean conceit. In his own reading of Jacques Derrida, Blincoe writes:

> History in an academic sense always means 'recorded history'; ie it must have been something that happened to someone and was noted down, like a tax record, or newspaper report, or eyewitness account, and by extension other cultural marks such as pottery sherds with identifiable patterned features. This means, history is always the history of recorded stuff ('text' in its very broadest sense meaning 'universal database'). This brings in a paradox that history is the marks of present-day, when the present-day is gone. These textual traces of the 'always already past' are Derrida's main interest.[167]

Derrida's concern, with which I agree, therefore necessitates the recalibrating of the significance of this pulp fiction, accelerating up through Bourdieu's hierarchies of taste, achieving critical mass as it does so. In this way, Dancefloor-Driven Literature might then take its rightful place along with Beat Generation and Gonzo fictions in the broader corpus of *cult fiction*, defined by Calcutt and Shephard as 'literature from the margins and extremes'.[168] Blincoe would seem to concur: 'Pulp fiction is the aim to write a kind of brave, intelligent, yet extremely partisan fiction; partisan for a political agenda. And I did think I was writing fiction that would have a cult appeal.'[169] Pulp might refer ostensibly to the quality of the paper in these paperbacks, but not the resilience of this literature in passing through history, preserving cultural code from the underground in a way that much sturdier fiction of the hardback 'canon' can, ironically, not.

This literary underpinning of the pulp requires a critical leap, and aesthetic reappraisal of Wilde's gutter, along with the cultural reinforcing of the seemingly ephemeral, so as to withstand the sometime pernicious passage of time. Blincoe remarks that 'the cultural significance of the 1990s is going to be a lot clearer for people once you get 20 to 25 years past it. It will prove to be of cultural and political significance so people will want to go back to these books.'[170] It is the conclusion, and contention, of this chapter that twenty years beyond the publication of these novels (at the time of writing) people will not only want to go 'back to these books' but that they will *have to*, if they are to understand the processes of EDMC, a music scene of such singular visual spectacle that its homological impulses could sustain not one, but a series of novels, from authors in sufficient number to then further congregate as the literary movement supported in this book.

Returning to an important aspect of the New Puritan Manifesto, Clause Seven contends: 'We recognize that published works are also historical documents. As fragments of our time, all our texts are dated and set in the present day. All products, places, artists and objects named are real.'[171] Here, the verisimilitude, pointillism and what this research has defined as acid naturalism of Blincoe's fiction map perfectly upon the central argument of this book, in terms of the broader resonance of the sonic, then literary, beat from the dancefloor. Important for both archival and literary reasons, the earlier novels of Blincoe stand as archaeological 'fragments' of this era, textual traces, subterranean pottery sherds.

9

Conclusion

Towards subterranean systems theory

Following directly on from the previous chapter, the key question remains: In our current age what is the import, and what in fact are we to do, with these literary pottery shards, now unearthed from the subterranean underground? That is certainly what I set out to explore, in writing this book. I opened this study with the story of my own motivation in conducting this research, in my desire to dig down; X marking the spot of a very precise intersection, this dark and magical crossroads that mark the point where the twin trails of words and music meet, and cross, that has fascinated me throughout my life. It fascinated me as a student of literature in Manchester, consumed at the same time by the beat of electronic dance music in the city; it fascinated me as a music journalist, giving me my first career in attempting to capture that music in words; it fascinated me as a PR, looking to describe music in order to explain it commercially; it fascinated me as a lecturer, entrusted with the task of teaching others how to write about music; and finally, it continues to fascinate me as writer and academic.

It is in this final stage that I am now trying to wrestle some kind of logic and sense onto this essential relationship, interested in looking at one particular scene to reveal how music is sustained, and nurtured by the English language. The ultimate endgame is to conceive of some new approach to analysing this crossroads, and that is what this final concluding chapter will do, driving a new stake into the ground, marking the spot. As I conceded in the Introduction, I am not the first to reach these crossroads. From Calvin Brown's intermedial urtex of 1948, through Wolf and Scher and the word and music studies of the 1990s to the concurrent publication of a number of key texts in recent years, other writers have shared my fascination with how, and indeed why, we write about music. We can even take this discourse back to Walter Pater's aphorism of 1877 that opened this book. Perhaps writing, like all art, truly does aspire to the condition of music. After all, Edison invented the phonograph, the antecedent of the Technics 1210 turntable, in the exact same year Pater penned those words. None of these writers, however, and none of these texts, have truly considered this intermedial intersection in the context of the beat of a specifically electronic dance music, and its broader subterranean culture, or indeed dug down into that corpus of literature to the depth that I have attempted in this book.

Certainly, I must first re-emphasize that the overarching strategic ambition of this book was not to assess or pass judgement on the literary quality of the work of Welsh, Noon, Blincoe or indeed any of the other Dancefloor-Driven authors highlighted in this research. Instead, I aimed first to detect the beat of a specifically electronic dance music within literature and then further to consider what role such music might play in that literary text. By bringing together these texts for the first time under the banner of Dancefloor-Driven Literature, this study has also been able to explore how they collectively serve to produce and reproduce the social identities and behaviours associated with a cohesive music culture, bringing new light to what Steve Redhead described as 'the most misunderstood youth cultural phenomenon of the 1990s'.[1]

I will now return to the central questions that drove the research of this book, although my findings will be further developed through this concluding chapter. First, and fundamentally, in authentically telling the story of the dancefloor and the wider subterranean sonic scene evident in the UK between 1988 and 2000, I have argued strongly that – beyond the beat, and towards a more systematic approach – it is entirely possible to appreciate and understand a popular music culture by reference purely to its literary re/presentation. Further, such an understanding operates across two temporal planes: first, in the contemporaneous enculturation of a subterranean scene and beyond that, to the archival role of that literary corpus, moving forwards. This is new terrain. In gathering together these Dancefloor-Driven writers for detailed analysis from a very particular literary approach, I have also been able to define a culturally historic genre that might usefully accommodate these texts. Further, I call for the elevation of that genre within a broader grouping of cult fiction, because of its ability to inculcate and carry cultural code, and thereby evolve this archival role, and importance. In this way, this new corpus might be later received, and processed, with the same reverence saved for more demonstrably 'high culture' texts.

Moving on from that central finding, in further delineating the varied ways in which authors use music within their texts, the book defined, and then deployed, a unique and original taxonomy for the uses of music in literary artefacts: the *figurative*, *mechanical* and *diegetic* use of music in the work of, respectively, Irvine Welsh, Jeff Noon and Nicholas Blincoe. In the twenty-first century, listening to music is as private as reading ever was, although music offers no inherent context. However, having explored, identified and interrogated the different roles that music plays within these texts, and within the broader subterranean scene, the music in Dancefloor-Driven Literature has been proven to stand as content *plus context*. I have also sought to prove that it is possible to detect the beat of electronic dance music in this literature. On occasion this music was indeed literal, and perfectly audible (partly addressing Wolf's claim for 'the theoretical fact that an actual "translation" of music into fiction is impossible'),[2] in the paratextual material of publications from Trevor Miller's *Trip City* to Irvine Welsh's *Ecstasy*. What is more interesting, and ultimately more valuable, however, is the varied ways the writers chosen as case studies have used electronic music tropes within the fiction itself.

It is only now, with the benefits of time, hindsight and an expanding collection of both primary Dancefloor-Driven texts and secondary academic works, that serious attempts can be made to understand the cultural underground's last stand in the twentieth century. Broadly taking place between the Second Summer of Love in 1988 and the change of the millennium, this book has proposed that authors were able to initially tell, and then preserve, stories of the dancefloor, in a prism formed of these secondary cultural artefacts. As noted in Chapter 5, Sarah Champion recollects how someone once told her, 'surely people who go clubbing don't read',[3] compounded by the assertion within the UK's 'style bible' *The Face* that 'the novel form is peculiarly unsuited to tales of club culture'.[4] Similarly, the Blincoe academic José Francisco Fernández cites novelist and literary critic Malcolm Bradbury in detailing how

> British authors were continuing with the old forms, unaware of the fact that the approaching end of the millennium demanded a new literary conscience: 'The world has changed far more than writing has and we haven't yet generated the new writing.'[5]

The Dancefloor-Driven Literature that emerged – as this book contends – with Trevor Miller's *Trip City* in 1989, and developed through the 1990s, disproves the perspective of *The Face*, at the same time supplying precisely the innovative literature Bradbury demanded.

Within this book, I have also demonstrated how such literature, whether short stories or novels, can be gathered together as a distinct genre; indeed, Appendix I is concerned with the process of gathering such texts together. I initially believed that this was the first time such a list had been collated, but was intrigued and excited to read, almost at the end of writing this book, that no less a figure than Steve Redhead had also compiled a list, called 'Further Reading on Clubcultures' at the end of the 'Clubcultures' chapter in his 1997 book *Subculture to Clubcultures*.[6] Although the list is rather short, containing only sixteen titles, and those titles are both fiction and non-fiction, it was nevertheless heartening to see Redhead's own early interest in gathering such literature together, and to see names such as A. D. Atkins, Nicholas Blincoe, Geraldine Geraghty and Douglas Rushkoff included. What Redhead began, Neil Transpontine added to with his *Datacide* article,[7] and I now continue, is only intended as a starting point: an organic list that might grow and evolve as more Dancefloor-Driven texts are published or unearthed, that can then be included.

Now able to be considered, more broadly, as a holistic entity, this corpus then serves these two critical and distinct functions in terms of further theoretical ramifications: the first in terms of contemporaneous enculturation and the society into which the literature was originally published, opening up this secret subterranean world for the non-cognate; the second, a historical function in documenting and preserving a popular culture. Each revolves around the relationship between the text – as potential fiction or as remembered fact – and the reader, always assisted by the presence of a soundtrack (whether implied, or very real). These two functions will now be considered in greater detail.

Contemporaneous enculturation

In terms of the first function, this book advances the theoretical framework of *enculturation* as the mechanism by which an underground popular music culture moves from 'the private to the public sphere' in Thornton's terms,[8] whether music recording or literary artefact. In reference to the processes of enculturation, it is important to acknowledge and articulate the different levels on which these novels operate, from the niche productions of self-published authors such as Pat W. Hendersen and A. D. Atkins to the more commercial distribution channels enjoyed by Irvine Welsh.[9] As Middleton remarks in *Reading Pop*, 'meaning is always socially and historically situated, and generally specific',[10] but whatever their specific affect, taken together as a holistic, transcendental corpus, such texts can be seen to exhibit important *effects* – in terms of communication, and penetration – of the scene beyond the *sub*terranean and out into the *supra*terranean machinations of hegemonic society.

It is the contention of this book that these cultural artefacts, or 'secondary artistic phenomena',[11] are the means by which a subterranean music culture moves from niche to dominant spheres, from underground to overground; the mechanic whereby – beyond the music itself – the homological variants of a culture are defined, and communicated to both participants and non-cognate cultural voyeurs. Within their pages, these club fictions reproduced and revealed the hitherto secret landscape of the nightclub: the habits of casual and recreational drug consumption, the machinations of the DJ and the impact of electronic dance music on the wider dancefloor, sonic waves that then rippled out across the broader society. Thus it must be argued that this literature – whether Redhead's 'repetitive beat literature',[12] Calcutt and Shephard's 'Chemical Generation literature',[13] or here, Dancefloor-Driven Literature – has revealed the dream of the dancefloor and enabled the cultural coronation of the DJ by unveiling this subterranean realm through words on the page. Once revealed in this way, the culture can then be not only celebrated by an exclusive realm of participant clubbers but also embraced by a circle of readers as broad as a book-buying audience might allow.

The archival function of the saved night

If EDMC in its 'rave' incarnation can be seen as having a defined historical immanence (the liminal thresholds of 1988 and 2000), I now progress in this chapter to a reinforcing of the archival function of that extant literature. With a plurality of voices and experiences, the dancefloor itself becomes a multi-authored text. Everyone adds their memories, or maybe their myths, but nevertheless contributes to the construction of the truth. One must appreciate, however, that memory is fragile and many stories will be lost with diminishing memories, others only preserved temporarily within the ephemeral realm of magazine media.[14] The voice of the novelist rings true, however, and their novels endure – their shelf life beyond that of a newspaper or magazine – where memories might now be more securely preserved in the phenomenological process of writing fiction.

As noted in Chapter 4, *The Face* – a bastion of aesthetic credibility conspicuous by its wealth of subcultural capital – reported that 'there's few things more solid than 200 pages of paperback'.[15] And, after all, that was the point: it *had* to be in literature that the coding of EDMC could be preserved, the novel, as compared to the magazine, proven to be a substantial enough medium to carry that subterranean code. At this point, it will be apposite to return one final time to journalist Hunter S. Thompson, who famously observes that 'the best fiction is far more true than any kind of journalism – and the best journalists have always known this',[16] while Redhead brings this idea to the club culture sphere when asking novelist Alan Warner if fiction is 'a way of telling contemporary history better'.[17] A central conclusion of this research is that one better understands the experience, the myths and the reality of EDMC through its *fictional* re/presentation; these literary artefacts robust enough to carry the coding for the scene in the words locked within, for future generations to decode.

Jacques Derrida deconstructs the specific foregrounding of written, rather than spoken, language and makes the attendant suggestion that the story of human society might be embedded, and decoded, through text. In terms of revealing the truths of, specifically, a popular music culture via its literary output, this process has been further identified in this study as *subterranean philology*, cultural-historical archaeology digging not into the ground, but into the words on the page. Passing back in time through the MIPC to the CCCS, Mark Duffett notes that Stuart Hall had an interest in 'the politically persuasive nature of texts',[18] arguing: 'He saw texts as carriers of dominant ideologies that were encoded by their makers and decoded by audiences.'[19] Language, like music, is indeed encoded in a series of signs – whether notes on the stave or words on the page – that might later be received and processed cerebrally, emotionally. While the printed page, even an empty dancefloor, might be said to be ostensibly flat and two-dimensional, the words and worlds described create the third dimension. Folded into the page, we can also add this fourth dimension. Time. Taking this into account, the reader can appreciate that what they are seeing in the words on the page of this literature is not the present, but rather the signifying light from the past. More broadly, cultural knowledge and understanding is itself also transferrable, across time, via its encoding in these durable texts – whether literature or music – and even better when sustained in a combination of the two.

Derrida describes his hypothesis of 'a total and remainderless destruction of the archive';[20] however, a more recent theorist, Nikolina Nedeljkov, conversely celebrates the *future archive*, in the 'redeemed past and reawakened present'.[21] In the context of hip hop as well as electronic dance music, Kodwo Eshun updates this concept with the notion of what might be called *future scratches* when, in terms of journalism, he writes: '*All* today's journalism is nothing more than a giant inertia engine to put the brakes on breaks, a moronizer placing all thought on permanent pause, a *futureshock absorber*, forever shielding its readers from the future's cuts, tracks, scratches.'[22] It was therefore these Dancefloor-Driven authors, and not the journalists of the time, who were preserving future history, future scratches carved in the linguistic grooves of their fictions. Thus, subterranean, underground 'cult' fiction preserves the cultural DNA of dead and dying cultures within its encoded semiotics, within its future scratches. A central conclusion of this book is therefore that Dancefloor-Driven Literature stands as the *archive* of this particular popular music culture, literary amber.

Paul Crosthwaite discusses, in at times pejorative terms, the dangers inherent in an imaginative historicism that might make grand claims when connecting text to context, in his case when examining the hagiographic pop criticism that surrounds the band Joy Division, encoding the 'city's hauntology'.[23] In Liverpool, for instance, the Cavern Club was pulled down, only to be rebuilt, on Matthew Street.[24] In an interview I once conducted with Anthony H. Wilson of Factory Records,[25] he argued that he did not want Manchester to become a cultural mausoleum in the same way, entombing its musical heritage, and Chapter 3 considered how the Haçienda, once built (as the Situationists demanded), was indeed torn down, only to be rebuilt as film set. However, with the Factory Records offices on Charles Street now open as a nightclub (named Fac252, following the Factory cataloguing system), and the planned opening of a theme bar called MADchester, it might be argued that indeed that is now happening to the city.[26] In this sense, even though culture might apparently be torn down architecturally, we still have the authenticity of the literature, in a vault where the veracity of EDMC might be more securely sealed. While the physical infrastructure, and the human participants, of EDMC has changed, therefore – the buildings, as with the memories, eroded – this literature remains trapped in the time of its creation, Blincoe's 'marks of present-day'. One need only open the page to travel back into this time in cultural history. Here, it is also worth noting Middleton's intriguing research on the phonograph, particularly in the way it was initially associated with death, and designed to preserve dead voices.[27] Etymologically, Middleton notes how closely 'groove' and 'grave' are linked, and he cites Friedrich Kittler's notion that 'record grooves dig the grave of the author',[28] in itself echoing Barthes's own 'Death of the Author'.[29] Writing on hauntology, Mark Fisher comments, 'Hauntology is a political gesture: a sign that the dead will not be silenced',[30] and collectively, the members of this generation were all wearing their grooves into the same typographic graves, writing books set to haunt their future in Derridean terms, for a distant post-millennial and post-subcultural readership to discover, dig up, decode.

In terms of the locating of sub- and supra-terranean realms, between the knowing and unknowing reader, someone interested in the UK of the 1990s might well turn to the more literary and readerly texts (in Barthes' terms) of Martin Amis, Julian Barnes and the wider Granta set,[31] although it is arguable what one might truly glean in terms of the specifics of that time in societal history, and certainly its subcultural shadow. Instead, and in order to fully decode and decipher society as it operated within its underground level, a cultural archaeologist, or subterranean philologist might find out about the culture of the street, or indeed what lies beneath the street – that Unholy Trinity of music, literature and intoxication – in turning to the writerly texts of Welsh, Noon and Blincoe. John Berger states that 'art has a historical function, "entirely opposed to art for art's sake". It restores to memory that which has been, or is being, eliminated',[32] while Wolf argues for 'the historical fact that musicalization has indeed repeatedly been attempted in fiction [...] which, due to its manifold uses, sheds light both on individual authors or work and on whole epochs or aesthetic tendencies'.[33] Following Berger's ideas, EDMC and its associated literature and secondary cultural re/presentation has been shown in this book to be fundamental in constructing a sociocultural archive by which that scene might be accessed and understood, once the 'dancers from the dance' have long stepped away from the dancefloor, and the participants have left their nightclubs. I have already introduced Walter Benjamin's notion of the 'saved night' (for Matthew Calarco, in reference to a 'natural world that is sufficient in itself, a world that has value independent of the role it may play as a dwelling place for human beings or as the stage where human history is acted out').[34] Progressing this conceit from nature and on to culture, we find that Benjamin, if unintentionally, provides a conceptual framework for the archival function of these texts. This literature is, in essence, a *save button* for the nocturnal: an archive of subjective, subterranean history – books as subcultural backup – where to access the files one need merely open the page and turn up the volume.

Spectacular subcultures and the dying of the light

In purely visual terms, rave culture may well have hidden from the linear glare of daylight, preferring the artificiality of the illuminated dancefloor. But if we also read 'spectacular' to mean impressive, or astonishing, then certainly this popular music culture successfully integrated both spectacular and countercultural impulses, to weave a locally coherent homology defined by music, fashion and drug practices. As I articulated in Chapter 3, rave culture also contained an inherent political agenda more evolved than that acknowledged by, for example, music writer Simon Reynolds who argues, reductively, against the scene's 'sensations rather than truths, fascination rather than meaning'.[35] To that end it was therefore useful – in terms of my argument and ideological position – to watch the 2019 Jeremy Deller documentary *Everybody in the Place: An Incomplete History of Britain 1984-1992*,[36] and note the very overt 1980s political context for the rave scene established by Deller in that account.

Here it should also be noted that the story of EDMC (even in its more specific rave incarnation) is still ongoing, certainly outlasting other music-based cultures. Media reports of the resurgence of the 'rave' scene in the United States have seen dance music and its broader club culture now repositioned and repurposed as 'EDM', for electronic dance music (in itself, causing an unfortunate overlap with the broader academic study of EDMC).[37] Further, we find this EDM scene centred, somewhat incongruously, around the desert city of Las Vegas, a locus arguably as stranded geographically as it is culturally. In reference to consideration of Ibiza in Chapter 3, in a 2012 *Guardian* article Simon Reynolds argues that Vegas has become 'the Ibiza of North America',[38] and the fact that American revellers in Vegas club spaces, such as Hakkasan and Omnia, now believe that the music of DJs like Tiesto, the Swedish House Mafia and David Guetta forms a new European invasion, rather than what it actually is – a slightly plastic appropriation and reassembling of America's own electronic nu-folk beat – merely the latest misunderstanding in a long line of cultural obfuscation. As detailed in Chapter 3, this misunderstanding is in itself deeply ironic, since this music culture initially emerged from New York, Detroit and Chicago and as such, American audiences are arguably receiving their own culture, reconstituted. However, such a resurgence, still taking place into the third decade of this century, undoubtedly makes this book particularly timely, in terms of its contribution to the ongoing discourse in this area.[39] Indeed, a *New Statesman* article of August 2019, trailed as 'Rebel Energy: The Return of Rave Culture', highlights both the political arguments of the Deller documentary, alongside cultural events such as the *Sweet Harmony: Rave Today* exhibition at the London Saatchi Gallery in 2019, and the movie *Beats*,[40] released in the same year. The standfirst reads: 'The spirit of rave culture is returning to music, film, art and even political protest.'[41]

Beyond EDM, a further conclusion of this book (from a basis of current research and worldwide retro-participant observation) is that – accepting the mutability of a fluid, postmodern context – cultural conditions in our post-millennial digital age will likely not allow for such homogenous subcultural formation in the future, the very term itself now redundant in the post-subcultural theoretical landscape outlined in Chapter 1. EDMC, in its rave format, will then be considered not only a spectacular subculture but also the very last subculture of a scope and scale to be considered such, in Hebdige's terms.[42] Redhead certainly agrees that the rave scene was 'the last counter culture – and much much, more – of the twentieth century'.[43] Necessarily and determinedly culturally historic in this view, and building on Redhead's statement, it is the further conclusion of this book that it is now impossible, in an age of global communities, neo-tribes and hyper-locality, for a subcultural system to assemble with the requisite cultural density to appear 'spectacular'. For a subculture to become spectacular it requires mass; to receive the opprobrium of mass moral panic it requires an essential visibility. Now, and in the future, popular music cultures are likely to be smaller – neo-tribes connecting digitally – hyper-localized and yet globally emancipated, enabled and empowered.[44] Such hyper-locality and global connectivity creates micro-scenes operating in micro-cultural climates; at times almost anonymous and the very antithesis of mass spectacle, as connections are now established across the global, rather than local, village.[45] No longer, therefore, is there the need to dress in the certain way that defines the subcultural tribe to which you swear allegiance, to buy the indispensable magazine that contains the code for how to behave and communicates the co-ordinates for where to assemble. As with the re-birthing of all cultures, the Unholy Trinity of words, beats and intoxicants identified in the Introduction will undoubtedly reform and re-emerge again. It is more that – while equipping the young members of a future society with the requisite subcultural tools – they will likely make a more modest, and localized, noise: connected digitally, if not sartorially.

In a sense, the twenty-year step progression in this study describes an evolution from a music culture that was acoustic (1940s) to electric (1960s) to electronic (1980s). By the time we reach the noughties, the revolution is arguably no longer musical at all, but technological: digital. Society now has to look somewhere other than music to form context for its latest moral panic, in a technological environment where you are more likely to upset your neighbourhood via your phone, than your hi-fi speakers. Theorists outline this new landscape as either *post*-subcultural[46] or *beyond subcultural*,[47] and as outlined earlier, post-subcultural theorists are entirely correct to state that our inexorable drift into a fractured, post-millennial postmodernity has created a mutable set of conditions that no longer allow for analogue, homogenous subcultural formation. In a sense, that is precisely why, in terms of the pre-millennial popular culture analysed in this account, it was ultimately more useful to return to the original subcultural theorists of the CCCS and MIPC, rather than the post-subcultural theorists who, and at times pejoratively, sought to unpack that work. That brings my thinking in line with that of Shildrick and MacDonald who argue: 'Whilst in need of theoretical refinement and empirical renewal, we think some of the broader goals of the CCCS subcultural approach remain valid ones'.[48] To sum up, in a post-millennial and essentially digital environment, I concur with Redhead not only that this was the last great scene of the twentieth century but further that, in our current cultural and technological landscape, it was also the last great subculture we have witnessed, approaching the third decade of this new century.

Subterranean systems theory

I will now consider the implications and possible future utility of the research conducted for this book. In his study, Wolf comments that 'a systematic theory of intermediality has to a large extent as yet to be developed'.[49] This conclusion now provides that theory, addressing the lacuna identified by Wolf in terms of both the taxonomy designed to ascribe the uses of music in Dancefloor-Driven Literature, within a broader subterranean systems theory that reinforces the structural weaknesses in subcultural theory. Taken together, this provides a suitably robust framework for the analysis of the cultural-historic impact of this literature.

In constructing this framework, I made an early methodological decision to firmly reject a structuralist approach, which might seek only to look down to the linguistic nuances of the text and disconnect text from both context and author. In a sense, this research is concerned less with isolating and incubating texts, but in creating links, intertextual, intermedial and intergenerational. Instead, throughout this book a claim has been made for larger systems at work behind the individual function of these works of fiction, building systems that might create dialogic links between, and beyond, those texts. As cultural theorists and linguists we might operate in an environment that is post-structural in many ways, but that does not preclude the construction of such *systems*, which stands, in a postmodern age, as a more satisfying term. This book therefore concerns itself not with structures, but root systems that might, even in terms of semantics, have a more useful application in the twenty-first century. Repositioning a theoretical framework from marketing,[50] systems theory argues that organizations do not operate in a void, and devoid of external factors; rather, they are under the influence of forces that influence both the way they operate within themselves and how they exert influence upon one another. Perhaps the simplest way of explaining systems theory is to imagine our solar system functioning as just such a system. In itself this is nothing more than Einstein posited with his theory of relativity: bodies have mass, they affect one another, and this must be extended to literary bodies, and cultural mass, operating within their own system, exerting gravity, and gravitas. No text can, therefore, be considered to exist in a vacuum; it is necessarily the result of stakeholder forces, both under the influence of, and exerting influence on, other texts.

In Chapter 5, I drew on Oscar Wilde's aphorism that we 'are all in the gutter, but some of us are looking at the stars', constantly drawn by both the magic of our solar system, even when our own reality might be more base, and basic. In that chapter I also cited Jean Baudrillard, who writes in *Fatal Strategies*: 'We can no longer observe the stars in the sky; we must now observe the subterranean deities that threaten a collapse into the void.'[51] Crucially, if we now follow Baudrillard's advice and now turn our attention from systems in the stars to those of our own world, we can first look to see the beauty in Wilde's gutter, and then further down, to the muddy milieu of the cultural underground analysed in this book, where Baudrillard's subterranean deities might be found. The aesthetic objective must then be to appreciate these subterranean deities with the same devotion we offer to those perceived in the heavens, Wolfe's *nostalgie de la boue*, a longing for the mud.[52] And just as with the stars in the sky we can also divine *subterranean systems* connecting texts, connecting scenes, within this cultural underground.

Cultural production is not random, and these music scenes are, instead, organically wired into larger subterranean systems, rooted to one another through the cultural underground, communicating in mycorrhizal networks.[53] Sarah Thornton agrees, at least in part, with this horticultural model and necessary balance of forces when she writes (intriguingly using the same metaphor) that

> subcultures do not germinate from a seed and grow by force of their own energy into mysterious movements, only to be belatedly digested by the media. Rather, media, and other cultural industries are there and effective right from the start.[54]

I concur with Thornton that cultural life, and indeed subterranean cultural life, is necessarily the balance of various inputs, and forces. As outlined in the opening of this book there stands an Unholy Trinity of effects – beats, words and intoxicants – that align in order to birth a new subterranean system. Like light, earth and water, there can be no scene in the absence of any one of these essential elements: the music core, the pharmaceutical accelerant and the literary mechanism for recording the resulting effect. If we therefore now imagine EDMC to be one such system, we have located in Chapter 3 the electronic beat – the sonic seed – spurned on by its own artificial accelerant. We might then further imagine these cultural artefacts enfolding that scene, like roots – a culture drawing sustenance, and substance, by virtue of these secondary literary re/presentations. In this way, such representations might influence the growth and decay of the sonic scene, while also bestowing historical integrity in then calcifying to form a literary legacy, preserved as a robust sociocultural archive moving forwards. The cycle of germination, life and decay horticulturalists will tell you is simply nature's system, that it is the natural order of things, a life cycle for organic life that might equally, and phenomenologically, be ascribed to subterranean music cultures. When one decays, it feeds the next that is set to break through.

This discourse builds from Bakhtin's work on dialogics, in considering how texts must be seen to relate to one another intertextually, rather than existing in a monologic void. The concern now is with looking not in to, but out from, the text, in order to draw links and construct systems of congruence where, in Whiteley's words, 'everything means, is understood, as part of a greater whole'.[55] Meaning is produced in the process of dialogue, between author, text and reader and between music scenes and literary generations; in Middleton's words, 'between text, style, and genre and other texts, styles, genres; between discourses, musical and other; between interpretations, mediators and other involved social actors'.[56] This dialogic approach informed the design of subterranean systems theory, enabling connections to be made in the system of a culture, to then further understand a popular culture by reference to others rooted to it – an entire subterranean cultural ecology.

Through these different reformations of music, literature and intoxicants, an essential countercultural beat, or impulse, remains constant. The rave scene was, in this life cycle, a model of subterranean growth and decay; simply the latest reincarnation of resistance to hegemony, the resistance of that generation felt in its electronic beats, chronicled in its Dancefloor-Driven Literature. If we now extrapolate this subterranean system analysis of this particular sonic scene, other popular cultures might similarly be analysed across time, in order to examine how these music scenes also gained substance, integrity and sustainability by virtue of the light bestowed by their own secondary re/presentation in literature. Thus, we can further draw back and reaffirm how these three-way systems – built of words, music and an intoxicatory accelerant – not only operate within their own immured space but also exert influence and aesthetic nutrients, underground, and across time, in directly affecting, connecting and influencing other systems. Fundamental to the ontological functioning of this particular book, for instance, a lineage in subterranean systems has been identified, linking rave back to rock back to Beat generations. Reuniting the elements of the Unholy Trinity, but now within the context of subterranean systems theory, if you therefore want to know about bebop and Benzedrine, the answer lies not in the clubs themselves (now lost to time) or even the music of Thelonious Monk, but in the words of Jack Kerouac, where that smoky atmosphere remains locked in. Similarly, we can divine what life was like in San Francisco in the late 1960s not necessarily from the music of Jefferson Airplane, but from the bombastic words of Hunter S. Thompson. It follows that if one wants to understand Manchester in the late 1980s, the answer is not necessarily in the conservatoire (such as Manchester's own Royal Northern College of Music),[57] or even in the pulsing 4/4 soundtrack of the rave scene itself; instead, it is within the pages of these novels by Welsh, Noon and Blincoe.

Subterranean systems theory can help to trace the sigmoidal curve of the life cycle of EDMC,[58] this particular system nurtured, supported and encouraged into life by the decayed matter of previous systems. Cultural compost. And when each subterranean system dies back, we are left with two things: the music and the cultural artefacts that accompany it, these musical texts, yes, but also the literary context that provides the linguistic keys by which to decode it. Smyth argues that 'music has been fundamental to the evolution of the modern British novel, and therefore it remains fundamental to the understanding of that discourse down to the present day'.[59] Where the diegetic soundtrack of the text is key in this encoding, there must now be a firm musicological appreciation of the digital beat of EDMC, and also beyond musicology, an appreciation of the wider cultural resonance of that beat, beyond the page. This theoretical framework is a key outcome of my research for this book, providing a useful systematic tool for decoding the importance of countercultural literature. Subterranean systems theory might be deployed, for instance, in making comparative studies of texts, for the individual analysis of other music scenes, or for considering how different subterranean scenes connect, in considering what draws them together, and affords congruence, as though returning to that staircase in the Haçienda where William S. Burroughs and Nicholas Blincoe once passed one another.

Using such systemic, dialogic connectivity – alongside theoretical tools of the Unholy Trinity such as those provided by Marcus Boon and Harry Shapiro – a researcher might unpack a scene by reference to these spheres of influence, and examine how the revolving, evolving and heady influences of music, literature and intoxications have impacted on that scene,[60] or conversely, consider the impact of one element that is missing from a scene. Grunge, for instance, was a more recent subterranean scene, but did it come with a literary corpus, as this book has demonstrated took place with the rave scene? Or rather, does this lack of literary light leave it etiolated, and less likely to survive through the passage of time? The next step is therefore to understand and value the impact each self-contained scene has on others in the wider system, so that subterranean systems theory itself expands. Even if, as described earlier, future subterranean systems are likely to be smaller in mass, there is always an onwards evolution as music, intoxicants and the literature that chronicles it changes and mutates, in an organic and continually transformative process.

Elevating the cult

Thornton remarks that 'high culture is generally conceived in terms of aesthetic values, hierarchies and canons, while popular culture is portrayed as a curiously flat folk culture'.[61] It has been argued throughout this book that Dancefloor-Driven writers such as Welsh, Noon and Blincoe sit within a lineage of writers of low, 'curiously flat' cult fiction. Nevertheless, they each draw on specific literary techniques and representational modes in order to authentically capture the spirit and energy of their particular subterranean milieu, writers Calcutt and Shephard ultimately eulogize as 'gatekeepers and holy dealers of particular fictional worlds',[62] that gate leading directly down to the cultural underground, the literary basement. Whether Kerouac on jazz, Thompson on rock or Welsh on acid house, when writing about music – from trumpet players to guitar gods to masters of the turntable – these writers had to reach for a kind of aesthetic synaesthesia to find a voice with which to describe the music in words, that very particular melopoetic process of sonification explored in detail in each case study.

Pierre Bourdieu suggests that what he calls 'cheap paperbacks' allow for 'a promise of popularity for the author, a threat of vulgarization for the reader,'[63] and further that 'the distinctive power of cultural possessions or practices [...] tends to decline with the growth in the absolute number of people able to appropriate them'.[64] Meanwhile, in terms of this modelling and the vertical axis of culture, or 'taste' in Bourdieu's terms, these authors working within EDMC choose deliberately, perhaps provocatively, to locate their fiction firmly in society's subterranean level, culturally located within Bakhtin's lower bodily stratum. That does not preclude, however, the seriousness with which such pulp literature might be considered both in this book and in the research of other theorists.[65] Indeed, if club fiction, as cult fiction, falls squarely in the category of low and popular culture, a further conclusion of this book is that we actually learn more about our society from an appreciation of Thornton's 'flat folk culture'. In *Repetitive Beat Generation*, Blincoe also resists the notion of canon: 'The whole pulp thing to me was suddenly realising that instead of this tradition there's a whole other tradition. And you can take it all the way back to Daniel Defoe.'[66] Indeed, if pulp fictions can be critically reinforced for the journey along Bourdieu's vertical taste hierarchy, they can also become robust enough to survive the horizontal axis of time, and thereby carry the pulse of this code through history. Bakhtin argues that 'official culture is founded on the principle of an immoveable and unchanging hierarchy in which the higher and the lower never merge',[67] but this book necessarily proposes, and concludes, that because of this central importance in chronicling a popular culture, this literature must be elevated to higher ground – the abject rendered sacred, even – where Dancefloor-Driven Literature can truly be, for Calcutt and Shephard, 'something that could be talked about with the reverence traditionally reserved for all things classical'.[68] From a perspective of passing time, this book therefore now calls for a more flexible reading of the high/low axis to literature. One must also bear in mind that such distinctions were, in any case, an artificial construct to make the study of literature by men seem more socially acceptable in the early decades of the last century, the likes of literary critics such as F. R. Leavis dividing literature into rather arbitrary high, and low, cultural piles.[69]

I therefore contend, perhaps controversially, that Dancefloor-Driven Literature should be treated with similar reverence to the more established genres, perhaps *because* of the very way it resists those more canonical genres, and in political terms runs counter to hegemonic culture. Here I also, and necessarily, argue against Theodor Adorno in asserting the qualitative value of an essentially consumer literary culture in communicating and preserving the preoccupations of that society. Mass culture has cultural mass, and that value has stood as an aesthetic worth identifying, investigating and celebrating in the course of my research. Centrally, this book therefore concludes with a call for the elevation of Dancefloor-Driven Literature as a subset of cult fiction,[70] in Calcutt and Shephard's terms, and further, seeks to elevate that corpus so as to treat it with reverence, even flattening out, or concertinaing, the now politically redundant notion of a high/low art binary axis, where liter*ary* signifies highbrow, liter*ature* less so.

Smyth further locates 'the value of popular culture relative to established canons of taste',[71] continuing:

> The questions proliferate: Must the popular cultural text be likened to the icons of high culture? Must the terms of the debate be set by those in command of a

particular critical discourse? Most significantly of all, who gets to set the criteria regarding what is beautiful and what is not?[72]

Smyth further adds that

> 'proper' literary writing does have a place, although it is ranged alongside other forms of fiction (fantasy, graphic, crime, and so on). In this way, my scepticism towards the paradigmatic exemplariness of classical music shall be shown to be of a piece with my scepticism towards the privileged status of literary fiction.[73]

Intermediality – fundamental in terms of this cultural decoding and enquiry – cannot be restricted to classical music, and the literary canon as defined by Leavis and supported by the academy. It must, instead, apply to all music, and in this case to the music, and consequent literature, of the subterranean dancefloor. As the editors remark in their introduction to the *New Puritan* collection, 'Fiction writers should at least be the ones who legislate what is and what is not fine writing.'[74]

This book has demonstrated how, taken together, electronic music and fine writing can be integral to the creation and maintenance of popular cultures through time, aided by the accelerating agent of intoxicants. Citing Greenberg, Wolf suggests:

> It would be inappropriate to denounce intermedial experiments as a 'confusion of the arts' (Greenberg 1940/86: 23): rather than engendering medial 'purity', which is a questionable value anyway, these experiments may lead to an enriching and interesting opening up of established media to something 'other' which seems particularly remote, and this is certainly a major reason for the minoritarian status of musicalized fiction. Yet, owing to this very remoteness, it turned out to be significant for a number of aesthetic tendencies in the development of fiction as a whole.[75]

I conclude that the progressive aesthetic of the club scene engendered the right environment for musico-literary experiments and the mixing of forms, in creating Wolf's 'other', as though the dancefloor itself were a laboratory for birthing inventive cultural hybrids. In so doing, the Dancefloor-Driven fiction of the 1990s was not a 'minor' concern, but rather (in the success, especially, of Welsh and the *Disco Biscuits* collection) the essential cultural story of that decade. Now, beyond two decades into the future, it stands as a way of retrospectively viewing that subterranean world. My hope is that this penetrative consideration of that literature – its micro aesthetics and macro world view – might itself add to the shaping of that story and its ongoing discourse.

Smyth reports: 'The contemporary British music-novel is, in this sense, a portal (albeit one of many) through which we may access some of the defining concerns of our period',[76] and in this book I have developed a theoretical framework for unlocking Smyth's portal, and defining the rave scene – and other historic music-based popular concerns – via their surviving literary artefacts. As such, I strongly hope that the ideas in this book have future applications, supporting Steve Redhead in reasserting the importance of cultural studies in the academy,[77] and adding to the ongoing discourse of musico-literary intermediality: that central concern for how, and why, we write about music. The emergence, and continued presence, of these secondary literary phenomena on the bookshelves directly addresses Reynolds's reductive questioning as to 'whether any form of recreational drug use is an adequate basis for a culture'.[78] Understanding that the sonic could become linguistic, these Dancefloor-Driven writers wrote to the beat of their time. Taken together, their work then encoded that beat, locked into words, ensuring now, when we open up these books, we are more aware of what we learn, and indeed what we *hear*, when we read about a music scene.

Glossary of terms and theories

This book is concerned with a niche (and now, broadly speaking, historic) subterranean scene. As such, there are many titles and phrases that might appear alien to the objective reader. Similarly, pre-existing theories must be unpacked and, where no theories exist for decoding these texts, new frameworks must be constructed in order to fully analyse this subculture and its varied literature.[1] These phrases and theories will now be defined, providing a useful theory overview to refer back to when reading the book. The following theories have in most cases been devised as entirely original frameworks during the research for this book, or occasionally modified pre-existing ideas, as a method of decoding the literature under review:

Cultural relevance theory

In another example of interdisciplinary bricolage, a theory will also be appropriated from the field of linguistics: relevance theory.[2] We hear music differently, and interpret that text in various ways. Similarly, we respond to what might be called 'in-text music' very differently, very much depending on our a priori understanding, or current balance of 'subcultural capital' in Thornton's terms,[3] and our ability to use that capital to add volume to the music track, as described. In *LitPop*, Rachel Carroll argues that 'a literary soundtrack can arguably only function on an intertextual level whereby the citation serves to activate meanings signified by the music'.[4] The reader therefore needs to come to the text equipped with an understanding of the subculture and its musical and technological practices, to enjoy a truly penetrative understanding of the text.

Dancefloor

Often referred to as two separate words (dance floor), this is the locus that lies at the centre of this entire book, and certainly provides the origins of the literature of this scene. As it therefore coheres as one entity, with a contained essentialism, the word has been conflated into one word within this book.

Dancefloor-Driven Literature

In the process of analysing these texts, this book gathers such works within the new genre of Dancefloor-Driven Literature – fiction born of the dancefloor. The printed page is indeed as flat as the dancefloor, and yet worlds of imagination are found to operate within its sphere. Further, in researching this book the author reached out to those writers determined to capture the essence of this electronic dance music culture within the rather more restrictive parameters of the written word. As part of that research process, and in order to better consider these works collectively, this book will call for the elevation of such texts within the broader realm of cult fiction. Appendix I will then gather together the key texts within this genre.

Ecstasy

First patented by pharmaceutical giant Merck in 1912,[5] Methylenedioxymethamphetamine (MDMA) was then further synthesized by chemist Alexander Shulgin in America. But street-level marketers realized they needed a more immediate and powerful street name for this intoxicant and settled on, in the words of Collin, 'a seductive new brand name: *Ecstasy*',[6] famously further shortened to 'E'.

EDMC

Electronic Dance Music Culture is the academic discipline that considers the varied aspects of the club scene. This book looks particularly at EDMC in its 'rave' incarnation, but that must be seen as only one form of music subculture that might be considered within the broader EDMC diaspora. Distinction will be made between the 'rave' scene, in particular, and the 'club' scene more broadly, although these terms are often interchangeable. EDMC should not be confused with the contemporary music genre EDM, which references a very particular style of high-tempo trance music particularly popular in the United States, produced and distributed by European DJs such as David Guetta and Tiesto.

Enculturation

Sarah Thornton describes the process of enculturation as the cultural mechanism by which an artefact, such as a music recording or indeed cultural intelligence itself, moves from 'the private to the public sphere'.[7] Similarly, club fictions reproduce the landscape of the nightclub, the habits of casual and recreational drug consumption and the hitherto secret, almost magical machinations of the DJ. As such, this term can be more broadly related to the mechanism by which Dancefloor-Driven Literature enables the distribution of subcultural knowledge, just as it describes how a niche, stripped-down, post-industrial sound from Detroit, New York and Chicago became the ubiquitous soundtrack of the late twentieth century.

Literary diegesis

In terms of the blurring of subjectivity and narrowing the connection between character, setting and reader (especially important in the authentic portrayal of the transformative effects of a drug experience), the notions of diegesis and metadiegesis, more associated with cinematic theory, have been incorporated. Diegetic music can broadly be defined as that which occurs within the environment of the film – for instance a car stereo, or radio – whereas non-diegetic music is likely to be the underscore or incidental music to the piece, designed to be detected by the audience in the cinema but not the actors within the narrative. This might be transferred to a literary rather than cinematic text, to describe the way music is used – almost behind the words, as silent soundtrack – where authors might instruct their fictional DJs to deploy music, for instance in nightclub scenes, in order to render the scene naturalistically.

Musico-literary intermediality

Werner Wolf describes the concept of intermediality as the relation of at least two media in one artefact, both exhibiting their typical signifiers[8] and later describing this as 'cross-medial intersemiotic relations',[9] working together to create a 'medial hybrid'.[10] Distinct from intertexuality, the two collaborating media in this study are music and literature, hence musico-literary intermediality.

Narrative Arc

Roland Barthes argues that all narratives share structural similarities,[11] and certainly in reading works of Dancefloor-Driven Literature a narrative structure emerges for many of these stories, which will be referenced throughout this book as their Narrative Arc. These discursive traits haunt many EDMC texts – the same parabolic storyline arc that carves the trajectory the author Thomas Pynchon famously described as 'Gravity's Rainbow' – in reference to V2 rockets.[12] This arc maps the genesis, zenith and nadir of the narrative: the anticipation, the actuality, the aftermath that orientates us through the story. This structure is also the journey of a night out: going out, coming up, coming down. Indeed, it is the story of club culture itself: the first flowering of the rave scene up to 1992, through the vainglorious commercial mutations of the 1990s, to a demise Dom Phillips very precisely pinpoints as 31 December 1999 – the commercial club scene now bloated, solipsistic, mired in money and violence.[13]

Rave

The rave scene was the last stand of the counterculture against the hegemonic dominance of late capitalism in the final years of the twentieth century, also representing the last of Dick Hebdige's 'spectacular subcultures'.[14] This book will argue that it was the spiritual successor to both the Beat Generation – exhibiting the same underground sensibilities, high-energy music, philosophy and club sessions – and the counterculture, in the sense of a desire to opt out of society and seek something 'other'. Beatniks, hippies and ravers reacted to, and resisted, the norms of society,[15] choosing instead intoxication and the beat of late-night music.

Re/presentation

A graphological neologism, this term is further explored in Chapter 4. However, broadly speaking it denotes the method by which a culture might be described, and then preserved, via its cultural artefacts. Re/presentation therefore refers to not only music text but also subcultural *con*text, the slash denoting a certain modernity in terms of graphology and an 'and/or' situation, rather than a simple stress on the 're' of representation. In this way the literature can present a culture, in creating and distributing stories to a contemporaneous audience, but it can also re/present that culture in terms of a broader communicative function, curating stories which might also encode a knowledge transfer to both a future and a contemporary readership.

The saved night

EDMC and its associated literature and secondary cultural representations will be shown to be fundamental in terms of constructing a sociocultural archive by which that scene might be accessed and decoded, once the actual participants have long stepped away from the dancefloor. Dancefloor-Driven Literature can thereby be seen as carrying the coding for the subculture itself. Walter Benjamin presents a useful term in discussing, in zoological terms, the notion of the 'saved night',[16] and this might be repurposed in more technological terms for this literature, which is, in essence, an archive of subjective, subcultural history – books as subcultural backup.

The Second Summer of Love

Electronic Dance Music has its 'rave' epiphany in the middle months of 1988, popularly termed 'The Second Summer of Love'. The summer of 1988 exhibited the perfect storm of cultural, political and pharmaceutical effects. Imported house music – DJ-driven music productions defined by a minimalist electronic four-to-the-floor beat – fused with a new dance drug to create a so-called Chemical Generation of young people disenfranchised by the hard-edged politics of Thatcherism. Margaret Thatcher, the UK's prime minister at the time, infamously claimed that there was 'no such thing as society'.[17] While this may have been perceived as true within the UK's hegemonic realms, on the dance fields and in the party warehouses and nightclubs of the UK, young adults found their sense of society on the dancefloor.

Subterranean versus supraterranan

Society can be critiqued as operating on (at least) two levels: the darker shadow of the subterranean and nocturnal world interrogated in this book, set against the reality of a more visible, dominant daylight society operating 'overground'.[18] To traverse the problematic use of the term 'subculture' (further explored in Chapter 2), this book proposes the use of 'supraterranean' to denote the world operating overground, set against the operations of the 'subterranean' underworld, in keeping with Latin derivations. Equally, the interest of theorists such as Jacques Lacan and Julia Kristeva in their articulation of the 'other' as a cultural construct will be useful in the central positioning of this musical underworld as antithetical to supraterranean, hegemonic culture.[19]

Subterranean life-cycle model/subterranean continuum

Building on Steve Redhead's ideas of 'the subcultural chain',[20] we can trace how each generation evolves its own cultural forms, narratives and identities. Equally, each generation wrestles, tries to contain and is ultimately overwhelmed by a darker shadow: the subterranean id to the supraterranean ego. In aesthetic terms, subterranean cultures act as the creative engine that drives the varying modes of art forwards, each generation eager to define itself and its cultural forms as new, energetic and ultimately different from the one that bore it. As such, a generation can view its culture within a hermetic bubble, without consideration of what has gone before. This book instead counters that links are strong, visible and desirable. Instead, one subterranean scene actually builds from that which preceded.

This book therefore argues for a subterranean continuum and, borrowing a theory from marketing, suggests that such cultures exhibit the same life-cycle model of growth and entropic collapse that more commercial products might follow. This theory articulates how music cultures cannot exist in a vacuum; rather, there is an essential countercultural lineage that runs between each form, continually subverting and influencing dominant culture as though in a perpetual helix. EDMC cannot, therefore, be considered to operate in a historical-cultural vacuum. Instead, one must necessarily, and dialogically, regard it in relation to the influences of other subterranean formations, each the same combination of literature, music and intoxicants.

Subterranean systems theory

Subterranean systems theory forms the key theoretical framework for this book,[21] considered largely in its concluding chapter. The word 'system' is used deliberately, a more robust and contemporary word than 'structure' where, even in its 'post-structural' usage, the words cannot accommodate what this book requires them to. Here, it is a matter not of texts forming structures in and of themselves but, rather, of systems that then connect with other systems. Such a theory involves a dialogic approach to subcultures, in line with that of Soviet-era theorist Mikhail Bakhtin. As the late Sheila Whiteley writes in *LitPop*, 'Dialogism is the characteristic epistemological mode of a world dominated by heteroglossia. Everything means, is understood, as part of a greater whole.'[22]

Unholy Trinity

In detecting patterns, frameworks and – more broadly – systems, this book has noted the presence of trinities: three cultural movements across time, and then further, three homological components within each of those movements. This account therefore proposes another central argument: that there exists an Unholy Trinity of cultural and pharmaceutical effects that coalesce to define a subterranean culture: the linking interplay of literature, music and intoxicants. Any such culture must, then, be considered a reaction between forces,[23] cultural formation necessarily the result of the collision of music and an accelerant formed of the chosen intoxicant of the day, subsequently reported, and recorded, in literature. These cultural ingredients have been explored before,[24] but never in this particular constitution.

This book further contends that within each subterranean scene, one element of this Unholy Trinity is foregrounded. The Beat scene was defined primarily by its literature; with rock, it was music; and with rave it was the drug itself – Ecstasy, or 'E' – that defined the scene, and gives the book its title.[25] Perhaps (and as a consequence of the critical focus on the music, and then the drug within the rave scene) there has, up until now, been a lacuna in the study of the third element of this Unholy Trinity, what is now defined as a Dancefloor-Driven Literature, that considers the scene from an apparently fictional perspective.

Notes

Epigraph

Walter Pater, 'The School of Giorgione', *Fortnightly Review*, 22.130 (October 1877), p. 528.

Chapter 1

1. Andrew Holleran, *Dancer from the Dance* (New York: Perennial, 2001), p. 35.
2. Hakim Bey, *T.A.Z.: The Temporary Autonomous Zone, Ontological Anarchy, Poetic Terrorism*, 2nd edn (Brooklyn, NY: Autonomedia, 2003).
3. See particularly Matthew Collin, *Altered State: The Story of Ecstasy Culture and Acid House* (London: Serpent's Tail, 2009); Bill Brewster and Frank Broughton, *Last Night A DJ Saved My Life: The History of the Disc Jockey* (London: Headline, 1999); Jeremy Gilbert and Ewan Pearson, *Discographies: Dance Music, Culture and the Politics of Sound* (London: Routledge, 1999); and Simon Reynolds, *Generation Ecstasy: Into the World of Techno and Rave Culture* (New York: Routledge, 1999).
4. Steve Redhead notes that 'Chemical Generation' is a term now broadly applied to this group of writers, playing on notions of drug consumption associated with the rave scene. In Steve Redhead ed., *Repetitive Beat Generation* (Edinburgh: Canongate, 2000), p. xxi he remarks: 'These were said by fashionable media cultural commentators to be the youth cultures which came after the 80s "boomers", "yuppies" and "thirtysomethings".'
5. The summer of 1988 became known as the Second Summer of Love in reference to the first, in 1967, itself associated with that decade's countercultural music scene.
6. Redhead, *Repetitive Beat Generation*, p. 16.
7. Simon A. Morrison, *Discombobulated: Dispatches from the Wrong Side* (London: Headpress, 2010).
8. See Glossary for a short definition of my term 're/presentation'.
9. This is the city where I myself moved, from London, to start my own literary studies in 1989, the heart of the MADchester era. At some stage at the very tail end of the 1980s, I went to a nightclub called the Haçienda (analysed further in Chapter 3), and in the lexicon natural to a book about books, the 'short story' is that Manchester is still the city I call home, where I live in its very heart, ironically opposite an infamous nightclub once called Home.
10. See, for example, Rebekah Farrugia, *Beyond the Dance Floor: Female DJs, Technology and Electronic Dance Music Culture* (Bristol: Intellect, 2012).
11. See also Susan R. Suleiman, *The Reader in the Text* (Princeton: Princeton University Press, 1980); Robert Holub, *Reception Theory* (London: Routledge, 2003); and Hans

Jauss, 'Literary History as a Challenge to Literary Theory', *New Literary History* 2 (1970–1), pp. 7–37.
12 The intersection of football and popular culture was a particular interest of the Manchester Institute of Popular Culture, explored in more detail further in the following chapter, and indeed remained so for Steve Redhead until the end of his life.
13 D. C. Gallin, *Kiss the Sky* (n.p.: Telemachus Press, 2012).
14 Pat W. Hendersen, *Club* (uncorrected galley proof). Also interviewed in the early stages of this research, the copy used was an unpublished manuscript donated by the author. *Club* was eventually self-published.
15 Nick Hornby, *How to Be Good* (London: Penguin, 2001), p. 108.
16 Alex Garland, *The Beach* (London: Penguin, 1997).
17 Hanif Kureshi, *The Black Album* (London: Faber & Faber, 1995).
18 Frank Owen, *Clubland Confidential* (London: Ebury Press, 2004).
19 James St. James, *Disco Bloodbath* (London: Sceptre, 1999).
20 Douglas Rushkoff, *The Ecstasy Club* (London: Sceptre, 1997).
21 Sarah Champion, ed., *Disco Biscuits: New Fiction from the Chemical Generation* (London: Sceptre, 1997).
22 Alan Warner, *Morvan Callar* (London: Vintage, 1996).
23 Redhead, *Repetitive Beat Generation*.
24 Mention must also be made of a later collection, Toni Davidson, ed., *Intoxication: An Anthology of Stimulant-Based Writing* (London: Serpent's Tail, 1998). However, as this collection is not specifically concerned with the dancefloor, it has less relevance to this research.
25 The author of this book actually first saw Irvine Welsh on the dancefloor of the Haçienda nightclub in Manchester, in the mid-1990s.
26 Irvine Welsh, interviewed in person at Molly Malone's pub, Glasgow, 19 February 2012 and via a 45-minute phone call to Miami, 23 February 2012.
27 Irvine Welsh, *The Acid House* (London: Vintage Press, 1995), *Ecstasy: Three Tales of Chemical Romance* (London: Jonathan Cape, 1996), and *Glue* (London: Vintage, 2002).
28 Jeff Noon, *Pixel Juice* (London: Anchor, 2000) and *Needle in the Groove* (London: Black Swan, 2001).
29 Nicholas Blincoe, *Acid Casuals* (London; Serpent's Tail, 1998), *Manchester Slingback* (London: Pan, 1998), and *Jello Salad* (London: Serpent's Tail, 1997).
30 Calvin S. Brown, *Music and Literature: A Comparison of the Arts* (Athens, Georgia: The University of Georgia Press, 1949).
31 Werner Wolf, *The Musicalization of Fiction: A Study in the Theory and History of Intermediality* (Georgia: Rodolphi, 1999).
32 See Walter Bernhart, Steven Paul Scher and Werner Wolf, eds, *Word and Music Studies: Defining the Field* (Amsterdam: Rodopi, 1999), the Proceedings of the First International Conference on Word and Music Studies at Graz, 1997. See also Steven Paul Scher, *Essays on Literature and Music (1967–2004)*, eds Walter Bernhart and Werner Wolf (Amsterdam: Rodopi, 2004).
33 Wolf, *The Musicalization of Fiction*, p. 229.
34 Gerry Smyth, *Music in Contemporary British Fiction: Listening to the Novel* (New York: Palgrave Macmillan, 2008), p. 4.
35 John Street, 'Introduction to "Literature and Music" special issue', *Popular Music* 24, no. 2 (2005), p. 163.

36 Michael Allis, 'Reading Music through Literature: Introduction', *Journal of Musicological Research*, 36, no. 1 (2017), pp. 1–5 (p. 1). See also Steven Paul Scher, 'Einleitung: literature und Musik: Entwickung und Stand der Forschung', in Steven Paul Scher (ed.), *Literatur und Musik: Ein Hanbuch zur Theorie und Praxis eines komparatistichen Grenzgbietes* (Berlin: Eric Schmidt, 1984), pp. 9–25.
37 Wolf, *The Musicalization of Fiction*, p. 37.
38 Gerry Smyth, *Music in Contemporary British Fiction: Listening to the Novel* (New York: Palgrave Macmillan, 2008), p. 16.
39 Wolf, *The Musicalization of Fiction*, p. 233.
40 Sarah Champion, ed., *Disco Biscuits: New Fiction from the Chemical Generation* (London: Sceptre, 1997).
41 Trevor Miller, *Trip City* (London: Avernus, 1989).

Chapter 2

1 See Rupa Huq, *Beyond Subculture: Pop, Youth and Identity in a Postcolonial World* (London: Routledge, 2006), p. 9.
2 See Simon Reynolds, 'Rave Culture: Living Dream or Living Death', in Steve Redhead (ed.), *The Clubcultures Reader: Readings in Popular Cultural Studies* (Oxford: Blackwell,1998); Huq, *Beyond Subculture*.
3 See Bibliography.
4 Matthew Cheeseman and David Forrest, 'The Narrative Nightclub', in Nick Bentley, Beth Johnson and Andrzej Zieleniec (eds), *Youth Subcultures in Fiction, Film and Other Media* (London: Palgrave Macmillan, 2018), p. 93.
5 Ibid.
6 Andy Bennett, 'Sub-Cultures or Neo-Tribes? Rethinking the Relationship between Youth Style Musical Taste', *Sociology* 33, no. 3 (1999), pp. 599–617.
7 Will Straw, 'Systems of Articulations, Logics of Change: Communities and Scenes in Popular Music', *Cultural Studies* 5, no. 3 (1991), 368–88.
8 David Hesmondhalgh, 'Subcultures, Scenes or Tribes? None of the Above', *Journal of Youth Studies* 8, no. 1 (2005), pp. 21–40 (p. 22).
9 Personal communication with Matthew Worley, via telephone on 22 July 2019.
10 Paul Hodkinson, *Goth: Identity, Style and Subculture* (Oxford: Berg, 2002), p. 7.
11 Tracy Shildrick and Robert MacDonald wrote 'In Defence of Subculture: Young People, Leisure and Social Divisions', *Journal of Youth Studies* 9, no. 2 (2006), pp. 125–60 (p. 136).
12 Hesmondhalgh, 'Subcultures, Scenes or Tribes?', p. 125.
13 Hodkinson, *Goth*, p. 23.
14 See Foucault's notion of the 'panopticon' in Michel Foucault, *Discipline and Punish: The Birth of the Prison* (London: Penguin, 1991), and further discussion in Chapter 7.
15 For further reading, notably around Gramsci's notions of cultural hegemony, please see his essays contained in Antonio Gramsci, *Selections from the Prison Notebooks* (London: Lawrence & Wishart, 2005).
16 Tracey Thorn, 'Off the Record: In Italy, I Swap the Gloom of Home for the Euphoria of the Gay Disco Scene of 1970s New York', *New Statesman*, 2 August–15 August 2019, p. 95.

17 Ibid.
18 Julia Kristeva, *Powers of Horror: An Essay on Abjection* (New York: Columbia Press, 1982); Jacques Lacan, *Ecrits: The Complete Edition in English* (New York: W. W. Norton, 2007).
19 Hesmondhalgh, 'Subcultures, Scenes or Tribes?' p. 38.
20 See Matthew Collin's *Altered State*, Bill Brewster and Frank Broughton's *Last Night A DJ Saved My Life*, Dave Haslam's *Adventures on the Wheels of Steel: The Rise of Superstar DJs* (London: Fourth Estate, 2001) and Dom Phillips's *Superstar DJs Here We Go! The Incredible Rise of Clubland's Finest* (London: Ebury Press, 2009). In addition, Simon Reynolds has been a notable, if populist, commentator on the club scene. His text *Generation Ecstasy: Into the World of Techno and Rave Culture* remains an extremely thorough account of both the historical context of this cultural formation and particularly his musicological understanding of the various electronic music genres that developed from the founding fathers of house, garage and techno. Interestingly, this text was published in the UK as *Energy Flash* (London: Picador, 1998) with a covermount CD soundtrack and differences between the two texts.
21 Steve Redhead, *The End-of-the-Century Party: Youth and Pop Towards 2000* (Manchester: Manchester University Press, 1990), p. 1.
22 This theory of twenty-year cultural shifts has also been made by Factory Records' Anthony H. Wilson, in conversation with the author, and by DJ Annie Nightingale (BBC 5Live, 13 July 2015).
23 Jack Kerouac, *The Subterraneans* (New York: Grove Weidenfeld, 1981), p. 1. The quote references the modernist poet Ezra Pound.
24 For clarification see Andy Bennett, 'Reappraising Counterculture', in Jedediah Sklower and Sheila Whiteley (eds), *Countercultures & Popular Music* (Farnham: Ashgate, 2014).
25 Hunter S. Thompson, *Fear and Loathing in Las Vegas* (London: Paladin, 1985), p. 67.
26 'Acid house' became a common descriptor for this scene, a combination of the drug LSD or 'acid' that fuelled the parties and its soundtrack of 'house' music. Participators also became known as 'ravers', interestingly also a phrase in common use in the 1960s, and the name of a pop music magazine of that decade.
27 Drawing first on established cultural contingencies, see Dick Hebdige, *Subculture: The Meaning of Style* (London: Methuen, 1983); Sarah Thornton, *Club Cultures: Music, Media and Subcultural Capital* (Cambridge: Polity, 1995); and David Muggleton and Rupert Weinzierl, eds., *The Post-Subcultures Reader* (Oxford: Berg, 2003).
28 For instance, Marcus Boon considers literature and intoxicants in *The Road of Excess: A History of Writers on Drugs* (Cambridge, MA: Harvard University Press, 2002) while Harry Shapiro considers music and intoxicants in *Waiting for the Man: The Story of Drugs and Popular Music* (London: Helter Skelter, 2003).
29 In respect of the prominence of the letter *E*, the reader might refer to the now iconic cover shot by Kevin Cummins, in the *NME* published 31 March 1990. This image sees the Happy Mondays' frontman Shaun Ryder hanging from the letter *E* on the rooftop of an Ibiza hotel. The Happy Mondays' sensibilities blended rock with a baggy rave aesthetic, and at the 2014 Louder than Words festival in Manchester, Cummins argued that the cover image encapsulated the moment.
30 Richard Middleton, *Reading Pop: Approaches to Textual Analysis in Popular Music* (Oxford: Oxford University Press, 2000), p. 3.

31 Ibid., p. 9.
32 Gerry Smyth, *Music in Contemporary British Fiction: Listening to the Novel* (New York: Palgrave Macmillan, 2008), p. 5.

Chapter 3

1   For instance, the author was able to interview Danny Krivit, a seminal DJ in New York from the 1960s onwards and a fundamental part of the Body & Soul club event of the 1990s.
2   Bey, *T.A.Z.*, p. 100.
3   See Michel Foucault, *Discipline and Punishment* (London: Penguin, 1991), p. 195, and further discussion in Chapter 8.
4   As an aside, Manchester's club promoters Colors created the 'Tower of Power' in the late 1990s, a cylindrical DJ booth constructed from speakers and designed to stand in the centre of the dancefloor. Ironically, this resembles a panopticon, in affording the DJ a 360-degree view of the dancefloor.
5   See Sara Cohen, *Rock Culture in Liverpool: Popular Music in the Making* (Oxford: Clarendon Press, 1991); Andy Bennett, 'Consolidating the Music Scenes Perspective', *Poetics* 32 (2004), pp. 223–34; and Robert Knifton, Marion Leonard and Les Roberts, eds. *Sites of Popular Music Heritage: Memories, Histories, Place* (New York and London: Routledge, 2015).
6   Sarah Thornton, *Club Cultures: Music, Media and Subcultural Capital* (Cambridge: Polity, 1995), p. 57.
7   *Saturday Night Fever*, dir. John Badham (USA: RSO, 1977).
8   *New York* magazine, 7 June 1976. See http://nymag.com/nightlife/features/45933/ [last accessed 8 August 2017].
9   See Charlie Leduff, 'Saturday Night Fever: The Life', in *New York Times*, 9 June 1996. http://www.nytimes.com/1996/06/09/nyregion/saturday-night-fever-the-life.html [last accessed 1 November 2017].
10 A critique of Adorno on these lines is complicated by the fact that he, himself, also criticized some classical music. See Theodor Adorno, 'On the Fetish Character of Music and the Regression of Listening', in *The Culture Industry: Selected Essays on Mass Culture* (London: Routledge, 2001) and Adorno, *In Search of Wagner* (London: Verso, 2009).
11 Gilbert and Pearson, *Discographies*, p. 116.
12 Simon Frith, 'Can Music Progress? Reflections on the History of Popular Music'. Originally a key note speech at the postgraduate conference 'Evolutions', a transcript can be found in *Musicology* 7 (2007), Serbian Academy of Sciences and Arts, p. 250.
13 Peter Conrad, cited in Stuart Walton, *Out of It: A Cultural History of Intoxication* (London: Penguin, 2002), p. xxi.
14 Boon, *The Road of Excess*, p. 204.
15 Mike Jay, *High Society: Mind-Altering Drugs in History and Culture* (London: Thames & Hudson, 2010), p. 46.
16 See Walton, *Out of It*; Jay, *High Society*; Thomas Lyttle and Michael Montagne, 'Drugs, Music, and Ideology: A Social Pharmacological Interpretation of the Acid House Movement', *International Journal of the Addictions*, 27, 10 (1992), pp. 1199–77.

17 Jacques Attali, *Noise: The Political Economy of Music* (Minneapolis: The University of Minnesota Press, 2009).
18 Ibid., p. 106.
19 For more musicological detail of EDMC, see Bernardo Alexander Attias, Anna Gavanas and Hillegonda C. Rietveld, eds, *DJ Culture in the Mix: Power, Technology and Social Change in Electronic Dance Music* (London: Bloomsbury, 2013).
20 Inventor of MIDI and founder of the Japanese electronics company Roland, Ikutaro Kakehashi, died during the course of this research, on 1 April 2017.
21 Ibid., p. 112.
22 Bernardo Attias, 'Subjectivity in the Groove: Phonography, Digitality and Fidelity', in Attias et al. *DJ Culture in the Mix*, p. 40.
23 Bernado Attias, 'Subjectivity in the Groove', p. 40.
24 For fuller details, please refer to the Discography.
25 Gilbert and Pearson, *Discographies*, p. 111.
26 Graham Massey on 'The Today Programme', BBC Radio 4, 21 March 2014.
27 The author interviewed Frankie Knuckles for *Ministry in Ibiza* in 1999.
28 Thornton, *Club Cultures*, p. 53.
29 See Vicky-Ann Cremona et al., *Theatrical Events: Borders, Dynamics, Frames* (Amsterdam: Rodopi, 2004).
30 Thornton, *Club Cultures*, p. 29.
31 See Alvin Toffler, *Future Shock* (New York: Random House, 1970) and Martin James, 'A silent voice across the MEdiaverse: *The Next Day* as identities presumed', *Celebrity Studies* 4, no. 3 (2013), pp. 387–9.
32 A central narrative thrust of this research is to elevate the music of the street to the realms of the conservatoire.
33 See Walter Benjamin, 'The Work of Art in the Age of Mechanical Reproduction', in *Illuminations* (London: Pimlico, 1999).
34 John Scannell, 'Working to Design: the Self-Perpetuating Ideology of Rock or … "The New Bob Dylan"', in *Portal: Journal of Multidisciplinary International Studies* 8, no. 1 (2011), p. 60.
35 Frith, 'Can Music Progress', p. 254.
36 Graham Massey, in conversation with the author for *Clash* magazine, n.d. Massey has also since reunited with producer A Guy Called Gerald, producing purely analogue music.
37 UK sales of vinyl were 1.2 million in the first half of 2014, 50 per cent up on the same period the previous year and 2015 saw the first ever specifically vinyl chart, its first Number One a house record, ironically a Farley and Heller reworking of Frankie Knuckles's 'Baby Wants To Ride'. More recently, a BBC report of 2017 cited the BPI's (British Phonographic Industry) own findings that sales of vinyl that year were 3.2 million, up 53 per cent on the previous year, the highest UK total in twenty-five years.
38 A concern of the 1950s Lettrist International, see www.psychogeography.co.uk.
39 Bennett, 'Consolidating the Music Scenes Perspective', p. 225.
40 Ibid., p. 223.
41 Ibid., p. 224.
42 Mark Fisher, *Ghosts of My Life: Writings on Depression, Hauntology and Lost Futures* (Alresford, Hants: Zero Books, 2013), p. 130.

43 Ibid., p. 125.
44 In New York, the author was able to visit the spaces where these grand nightclubs once stood, and follow, in psychogeographic terms, spaces such as Studio 54, Paradise Garage and Limelight.
45 Danny Krivit, interviewed in person by the author, in a coffee shop and in his car, 30 March 2015, New York.
46 Just one example: New York's Webster Hall opened in 1886 as a social space, survived prohibition (perhaps largely because of the patronage of a certain Al Capone) and was still functioning as a nightclub when the author visited in 2007, having survived complaints from neighbours as far back as 1918.
47 Lisa Robinson, 'Boogie Nights', *Vanity Fair*, February 2010, https://www.vanityfair.com/culture/2010/02/oral-history-of-disco-201002 [last accessed 3 November 2017].
48 Robinson, 'Boogie Nights'.
49 In an overt quest for Barthes's mythology, the most iconic image from the club is that of Bianca Jagger arriving for her birthday party on the back of a white horse. She later admitted she only climbed onto the horse at the door of Studio 54.
50 Bey, *T.A.Z.*, pp. x–xi. Grammar as per original.
51 Ibid., p. 104.
52 Ibid., p. 122.
53 Haden-Guest, *The Last Party: Studio 54, Disco & The Culture of the Night* (New York: It Books, 2009), p. 53.
54 Thomas Pynchon also uses the notion of the 'zone' in *Gravity's Rainbow*.
55 Richard Middleton, '"Last Night a DJ Saved My Life": Avians, Cyborgs and Siren Bodies in the Era of Phonographic Technology', in *Radical Musicology* 1 (2006), p. 15.
56 Danny Krivit, author interview.
57 Haden-Guest, *The Last Party*, p. 347.
58 Ibid., p. 212.
59 The research trip to Chicago enabled the author to visit 206 South Jefferson and photograph the building where these parties took place, with the cross-street now renamed The Honorary Frankie Knuckles Way.
60 A huge name in this developing story of club culture, Frankie Knuckles died during this research, on 31 March 2014, receiving obituaries from people including US president Barak Obama. 25 August is now Frankie Knuckles Day.
61 Graeme Park, interviewed in the author's garden, Stockport, 23 March 2011.
62 Thornton, *Club Cultures*, p. 46.
63 Bennett, 'Consolidating the Music Scenes Perspective', p. 230.
64 Haden-Guest, *The Last Party*, p. 26.
65 In conversation Krivit recalls there were around 4,000 cabaret licenses in the city in those years and 'all of those clubs were packed'; he estimates there are now around forty and 'those clubs are struggling'.
66 Beyond more significant connections, the *Saturday Night Fever* soundtrack was largely built on the music of The Bee Gees, a band that itself came, like the two interview subjects in Chapter 4, from Chorlton-cum-Hardy, in Manchester.
67 Interview between the author and New Order on behalf of the UK club culture magazine *Muzik*, recorded at the Malmaison Hotel, Manchester, ahead of the release of their 2001 album *Get Ready*. The audio can be found at https://www.rocksbackpages.com/Library/Article/new-order-2001.

68 The Situationist International Manifesto, *Internationale Situationniste* #4 (June 1960) can be found at http://www.cddc.vt.edu/sionline/si/manifesto.html [last accessed 24 June 2016].
69 Ivan Chtcheglov's 'Formulary for a New Urbanism' can be found at http://www.bopsecrets.org/SI/Chtcheglov.htm [last accessed 27 April 2017]. Italics in original.
70 The author produced a documentary about the Haçienda on its fifteenth anniversary in 1997, for the Manchester radio station *Kiss Radio*. Including interviews with Tony Wilson, Rob Gretton and members of The Smiths and the Happy Mondays, the author's copy is now sadly lost.
71 Full Factory catalogue numbers can be found at www.factoryrecords.net/catalogue/ [last accessed 24 June 2016].
72 For further reading see Dave Haslam, *Manchester, England: The Story of the Pop Cult City* (London: Fourth Estate, 2010).
73 Tracks chosen from the 87-91 CD of the album *Viva: Fifteen years of Haçienda nights* (UK: Deconstruction, 1997).
74 Thornton, *Club Cultures*, p. 15.
75 In Jon Savage, *The Hacienda Must Be Built* (Woodford Green: International Music Publications, 1992), p. 38.
76 Pierre Bourdieu, *Distinction: A Social Critique of the Judgement of Taste* (London: Routledge, 2010).
77 The Happy Mondays released their 'MADChester Rave On' EP in November 1989 through Factory Records, the track 'Hallelujah' proving to be a breakthrough hit.
78 The Happy Mondays, 'Loose Fit' (UK: Factory, 1991).
79 Mick Middles, *Factory: The Story of the Record Label* (London: Random House, 2011), p. 326.
80 These comments are from a contemporaneous documentary, broadcast as part of the programme *Riverside*, BBC, 1983, which can be found at https://www.youtube.com/watch?v=YvUwmKDGhC8 [last accessed 1 November 2017].
81 Chtcheglov, 'Formulary for a New Urbanism'.
82 In a sense, commercial psychogeography even now drives club operators to reopen Factory's offices as a nightclub, or for Crosby Homes to buy the site of the Haçienda club and, playing on these acid house notions, rebuild it as a block of 'luxury' loft apartments. Perhaps such structures need to be destroyed by commerce to survive in perpetuity in the myth. This would almost certainly be Barthes's contention.
83 A misspelling of Durruti, The Durutti Column were a Factory band for many years, featuring guitarist Vini Reilly.
84 The process of its architectural deconstruction and subsequent commercial redistribution is in itself reported in the documentary *Do You Own the Dancefloor*, dir. Chris Hughes (UK: Heehaw Films, 2015).
85 Simon Reynolds, 'Rave Culture: Living Dream or Living Death', in Steve Redhead (ed.), *The Clubcultures Reader: Readings in Popular Cultural Studies* (Oxford: Blackwell, 1998), p. 85.
86 See Roger McKeon, ed., *Driftworks* (New York: Semiotext(e), 1984), a translation of the essays contained in Jean-François Lyotard, *Dérive à partir de Marx et Freud* (Paris: Union Général d'Editions, 1973).
87 Bey, *T.A.Z.*, p. 104.
88 Graham St. John, *Technomad: Global Raving Countercultures* (London: Equinox, 2009).

89   Bennett, 'Consolidating the Music Scenes Perspective', p. 230.
90   See Simon A. Morrison, 'Manumission', *Ministry in Ibiza*, 14 August–27 August 1999, p. 20.
91   In 1997 EDMC magazine *Mixmag* ran a cover titled 'Gunchester', featuring an image of a hooded man holding up a gun. It proved both controversial and damaging to the city at that time.
92   Although a tragic change in pace, this was also a fecund period for the researchers at the Manchester Institute for Popular Culture, which functioned through these years. See Redhead, *The Clubcultures Reader*.
93   Morrison, 'Manumission', p. 21.
94   Equally it might be seen as a 'carnival', in Bakhtin's terms, theories that will be incorporated into the analysis of Irvine Welsh in Chapter 6.
95   Bey, *T.A.Z.*, p. xi.
96   Ibid.
97   Bey compares this free state to a Pirate Utopia, adding how fond of music pirates seem to be. And indeed Ibiza was once a base for pirates.
98   This was where Freddie Mercury would famously perform the 1992 Olympic theme 'Barcelona' with Montserrat Caballé, and Grace Jones (fêted at Studio 54) would also appear.
99   Morrison, 'Manumission', p. 23.
100   Sheila Henderson, *Ecstasy: Case Unsolved* (London: Pandora, 1997), p. 48.
101   Ibid., p. 119.
102   The title for this section derives from the track 'The Politics of Dancing' (UK: EMI, 1983), in which the band Re-flex sang: 'We got the message / I heard it on the airwaves / The politicians / Are now DJs', in a decade defined by recession and industrial strife.
103   The scientific basis for this research is the article 'Express Yourself', written in the late 1990s by the author for *DJ* magazine, n.d.
104   Simon Morrison, 'Express Yourself', interview with Dr Neil Todd conducted at the University of Manchester for *DJ* magazine.
105   Certainly, some electronic tracks are specifically built with that thought in mind, for instance the orgiastic female vocal on the Lil Louis track 'French Kiss' (US: Diamond Records, 1989).
106   Such a function is exemplified by Manumission promoter Mike McKay, having sex on stage with his partner, Claire Davies. Initially a philosophical statement that added to the myth of proceedings, it ultimately became a seedy spectacle that tarnished the reputation of the night, as voyeurs were attracted for that event, rather than the night itself.
107   Holleran, *Dancer from the Dance*.
108   Huq, *Beyond Subculture*, p. 100.
109   Simon Reynolds, 'Rave Culture: Living Dream or Living Death?', p. 91.
110   Irvine Welsh, interviewed in person by the author at Molly Malone's pub, Glasgow, 19 February 2012 and via a 45-minute phone call to Miami, 23 February 2012.
111   Shapiro, *Waiting for the Man*, pp. 246–7.
112   Douglas Keay, 'Aids, Education and the Year 2000', *Woman's Own* (31 October 1987), pp. 8–10.
113   As a personal recollection of these parties, Anthony Wayne's *Class of 88: The True Acid House Experience* (London: Virgin Book, 1998) is a very compelling study.

114 Simon Frith, 'The Cultural Study of Popular Music', in Lawrence Grossberg, Cary Nelson and Paula Treichler, eds., *Cultural Studies* (New York: Routledge, 1992), p. 177.
115 The Beastie Boys, '(You Gotta) Fight for Your Right (to Party)' (USA: Def Jam Recordings, 1986).
116 Bey, *T.A.Z.*, p. 103.
117 Henderson, *Ecstasy*, p. 120.
118 This position was reinforced at the 2016 Louder than Words conference. In a panel entitled The Politics of Dancing, convened by the author, it was interesting to note that, by a show of hands, the audience and panel did feel the club scene was politicized, notably following events in 2016 including the mass shooting at Florida gay club Pulse, and the closing of the Fabric nightclub in London.
119 UK Government (1994) Criminal Justice and Disorder Act: www.legislation.gov.uk/ukpga/1994/33/section/63 [last accessed 29 December 2012].
120 Walton, *Out of It*, p. 271.
121 Reynolds, 'Rave Culture: Living Dream or Living Death?', p. 86.
122 Walton, *Out of It*, p. xxii.
123 In the early hours of 28 June 1969 police raided the Mafia-owned gay club the Stonewall Inn, located by Christopher Park in Greenwich Village, New York. The resulting riots functioned as a resistance against authority delivered by the community itself.
124 The Happy Mondays included a track 'God's Cop' on their album *Pills 'n' Thrills and Bellyaches* (UK: Factory Records, 1990).
125 Anderton's comments were made during a speech at a policing seminar, December 1986.
126 Nicholas Blincoe, *Manchester Slingback* (London: Pan, 1998).
127 Walton, *Out of It*, p. 118.
128 At the Politics of Dancing talk at Louder than Words, panellists touched on this discourse, detailing how the policy of Mayor Giuliani in New York, and a similar policy in London, are stripping those cities of their cultural vitality.
129 It is worth noting how both of the latter draw their names from politically charged sources.
130 See Phillips, *Superstar DJs Here We Go!*
131 Mikhail Bakhtin, *Rabelais and His World* (Bloomington: Indiana University Press, 1984).
132 The author once reviewed a Singapore nightclub, for instance, owned and operated (it transpired) entirely by the Singapore government. Bakhtin's theories are here made manifest.
133 Bey, *T.A.Z.*, p. 99
134 Ibid., p. 124.
135 Henderson, *Ecstasy*, p. 6.
136 For further information on Spiral Tribe, see Simon Reynolds, *Generation Ecstasy*; Matthew Collin, *Pop Grenade* (London: Zero Books, 2015).
137 Bey, *T.A.Z.*, p. 100. Italics in original.
138 Henderson, *Ecstasy*, p. 4.
139 It is this spirit Alex Garland taps for his novel *The Beach*, an important, early and commercially successful work of Dancefloor-Driven Literature.
140 Henderson, *Ecstasy*, p. xxvi.

Chapter 4

1. Stuart Hall, *Representation: Cultural Representation and Signifying Practices* (London: Sage, 2003).
2. Bey, *T.A.Z.*, p. 128.
3. Ibid., p. 130. Italics in original.
4. Held in Kassel, Germany, the author presented his own theories of re/presentation at this conference.
5. Wolf, *The Musicalization of Fiction*, p. 237.
6. Here Fisher channels Ian Penman writing about dub music in Fisher, *Ghosts of My Life*, p. 132.
7. Thornton, *Club Cultures*, p. 34.
8. Bibliographic details for these titles will follow in subsequent footnotes.
9. Redhead, *Repetitive Beat Generation*, p. xxii. Ellipses in original.
10. Stan Beeler, *Dance, Drugs and Escape: The Club Scene in Literature, Film and Television Since the Late 1980s* (North Carolina: McFarland & Co., 2007), p. 182.
11. Ibid., p. 25.
12. Henderson, *Ecstasy*, p. 9.
13. Alan Partridge: https://www.youtube.com/watch?v=NGvzlf-4PJQ&t=10s [last accessed 16 August 2017], *Family Guy*: https://www.youtube.com/watch?v=ZaT_hqGUP7U [last accessed 22 January 2018].
14. *It's All Gone Pete Tong*, dir. Michael Dowse (UK: Vertigo, 2004).
15. *24 Hour Party People*, dir. Michael Winterbottom (UK: Pathé, 2002).
16. *Kevin & Perry Go Large*, dir. Ed Bye (UK: Icon, 2000).
17. One might look, for instance, at a subset of Ibiza-based TV vehicles, from the TV version of Colin Butts's fiction *Is Harry on the Boat?* (London: Orion, 1997) through to reality series such as London Weekend Television's *Ibiza Uncovered* of the late 1990s and documentaries such as the Jimi Mistry–produced documentary *And the Beat Goes On* (2009) and 2019's *Ibiza: The Silent Movie*, directed by Julien Temple. Indeed, during his time living on the island, the author of this book had some personal experience of this area, writing, researching and appearing in the *Club-A-Vision* Ibiza Specials for ITV and also presenting a gossip segment for Rapture TV.
18. 'Cherubim and Seraphim', *Inspector Morse*, dir. Danny Boyle (UK: ITV, 15 April 1992). Danny Boyle would go on to direct both *Trainspotting* (1996) and *The Beach* (2000), both of which have EDMC resonances.
19. Quoted in Beeler, *Dance, Drugs, Escape*, p. 174.
20. 'Cardigan', *Men Behaving Badly*, dir. Martin Dennis (UK: BBC1, 18 July 1996), https://www.youtube.com/watch?v=AKIADiVLT1c, [last accessed 14 August 2017].
21. 'Cardigan', 13:30.
22. The 1990s were also the decade of 'laddism', defined by interests in football, music and lager, perhaps most perfectly encapsulated in the magazine *Loaded*.
23. 'Cardigan', 26:13.
24. See Roland Barthes, 'Introduction to the Structural Analysis of Narratives', in Roland Barthes, *Image, Music, Text* (London: Fontana Press, 1977), pp. 79–124.
25. Thomas Pynchon, *Gravity's Rainbow* (London: Vintage, 2000).
26. See Phillips, *Superstar DJs Here We Go!*

27 Kembrew McLeod, 'Genres, Subgenres, Sub-Subgenres and More: Musical and Social Difference within Electronic Dance Music Communities', *Journal of Popular Music Studies* 13 (2001), pp. 59–75 (p. 64).
28 Collin, *Altered State*, pp. 36–7.
29 'Epiphanies', *Spaced* (UK: dir. Edgar Wright, Channel 4, 29 October 1999).
30 Ibid., 03:30.
31 Ibid., 00:01.
32 Ibid., 08:45, emphasis is the author's to suggest the expression of the dialogue.
33 Ibid., 21:10.
34 Ibid., 23:35.
35 Simon Pegg, 'Kermode and Mayo Film Review', *BBC 5Live*, February 2011.
36 Allan Moore, 'Authenticity as Authentication', *Popular Music* 21, no. 2 (2002), pp. 209–23 (p. 214).
37 Beeler, *Dance, Drugs, Escape*, p. 153.
38 Bey, *T.A.Z.*, p. xi.
39 *Rock around the Clock*, dir. Fred F. Sears (USA: Clover Productions, 1956).
40 For further reading, please see Simon A. Morrison, '"Clubs Aren't Like That" Discos, Deviance and Diegetics in Club Culture Cinema', *Dancecult: Journal of Electronic Dance Music Culture* 4, no. 2 (2012), pp. 48–66.
41 Aspects of this section on cinema appeared in a different form in Morrison, 'Clubs Aren't Like That', pp. 48–66.
42 Sean Nye, 'Review Essay: Berlin Calling and Run Lola Run', *Dancecult* 1, no. 2 (2010), pp. 121–7 (p. 121).
43 *54*, dir. Mark Christopher (USA: Dollface, 1998).
44 Graeme Park interviewed by the author, home of the author, 23 March 2011.
45 *24 Hour Party People*, dir. Michael Winterbottom.
46 From the perspective of participant observation, and as an extra in the filming, the author therefore enjoyed the rather peculiar ethnographic position of researching a club in its fictional reconstruction. This experience, some of which was spent with Graeme Park, was recounted in the chapter '24 Hour Party People', in Morrison, *Discombobulated*, pp. 198–202.
47 See comments of Greg Harrison, director of the 2000 American EDMC film *Groove* (USA: Sony Pictures, 2000), in a documentary included with the DVD extras.
48 However, in further analysing tropes of authenticity, it was not Haslam who shared the booth with Mike Pickering at actual Haçienda events, but Graeme Park who, during the filming, was, instead, at the bar with the author of this book.
49 Park, author interview.
50 *Ecstasy*, dir. Lux (Canada: Dolce Cielo, 2011).
51 *Irvine Welsh's Ecstasy*, dir. Rob Heydon (Canada: Silver Reel, 2012).
52 In terms of the Heydon film, the journalism work of the author of this book led to invitations to two screenings prior to distribution (one in London and one at the 2012 Glasgow Film Festival) as well as the opportunity to spend time with the author of the source material, Irvine Welsh, the film's director Rob Heydon and principal male lead, Adam Sinclair.
53 The Lux film had a limited release in North America, via DVD and streaming methods. Although the copy used for this research is marked as a final cut, it appears the film has subsequently been re-edited.

54 Although in terms of Heydon's film, one must also remember the importance of Irvine Welsh's source text, and the central role of Edinburgh and Edinburgh characters.
55 Rob Heydon, interviewed in person by the author, Novotel hotel, Glasgow, 19 February 2012.
56 Redhead, *Repetitive Beat Generation*, p. xxii.
57 *Weekender*, dir. Karl Golden (UK: Benchmark Films, 2011). Although released in 2011, this film takes as historic context the rave scene of 1990.
58 In terms of semantics, the word 'genesis' itself formed the name to one of the original key raves. See Anthony, *Class of 88*.
59 Richard Middleton, *Studying Popular Music* (Open University Press: Milton Keynes, 1997), p. 9.
60 Hebdige, *Subculture*, p. 101.
61 Middleton, *Studying Popular Music*, p. 9.
62 In Hebdige, *Subculture*, p. 90.
63 Thornton, *Club Cultures*, p. 146.
64 Redhead, *Repetitive Beat Generation*, p. xxi.
65 Irvine Welsh, 'The Undefeated', in *Ecstasy: Three Tales of Chemical Romance* (London: Jonathan Cape, 1996).
66 Collin, *Altered State*, p. 302.
67 Irvine Welsh, *Trainspotting* (London: Minerva, 1994).
68 *Trainspotting*, dir. Danny Boyle (Channel 4 Films, 1996).
69 Simon A. Morrison, 'Irvine's Ecstasy', *Mixmag*, May 2012.
70 Mark Cousins, *The Story of Film* (London: Pavilion Books, 2011), p. 494.
71 Ibid.
72 Heydon, *Irvine Welsh's Ecstasy*, 0:53. Note the use of the phrase 'disco biscuits', which will become significant in Chapter 4.
73 This cinematic theory will, later in this book, be appropriated for more literary means.
74 Claudia Gorbman, *Unheard Melodies: Narrative Film Music* (London: BFI Publishing, 1987), p. 21.
75 James Monaco, *How to Read a Film: Movies, Media, Multimedia*, 3rd edn (Oxford: Oxford University Press, 2000), p. 155.
76 Hussey remarks that the process was further complicated by subsequent re-edits of the film, which have recut certain scenes and therefore further disturbed the synergy between the mise en scène and diegetic soundtrack.
77 Nick Hussey, interviewed in person by the author, All Bar One, Manchester, 25 March 2011.
78 Rob Heydon, author interview.
79 Heydon, *Irvine Welsh's Ecstasy*, 1:28.
80 Adam Sinclair, interviewed in person by the author, Novotel hotel, Glasgow, 19 February 2012.
81 Ibid.
82 Heydon, *Irvine Welsh's Ecstasy*, 1:02:14. The night is called Musica and features real-world DJ John Digweed, who also makes a cameo, playing himself, in the American film *Groove*.
83 Heydon, author interview.

84 Gorbman, *Unheard Melodies*, p. 11.
85 Heydon, *Irvine Welsh's Ecstasy*, 31:02.
86 Heydon, author interview.
87 Heydon, *Irvine Welsh's Ecstasy*, 57:01.
88 Monaco, *How to Read a Film*, p. 158.
89 Beeler, *Dance, Drugs, Escape*, p. 49.
90 Andrew Calcutt and Richard Shephard, *Cult Fiction: A Reader's Guide* (London: Prion, 1998), p. xvi.
91 David Muggleton, 'The Post-subculturalist', in Redhead, *The Club Cultures Reader*, p. 91.
92 McLeod, 'Genres, Subgenres, Sub-Subgenres and More', pp. 59–75 (p. 59).
93 Irvine Welsh, interviewed in person at Molly Malone's pub, Glasgow, 19 February 2012 and via a 45-minute phone call to Miami, 23 February 2012.
94 One such media would be radio and indeed the author has worked extensively in this medium, for stations including BBC Radio 1 and Kiss 102 Radio. A study of greater length would enable a consideration of such broadcasters, alongside inner-city pirate radio; however, that is not possible in a study of this scale.
95 Sarah Champion, in Redhead, *Repetitive Beat Generation*, p. 18.
96 Ibid., p. 16.
97 Aspects of this section appear in a different form in Simon A. Morrison, '"Surely People Who Go Clubbing Don't Read": Dispatches from the Dancefloor and Clubland in Print', *IASPM Journal*, ed. C. Jacke, M. James and Ed Montano, 4, no. 2 (2014).
98 Defined by Tom Wolfe in his celebrated 1973 collection *The New Journalism* (London: Picador, 1990), it was estimated by New Journalism theorist Marc Weingarten to have taken place in America between 1962 and 1977, popularized by writers such as Wolfe himself, Joan Didion, Gay Telese, Terry Southern, Norman Mailer and Hunter S. Thompson.
99 The author shared a questionnaire with several key industry professionals in June and July 2013. The questionnaire appears as appendix III, while relevant comments are included in-text.
100 Thornton, *Club Cultures*, p. 120, cited in Hodkinson, *Goth*.
101 Steve Redhead, *Subculture to Clubcultures: An Introduction to Popular Cultural Studies* (Oxford: Blackwell, 1997), p. 103.
102 For further reading, see Morrison, 'Surely People Who Go Clubbing Don't Read', pp. 71–84.
103 Stanley Cohen, *Folk Devils and Moral Panics* (London: Routledge, 2002).
104 As defined by The Criminal Justice and Public Order Act, 1994.
105 'Spaced Out', *The Sun*, 24 June 1989.
106 Interestingly – and despite the protestations that will be considered in the following chapter – *The Face* magazine did publish Richard Benson, ed., *Nightfever: Club Writing in the Face 1980–1997* (London: Boxtree, 1997), in the same year Champion's own edition of short stories, *Disco Biscuits*, was published.
107 Thornton, *Club Cultures*, p. 158.
108 This book will also evidence how Irvine Welsh cited such magazines to engender authenticity in his fiction, as did author Trevor Miller who, on page 23 of his 1989 clubland novel *Trip City* (further considered in the following chapter), discusses the

109 life cycle of a club, The Underground, and the influence of the media: 'Articles in *The Face* and *i-D*. Big money taken on the door. Then it crashed.'
109 Tony Prince, response to questionnaire, 2 September 2013. Note that questionnaire responses are reproduced with their original grammar.
110 Chris Mellor, ex-editor of *Jocks* and *DJ*, response to questionnaire, 29 July 2013.
111 International Publishing Corporation, a UK publishing house now subsidiary of Time Inc.
112 These figures are from *Ministry* editor Scott Manson, but correlate with the recollection of the author. Historical figures can be found with the Audit Bureau of Circulation at www.abc.org.uk.
113 Tony Prince, response to questionnaire.
114 Dan Prince, editor of *DMCWorld.Com*, response to questionnaire, 2 September 2013.
115 Huq, *Beyond Subculture*, p. 104.
116 Redhead, *Repetitive Beat Generation*, p. xx.
117 See Eamonn Forde, 'From Polyglottism to Branding: On the Decline of Personality Journalism in the British Music Press', *Journalism: Theory, Practice, Criticism* 2, no. 1 (2001), pp. 37–56.
118 'Fear and Loathing in Las Vegas' first appeared in *Rolling Stone* issue 95, 11 November 1971 and issue 96, 25 November 1971. Thompson will be discussed in more detail later in this chapter.
119 Sarah Champion, interviewed in person by the author, the Leadstation, Chorlton, Manchester, 29 May 2013.
120 Champion, author interview.
121 See Dan Sperber and Deirdre Wilson, *Relevance: Communication and Cognition*, 2nd edn (Oxford: Blackwell, 1995); Adam Gargani, 'Poetic Comparisons: How Similes Are Understood' (unpublished doctoral book, University of Salford, 2014).
122 Roland Barthes, *Mythologies* (London: Vintage, 2009), p. 138.
123 Champion, author interview.
124 Hunter S. Thompson, *Fear and Loathing in America: The Brutal Odyssey of an Outlaw Journalist 1968–1976* (London: Bloomsbury, 2000), p. xiv.
125 John Hollowell, *Fact & Fiction: The New Journalism and the Nonfiction Novel* (Chapel Hill: The University of North Carolina Press, 1977), p. 52.
126 Marc Weingarten, *Who's Afraid of Tom Wolfe? How New Journalism Rewrote the World* (London: Aurum, 2005), p. 8.
127 Hollowell, *Fact & Fiction*, p. 52.
128 Champion, author interview.
129 Manson was also editor of *Loaded*, a 'lad's mag' that certainly did express, to a certain extent, the gonzo sensibilities of the 1990s, mirrored in the TV programme *Men Behaving Badly*, analysed earlier.
130 Scott Manson, ex-editor of *Ministry*, response to questionnaire, 24 July 2013.
131 James 'Disco' Davis, ex-Clubs Editor of *Ministry*, response to questionnaire, 11 July 2013.
132 Duncan Dick, deputy editor of *Mixmag*, response to questionnaire, 16 September 2013.
133 Skrufff, DJ and writer, response to questionnaire, 15 July 2013.
134 Amol Rajan, 'The Diary: Techno in Barcelona, the Indie's Founding Fathers, and My Advice to Australia's Cricket Team', *New Statesman*, 28 June–4 July 2013, p. 20.

135 When the collection of these columns, *Discombobulated*, was reviewed in the EDMC journal *Dancecult*, they registered this Gonzo impulse: 'Enjoying the ride is not viewed as a distraction or something to be editorially cut from his clubland tales but instead forms an integral part of his adventures. Often discussed in relation to drugs research is the tendency for writers to produce sanitised accounts of their fieldwork whilst neglecting the role of pleasure (Holt and Treloar 2008); this aspect of clubland is a feature most definitely not omitted from Morrison's accounts', *Dancecult: Journal of Electronic Dance Music Culture* 4, no. 1 (2011), pp. 107–18 (pp. 113–14).
136 Forde, 'From Polyglottism to Branding'.
137 John Hellman, *Fables of Fact: The New Journalism as New Fiction* (Chicago: University of Illinois Press, 1981), p. 22.
138 Ibid., p. 23.
139 Barthes, *Mythologies*, p. 152.
140 Ibid., p. 131.
141 After our meeting, the author of this book gave Champion a copy of his book, *Discombobulated*. She subsequently read it and on 25 June 2013 sent the following text message: 'Did i tell you how much i love you book. That's gonzo'.
142 Hunter S. Thompson, *The Great Shark Hunt* (London: Summit Books, 1979), jacket cover.
143 Redhead, *Repetitive Beat Generation*, p. 128.
144 Mick Farren, *Elvis Died for Somebody's Sins but Not Mine* (London: Headpress, 2013), p. 178.
145 Ibid.
146 Norman Mailer, *Armies of the Night* (London: Penguin, 1970).
147 In this digital age, that is partly alleviated by the archives of Rock's Backpages (www.rocksbackpages.com), although undoubtedly many of those club culture publications will only survive in the cellars and attics of the most devoted collectors and aficionados.

Chapter 5

1 Holleran, *Dancer from the Dance*, p. 35.
2 Aspects of this chapter appear in a different form in Simon A. Morrison, 'Dancefloor-Driven Literature: Subcultural Big Bangs and a New Center for the Aesthetic Universe', *Popular Music* 36, no. 1 (The Critical Imperative) (January 2017), pp. 43–54.
3 Miller, *Trip City*.
4 Champion, *Disco Biscuits*.
5 Reported in Redhead, *Repetitive Beat Generation*, p. xxii. Unfortunately, Redhead does not include a reference to the edition of the magazine in which this featured.
6 'E' in reference to the drug Ecstasy that was widely seen as the pharmaceutical driver of the rave scene. For further reading, refer to Chapter 3.
7 First published in 1948, the edition used in this research is Brown, *Music and Literature*. See also Scher, *Essays on Literature and Music (1967–2004)*; Wolf, *The Musicalization of Fiction*.

8   Smyth, *Music in Contemporary British Fiction*; Rachel Carroll and Adam Hansen, eds., *LitPop: Writing and Popular Music* (Farnham: Ashgate, 2014); Eric Hertz and Jeffrey Roessner, *Write in Tune* (New York: Bloomsbury, 2014).
9   Doing Nightlife and EDMC Fieldwork Special Issue, *Dancecult* 5, no. 1 (2013).
10 Morrison, 'Surely People Who Go Clubbing Don't Read', pp. 71–84 (p. 74).
11 Scher, *Essays on Literature and Music*.
12 Smyth, *Music in Contemporary British Fiction*.
13 Middleton, *Reading Pop*, p. 3.
14 The author presented a paper at the 2017 biannual IASPM conference and was interested to note discourse in this area continues.
15 'Mancunian' in the sense from, or of, Manchester.
16 The Lost Generation were principally American writers working in the post First World War period, including Ernest Hemingway and F. Scott Fitzgerald.
17 José Francisco Fernández, *The New Puritan Generation* (Canterbury: Gylphi, 2013), p. 6.
18 Redhead, *Repetitive Beat Generation*, p. 4.
19 Jeff Noon, interviewed in person by the author: Pizza Express, Charing Cross, London, 7 April 2014.
20 Irvine Welsh, interviewed in person by the author: Molly Malone's pub, Glasgow, 19 February 2012, and by telephone, 23 February 2012.
21 Nicholas Blincoe, interviewed in person at Le Pain Quotidien, Victoria, London, 12 April 2013.
22 Sarah Champion, interviewed in person at the Leadstation, Chorlton, Manchester, 29 May 2013.
23 Ibid.
24 Chares Bukowski, 1920–94, was an American author and poet who focused on the downtrodden of Los Angeles for character and subject matter.
25 Champion, author interview.
26 The Criminal Justice and Public Order Act, November 1994.
27 Redhead, *Repetitive Beat Generation*, p. xxvi.
28 Ibid., p. xxvi.
29 Ibid., p. xxv.
30 Champion, *Disco Biscuits*, p. xiv.
31 Redhead, *Repetitive Beat Generation*, p. 14.
32 Ibid., p. 14.
33 Champion, *Disco Biscuits*, p. xvi.
34 Champion, author interview.
35 Indeed the phrase forms one of the list of slang terms that are read out at the start of the film *Irvine Welsh's Ecstasy*, dir. Rob Heydon (Canada: Silver Reel, 2012), discussed in the last chapter.
36 Champion, author interview.
37 Hebdige, *Subculture*, p. 97.
38 Jonathan Brook, 'Sangria', in Champion, *Disco Biscuits*, p. 128.
39 Matthew de Abaitua, 'Inbetween', ibid., p. 245.
40 Michael River, 'Electrovoodoo', ibid., p. 102.
41 Mike Benson, 'Room Full of Angels', ibid., p. 24.
42 Brook, 'Sangria', ibid., p. 134.

43 Ibid., p. 136.
44 Nicholas Blincoe, 'Ardwick Green', ibid., p. 9.
45 Charlie Hall, 'The Box', ibid., p. 153.
46 Ben Graham, 'Weekday Service', ibid., p. 164.
47 Ibid., pp. 73, 73, 151, 151, 210, 210, 210.
48 Ibid., pp. 67, 67, 72, 72, 72, 72, 72, 73, 73, 111, 111, 154.
49 Alan Warner, 'Bitter Salvage', ibid., p. 263.
50 Puff, 'Two Fingers', ibid., p. 211.
51 Ibid., p. 212.
52 Simon Frith, *Sound Effects: Youth, Leisure, and the Politics of Rock'n'Roll* (New York: Pantheon, 1981), p. 5.
53 Champion, author interview.
54 Ibid.
55 See Chapter 7.
56 Champion, author interview.
57 For further information on the Haçienda, see Chapter 3.
58 Redhead, *Repetitive Beat Generation*, p. xii. The Arthrob parties are discussed again in Chapter 6.
59 Champion, author interview.
60 Ibid.
61 Ibid.
62 Champion, author interview.
63 Smyth, *Music in Contemporary British Fiction*, p. 119.
64 Paul Mathur, 'Trip City Is Green', *The London Evening Standard*, 12 October 1989.
65 Jack Barron, 'Tripping Yarns', *New Musical Express*, 2 December 1989, p. 48.
66 Miller, *Trip City*, p. 1.
67 New Order, 'Blue Monday', Factory Records, 1983.
68 Miller, *Trip City*, pp. 180–1.
69 Jim Burns, interviewed in person by the author: Red Bull pub, Stockport, 16 June, 2011.
70 Smyth, *Music in Contemporary British Fiction*, p. 3.
71 Ibid.
72 *Huffington Post*, 2015.
73 Miller, *Trip City*, p. 93.
74 Twenty-five years after its publication, Trevor Miller attempted to publish an anniversary edition (see Figure 5.2). The author of this book arranged for a reunion of Miller and Gerald at the 2014 Louder than Words literature festival in Manchester to mark the occasion. Several years down the line it is now perhaps fitting, even amusing, that (quite independently) neither of them turned up.
75 A Guy Called Gerald, *Trip City* (UK: Avernus, 1989). The tracks remain available through more contemporary digital media portals.
76 A conflation of 'producer' and 'consumer', Alvin Toffler's term implies the consumer is more active in the process of production and consumption of the artefact.
77 This might have even further ramifications in the current digital age, where YouTube can provide an audio key to the consumption of a literary novel. Pursuing these intermedial thoughts, I myself published a soundtrack on *Mixcloud* to accompany the reading of my article 'Dancefloor-Driven Literature', pp. 43–54, mixed by Nick Hussey.

78 This reading is a result of a close listening to the music, 16 May 2016.
79 *Disco Biscuits* (UK: Coalition, 1997). Compiled by Sarah Champion herself (although in conversation she explains the addition of 'Groovy Train' by indie band the Farm was a late and unwelcome addition by record label Coalition), the double album contains tracks including 'Pacific State' by 808 State, 'Not Forgotten' by Leftfield, 'Strings of Life' by Rhythim Is Rhythim and what is badged on the cover as an 'Exclusive Andrew Weatherall track', the Two Lone Swordsmen cut 'Kicking In and Out'.
80 *Energy Flash* (UK: No Label, 1998). This CD includes tracks such as 'Aftermath' by Nightmares on Wax, DJ Hype's 'Shot in the Dark', 'The Element' by 4Hero and the titular 'Energy Flash' by Joey Beltram.
81 Calcutt and Shephard, *Cult Fiction*, p. xv.
82 See Chapter 1 for a full definition of diegesis.
83 Miller, *Trip City*, pp. 16, 20, 108, 167, 173, 175, 240.
84 Ibid., pp. 8, 8, 173, 173, 177.
85 Ibid., p. 100.
86 Ibid., p. 108.
87 Ibid., pp. 108, 108, 137, 137, 174.
88 Ibid., p. 167.
89 Ibid., p. 2.
90 At the same time, one must accept that non-diegetic music can only exist in the paratextual material to literature, for instance, as soundtrack to accompany its reading, as identified earlier.
91 Miller, *Trip City*, p. 173.
92 Ibid., p. 100.
93 Ibid., p. 108.
94 Ibid., p. 137.
95 Stephen Benson, *Literary Music* (Farnham: Ashgate, 2006), p. 4.
96 The concert with Ornette Coleman took place at La Villette, Paris, 1 July 1997.
97 Cited in Peter Dayan, 'The Force of Music in Derrida's Writing', in Delia da Sosa Correa (ed.), *Phrase and Subject: Studies in Literature and Music* (Oxford: Legenda, 2006), p. 46.
98 Ibid., p. 45.
99 Ibid., p. 46.
100 Trevor Miller, interviewed by the author at the Leadstation, Chorlton, 12 February 2014.
101 Miller, *Trip City*, p. 96.
102 Ibid.
103 Ibid., p. 174.
104 *Day of the Jackal*, dir. Fred Zinnemann (UK & France: Warwick Films, 1973).
105 Miller, *Trip City*, p. 31.
106 Miller, author interview.
107 Ibid.
108 Ibid.
109 Ibid.
110 Ibid.
111 Ibid.

112 Personal communication between Trevor Miller and the author, 2 August 2019.
113 Miller, author interview.
114 Ibid. As detailed in Chapter 2, Anthony H. Wilson, or Tony Wilson, was one of the founders of Factory Records in Manchester and a well-known presenter on the region's Granada Television, hosting important music television shows.
115 *i-D* review of Welsh's 1996 novel *Maribou Stork Nightmares*, cited in end matter of Welsh, *Glue*.
116 Miller, author interview.
117 Jonathan Bate, 'Reading for Your Life: How Books Help Us to Become Better Human Beings', *New Statesman*, 14–20 August 2015.
118 Neil Gaiman, '"Let's Talk about Genre": Neil Gaiman and Kazuo Ishiguro in Conversation', *New Statesman*, 29 May–4 June 2015.
119 Wolf, *The Musicalization of Fiction*, p. 234.
120 Martin Millar, 'How Sunshine Star-Traveller Lost His Girlfriend', in Champion, *Disco Biscuits*, p. 90.
121 Ibid., p. 96.
122 Jean Baudrillard, *Fatal Strategies* (New York: Semiotext(e), 1990), p. 195.
123 For further expansion on this notion of an interstellar intermediality, see Morrison, 'Dancefloor-Driven Literature'.
124 Building on these thoughts, EDMC producer Fatboy Slim released an album titled *Halfway Between the Gutter and the Stars*.
125 Cited in Middleton, 'Last Night a DJ Saved My Life', p. 26.
126 This idea will be further explored in Chapter 9.

Chapter 6

1 Irvine Welsh, in an interview with the author of this book for *Muzik* magazine, c. 2001, for the launch of the novel *Glue*.
2 Champion, *Disco Biscuits*.
3 Redhead, *Repetitive Beat Generation*.
4 Collin, *Altered State*, p. 302.
5 Ibid., p. 303.
6 Beeler, *Dance, Drugs and Escape*, p. 56.
7 Calcutt and Shephard, *Cult Fiction*, p. 285.
8 For further information on this concept, please see Mikhail Bakhtin, *The Dialogic Imagination: Four Essays* (Austin: University of Texas Press, 2006). This theory will be discussed in more detail later in this chapter.
9 Redhead, *Repetitive Beat Generation*, p. xxiii.
10 Personal communication with the author. Irvine Welsh, interviewed in person at Molly Malone's pub, Glasgow, 19 February 2012 and via telephone on 23 February 2012.
11 Carroll and Hansen, *LitPop*, p. 21.
12 Welsh, *Ecstasy*.
13 Heydon, *Irvine Welsh's Ecstasy*.
14 Welsh, *Glue*.
15 Redhead, *Repetitive Beat Generation*, p. xxv.

16 Indeed, reports suggest that Welsh is writing a TV series based on Manchester's Donnelly brothers, and the story of their Gio Goi fashion label.
17 Welsh, author interview.
18 Redhead, *Repetitive Beat Generation*, xi. This was also the subtitle for the 1998 short story collection *Intoxication*, identified in the Literature Review of this book.
19 Calcutt and Shephard, *Cult Fiction*, p. 286.
20 Shapiro, *Waiting for the Man*, p. 252.
21 Redhead, *Repetitive Beat Generation*, p. xxvii.
22 Ibid., p. xv.
23 Welsh, author interview.
24 Reynolds, *Generation Ecstasy*, p. 9.
25 Smyth, *Music in Contemporary British Fiction*, p. 216.
26 Redhead, *Repetitive Beat Generation*, p. xv.
27 Welsh, author interview.
28 Ernesto Leal and his brother Juan were Chilean political refugees based initially in Scotland. They founded Arthrob in 1995. Welsh references Andrew Weatherall in his short story 'The Undefeated', explored in greater depth later in this chapter.
29 Bebop was a more improvisational, contemporary and upbeat form of jazz popularized by musicians such as Charlie Parker, Thelonious Monk and Dizzy Gillespie. Their music was hugely influential on Beat Generation writers such as Jack Kerouac.
30 Redhead, *Repetitive Beat Generation*, p. xv.
31 From a conversation with Carl Loben, the Wagon & Horses pub, Brighton, 18 July 2019.
32 Carroll and Hansen, *LitPop*, p. 193.
33 Welsh, *Ecstasy*, p. 38.
34 D-Mob, 'We Call It Acieed' (UK: FFRR, 1988).
35 Welsh, *Glue*, p. 284.
36 Carroll and Hansen, *LitPop*, p. 193.
37 Hertz and Roessner, *Write in Tune*, p. 3.
38 Ibid., p. 60.
39 Nikolina Nedeljkov, 'Creation, Resistance, and Refacement: Postfuturist Storytelling, Cultural Flows, and the Remix' (New York: CUNY Academic Works, 2015), p. 92.
40 Many of these issues were discussed with Nedeljkov during a visit with the author to the British Library, 19 August 2016.
41 Nedeljkov, 'Creation, Resistance, and Refacement', p. 93.
42 Redhead, *Repetitive Beat Generation*, p. xxvii.
43 Smyth, *Music in Contemporary British Fiction*, p. 50.
44 Welsh, author interview.
45 Welsh, *Glue*, p. 225.
46 Smyth, *Music in Contemporary British Fiction*, p. 164.
47 Nikolina Nedeljkov, 'Enduring Schooling: Against Noise, and in the Service of the Remix', *Genero*, 18 (2014), pp. 65–88 (p. 81).
48 Redhead, *Repetitive Beat Generation*, p. 139.
49 Welsh, author interview.
50 Bakhtin, *Rabelais and His World*, p. 380.
51 Welsh, author interview.

52 Bakhtin, *Rabelais and His World*, p. 187.
53 Ibid., p. 188.
54 The author is intrigued to note here the use of the phrase 'the wrong side', since it formed part of the subheading of his own 2010 collection *Discombobulated*, itself often concerned with a grotesque realism.
55 Bakhtin, *Rabelais and His World*, p. 161.
56 Fernández, *The New Puritan Generation*, p. 7.
57 James Boswell (1740–95), diarist and biographer, best known as the biographer of Samuel Johnson.
58 Welsh, author interview.
59 Redhead, *Repetitive Beat Generation*, p. 148.
60 Bakhtin, *Rabelais and His World*, p. 318.
61 See Julia Kristeva, *Powers of Horror*.
62 Magic realism is a literary genre that fused elements of the supernatural into realist fiction, popularized by South American writers such as Gabriel García Márquez.
63 Carroll and Hansen, *LitPop*, p. 231.
64 A Scottish term denoting football fan, or perhaps hooligan, based on the style of clothes they are perceived to wear.
65 Irvine Welsh, 'The State of the Party', Champion, *Disco Biscuits*, p. 39.
66 Ibid.
67 Ibid., p. 33.
68 Ibid.
69 Ibid.
70 Ibid., p. 36.
71 Ibid., p. 42.
72 Bakhtin, *Rabelais and His World*, p. 155.
73 Ibid., p. 303.
74 Welsh, 'The State of the Party', p. 59.
75 Ibid., p. 154.
76 Ibid., pp. 34–5.
77 The emo band My Chemical Romance has cited the text as the inspiration for its name.
78 Barbara Cartland (1901–2000), English writer of principally commercially orientated romance.
79 Jimmy Savile was a UK television star, dramatically discovered, after his death, to have been a long-standing and aggressive paedophile.
80 Thalidomide was a pharmaceutical drug for pregnant women to ease morning sickness which was first manufactured in Germany in the 1950s and marketed in the UK by the Distiller's Company. It was ultimately found to have serious physical consequences on the limb development of babies in utero.
81 Redhead, *Repetitive Beat Generation*, p. 140.
82 Collin, *Altered State*, p. 301.
83 Marcus Boon, *The Road of Excess: A History of Writers on Drugs* (Cambridge, MA: Harvard University Press, 2002), p. 276.
84 Calcutt and Shephard, *Cult Fiction*, p. 286. It should be noted the correct year of publication is 1996.
85 Beeler, *Dance, Drugs and Escape*, p. 4.

86 Ibid., p. 62.
87 Sarah Champion, interviewed in person by the author at the Leadstation, Chorlton, Manchester, 29 May 2013.
88 See Stanley Fish, *Is There a Text in This Class?: The Authority of Interpretive Communities* (Cambridge, MA: Harvard University Press, 1980).
89 Mark Duffett, *Understanding Fandom: An Introduction to the Study of Media Fan Culture* (New York and London: Bloomsbury, 2013), p. 79. Italics in original.
90 Ibid., p. 63.
91 Redhead, *Repetitive Beat Generation*, p. 141.
92 I understand the commercial processes involved very well, having had to battle over the cover of *Discombobulated*, which at one point was to feature a semi-naked woman, for reasons I never really understood.
93 Bakhtin, *Rabelais and His World*, p. 329. Such subterranean semantic connotations also link to the EDMC band Underworld.
94 Ibid., p. ix.
95 Ibid., p. 165.
96 Beeler, *Dance, Drugs and Escape*, p. 59.
97 Smyth, *Music in Contemporary British Fiction*, p. 7.
98 Ibid., p. 116. For a detailed analysis of Forster and music, see Michelle Fillion, *Difficult Rhythm: Music & the Word in E. M. Forster* (Urbana, Chicago: University of Illinois Press, 2010); Fillion explores Forster's reference to specific works by Beethoven, for example, to denote the relative depth of particular characters.
99 Welsh, author interview.
100 Ibid.
101 Hertz and Roessner, *Write in Tune*, p. 3.
102 Ibid.
103 For a further definition of anempathetic music see Michel Chion, cited in Carroll and Hansen, *LitPop*, p. 190.
104 Welsh, author interview.
105 Brett Easton Ellis, *American Psycho* (New York: Vintage Books, 1991).
106 In the Heydon film version of 'The Undefeated' (see Chapter 4 for a more detailed interrogation of *Irvine Welsh's Ecstasy*), this is represented by Hugh's love of country music.
107 Welsh, 'The Undefeated', p. 171.
108 Ibid., p. 236.
109 Ibid.
110 Ibid., p. 237.
111 Ibid., p. 215.
112 Ibid., p. 206.
113 Nedeljkov, *Creation, Resistance, and Refacement*, p. 97.
114 Smyth, *Music in Contemporary British Fiction*, p. 33.
115 Hertz and Roessner, *Write in Tune*, p. 3.
116 Ibid., pp. 169, 176, 194.
117 Ibid., p. 169.
118 Welsh, 'The Undefeated', p. 275.
119 Ibid., p. 267.
120 Ibid., p. 267.

121 Ibid., p. 192.
122 Ibid., p. 265.
123 Ibid., p. 263.
124 As the listings editor of *DJ* magazine in the late 1990s, the author recalls typing out the name of many of these club nights in the magazine.
125 Welsh, 'The Undefeated', p. 204.
126 Ibid., pp. 176, 195, 205, 226, 245, 252, 253, 259, 260, 263.
127 Ibid., pp. 174, 181, 254.
128 Ibid., pp. 169, 185, 188, 189, 200, 225, 235, 230.
129 Ibid., p. 244. These magazines formed part of Chapter 3.
130 Beeler, *Dance, Drugs and Escape*, p. 60.
131 Welsh, 'The Undefeated', p. 155.
132 Parallels might also be drawn to Aldous Huxley's attempts to describe his listening experiences having taken LSD. See Aldous Huxley, *Island* (London: Panther, 1978) and Aldous Huxley, *Moksha: Aldous Huxley's Classic Writings on Psychedelics and the Visionary Experience*, eds, Michael Horowitz and Cynthia Palmer (Rochester, VT: Park Street Press, 1999).
133 Henderson, *Ecstasy*, p. 48.
134 Beat writers such as Jack Kerouac and Gonzo-orientated journalists such as Hunter S. Thompson, Lester Bangs and Tom Wolfe would certainly occupy this ground, and stylistic links can be drawn between all of these authors.
135 Champion, author interview.
136 Welsh, 'The Undefeated', p. 254.
137 Dave Haslam, 'DJ Culture', in Redhead, *The Clubcultures Reader*, p. 160.
138 Wolf, *The Musicalization of Fiction*, p. 238.
139 Ibid., p. 236.
140 For Bakhtin, the notion of heteroglossia foregrounds the importance of social and historical context in the understanding of text. See Bakhtin, *The Dialogic Imagination*.
141 Welsh, author interview.
142 Welsh, *Glue*, p. 276.
143 The November 2011 issue of *Mixmag* threatened to 'out' the real person that Welsh's DJ was based upon, but in conversation with the author of this book Welsh suggested that this person would 'sue my arse off' if his identity were revealed, adding: 'It is based on somebody but I'm not saying who. Keep it enigmatic, like.'
144 Welsh, author interview.
145 Welsh, *Glue*, p. 22.
146 Ibid., p. 25.
147 Ibid., p. 192.
148 Beeler, *Dance, Drugs and Escape*, p. 65.
149 Welsh, author interview.
150 Welsh, *Glue*, p. 31.
151 Ibid., p. 311.
152 Ibid., p. 276.
153 Irvine Welsh in Redhead, *Repetitive Beat Generation*, p. 148. This notion will be discussed further later in this chapter.
154 Welsh, *Glue*, p. 332.

155 Hebdige, *Subcultures*, p. 168.
156 Adam Brown, 'Let's All Have a Disco? Football, Popular Music and Democratization', in Redhead, *The Clubcultures Reader*, p. 78.
157 Welsh, author interview.
158 Ben Malbon, *Clubbing: Dancing, Ecstasy and Vitality* (London: Routledge, 1999), p. 6.
159 Reynolds, 'Rave Culture: Living Dream or Living Death?', p. 86.
160 Hillegonda Rietveld, 'Living the Dream', in Steve Redhead (ed.), *Rave Off: Politics and Deviance in Contemporary Youth Culture* (Aldershot: Avebury, 1993), p. 58.
161 Reynolds, 'Rave Culture: Living Dream or Living Death?', p. 90.
162 See Barthes, *Mythologies*.
163 Tom Wolfe, *Radical Chic and Mau-mauing the Flak Catchers* (London: Cardinal, 1989), p. 42.
164 Bakhtin, *Rabelais and His World*, p. 309.
165 Ibid., p. 319.
166 Ibid., p. 378.
167 Both the film and the book of *Trainspotting* feature a scene in which the character Renton finds that the only opiates he can find are suppositories.
168 Welsh, *Glue*, p. 263.
169 Ibid., p. 290.
170 Ibid., p. 298. This section is actually subtitled 'Foreskin'.
171 Bakhtin, *Rabelais and His World*, p. 315.
172 Thornton, *Club Cultures*, p. 146.
173 Theodor Adorno, *The Jargon of Authenticity* (London: Routledge Classics, 2003), p. xix.
174 Hebdige, *Subcultures*, p. 91.
175 Welsh, *Glue*, p. 327.
176 Welsh, author interview.
177 Welsh, *Glue*, p. 399.
178 Welsh, author interview.
179 Redhead, *Repetitive Beat Generation*, p. 148.
180 Welsh, *Glue*, p. 473.
181 Ibid., p. 554.
182 Ibid.
183 Ibid., p. 275.
184 Wolf, *The Musicalization of Fiction*, p. 236.
185 Haslam, 'DJ Culture', p. 157.
186 Welsh, *Glue*, p. 328.
187 Beeler, *Dance, Drugs and Escape*, p. 64.
188 Middleton, *Studying Popular Music*, p. 172.
189 Calcutt and Shephard, *Cult Fiction*, p. xi.
190 Bakhtin, *Rabelais and His World*, p. 10.
191 Boon, *The Road of Excess*, p. 276.
192 Calcutt and Shephard, *Cult Fiction*, p. iv.
193 Bakhtin, *Rabelais and His World*, p. 159.
194 Ibid., p. 167.
195 Ibid., p. 109.

196 Ibid., p. 160.
197 Redhead, *Repetitive Beat Generation*, p. 14.
198 Frederic Jameson, *Archaeologies of the Future: The Desire Called Utopia and Other Science Fictions* (London and New York: Verso, 2005).

Chapter 7

1. Champion, *Disco Biscuits*.
2. Redhead, *Repetitive Beat Generation*.
3. The phrase 'mashup' is a relatively recent development in both music and cinema, in which one established genre is merged with another, in order to create something entirely new. An example might be the uniting of romance and zombie genres in the 2016 film *Pride and Prejudice and Zombies*, dir. Burr Steers (UK: Cross Creek Pictures, 2016).
4. Aspects of this chapter previously appeared in a different form in Morrison, 'DJ-Driven Literature', pp. 219–314.
5. For further information, Noon's manifesto can be found at: http://jeffnoon.weebly.com/the-ghost-on-the-b-side.html [last accessed 29 August 2019].
6. Jeff Noon, 'Film-Makers Use Jump Cuts, Freeze Frames, Slow Motion. Musicians Remix, Scratch, Sample. Can't We Writers Have Some Fun as Well?', *The Guardian*, 10 January 2001. This article can be found at http://www.theguardian.com/books/2001/jan/10/fiction.film [last accessed 25 July 2017].
7. William Burroughs, 'The Cut Up Method', in Leroi Jones (ed.), *The Moderns: An Anthology of New Writing in America* (London: MacGibbon & Kee, 1965), pp. 345–8.
8. Jack Kerouac's 'Essentials of Spontaneous Prose' can be found at: http://www.writing.upenn.edu/~afilreis/88/kerouac-spontaneous.html [last accessed 29 July 2015].
9. Jeff Noon, 'DJNA', in Champion, *Disco Biscuits*.
10. Noon, *Needle in the Groove*.
11. Noon, *Pixel Juice*.
12. For further reading see Ismo Santala, '"Dub Fiction": The Musico-Literary Features of Jeff Noon's *Cobralingus*' (unpublished PhD book, University of Tampere, 2010); Andrew Wenaus, '"Spells Out the Word of Itself, and Then Dispelling Itself": The Chaotics of Memory' and 'The Ghost of the Novel in Jeff Noon's *Falling Out of Cars*', *Journal of the Fantastic in the Arts* 23, no. 2 (2012), pp. 260–84.
13. Jeff Noon, interviewed by the author: Pizza Express, Charing Cross, London, 7 April 2014.
14. Jeff Noon, 'Pixel Dub Juice', in *Pixel Juice*, p. 343.
15. Like Blincoe, Noon ultimately left Manchester geographically behind, choosing to live in Brighton, reporting in his interview that 'when I left Manchester I made a conscious decision not to write about it'. His biography in *Disco Biscuits* states he 'is wanting to give a voice to Manchester. Is not wanting to die in Manchester', in Champion, *Disco Biscuits*, p. 237. Interestingly, as of 2019 Irvine Welsh is also partly based in Brighton.
16. Noon, author interview.
17. Ibid.
18. Redhead, *Repetitive Beat Generation*, p. 113.

19 Artist Sara Abbott held an exhibition of her figurative paintings of Noon characters in a Todmordern, Lancashire, gallery in July 2015, suggesting art and literature might continue to offer the same intermedial revelations as music and literature.
20 Jeff Noon, *Woundings* (London: Oberon, 1986).
21 The 2016 social media posts from Noon suggest that he is launching a computer game based on *Vurt*.
22 Nedeljkov, 'Creation, Resistance, and Refacement', p. 40.
23 Jeff Noon, *Pollen* (London: Pan, 2001).
24 Jeff Noon, *Automated Alice* (London: Corgi, 1997).
25 Noon, author interview.
26 Sarah Champion, interviewed in person by the author: Chorlton, Manchester, 29 May 2013.
27 Noon, author interview.
28 Ibid.
29 Jeff Noon, *Nymphomation* (New York: Doubleday, 1997).
30 Noon, author interview.
31 For further reading relating to bricolage, see Hebidge, *Subculture*, pp. 103–4.
32 Smyth, *Music in Contemporary British Fiction*, p. 151.
33 Champion, author interview.
34 Hannah Priest, 'Steampunk, Cyberpunk, Whimsy: Generic Definition and Jeff Noon's *The Automated Alice*', unpublished conference paper. The only copy in the possession of the author is a Word document, with no details beyond the title and author, emailed to the author by Jeff Noon, 2 June 2015.
35 Ibid.
36 Karen Collins, 'Dead Channel Surfing: The Commonalities between Cyberpunk Literature and Industrial Music', *Popular Music* 25, no. 2 (2005), p. 165. Although initially established as an electronic genre, industrial music is more broadly characterized by a foregrounding of noise over melody, for instance through distorted guitars.
37 Bruce Sterling, *Cyberpunk in the Nineties* (Cambridge: Interzone, 1991), p. 345.
38 Middleton, 'Last Night a DJ Saved My Life', p. 18.
39 Noon, author interview.
40 Ibid.
41 Ismo Santala, 'Dub Fiction', p. 44.
42 Wenaus, 'Spells Out the Word of Itself', p. 261.
43 Noon, *Falling Out of Cars* (London: Black Swan, 2003).
44 For further reading, see William Burroughs, 'The Cut Up Method'.
45 Wolf, *The Musicalization of Fiction*, p. 235.
46 Andrew Wenaus, '"You are cordially invited to a / CHEMICAL WEDDING": Metamorphiction and Experimentation in Jeff Noon's Cobralingus', http://www.electronicbookreview.com/thread/electropoetics/postfuturist [last accessed 6 September 2017].
47 Ibid.
48 Another Manchester writer, Anthony Burgess, is also concerned with this evocation of language used to resist oppression. See Anthony Burgess, *A Clockwork Orange* (London: Penguin, 1972), a novel where music is also central.
49 Cited in Collins, 'Dead Channel Surfing', p. 165.

50 Noon, 'DJNA', p. 173. Italics in original.
51 Ibid.
52 Ibid.
53 Ibid., p. 176.
54 Ibid., p. 174.
55 Ibid., p. 175.
56 See Chapter 3 for a further expansion on these points.
57 See Huq, *Beyond Subculture*; Reynolds, 'Rave Culture: Living Dream or Living Death?'.
58 Noon, 'DJNA', p. 175.
59 Ibid., p. 186.
60 Ibid., p. 173.
61 Ibid.
62 A Situationist concept, détournement involves the reordering of existing cultural assets in order to create something new, and often in opposition to the original form.
63 Noon, 'DJNA', p. 176.
64 Ibid., p. 185.
65 *Pixel Juice* was published in 1998, *Needle in the Groove* in 2000.
66 Wolf, *The Musicalization of Fiction*, p. 232.
67 Interview with the author. Here Noon refers to Manchester's gang problem, discussed in Chapter 3.
68 Local legislation only allowed cabaret clubs in Manchester in the 1960s. For further reading, see C. P. Lee, *Shake, Rattle & Rain: Popular Music Making in Manchester, 1950-1995* (London: Hardinge Simpole, 2002).
69 Interview with the author.
70 Ibid.
71 For stylistic reasons Noon chooses to use lower case throughout this novel, as well as creating his own words. Like Welsh he also deploys unconventional grammar, replacing speech marks with dashes for instance. This will be further analysed later into the chapter.
72 Noon, *Needle in the Groove*, p. 97.
73 Ibid., p. 13. Ian Curtis was lead singer with Factory band Joy Division. He committed suicide on 18 May 1980.
74 Ibid., p. 18.
75 Nikolina Nedeljkov, 'Wired to a Maze: Pixel Saturnalia and Refacement' (unpublished PhD book, The City University of New York, 2015), p. 45.
76 Charles Shaar Murray, *The Hellhound Sample* (London: Heapdress, 2011).
77 Sean Coombs, AKA Puff Daddy, is a contemporary hip-hop star and businessman. This structure is also quite redolent, in some ways, of the E4 television series *Empire*, based around a family involved in the hip-hop music industry (USA: Imagine Television, 2015).
78 Noon, *Needle in the Groove*, p. 68.
79 Noon also contends that like musical ability, addiction is also genetic – that it can be encoded and passed down.
80 Noon, *Needle in the Groove*, p. 119.
81 Noon, author interview.
82 Noon, *Needle in the Groove*, paratextual material. Grammar as per original.

83 Ibid.
84 Benson, *Literary Music*, p. 74.
85 Smyth, *Music in Contemporary British Fiction*, p. 151.
86 Kerouac, 'Essentials of Spontaneous Prose'.
87 Noon, *Needle in the Groove*, p. 107.
88 *Nothing Here Now but the Recordings* (UK: Industrial Records, 1981). Industrial Records was Throbbing Gristle's label. In terms of EDM connections, producer Paul Oakenfold also worked with Burroughs, creating a link between the beat of bop and electronica, while Nirvana frontman Kurt Cobain also recorded with the Beat author.
89 Jeff Noon and David Toop, *Needle in the Groove* (UK: Sulphur Records, 2000).
90 Usefully, as an 'open source' resource, Noon includes these filters within the article 'Cobralingus Engine – Metamorphiction Process', http://www.languageisavirus.com/articles/articles.php?subaction=showcomments&id=1099110704&archive=&start_from=&ucat=&#.VZ5Q08YdLlI [last accessed 29 August 2019].
91 Noon, author interview.
92 Here Toop refers to David Toop, *The Rap Attack: African Jive to New York Hip Hop* (London: Pluto Press, 1984).
93 David Toop, email response to author, 11 February 2015. Grammar as per original email.
94 For further reading on these first two pairings, see Simon Warner, *Text and Drugs and Rock 'n' Roll* (New York: Bloomsbury, 2013).
95 Noon, author interview.
96 Noon declined to attend the 2013 Louder than Words literary event in Manchester, for instance, after an invitation from the author.
97 Noon, author interview.
98 Ibid.
99 Encompassing literature and visual art, Dada was an early twentieth century, initially European, movement that prioritized irreverence and irrationality within a 'trash' aesthetic. The connection between Dada and 'low culture' is explored in the *Journal of Popular Music*, 25, no. 2 (2005); and Simon Warner, 'The Banality of Degradation: Andy Warhol, the Velvet Underground and the Trash Aesthetic', in Jedediah Skowler and Sheila Whiteley (eds), *Countercultures and Popular Music* (Farnham: Ashgate, 2014).
100 For further reading around Gramsci notions of cultural hegemony, please see the essays contained in Gramsci, *Selections from the Prison Notebooks*.
101 Farrugia, *Beyond the Dance Floor*.
102 Cited in Simon Frith and Jon Savage, 'Pearls and Swine: Intellectuals and the Mass Media', in Steve Redhead, Derek Wynne and Justin O'Connor (eds), *The Clubcultures Reader: Readings in Popular Cultural Studies* (Oxford: Blackwell, 1998), p. 12.
103 Noon, *Pixel Juice*, p. 312.
104 Ibid., p. 310.
105 Ibid., p. 312.
106 Ibid., p. 310.
107 Ibid., p. 314.
108 Jeff Noon, 'Dub Fiction', in Redhead, *Repetitive Beat Generation*, pp. 111–18.
109 For further reading see Dave Thompson, *Reggae & Caribbean Music* (London: Backbeat Books, 2002).

110 Noon, *Pixel Juice*, p. 91.
111 Ibid., p. 92.
112 Ibid.
113 Perhaps this also further plays on Lacan's notion that, in terms of gender coding, as a female DJ she requires artificial enhancement to replace a phallic 'lack'.
114 Donna Haraway, ed., *Simians, Cyborgs and Women: The Reinvention of Nature* (New York: Routledge, 1991), cited in Jeremy Gilbert and Ewan Pearson, *Discographies: Dance Music, Culture and the Politics of Sound* (London: Routledge, 1999), p. 115.
115 Jonathan Yu, 'Electronic Dance Music and Technological Change: Lessons from Actor-Network Theory', in Bernado Alexander Attias, Anna Gavanas and Hillegonda C. Rietveld (eds), *DJ Culture in the Mix: Power, Technology and Social Change in Electronic Dance Music* (London: Bloomsbury, 2013), p. 166.
116 Cited in ibid., p. 24.
117 Middleton, '"Last Night a DJ Saved My Life": Avians, Cyborgs and Siren Bodies in the Era of Phonographic Technology', *Radical Musicology* 1 (2006), p. 27.
118 Noon, author interview.
119 Tony Mitchell, 'Terpsichorean Architecture: Editor's Introduction', *Portal: Journal of Multidisciplinary Studies* 8, no. 1 (2011), p. 2.
120 Jeff Noon and Lauren Beukes: 'The Five Question Interview', Tor Books, 8 April 2013, http://www.torbooks.co.uk/blog/2013/04/08/jeff-noon-and-lauren-beukes-the-five-question-interview [last accessed 24 July 2017].
121 Wolf, *The Musicalization of Fiction*, p. 239.
122 Noon now pens short creative works in Facebook posts. A post of 28 December 2016 reads, 'William Burroughs was a poacher in the word orchard, slicing the roots and folding leaf upon leaf, searching for new grafts, new flowers, new seeds', evidencing a continued interest in the Beat author while also interestingly metaphorically linking to horticulture.
123 Noon, author interview.
124 Ibid.
125 Smyth, *Music in Contemporary British Fiction*, p. 42.
126 Champion, *Disco Biscuits*, p. 295.
127 Smyth, *Music in Contemporary British Fiction*, p. 22.
128 Although defined by Derrida in *Spectes of Marx*, hauntology has since been adopted by UK commentators such as Simon Reynolds and Mark Fisher to relate to a specific genre of music, the haunting conveyed by, for instance, the crackle of records and samples from television of the 1960s and 1970s. In papers I have given, for instance at the IASPM conference in Canberra, Australia, in 2019, I have looked to move the notion of hauntology on, or perhaps back, to denote this more cultural sense of a spectre or haunting.
129 Noon, author interview.
130 For further reading, see Thornton, *Club Cultures*; Brewster and Broughton, *Last Night a DJ Saved My Life*; Malbon, *Clubbing*; Attias et al., *DJ Culture in the Mix*.
131 Noon, author interview.
132 In itself this choice is interesting, as Bowie has himself used the Burroughs/Gysin cut-up method in creating his own lyrical content.
133 Santala, *Dub Fiction*, p. 44.
134 Jeff Noon, 'Blurbs', in Noon, *Pixel Juice*, p. 158.

135	Ibid., p. 161.
136	Ibid., p. 163.
137	Lauren Beukes, 'The Five Questions Interview'.
138	See Thompson, *Reggae & Caribbean Music*.
139	Noon, author interview.
140	Jeff Noon, 'Homo Karaoke', in Noon, *Pixel Juice*, p. 93.
141	A haiku is a Japanese poetic form in which each poem is formed of seventeen syllables.
142	Noon, 'Homo Karaoke', p. 97.
143	Ibid.
144	Early examples of hip-hop DJs who used this technique include DJ Kool Herc, Grandmaster Flash, Afrika Bambaataa and Grand Wizard Theodore.
145	Noon, 'Orgmentations', in *Pixel Juice*, p. 309.
146	For turntable technique, see Stephen Webber, *DJ Skills: The Essential Guide to Mixing and Scratching* (Burlington, MA: Focal Press, 2008).
147	Brewster and Broughton, *Last Night a DJ Saved My Life*, p. 19.
148	Ibid., p. 141.
149	Noon, 'Orgmentations', in *Pixel Juice*, p. 309.
150	Noon, 'Hands of the DJ', in *Pixel Juice*, p. 310.
151	Santala, 'Dub Fiction', p. 48.
152	Jack Kerouac, 'The Beginning of Bop', *Readings by Jack Kerouac on the Beat Generation*, Verve, LP150-05, 1960. This version 'Fantasy: The Early History of Bop (section 1)', *Jazz of the Beat Generation* (Jazzfm Recordings, 2003).
153	Noon, 'Film-Makers Use Jump Cuts'.
154	Noon, cited in Santala, 'Dub Fiction', p. 37.
155	This is drawn from a conversation the author had with electro-acoustic composer and academic David Berezan.
156	Santala, 'Dub Fiction', p. 38.
157	Personal communication with the author, 25 July 2017.
158	Middleton, 'Last Night a DJ Saved My Life', p. 24.
159	Cited in Attias, 'Subjectivity in the Groove', p. 40.
160	Noon, author interview.
161	Ibid.
162	Ibid.
163	Ibid.
164	Holleran, *Dancer from the Dance*, p. 35.
165	Noon, author interview.
166	George Melly, *Revolt into Style: The Pop Arts in the 50s and 60s* (Oxford: Oxford University Press, 1989). Jeff Noon introduced this title himself at this point in the conversation.
167	Noon, author Interview.
168	Jeff Noon, *Channel SK1N* (Smashwords, 2012), eBook.
169	Wenaus, 'You are cordially invited to a / CHEMICAL WEDDING'.
170	Noon, cited in Santala, 'Dub Fiction', p. 45.
171	Wenaus, 'Spells Out the Word of Itself', p. 267.
172	Noon, *Pixel Juice*, p. 311.
173	Wenaus, 'Spells Out the Word of Itself', p. 265.

174 Noon, *Needle in the Groove*, p. 16.
175 Noon, *Pixel Juice*, p. 160.
176 Ibid., p. 163.
177 Wenaus, 'Spells Out the Word of Itself', p. 267.
178 Cited in Middleton, 'Last Night a DJ Saved My Life', p. 26.
179 Wenaus, 'Spells Out the Word of Itself', p. 268.
180 Noon, author interview.
181 Noon, 'Film-Makers Use Jump Cuts'.
182 More recent social media contact would suggest that the relationship has survived this difference of creative opinion.
183 Noon, 'Film-Makers Use Jump Cuts'.
184 Famously Tolstoy challenged his fellow Russian novelist to a duel.
185 Noon, 'Film-Makers Use Jump Cuts …'.
186 Ibid.
187 Ibid.
188 Ibid.

Chapter 8

1 Champion, *Disco Biscuits*.
2 As a personal aside, this well-thumbed copy of *Disco Biscuits* has now been signed by Jeff Noon and Nicholas Blincoe, as well as Sarah Champion. The latter has even suggested this book might provide a reason for a reunion of these authors.
3 Nicholas Blincoe, interviewed in person by the author: Le Pain Quotidien, London, 12 April 2013.
4 Ibid.
5 Champion, interview with the author, 29 May 2013, in reference to Blincoe, *Acid Casuals* and Blincoe, *Manchester Slingback*. As of 2019, there are plans to turn *Acid Casuals* into a TV series, with Sarah Champion consulting on that project at the time of writing.
6 Blincoe, *Jello Salad*.
7 Following an initial interview on 12 April 2013, Blincoe accepted an invitation to join the club culture panel, convened by the author of this book, of the 2014 iteration of the Louder than Words festival of music and writing in Manchester. Email communication has since been ongoing.
8 Jean-Jacques Lecercle, *Philosophy Through the Looking Glass: Language, Nonsense, Desire* (London: Hutchison, 1985).
9 Blincoe's place in the corpus of Dancefloor-Driven Literature is further confirmed by the fact he actually appears as a character, Mr Bingo, in a later King novel, *Jim Giraffe*, as indicated by Blincoe in email correspondence with the author.
10 Nicholas Blincoe and Matt Thorne, eds., *All Hail the New Puritans* (London: 4th Estate, 2001).
11 Judith Shulevitz, 'The Close Reader; The Puritan Ethic', *The New York Times*, 11 March 2001. http://www.nytimes.com/2001/03/11/books/the-close-reader-the-puritan-ethic.html [last accessed 15 March 2017].

12 James Wood, 'Celluloid Junkies', *The Guardian*, 16 September 2000, https://www.theguardian.com/books/2000/sep/16/fiction.reviews1 [last accessed 15 March 2017].
13 Alex Clark, 'No Dancing, No Music', *The London Review of Books* 22, no. 21 (2 November 2000), pp. 28–9, https://www.lrb.co.uk/v22/n21/alex-clark/no-dancing-no-music [last accessed 15 March 2017].
14 Fernández, *The New Puritan Generation*. Personal email communication between the author of this book and Fernández has also proved useful to this research.
15 David Owen, 'Writing by Numbers: Disavowing Literary Tradition in *All Hail the New Puritans*', in Fernández (ed.), *The New Puritan Generation*, p. 50.
16 Blincoe, author interview.
17 Most recently, Blincoe has moved his focus to issues around the Palestine/Israel situation. Intriguingly, his last book considers that conflict in terms of football, just as Steve Redhead and many MIPC commentators placed football in a sociopolitical context. Please see Nicholas Blincoe, *More Noble than War: The Story of Football in Israel and Palestine* (London: Little Brown, 2019).
18 Champion, *Disco Biscuits*, p. 291.
19 Blincoe, author interview.
20 Blincoe studied art at Middlesex University, before undertaking postgraduate study at Warwick.
21 Blincoe, author interview.
22 Catalogue details of that single can be found here: http://factoryrecords.org/meatmouth.php [last accessed 25 September 2015].
23 Blincoe, author interview.
24 Ibid.
25 Where 'social realism' is taken to be a specific literary genre, and 'naturalism' a stylistic technique in the service of the authentic rendering of that genre.
26 Margaret Drabble, ed., *The Oxford Companion to English Literature* (Oxford: Oxford University Press, 2000), p. 713.
27 Adorno, *The Jargon of Authenticity*.
28 Beeler, *Dance, Drugs and Escape*, p. 52.
29 Ibid.
30 Featuring a cover image of a hooded man holding out a gun as though from the page itself, this issue was published in 1998.
31 In terms of the crossover between crime and clubland, see Simon A. Morrison, 'Interview with the Gangster', in *Discombobulated: Dispatches from the Wrong Side* (London: Headpress, 2010), pp. 143–7.
32 Blincoe, author interview.
33 Beeler, *Dance, Drugs and Escape*, p. 54.
34 The notion of the 'Sunday Social' would be immediately understood by a cognizant, participant readership.
35 See Owen, 'Writing by Numbers'.
36 Blincoe, author interview.
37 Beeler, *Dance, Drugs and Escape*, p. 73.
38 Blincoe, author interview.
39 In keeping with Point 7 of the New Puritan Manifesto, which suggests 'all products, places, artists and objects named are real'.

40 Nicholas Blincoe, 'Ardwick Green', in Champion, *Disco Biscuits*, p. 8. Italics are Blincoe's own.
41 Ibid., p. 10.
42 Ibid., p. 5. Spelling of Haçienda is Blincoe's own.
43 Ibid., p. 7. Italics are Blincoe's own.
44 Ibid.
45 Blincoe, author interview.
46 Blincoe, 'Ardwick Green', p. 13.
47 Blincoe, author interview. HMV is a famous UK high street music retailer.
48 Ibid.
49 Ibid.
50 Blincoe indicates he performed at the *Disco Biscuits* club events at Turnmills, London; 'the Hoxton Square one' (also London) and Paradise Factory, Manchester. Personal email communication with the author, 6 August 2019.
51 Ibid.
52 'Acid Casual' is therefore a confluence of terms. As described in Chapter 5, a 'football casual' is a principally Scottish term for a football fan, where an 'Acid Ted' is a lightly pejorative term for late-adopters of EDMC.
53 Blincoe, *Acid Casuals*, p. 168.
54 It was perhaps no coincidence that Blincoe requested we meet in Le Pain Quotidien.
55 Lecercle, *Philosophy through the Looking Glass*, p. 44.
56 Ibid., p. 43.
57 Ibid.
58 Ibid., p. 37.
59 See Roland Barthes, *The Pleasure of the Text* (New York: Farrar, Straus Giroux, 1980).
60 Interview with the author.
61 This was confirmed by Blincoe in an email of 22 September 2015.
62 Blincoe, *Acid Casuals*, p. 226.
63 None of Blincoe's novels, for instance, were published with a soundtrack to accompany their reading, as was the case with Miller's *Trip City* and Welsh's *Ecstasy*.
64 Gerry Smyth, *Music in Contemporary British Fiction: Listening to the Novel* (New York: Palgrave Macmillan, 2008), p. 5.
65 Blincoe, *Acid Casuals*, p. 4.
66 Ibid.
67 Ibid.
68 Ibid., p. 5.
69 See Ferdinand de Saussure, *Course in General Linguistics* (London: Open Court, 1986).
70 See Mark Duffett, *Understanding Fandom: An Introduction to the Study of Media Fan Culture* (New York and London: Bloomsbury, 2013).
71 Mark Fisher, *Ghosts of My Life: Writings on Depression, Hauntology and Lost Futures* (Winchester, UK: Zero Books, 2014), p. 120.
72 Ian Penman, '[the Phantoms of] TRICKNOLOGY [versus a Politics of Authenticity]', *The Wire*, March 1995.
73 This reading is constructed from the author's own memories of PSV, as he visited the venue many times in the early 1990s. It was subsequently confirmed in an email from Nicholas Blincoe, dated 22 September 2015. Previously known as the Russell Club, this is where Factory Records began hosting gigs in the late 1970s.

74　Blincoe, *Acid Casuals*, p. 168.
75　Ibid.
76　Blincoe, *Acid Casuals*, p. 178.
77　Ibid., p. 39.
78　Lecercle, *Philosophy through the Looking Glass*, p. 45.
79　Where the Haçienda carried the Factory catalogue number 51, Dry, on Oldham Street (in what is now the Northern Quarter area), was 201.
80　Blincoe, author interview.
81　Blincoe, *Acid Casuals*, p. 37.
82　Blincoe, *Acid Casuals*, p. 37.
83　Ibid., p. 21.
84　Dry operated up until 2017, although towards the end it was not under the ownership of the now defunct Factory Records. News reports of March 2017 suggest it has been sold and will be turned into a boutique hotel.
85　Lecercle, *Philosophy through the Looking Glass*, p. 43.
86　Ibid.
87　Blincoe, *Acid Casuals*, p. 25.
88　Ibid., p. 11.
89　A photo of Anthony H. Wilson hung in the booth where the entrance money was taken at the Haçienda.
90　Lecercle, *Philosophy through the Looking Glass*, p. 12.
91　Roland Barthes, 'The Death of the Author', in *Image, Music, Text* (London: Fontana Press, 1977), p. 147.
92　Blincoe, author interview.
93　Redhead, *Repetitive Beat Generation*, p. 148.
94　Hanif Kureshi, *The Buddha of Suburbia* (London: Faber and Faber, 1990).
95　Rachel Carroll and Adam Hansen, ed., *LitPop*, p. 20.
96　Nicholas Blincoe and Matt Thorne, eds., *All Hail the New Puritans* (London: 4th Estate, 2001), p. xi.
97　Ben Kelly was the designer of the Haçienda nightclub, who incorporated an industrial aesthetic into his design ideas for the club.
98　Lecercle, *Philosophy through the Looking Glass*, p. 16.
99　Blincoe, *Acid Causals*, p. 176.
100　Blincoe, author interview.
101　Truman Capote, interviewed on the David Susskind programme *Open End*, 1959.
102　Redhead, *Repetitive Beat Generation*, p. 9. Blincoe no longer remembers this exchange with Redhead, and in conversation concludes: 'I don't know what I was moaning about.'
103　In reference to an earlier point about French philosophy, it is also worth noting the connection between the Beats and French writing and culture.
104　Blincoe, author interview.
105　In a blog for music magazine *NME*, Hook writes: 'That was one of those nights when there was hardly anyone in but it was quite intense because of what William Burroughs was doing. The funny thing was that one of Joy Division's first gigs abroad was with William Burroughs, a William Burroughs evening in the Plan K in Belgium so we had a little bit of history with him 'cos he'd told Ian to fuck off when he asked for a free book. Even at the Haçienda I didn't ask for a free book either. I was as scared of William Burroughs as he was.' Peter Hook, 'Hooky's Top 10 Hacienda [sic] Memories – Part 1', *NME*, 1 October 2009.

106 Redhead, *Repetitive Beat Generation*, p. 6.
107 Blincoe, author interview.
108 Smyth, *Music in Contemporary British Fiction*, p. 7.
109 Already mentioned in Chapter 3 in reference to the origins of Manumission, the Gay Village is located around Canal Street. Once a more hidden area of the city, it is now very much an important part of Manchester's social geography, and a focus for the city's gay community.
110 At this stage in his career Blincoe was evidently less Puritan about flashbacks, which were banned in the manifesto.
111 William Shakespeare, *Hamlet*, III, scene 2 (London: Routledge, 1990).
112 Collin, *Altered State*, p. 340.
113 Hebdige, *Subculture*, p. 54.
114 Blincoe, *Jello Salad*, p. 155.
115 Ibid., p. 96.
116 Ibid., pp. 226, 240, 237.
117 Ibid., p. 199.
118 Ibid., p. 226.
119 Blincoe, *Jello Salad*, p. 38.
120 Hebdige, *Subculture*, p. 10.
121 Smyth, *Music in Contemporary British Fiction*, p. 5.
122 Blincoe, author interview.
123 In his email of 22 September 2015, Blincoe confirms: 'The venue was napoleons, which seems to still exist, though I also used bits of Fufu's palace', by which he means Foo-Foo's Palace, subject of my own story with Foo-Foo in Morrison, *Discombobulated*, pp. 10–14.
124 Blincoe, *Manchester Slingback*, p. 27.
125 'God's Cop', *Pills 'n' Thrills and Bellyaches*.
126 Indeed it is widely felt that the commercial popularity of the Gay Village in recent years has been to the detriment of its inherent character.
127 Blincoe, *Manchester Slingback*, pp. 143–4.
128 The author lived in the Gay Village between 1997 and 2000, and Blincoe's description has particular resonance.
129 Blincoe, *Manchester Slingback*, p. 51.
130 Smyth, *Music in Contemporary British Fiction*, p. 89.
131 Blincoe, *Manchester Slingback*, p. 156.
132 Ibid., p. 157.
133 Blincoe, *Jello Salad*, p. 32.
134 Thornton, *Club Cultures*, p. 85.
135 Thornton, *Club Cultures*, p. 60.
136 Phillips, *Superstar DJs Here We Go!*.
137 Ibid.
138 Blincoe, *Jello Salad*, p. 226.
139 Ibid., p. 186.
140 Ibid., p. 226.
141 Blincoe, *Manchester Slingback*, p. 156.
142 Blincoe, *Jello Salad*, p. 22.
143 Ibid., p. 25.

144 I recall visits to a 1990s incarnation of the same space, as the nightclub Konspiracy.
145 Blincoe, *Jello Salad*, p. 27.
146 Smyth, *Music in Contemporary British Fiction*, p. 123.
147 See Theodor W. Adorno, *Aesthetic Theory* (London: Bloomsbury, 2013).
148 Usually perceived as a term in cinematic theory, noir draws on German expressionist cinema to denote films, often detective narratives, shot in a distinctive black-and-white style.
149 Jack Kerouac, *On the Road* (London: Penguin, 1987), p. 122.
150 Blincoe, author interview.
151 Dennis Broe, 'A Strike, Bloody and Poetic: French Film Noir and the Defeat of the Popular Front', *Avanca | Cinema, 2012*, pp. 790–5. The author of this book was in attendance for this paper, as he was also presenting research on EDMC cinema.
152 See Richard Osborne, *Clubland Heroes: A Nostalgic Study of the Recurrent Characters in the Romantic Fiction of Dornford Yates, John Buchan and 'Sapper'* (London: Hutchinson, 1983).
153 Growing up in Rochdale, on the very edge of the moors, Blincoe would be well aware of the Moors Murderers – Myra Hindley and Ian Brady – who between 1963 and 1965 murdered five children and buried them on the moors.
154 So called because of the ostensibly cheap, commercial nature of both the content and the form of this fiction, pulp fiction was deliberately designed to be ephemeral.
155 Blincoe, author interview.
156 Ibid.
157 See appendix IV, figures 5 and 6.
158 Katy Guest, 'Nicholas Blincoe: A Passionate Puritan', *The Independent*, 16 July 2004, http://www.independent.co.uk/arts-entertainment/books/features/nicholas-blincoe-a-passionate-puritan-47480.html [last accessed 11 September 2017].
159 Blincoe confirmed this in an email of 22 September 2015.
160 It is also redolent of Lou Reed on the front and back of the LP sleeve for the 1972 album *Transformer* (USA: RCA Victor, 1972).
161 Blincoe, *Acid Casuals*, paratextual material.
162 Blincoe, author interview.
163 Blincoe, author interview.
164 Wilde's conceit is explored in more detail in Chapter 6.
165 Smyth, *Music in Contemporary British Fiction*, p. 9.
166 Ibid.
167 Nicholas Blincoe, Facebook post, 13 March 2017.
168 Calcutt and Shephard, *Cult Fiction*, p. x.
169 Blincoe, author interview.
170 Ibid.
171 Blincoe and Thorn, *All Hail the New Puritans*, front matter.

Chapter 9

1 Redhead, *Subculture to Clubcultures*, p. 102.
2 Wolf, *The Musicalization of Fiction*, p. 229.
3 Champion, in Redhead, *Repetitive Beat Generation*, p. 18.

4   Redhead, *Repetitive Beat Generation*, p. xxii.
5   Fernández, *The New Puritan Generation*, p. 3.
6   Redhead, *Subculture to Clubcultures*, p. 103.
7   Neil Transpontine, '"These Days Are Not to Be Missed": 1990s Rave and Club Culture in Fiction', *Datacide Magazine*, n.d., https://datacide-magazine.com/these-days-are-not-to-be-missed-1990s-rave-and-club-culture-in-fiction/ [last accessed 9 August 2019].
8   Thornton, *Club Cultures*, p. 34.
9   See Appendix I for an evolving list of such titles.
10 Middleton, *Reading Pop*, p. 13.
11 Beeler, *Dance, Drugs and Escape*, p. 153.
12 This phrase is itself the title of the Redhead collection of 2000, published by Rebel Inc.
13 Calcutt and Shephard, *Cult Fiction*, p. 285.
14 It was for this very reason that the author of this book worked to collect his 'Dispatches from the Wrong Side' columns into the *Discombobulated* collection, where the stories would otherwise only have seen life during the short two-week duration *DJ* magazine was on the newsstand.
15 In Redhead, *Repetitive Beat Generation*, p. xxii.
16 Thompson, *The Great Shark Hunt*, jacket cover.
17 Redhead, *Repetitive Beat Generation*, p. 128.
18 Duffett, *Understanding Fandom*, p. 60.
19 Ibid.
20 Cited in Roger Sabin, ed., *Punk Rock: So What? The Cultural Legacy of Punk* (London: Routledge, 1999), p. 27.
21 Nedeljkov, 'Creation, Resistance, and Refacement', p. 97.
22 Kodwo Eshun, *More Brilliant than the Sun: Adventures in Sonic Fiction* (London: Quartet Books, 1999), p. **00**(–006). Emboldened, and italicized, in original.
23 Paul Crosthwaite, 'Trauma and Degeneration: Joy Division and Pop Criticism's Imaginative Historicism', in Carroll and Hansen (ed.), *LitPop*, p. 134.
24 The Cavern Club was the location for many of The Beatles' early gigs in Liverpool, from 1961 to 1963. I thoroughly enjoyed taking my Music Journalism students there, on a Beatles tour we joined in February 2019.
25 Interviewed by the author for a thirty-minute documentary on the fifteenth anniversary of the Haçienda, recorded and produced for Kiss Radio in 1997. Regrettably, any recording of that show has been lost.
26 This is a nostalgia industry that enables and emboldens Crosby Homes to play on the past of the Haçienda, in the creation of an apartment block of the same name, which has nothing to do with the nightclub aside from the corner of the two streets on which it resides.
27 Middleton, 'Last Night a DJ Saved My Life'.
28 Ibid., p. 6.
29 Barthes, 'The Death of the Author'.
30 Fisher, *Ghosts of My Life*, p. 132.
31 *Granta* is a literary magazine that famously publishes a 'Best of Young British Novelists' poll.
32 Quoted in Phillip Maughan, '"I Think the Dead Are with Us": John Berger at 88', in *The New Statesman*, 11 June 2015, p. 39.

33 Wolf, *The Musicalization of Fiction*, p. 240.
34 Matthew Calarco, *The Question of the Animal from Heidegger to Derrida* (New York: Columbia University Press, 2008), p. 100.
35 Reynolds, 'Rave Culture: Living Dream or Living Death?', p. 91.
36 *Everybody in the Place: An Incomplete History of Britain 1984–1992*, dir. Jeremy Deller (UK: BBC, 2019).
37 For further reading, see Simon Reynolds, 'How Rave Music Conquered America', *The Guardian*, 2 August, 2012; Luke Bainbridge, 'David Guetta: Lord of Dance', *The Observer*, 22 April 2012; Alexis Petrides, 'Las Vegas's Gamble with Dance Music', *The Guardian*, 17 July 2014.
38 Reynolds, 'How Rave Music Conquered America'.
39 Perceiving the EDM scene as a reconstituting of existing elements, with little new (aside from the massive wages DJs can now command), brings such discourse into line with commentators who argue it stands much as the 'Elvis in Vegas' period did for rock & roll, that in actuality it has little in common with the roots of the flowering of acid house in the Second Summer of Love.
40 *Beats*, dir. Brian Welsh (UK: Rosetta Productions, 2019).
41 Andrew Harrison, 'Wizards of the Sonic', *New Statesman*, 23 August–29 August 2019. Netflix also released a movie in 2018 entitled *Ibiza*, centring on three New York women finding liberation on the Mediterranean island considered more closely in Chapter 3. This film was the focus of my talk at the XX Biennial IASPM conference in Canberra, Australia, in June 2019. *Ibiza*, dir. Alex Richanbach (USA: Gary Sanchez Productions, 2018).
42 See Hebdige, *Subculture*, p. 97.
43 Redhead, *Repetitive Beat Generation*, p. xxvii.
44 See John, *Technomad*.
45 'The Global Village' was a term created by Marshall McLuhan, in *The Gutenberg Galaxy: The Making of Typographic Man* (Toronto: University of Toronto Press, 1962).
46 See Muggleton, 'The Post-subculturalist', pp. 167–85.
47 See Huq, *Beyond Subculture*.
48 Shildrick and MacDonald, 'In Defence of Subculture', pp. 125–60 (p. 137).
49 Wolf, *The Musicalization of Fiction*, p. 35.
50 A description and illustrative model of systems theory can be found in Ralph Tench and Liz Yeomans, *Exploring Public Relations* (Edinburgh: Pearson, 2006), p. 27. See also Jacquie L'Etang and Magda Pieczka, *Critical Perspectives in Public Relations* (London: International Thomson Business Press, 1996).
51 Baudrillard, *Fatal Strategies*, p. 195.
52 Wolfe, *Radical Chic and Mau-mauing the Flak Catchers*, p. 42.
53 If this is already sounding somewhat far-fetched, you may prefer not to read Richard Grant, 'Do Trees Talk to Each Other', in *Smithsonian Magazine*, March 2018, which can be found at https://www.smithsonianmag.com/science-nature/the-whispering-trees-180968084 [last accessed 30 August 2019].
54 Thornton, *Club Cultures*, p. 117.
55 Carroll and Hansen, *LitPop*, p. 234.
56 Middleton, *Reading Pop*, p. 13.
57 The Royal Northern College of Music is a well-established, higher education music institute based in Manchester. Tracing its origins back to Sir Charles Hallé in the late nineteenth century, it is greatly respected.

58 For further reading about the sigmoidal curve, see the work of physicist Geoffrey West, who applies the life-cycle model to both organisms and organizations, *The New Statesman*, 22–18 November 2013.
59 Smyth, *Music in Contemporary British Fiction*, p. 59.
60 See Boon, *The Road of Excess*; Shapiro, *Waiting for the Man*.
61 Thornton, *Club Cultures*, p. 8.
62 Calcutt and Shephard, *Cult Fiction*, p. xiii.
63 Bourdieu, *Distinction*, p. 227.
64 Ibid.
65 See Beeler, *Dance, Drugs, Escape*; Fernández, *The New Puritan Generation*; Nedeljkov, 'Creation, Resistance, and Refacement'; Redhead, *Repetitive Beat Generation*; and Santala, 'Dub Fiction'.
66 Blincoe, in Redhead, *Repetitive Beat Generation*, p. 9. Daniel Defoe was an eighteenth-century English writer, of prose and subversive satire.
67 Bakhtin, *Rabelais and His World*, p. 166.
68 Calcutt and Shephard, *Cult Fiction*, p. iv.
69 Certainly, the study of literature, notably in the work of Terry Eagleton (itself channelled effectively in the research of Nedeljkov), became more widely politicized in the 1960s.
70 The process of building this genre, while not comprehensive, begins in Appendix I.
71 Smyth, *Music in Contemporary British Fiction*, p. 118.
72 Ibid.
73 Ibid, p. 8.
74 Blincoe and Thorne, *All Hail the New Puritans*.
75 Wolf, *The Musicalization of Fiction*, p. 238.
76 Smyth, *Music in Contemporary British Fiction*, p. 9.
77 Steve Redhead, an important inspiration for this book, has himself called for such a recalibration: 'Remembering the Manchester Institute for Popular Culture', *Tara Brabazon's podcast*, 15 November 12015.
78 Reynolds, 'Rave Culture: Living Dream or Living Death?', p. 91.

Glossary of terms and theories

1 At the same time, these new theoretical frameworks might also provide useful tools for future culture scholars to use.
2 Much of the understanding of relevance theory was gleaned during illuminating and enjoyable conversations with the linguist and relevance theorist Dr Adam Gargani.
3 Thornton, *Club Cultures*, p. 60.
4 Carroll and Hansen, *LitPop*, p. 193.
5 For further reading see Jay, *High Society*.
6 Collin, *Altered State*, p. 28. Italics in original.
7 Thornton, *Club Cultures*, p. 34.
8 Wolf, *The Musicalization of Fiction*, p. 40.
9 Ibid., p. 47.
10 Ibid., p. 40.
11 See Barthes, 'Introduction to the Structural Analysis of Narratives', pp. 79–124.

12 Pynchon, *Gravity's Rainbow*.
13 See Phillips, *Superstar DJs Here We Go!*.
14 Hebdige, *Subculture*, p. 97.
15 Even in semantic terms it is interesting to note that this is a reappropriation of the 1960s term 'rave', only here rave becomes a verb, noun and locus for this new subcultural scene.
16 Cited in Middleton, 'Last Night a DJ Saved My Life', p. 26. In reference to Benjamin's original use of the term to denote 'a natural world that is sufficient in itself', see Calarco, *The Question of the Animal from Heidegger to Derrida*, p. 100.
17 Keay, 'Aids, Education and the Year 2000', pp. 8–10.
18 See Foucault's notion of the 'panopticon' in Foucault, *Discipline and Punish*, and further discussion in Chapter 7.
19 Kristeva, *Powers of Horror*; Lacan, *Ecrits*.
20 Redhead, *The End-of-the-Century Party*, p. 1.
21 A description and illustrative model of systems theory can be found in Tench and Yeomans, *Exploring Public Relations*, p. 27. See also L'Etang and Pieczka, *Critical Perspectives in Public Relations*.
22 Sheila Whiteley, 'Coda', in Carroll and Hansen (eds), *LitPop*, p. 234.
23 Drawing first on established cultural contingencies, see Hebdige, *Subculture*; Thornton, *Club Cultures*; and Muggleton and Weinzierl (eds), *The Post-Subcultures Reader*.
24 For instance, Marcus Boon considers literature and intoxicants in *The Road of Excess*, while Harry Shapiro considers music and intoxicants in *Waiting for the Man*.
25 In respect of the prominence of the letter *E*, the reader might refer to the now iconic cover shot by Kevin Cummins, in the *NME* published 31 March 1990. This image sees the Happy Mondays' frontman Shaun Ryder hanging from the letter *E* on the rooftop of an Ibiza hotel. The Happy Mondays' sensibilities blended rock with a baggy rave aesthetic, and at the 2014 Louder than Words festival in Manchester, Cummins argued that cover image encapsulated the moment.

Bibliography

Adorno, Theodor W., 'On the Fetish Character of Music and the Regression of Listening', in *The Culture Industry: Selected Essays on Mass Culture* (London: Routledge, 2001).
Adorno, Theodor W., *The Jargon of Authenticity* (London: Routledge, 2003).
Adorno, Theodor W., *In Search of Wagner* (London: Verso, 2009).
Adorno, Theodor W., *Aesthetic Theory* (London: Bloomsbury, 2013).
Allis, Michael, 'Reading Music Through Literature: Introduction', *Journal of Musicological Research* 36, no. 1 (2017), 1–5.
Anthony, Wayne, *Class of 88: The True Acid House Experience* (London: Virgin Books, 1998).
Attali, Jacques, *Noise: The Political Economy of Music* (Minneapolis: The University of Minnesota Press, 2009).
Attias, Bernardo Alexander, 'Subjectivity in the Groove', in Bernardo Alexander Attias, Anna Gavanas and Hillegonda C. Rietveld (eds), *DJ Culture in the Mix: Power, Technology and Social Change in Electronic Dance Music* (London: Bloomsbury, 2013).
Attias, Bernardo Alexander, Anna Gavanas and Hillegonda C. Rietveld, eds, *DJ Culture in the Mix: Power, Technology and Social Change in Electronic Dance Music* (London: Bloomsbury, 2013), pp. 15–49.
Bakhtin, Mikhail, *Problems of Dostoyevsky's Poetics* (Moscow: Khudozhestvennaja literature, 1963).
Bakhtin, Mikhail, *Rabelais and His World* (Bloomington: Indiana University Press, 1984).
Bakhtin, Mikhail, *The Dialogic Imagination: Four Essays* (Austin: University of Texas Press, 2006).
Bainbridge, Luke, 'David Guetta: Lord of Dance', *The Observer*, 22 April 2012.
Bangs, Lester, *Mainlines, Blood Feasts and Bad Taste* (London: Serpent's Tail, 2003).
Baron, Jack, 'Tripping Yarns', *NME*, 22 December 1989.
Barthes, Roland, 'The Death of the Author', in *Image, Music, Text* (London: Fontana Press, 1977).
Barthes, Roland, *Image, Music, Text* (London: Fontana, 1977).
Barthes, Roland, *The Pleasure of the Text* (New York: Farrar, Straus Giroux, 1980).
Barthes, Roland, *Mythologies* (London: Vintage, 2009).
Bate, Jonathan, 'Reading for Your Life: How Books Help Us to Become Better Human Beings', *New Statesman*, 14–20 August 2015.
Baudrillard, Jean, *Fatal Strategies* (New York: Semiotext(e), 1990).
Beeler, Stan, *Dance, Drugs and Escape: The Club Scene in Literature, Film and the Club Scene in Literature, Film and Television Since the Late 1980s* (Jefferson, NC: McFarland & Co, 2007).
Benjamin, Walter, 'The Work of Art in the Age of Mechanical Reproduction', in *Illuminations* (London: Pimlico, 1999), pp. 211–35.
Bennett, Andy, 'Sub-cultures or Neo-tribes? Rethinking the Relationship between Youth Style Musical Taste', *Sociology* 33, no. 3 (1999), 599–617.

Bennett, Andy, 'Consolidating the Music Scenes Perspective', *Poetics* 32 (2004), 223-34.
Bennett, Andy, 'Reappraising Counterculture', in Jedediah Sklower and Sheila Whiteley (eds), *Countercultures & Popular Music* (Farnham: Ashgate, 2014).
Bennett, Andy and Keith Kahn-Harris, *After Subculture* (London: Palgrave, 2004).
Bennett, Andy, Barry Shank and Jason Toynbee (eds), *The Popular Music Studies Reader* (London: Routledge, 2006).
Benson, Richard, *Nightfever: Club Writing in the Face 1980-1997* (London: Boxtree, 1997).
Benson, Stephen, *Literary Music* (Farnham: Ashgate, 2006).
Bernhart, Walter, Steven Paul Scher and Werner Wolf, eds, *Word and Music Studies: Defining the Field* (Amsterdam: Rodopi, 1999).
Beukes, Lauren, 'The Five Question Interview', Tor Books, 8 April 2013.
Bey, Hakim, *T.A.Z.: The Temporary Autonomous Zone, Ontological Anarchy, Poetic Terrorism*, 2nd edn (Brooklyn, NY: Autonomedia, 2003).
Blincoe, Nicholas, 'Ardwick Green', in Sarah Champion (ed.), *Disco Biscuits: New Fiction from the Chemical Generation* (London: Sceptre, 1997).
Blincoe, Nicholas, *Jello Salad* (London: Serpent's Tail, 1997).
Blincoe, Nicholas, *Acid Casuals* (London; Serpent's Tail, 1998).
Blincoe, Nicholas, *Manchester Slingback* (London: Pan, 1998).
Blincoe, Nicholas and Matt Thorne (eds), *All Hail the New Puritans* (London: 4th Estate, 2001).
Boon, Marcus, *The Road of Excess: A History of Writers on Drugs* (Cambridge, MA: Harvard University Press, 2002).
Bourdieu, Pierre, 'Forms of Capital', in John C. Richardson (ed.), *Handbook of Theory and Research for the Sociology of Education* (New York: Greenwood Press, 1986), pp. 241-58.
Bourdieu, Pierre, *Language and Symbolic Power* (Cambridge, UK: Polity, 1991).
Bourdieu, Pierre, *Distinction: A Social Critique of the Judgement of Taste* (London: Routledge, 2010).
Brewster, Bill and Frank Broughton, *Last Night a DJ Saved My Life: The History of the Disc Jockey* (London: Headline, 1999).
Broe, Dennis, 'A Strike, Bloody and Poetic: French Film Noir and the Defeat of the Popular Front', *Avanca | Cinema*, 2012, pp. 790-5.
Brown, Adam, 'Let's All Have a Disco? Football, Popular Music and Democratization', in Steve Redhead (ed.), *The Clubcultures Reader: Readings in Popular Cultural Studies* (Oxford: Blackwell, 2000), pp. 61-83.
Brown, Calvin S., *Music and Literature: A Comparison of the Arts* (Athens, GA: The University of Georgia Press, 1949).
Burgess, Anthony, *A Clockwork Orange* (London: Penguin, 1972).
Burroughs, William S., 'The Cut Up Method', in Leroi Jones (ed.), *The Moderns: An Anthology of New Writing in America* (London: MacGibbon & Kee, 1965), pp. 345-8.
Butts, Colin, *Is Harry on the Boat?* (London: Orion, 1997).
Calarco, Matthew, *The Question of the Animal from Heidegger to Derrida* (New York: Columbia University Press, 2008).
Calcutt, Andrew and Richard Shephard, *Cult Fiction: A Reader's Guide* (London: Prion, 1998).
Carroll, Rachel and Adam Hansen (eds), *LitPop: Writing and Popular Music* (Farnham: Ashgate, 2014).

Champion, Sarah, ed., *Disco Biscuits: New Fiction from the Chemical Generation* (London: Sceptre, 1997).
Champion, Sarah (ed.), *Disco 2000* (London: Hodder & Stoughton, 1998).
Champion, Sarah (ed.), 'Generation E', in Steve Redhead (ed.), *Repetitive Beat Generation* (Edinburgh: Canongate, 2000), pp. 13–23.
Chtcheglov, Ivan, 'Formulary for a New Urbanism', http://www.bopsecrets.org/SI/Chtcheglov.htm [last accessed 2 November 2017].
Cohen, Sara, *Rock Culture in Liverpool: Popular Music in the Making* (Oxford: Clarendon Press, 1991).
Cohen, Stanley, *Folk Devils and Moral Panics*, 3rd edn (London: Routledge, 2002).
Cohn, Nik, 'Tribal Rites of the New Saturday Night', *New York Magazine*, 1976.
Collin, Matthew, *Altered State: The Story of Ecstasy Culture and Acid House* (London: Serpent's Tail, 2009).
Collin, Matthew, *Pop Grenade* (London: Zero Books, 2015).
Collin, Matthew, *Rave On: Global Adventures in Electronic Dance Music* (London: Serpent's Tail, 2018).
Collins, Karen, 'Dead Channel Surfing: The Commonalities between Cyberpunk Literature and Industrial Music', *Popular Music* 25, no. 2 (2005), pp. 165–178.
Cremona, Vicki Ann, Peter Eversmann, Hans van Maanen, Willmar Sauter and John Tulloch, eds., *Theatrical Events: Borders, Dynamics, Frames* (Amsterdam: Rodopi, 2004).
Crosthwaite, Paul, 'Trauma and Degeneration: Joy Division and Pop Criticism's Imaginative Historicism', in Rachel Carroll and Adam Hansen (eds), *LitPop: Writing and Popular Music* (Farnham: Ashgate, 2014).
Cousins, Mark, *The Story of Film* (London: Pavilion Books, 2011).
Davidson, Toni (ed.), *Intoxication: An Anthology of Stimulant-Based Writing* (London: Serpent's Tail, 1998).
Dayan, Peter, 'The Force of Music in Derrida's Writing', in Delia da Sosa Correa (ed.), *Phrase and Subject: Studies in Literature and Music* (Oxford: Legenda, 2006).
Derrida, Jacques, *Glas* (Lincoln: University of Nebraska Press, 1986).
Derrida, Jacques, *Of Grammatology* (Baltimore: The John Hopkins University Press, 1976).
Derrida, Jacques, *Specters of Marx: The State of the Debt, the Work of Mourning, and the New International* (New York: Routledge, 1994).
Drabble, Margaret, *The Oxford Companion to English Literature* (Oxford: Oxford University Press, 2000).
Duffett, Mark, *Understanding Fandom: An Introduction to the Study of Media Fan Culture* (London: Bloomsbury, 2013).
Eagleton, Terry, *Literary Theory: An Introduction* (Oxford: Blackwell, 1993).
Easthope, Anthony, *Literary into Cultural Studies* (London: Routledge, 1991).
Easton-Ellis, Brett, *American Psycho* (New York: Vintage, 1991).
Farren, Mick, *Elvis Died for Somebody's Sins but Not Mine* (London: Headpress, 2013).
Farrugia, Rebekah, *Beyond the Dance Floor: Female DJs, Technology and Electronic Dance Music Culture* (Bristol: Intellect, 2012).
Fernández, José Francisco, ed., *The New Puritan Generation* (Canterbury: Glyphi, 2013).
Fikentscher, Kai, *You Better Work: Underground Dance Music in New York City* (Hanover, NH: Wesleyan University Press, 2000).
Fikentscher, Kai, '"It's Not the Mix, It's the Selection": Music Programming in Contemporary DJ Culture', in Bernardo Alexander Attias, Anna Gavanas and

Hillegonda C. Rietveld (eds), *DJ Culture in the Mix: Power, Technology and Social Change in Electronic Dance Music* (London: Bloomsbury, 2013), pp. 123-49.

Fillion, Michelle, *Difficult Rhythm: Music & the Word in E. M. Forster* (Urbana, Chicago: University of Illinois Press, 2010).

Fish, Stanley, *Is There a Text in This Class?: The Authority of Interpretive Communities* (Cambridge, MA: Harvard University Press, 1980).

Fisher, Mark, 'What Is Hauntology?', *Film Quarterly* 66, no. 1 (2012), 16-24.

Fisher, Mark, *Ghosts of My Life: Writings on Depression, Hauntology and Lost Futures* (Alresford, Hants: Zero Books 2014).

Forde, Eamonn, 'From Polyglottism to Branding: On the Decline of Personality Journalism in the British Music Press', *Journalism: Theory, Practice, Criticism* 2, no. 1 (2001), 37-56.

Foucault, Michel, *Discipline and Punish: The Birth of the Prison* (London: Penguin, 1991).

Frith, Simon, *Sound Effects: Youth, Leisure, and the Politics of Rock'n'Roll* (New York: Pantheon, 1981).

Frith, Simon, 'The Cultural Study of Popular Music', in Lawrence Grossberg, Cary Nelson and Paula Treichler (eds), *Cultural Studies* (New York: Routledge, 1992).

Frith, Simon, *Performing Rites: Evaluating Popular Music* (Oxford: Oxford University Press, 1998).

Frith, Simon, 'Can Music Progress? Reflections on the History of Popular Music', *Musicology* 7 (2007), Serbian Academy of Sciences and Arts.

Frith, Simon and Andrew Goodwin (eds), *On Record: Rock, Pop & the Written Word* (Abingdon: Routledge, 2007).

Frith, Simon and Jon Savage, 'Pearls and Swine: Intellectuals and the Mass Media', in Steve Redhead (ed.), *The Clubcultures Reader: Readings in Popular Cultural Studies* (Oxford: Blackwell, 1998), pp. 7-17.

Gaiman, Neil, '"Let's Talk about Genre": Neil Gaiman and Kazuo Ishiguro in Conversation', *New Statesman*, 29 May-4 June 2015.

Gallin, D. C., *Kiss the Sky* (n.p.: Telemachus Press, 2012).

Gargani, Adam, 'Poetic Comparisons: How Similes Are Understood' (unpublished doctoral thesis, University of Salford, 2014).

Garland, Alex, *The Beach* (London: Penguin, 1997).

Garratt, Sheryl, *Adventures in Wonderland: A Decade in Club Culture* (London: Headline, 1998).

Gendron, Bernard, 'Adorno Meets the Cadillacs', in Tania Modleski (ed.), *Studies in Entertainment: Critical Approaches to Mass Culture* (Bloomington: Indiana University Press, 1986).

Gilbert, Jeremy and Ewan Pearson, *Discographies: Dance Music, Culture and the Politics of Sound* (London, Routledge, 1999).

Gorbman, Claudia, *Unheard Melodies: Narrative Film Music* (London: BFI Publishing, 1987).

Gramsci, Antonio, *Selections from the Prison Notebooks* (London: Lawrence & Wishart, 2005).

Grossberg, Lawrence, Cary Nelson and Paula Treichler, eds, *Cultural Studies* (New York: Routledge, 1992).

Guest, Katy, 'Nicholas Blincoe: A Passionate Puritan', *The Independent*, 16 July 2004.

Haden-Guest, Anthony, *The Last Party: Studio 54, Disco & the Culture of the Night* (New York: It Books, 2009).

Hall, Stuart, ed., *Representation: Cultural Representations and Signifying Practices* (London: Sage, 2002).
Haraway, Donna, ed., *Simians, Cyborgs and Women: The Reinvention of Nature* (New York: Routledge, 1991).
Haslam, Dave, *Adventures on the Wheels of Steel: The Rise of Superstar DJs* (London: Fourth Estate, 2001).
Haslam, Dave, *Manchester, England: The Story of the Pop Cult City* (London: Fourth Estate, 2010).
Haslam, Dave, *Life After Dark* (London: Simon and Schuster, 2015).
Haslam, Dave, 'DJ Culture', in Steve Redhead (ed.), *The Clubcultures Reader: Readings in Popular Cultural Studies* (Oxford: Blackwell, 2000), pp. 150–61.
Hebdige, Dick, *Subculture: The Meaning of Style* (London: Methuen, 1983).
Hellman, John, *Fables of Fact: The New Journalism as New Fiction* (Chicago, IL: University of Illinois Press, 1981).
Hendersen, Pat W., *Decade* (London: Phoenix Publishing, 2009).
Hendersen, Pat W., 'Club' (Unpublished manuscript).
Henderson, Sheila, *Ecstasy: Case Unsolved* (London: Pandora, 1997).
Hertz, Eric and Jeffrey Roessner, *Write in Tune* (New York: Bloomsbury, 2014).
Hesmondhalgh, David, 'Subcultures, Scenes or Tribes? None of the Above', *Journal of Youth Studies* 8, no. 1 (2005), 21–40.
Hewitt, Paolo, *Heaven's Promise* (London: Heavenly, n.d.).
Hodkinson, Paul, *Goth: Identity, Style and Subculture* (Oxford: Berg, 2002).
Holleran, Andrew, *Dancer from the Dance* (New York: Perennial, 2001).
Hollowell, John, *Fact & Fiction, The New Journalism and the Nonfiction Novel* (Chapel Hill, NC: The University of North Carolina Press, 1977).
Holub, Robert, *Reception Theory* (London: Routledge, 2003).
Hornby, Nick, *How to Be Good* (London: Penguin, 2001).
Huq, Rupa, *Beyond Subculture: Pop, Youth and Identity in a Postcolonial World* (London: Routledge, 2006).
Huxley, Aldous, *Island* (London: Panther, 1978).
Huxley, Aldous, *Moksha: Aldous Huxley's Classic Writings on Psychedelics and the Visionary Experience*, ed., Michael Horowitz and Cynthia Palmer (Rochester, VT: Park Street Press, 1999).
James, Martin, *French Connections: From Discothèque to Discovery* (London: Sanctuary, 2003).
James, Martin, 'A Silent Voice Across the MEdiaverse: *The Next Day* as Identities Presumed', *Celebrity Studies* 4, no. 3 (2013), 387–9.
Jameson, Frederic, *Archaeologies of the Future: The Desire Called Utopia and Other Science Fictions* (London and New York: Verso, 2005).
Jay, Mike, *High Society: Mind-Altering Drugs in History and Culture* (London: Thames & Hudson, 2010).
Jauss, Hans, 'Literary History as a Challenge to Literary Theory', *New Literary History* 2 (1970–1), pp. 7–37.
Jenkins, Tony, 'Fear and Loathing in Las Vegas Author Takes His Own Life', in RK Puma, 20 February 2005, http://www.rkpuma.com/gonzo.htm.
Keay, Douglas, 'Aids, Education and the Year 2000', *Woman's Own*, 31 October 1987.
Kerouac, Jack, *On the Road* (London: Penguin, 1987).

Kerouac, Jack 'Essentials of Spontaneous Prose', in Leroi Jones (ed.), *The Moderns: An Anthology of New Writing in America* (London: MacGibbon & Kee, 1965), pp. 343–4, http://www.writing.upenn.edu/~afilreis/88/kerouac-spontaneous.html [last accessed 29 July 2015].
King, Darren, *Jim Giraffe* (Toronto: Anchor, 2005).
Knifton, Robert, Marion Leonard and Les Roberts, eds, *Sites of Popular Music Heritage: Memories, Histories, Place* (New York and London: Routledge, 2015).
Kristeva, Julia, *Powers of Horror: An Essay on Abjection* (New York: Columbia Press, 1982).
Kureshi, Hanif, *The Buddha of Suburbia* (London: Faber and Faber, 1990).
Kureshi, Hanif, *The Black Album* (London: Faber & Faber, 1995).
Lacan, Jacques, *Ecrits: The Complete Edition in English* (New York: W. W. Norton, 2007).
Lee, C. P., *Shake, Rattle & Rain: Popular Music Making in Manchester, 1950–1995* (London: Hardinge Simpole, 2002).
L'Etang, Jacquie and Magda Pieczka, *Critical Perspectives in Public Relations* (London: International Thomson Business Press, 1996).
Lindberg, Ulf, Gestur Guðmundsson, Morten Michelsen and Hans Weisethaunet, eds, *Rock Criticism from the Beginning: Amusers, Cruisers & Cool-Headed Cruisers* (New York: Peter Lang, 2011).
Lyttle, Thomas and Michael Montagne, 'Drugs, Music, and Ideology: A Social Pharmacological Interpretation of the Acid House Movement', *International Journal of the Addictions* 27, no. 10 (1992), 1159–77.
Mailer, Norman, *Armies of the Night* (London: Penguin, 1970).
Malbon, Ben, *Clubbing: Dancing, Ecstasy and Vitality* (London: Routledge, 1999).
Maughan, Phillip. '"I Think the Dead Are with Us": John Berger at 88', *The New Statesman*, 11 June 2015.
McKeon, Rogert, ed., *Driftworks* (New York: Semiotext(e), 1984), a translation of the essays contained in Jean-François Lyotard, *Dérive à partir de Marx et Freud* (Paris: Union Général d'Editions, 1973).
McInnes, Colin, *Absolute Beginners* (London: Allison & Busby, 2011).
McLeod, Kembrew, 'Genres, Subgenres, Sub-Subgenres and More: Musical and Social Differentiation Within Electronic/Dance Music Communities', *Journal of Popular Music Studies* 13 (2001), 59–75.
McLuhan, Marshall, *The Gutenberg Galaxy: The Making of Typographic Man* (Toronto: University of Toronto Press, 1962).
Melly, George, *Revolt into Style: The Pop Arts in the 50s and 60s* (Oxford: Oxford University Press, 1989).
Middles, Mick, *Factory: The Story of the Record Label* (London: Random House, 2011).
Middleton, Richard, *Studying Popular Music* (Milton Keynes: Open University Press, 1997).
Middleton, Richard, *Reading Pop: Approaches to Textual Analysis in Popular Music* (Oxford: Oxford University Press, 2000).
Middleton, Richard, '"Last Night a DJ Saved My Life": Avians, Cyborgs and Siren Bodies in the Era of Phonographic Technology', *Radical Musicology* 1 (2006): 31 pars. 17 May 2007, http://www.radical-musicology.org.uk>.
Millar, Martin, 'How Sunshine Star-Traveller Lost His Girlfriend', in Sarah Champion (ed.), *Disco Biscuits: New Fiction from the Chemical Generation* (London: Sceptre, 1997).
Miller, Trevor, *Trip City* (London: Avernus, 1989).

Mitchell, Tony, 'Terpsichorean Architecture: Editor's Introduction', *Portal: Journal of Multidisciplinary Studies* 8, no. 1 (2011): 1–16.
Monaco, James, *How to Read a Film: Movies, Media, Multimedia*, 3rd edn (Oxford: Oxford University Press, 2000).
Moore, Allan, 'Authenticity as Authentication', *Popular Music* 21, no. 2 (2002), 209–23
Morrison, Simon A., 'Manumission', *Ministry in Ibiza*, 14 August–27 August 1999.
Morrison, Simon A., Irvine Welsh interview, *Muzik* (IPC, 2001).
Morrison, Simon A., *Discombobulated – Dispatches from the Wrong Side* (London: Headpress, 2010).
Morrison, Simon A., '"Clubs Aren't Like That" Discos, Deviance and Diegetics in Club Culture Cinema', *Dancecult: Journal of Electronic Dance Music Culture* 4, no. 2 (2012), 48–66.
Morrison, Simon A., 'DJ-Driven Literature: A Linguistic Remix', in Bernardo Alexander Attias, Anna Gavanas and Hillegonda C. Rietveld (eds), *DJ Culture in the Mix: Power, Technology and Social Change in Electronic Dance Music* (London: Bloomsbury, 2013), pp. 291–314.
Morrison, Simon A., '"Surely People Who Go Clubbing Don't Read": Dispatches from The Dancefloor and Clubland in Print', *IASPM Journal* (Christophe Jacke, Martin James and Ed Montano, eds) 4, no. 2 (2014), pp. 71–84.
Morrison, Simon A., 'Dancefloor-Driven Literature: Subcultural Big Bangs and a New Center for the Aesthetic Universe', *Popular Music* 36, no. 1 (The Critical Imperative) (January 2017), 43–54.
Muggleton, David, 'The Post-subculturalist', in Steve Redhead (ed.), *The Clubcultures Reader: Readings in Popular Cultural Studies* (Oxford: Blackwell, 1998), pp. 167–85.
Muggleton, David and Weinzierl, Rupert, eds, *The Post-Subcultures Reader* (Oxford: Berg, 2003).
Murray, Charles Shaar, *The Hellhound Sample* (London: Heapdress, 2011).
Nedeljkov, Nikolina, 'Enduring Schooling: Against Noise, and in the Service of the Remix', *Genero*, 18 (2014), 65–88.
Nedeljkov, Nikolina, 'Creation, Resistance, and Refacement: Postfuturist Storytelling, Cultural Flows, and the Remix' (New York: CUNY Academic Works, 2015).
Nedeljkov, Nikolina, 'Wired to a Maze: Pixel Saturnalia and Refacement' (unpublished PhD thesis, The City University of New York, 2015).
Noon, Jeff, *Woundings* (London: Oberon, 1986).
Noon, Jeff, *Vurt* (London: Pan, 1994).
Noon, Jeff, *Automated Alice* (London: Corgi, 1997).
Noon, Jeff, 'DJNA', in Sarah Champion (ed.), *Disco Biscuits: New Fiction from the Chemical Generation* (London: Sceptre, 1997).
Noon, Jeff, *Nymphomation* (New York: Doubleday, 1997).
Noon, Jeff, 'Dub Fiction', in Steve Redhead (ed.), *Repetitive Beat Generation* (Edinburgh: Canongate, 2000), pp. 111–18.
Noon, Jeff, *Pixel Juice* (London: Anchor, 2000).
Noon, Jeff, *Cobralingus* (Mesquite, TX: Codex, 2001).
Noon, Jeff, 'Film-Makers Use Jump Cuts, Freeze Frames, Slow Motion. Musicians Remix, Scratch, Sample. Can't We Writers Have Some Fun as Well?', *The Guardian*, 10 January 2001.
Noon, Jeff, *Needle in the Groove* (London: Black Swan, 2001).

Noon, Jeff, *Pollen* (London: Pan, 2001).
Noon, Jeff, *Falling Out of Cars* (London: Black Swan, 2003).
Noon, Jeff, *Channel SK1N* (Smashwords, 2012), eBook.
Noon, Jeff, 'The Ghost on the B-Side', http://jeffnoon.weebly.com/the-ghost-on-the-b-side.html [last accessed 22 January 2018].
Nye, Sean, 'Review Essay: Berlin Calling and Run Lola Run', *Dancecult* 1, no. 2 (2010), 121–7.
Osborne, Richard *Clubland Heroes: A Nostalgic Study of the Recurrent Characters in the Romantic Fiction of Dornford Yates, John Buchan and 'Sapper'* (London: Hutchinson, 1983).
Owen, David, 'Writing By Numbers: Disavowing Literary Tradition in *All Hail the New Puritans*', in José Francisco Fernández (ed.), *The New Puritan Generation* (Canterbury: Glyphi, 2013), pp. 47–63.
Owen, Frank, *Clubland Confidential* (London: Ebury Press, 2004).
Paddison, Max, *Adorno, Modernism and Mass Culture: Essays on Critical Theory and Music*, 2nd edn (London: Kahn & Averill, 2004).
Petrides, Alexis, 'Las Vegas's Gamble with Dance Music', *The Guardian*, 17 July 2014.
Phillips, Dom, *Superstar DJs Here We Go!: The Incredible Rise of Clubland's Finest* (London: Ebury Press, 2009).
Priest, Hannah, 'Steampunk, Cyberpunk, Whimsy: Generic Definition and Jeff Noon's *The Automated Alice*' (unpublished conference paper).
Pynchon, Thomas, *Gravity's Rainbow* (London: Vintage, 2000).
Redhead, Steve, *The End-of-the-Century Party: Youth and Pop Towards* 2000 (Manchester: Manchester University Press, 1990).
Redhead, Steve, *Rave Off: Politics and Deviance in Contemporary Youth Culture* (Aldershot: Avebury, 1993).
Redhead, Steve, *Subculture to Clubcultures: An Introduction to Popular Cultural Studies* (Oxford: Blackwell, 1997).
Redhead, Steve, *The Clubcultures Reader: Readings in Popular Cultural Studies* (Oxford: Blackwell, 1998).
Redhead, Steve, *Repetitive Beat Generation* (Edinburgh: Rebel Inc., 2000).
Reynolds, Simon, 'Rave Culture: Living Dream or Living Death?', in Steve Redhead (ed.), *The Clubcultures Reader: Readings in Popular Cultural Studies* (Oxford: Blackwell, 1998), pp. 84–93.
Reynolds, Simon, *Generation Ecstasy: Into the World of Techno and Rave Culture* (New York: Routledge, 1999).
Reynolds, Simon, *Retromania: Pop Culture's Addiction to Its Own Past* (London: Faber & Faber, 2011).
Reynolds, Simon, 'How Rave Music Conquered America', *The Guardian*, 2 August 2012.
Rief, Silvia, *Club Cultures: Boundaries, Identities and Otherness* (London and New York: Routledge, 2009).
Rietveld, Hillegonda, 'Living the Dream', in Steve Redhead (ed.), *Rave Off: Politics and Deviance in Contemporary Youth Culture* (Aldertshot: Avebury, 1993).
Rietveld, Hillegonda, *This Is Our House; House Music, Cultural Spaces and Technologies* (Aldershot: Ashgate, 1998).
Rietveld, Hillegonda, 'Journey to the Light? Immersion, Spectacle and Mediation', in Attias, Bernardo Alexander, Anna Gavanas and Hillegonda C. Rietveld (eds), *DJ*

Culture in the Mix: Power, Technology and Social Change in Electronic Dance Music (London: Bloomsbury, 2013), pp. 79–102.

River, Michael, 'Electrovoodoo', in Sarah Champion (ed.), *Disco Biscuits: New Fiction from the Chemical Generation* (London: Sceptre, 1997).

Robinson, Lisa, 'Boogie Nights', *Vanity Fair*, February 2010.

Rushkoff, Douglas, *The Ecstasy Club* (London: Sceptre, 1997).

Santala, Ismo, '"Dub Fiction": The Musico-Literary Features of Jeff Noon's *Cobralingus*' (unpublished PhD thesis, University of Tampere, 2010).

de Saussure, Ferdinand, *Course in General Linguistics* (La Salle, IL: Open Court Classics, 1983).

Savage, Jon, *The Hacienda Must Be Built* (Woodford Green: International Music Publications, 1992).

Scannell, John, 'Working to Design: The Self-perpetuating Ideology of Rock or … "The New Bob Dylan"', *Portal: Journal of Multidisciplinary International Studies* 8, no. 1 (2011), pp. 1–15.

Scher, Steven Paul, 'Einleitung: literature und Musik: Entwickung und Stand der Forschung', in Steven Paul Scher (ed.), *Literatur und Musik: Ein Hanbuch zur Theorie und Praxis eines komparatisichen Grenzgbietes* (Berlin: Eric Schmidt, 1984), pp. 9–25.

Scher, Steven Paul, *Essays on Literature and Music (1967–2004)*, eds Walter Bernhart and Werner Wolf (Amsterdam: Rodopi, 2004).

Shapiro, Harry, *Waiting for the Man: The Story of Drugs and Popular Music* (London: Helter Skelter, 2003).

Shildrick, Tracy and Robert MacDonald, 'In Defence of Subculture: Young People, Leisure and Social Divisions', *Journal of Youth Studies* 9, no. 2 (2006), 125–40.

Situationist International Manifesto, Internationale Situationniste #4 (June 1960), http://www.cddc.vt.edu/sionline/si/manifesto.html [last accessed 24 June 2016].

Sklower, Jedediah and Sheila Whiteley, eds, *Countercultures & Popular Music* (Farnham: Ashgate, 2014).

Smyth, Gerry, *Music in Contemporary British Fiction: Listening to the Novel* (New York: Palgrave Macmillan, 2008).

da Sosa Correa, Delia (ed.), *Phrase and Subject – Studies in Literature and Music* (Oxford: Legenda, 2006).

Sperber, Dan and Deirdre Wilson, *Relevance: Communication and Cognition*, 2nd edn (Oxford: Blackwell, 1995).

St. James, James, *Disco Bloodbath* (London: Sceptre, 1999).

St. John, Graham 'Post-Rave Technotribalism and the Carnival of Protest', in *The Post-Subcultures Reader* (Oxford: Berg, 2003), pp. 65–82.

St. John, Graham, *Technomad: Global Raving Countercultures* (London: Equinox, 2009).

St. John, Graham, 'Astronauts, Psychonauts and Electronauts', *Dancecult* 6, no. 4 (2014).

Sterling, Bruce, *Cyberpunk in the Nineties* (Cambridge: Interzone, 1991).

Straw, Will, 'Systems of Articulations, Logics of Change: Communities and Scenes in Popular Music', *Cultural Studies* 5, no. 3 (1991), 368–88.

Street, John, 'Introduction to "Literature and Music" special issue', *Popular Music* 24, no. 2 (2005), pp. 163–164.

Suleiman, Susan R., *The Reader in the Text* (Princeton: Princeton University Press, 1980).

Tench, Ralph and Liz Yeomans, *Exploring Public Relations* (Edinburgh: Pearson, 2006).

Thompson, Dave, *Reggae & Caribbean Music* (London: Backbeat Books, 2002).

Thompson, Hunter S., *The Great Shark Hunt* (London: Summit Books, 1979).
Thompson, Hunter S., *The Fear and Loathing Letters Volume 1*, ed. Douglas Brinkley (London: Bloomsbury, 1997).
Thompson, Hunter S., *Fear and Loathing in America: The Brutal Odyssey of an Outlaw Journalist 1968–1976* (London: Bloomsbury, 2000).
Thompson, Hunter S., *Ancient Gonzo Wisdom* (Cambridge: Da Capo Press, 2009).
Thornton, Sarah, *Club Cultures: Music, Media and Subcultural Capital* (Cambridge: Polity, 1995).
Toffler, Alvin, *Future Shock* (New York: Random House, 1970).
Toop, David, *The Rap Attack: African Jive to New York Hip Hop* (London: Pluto Press, 1984).
Toop, David, *Oceans of Sound: Aether Talk, Ambient Sound and Imaginary Worlds* (London: Serpent's Tail, 2001).
Transpontine, Neil, '"These Days Are Not to Be Missed": 1990s Rave and Club Culture in Fiction', *Datacide Magazine*, n.d., https://datacide-magazine.com/these-days-are-not-to-be-missed-1990s-rave-and-club-culture-in-fiction/.
UK Government, Criminal Justice and Disorder Act (1994), www.legislation.gov.uk/uk pga/1994/33/section/63.
Waksman, Steve, *Instruments of Desire: The Electric Guitar and the Shaping of Musical Experience* (Cambridge, MA: Harvard University Press, 2001).
Walton, Stuart, *Out of It: A Cultural History of Intoxication* (London: Penguin, 2002).
Warner, Alan, *Morvern Callar* (London: Vintage, 1996).
Warner, Alan, 'Celtic Trails', in Steve Redhead (ed.), *Repetitive Beat Generation* (Edinburgh: Canongate, 2000), pp. 127–34.
Warner, Simon, *Texts and Drugs and Rock 'n' Roll* (New York: Bloomsbury, 2013).
Warner, Simon, 'The Banality of Degradation: Andy Warhol, the Velvet Underground and the Trash Aesthetic', in Jedediah Skowler and Sheila Whiteley (eds), *Countercultures and Popular Music* (Farnham: Ashgate, 2014).
Webber, Steve, *DJ Skills: The Essential Guide to Mixing and Scratching* (Burlington, MA: Focal Press, 2008).
Weingarten, Marc, *Who's Afraid of Tom Wolfe? How New Journalism Rewrote the World* (London: Aurum, 2005).
Weingarten, Marc, *The Gang That Wouldn't Shoot Straight* (New York: Crown, 2006).
Weinzierl, Rupert and David Muggleton, 'What Is "Post-subcultural Studies" Anyway?', in *The Post-Subcultures Reader* (Oxford: Berg, 2003), pp. 3–23.
Welsh, Irvine, *Trainspotting* (London: Minerva, 1994).
Welsh, Irvine, *The Acid House* (London: Vintage Press, 1995).
Welsh, Irvine, *Ecstasy: Three Tales of Chemical Romance* (London: Jonathan Cape, 1996).
Welsh, Irvine, *Maribou Stork Nightmares* (London: Jonathan Cape, 1996).
Welsh, Irvine, 'The State of the Party', in Sarah Champion (ed.), *Disco Biscuits: New Fiction from the Chemical Generation* (London: Sceptre, 1997).
Welsh, Irvine, 'Post-Punk Junk', in Steve Redhead (ed.), *Repetitive Beat Generation* (Edinburgh: Canongate, 2000), pp. 137–50.
Welsh, Irvine, *Glue* (London: Vintage, 2002).
Welsh, Irvine, *Filth* (London: Vintage, 2013).
Wenaus, Andrew, '"Spells Out the Word of Itself, and Then Dispelling Itself": The Chaotics of Memory' and 'The Ghost of the Novel in Jeff Noon's *Falling Out of Cars*', *Journal of the Fantastic in the Arts* 23, no. 2 (2012), 260–84.

Wenaus, Andrew, '"You Are Cordially Invited to a / CHEMICAL WEDDING": Metamorphiction and Experimentation in Jeff Noon's Cobralingus', http://www.electronicbookreview.com/thread/electropoetics/postfuturist [last accessed 1 November 2017].
West, Geoffrey, *The New Statesman*, 22–18 November 2013.
Whiteley, Sheila, 'Coda', in Rachel Carroll and Adam Hansen (eds), *LitPop: Writing and Popular Music* (Farnham: Ashgate, 2014).
Williamson, Kevin, *Drugs and the Party Line* (Edinburgh: Rebel Inc., 1997).
Wolf, Werner, *The Musicalization of Fiction: A Study in the Theory and History of Intermediality* (Amsterdam: Rodopi, 1999).
Wolfe, Tom, *Radical Chic and Mau-mauing the Flak Catchers* (London: Picador, 2009).
Wolfe, Tom and E. W. Johnson (eds), *The New Journalism* (London: Picador, 1990).
Yu, Jonathan, 'Electronic Dance Music and Technological Change: Lessons from Actor-Network Theory', in Bernado Alexander Attias, Anna Gavanas and Hillegonda C. Rietveld (eds), *DJ Culture in the Mix: Power, Technology and Social Change in Electronic Dance Music* (London: Bloomsbury, 2013), pp. 151–72.

Select EDMC discography

4Hero, 'The Element' (UK: Reinforced Records, 1993).
808 State, 'Pacific' (UK: ZTT, 1989).
A Guy Called Gerald, 'Trip City Mambo' (UK: Avernus, 1989).
A Guy Called Gerald, 'Valentine's Theme' (UK: Avernus, 1989).
Afrika Bambaataa, 'Planet Rock' (USA: Tommy Boy, 1982).
Black Grape, *It's Great When You're Straight, Yeah* (UK: Radioactive, 1995).
Cybotron, 'Clear' (USA: Fantasy, 1983).
D-Mob, 'We Call It Acieed' (UK: FFRR, 1988).
DJ Hype, 'Shot in the Dark' (UK: Suburban Base Records, 1993).
D.J. P.C, 'Insomniak' (Belgium: BITE Records, 1991).
Eek-A-Mouse, 'Ganja Smuggling' (Jamaica: Volcano, n.d.).
Farley 'Jackmaster' Funk, 'Love Can't Turn Around' (US: House Records, 1986).
Fatboy Slim, 'Everybody Needs a 303' (UK: Skint, 1995).
Hardfloor, 'Acperience' (USA: Moonshine Music, 1993).
Joey Beltram, 'Energy Flash' (USA: Transmat, 1990).
Josh Wink, 'Higher State of Consciousness' (USA: Strictly Rhythm, 1995).
Leftfield, 'Not Forgotten' (UK: Outer Rhythm, 1990).
Lil Louis, 'French Kiss' (USA: Diamond Records, 1989).
Nightmares on Wax, 'Aftermath #1' (UK: Warp Records, 1990).
Phuture, 'Acid Tracks' (USA: Trax Records, 1987).
The Prodigy, 'Charly' (UK: XL Recordings, 1991).
Richie Rich, 'Salsa House' (UK: FFRR, 1989).
Rhythim Is Rhythim, 'Strings of Life' (US: Trasmat, 1987).
Second Phase, 'Mentasm' (Belgium: R & S Records, 1991).
T-Coy, 'Carino' (Belgium: R & S Records, 1991).\
The Happy Mondays, 'MADChester Rave on EP' (UK: Factory, November 1989).
The Happy Mondays, 'Hallelujah' (Benelux: Factory, 1990).
The Happy Mondays, 'Loose Fit' (UK: Factory, 1991).
Two Lone Swordsmen, 'Kicking In and Out' (featured on *Disco Biscuits*, UK: Coalition Recordings, 1997).

Select EDMC filmography

UK and International Dancefloor-Driven film texts

24 Hour Party People, dir. by Michael Winterbottom (UK: Pathe, 2002).
54, dir. Mark Christopher (USA: Dollface, 1998).
Amnesia, dir. Barbet Schroeder (Switzerland and France: Vega Film, 2015).
Beats, dir. Brian Welsh (UK: Rosetta Productions, 2019).
Berlin Calling, dir. Hannes Stöhr (Germany: Sabotage Films, 2008).
Beyond the Rave, dir. Matthias Hoene (UK: Hammer Films, 2008).
Do You Own the Dancefloor, dir. Chris Hughes (UK: Heehaw Films, 2015).
Ecstasy, dir. Lux (Canada: Dolce Cielo, 2011).
Groove, dir. Greg Harrison (USA: Sony Pictures, 2000).
Human Traffic, dir. Justin Kerrigan (UK: Fruit Salad Films, 1999).
Ibiza, dir. Alex Richanbach (USA: Gary Sanchez Productions, 2018).
Ibiza: The Silent Movie, dir. Julien Temple (UK: Essential Arts, 2019).
Irvine Welsh's Ecstasy, dir. Rob Heydon (Canada: Silver Reel, 2012).
It's All Gone Pete Tong, dir. Michael Dowse (UK: Vertigo, 2004).
Kevin & Perry Go Large, dir. Ed Bye (UK: Icon, 2000).
Morvern Callar, dir. Lynne Ramsey (UK: Scottish Screen, 2002).
Run Lola Run, dir. Tom Tykwer (Germany: Arte, 1998).
Saturday Night Fever, dir. John Badham (USA: RSO, 1977).
Sorted, dir. Alexander Jovy (UK: Jovy Junior Enterprises, 2000).
The 51st State, dir, Ronny Yu (UK: Alliance Atlantis Communications, 2001).
Trainspotting, dir. Danny Boyle (UK: Channel 4 Films, 1996).
Weekender, dir. Karl Golden (UK: Benchmark Films, 2011).
XOXO, dir. Christopher Louie (USA: Netflix, 2016).

TV

Alan Partridge's Scissored Isle, https://www.youtube.com/watch?v=NGvzlf-4PJQ&t=10s, dir. Neil Gibbons and Rob Gibbons (UK: Online, 2016).
And the Beat Goes On, dir. Steve Jaggi (UK: Sepia Films, 2009).
'Cardigan', *Men Behaving Badly*, dir. Martin Dennis (UK: BBC1, 18 July 1996).
Club-A-Vision Ibiza Specials, dir. Russell Cleaver (UK: ITV, 1999).
'Cherubim and Seraphim', *Inspector Morse*, dir. Danny Boyle (UK: ITV, 15 April 1992).
'Epiphanies', *Spaced*, dir. Edgar Wright (UK: Channel 4, 29 October 1999).
'Model Misbehavior', *Family Guy*, dir. Sarah Frost and Peter Shin (USA: 20th Century Fox, 2006), https://www.youtube.com/watch?v=ZaT_hqGUP7U [last accessed 22 January 2018].

Appendix I
A Catalogue of Dancefloor-Driven Literature

Note: While outlining the basis of a corpus of Dancefloor-Driven Literature, this is designed to be an organic, evolving list. It also includes historically important fictions for the creation of this literature, and more commercial novels that contain demonstrative EDMC scenes. Focus is given to UK publications and special attention is paid to the texts used within this book, notably the stories from *Disco Biscuits*, although all stories within that collection should be considered Dancefloor-Driven texts.

Arnott, Jake, *True Crime* (London: Sceptre, 2004).
Atkins, A. D., *Ecstasy, Sorted & On One* (London: n.pub., 1995).
Benson, Mike, 'Room Full of Angels', in Sarah Champion (ed.), *Disco Biscuits: New Fiction from the Chemical Generation* (London: Sceptre, 1997).
Blincoe, Nicholas, 'Ardwick Green', in Sarah Champion (ed.), *Disco Biscuits: New Fiction from the Chemical Generation* (London: Sceptre, 1997).
Blincoe, Nicholas, *Jello Salad* (London: Serpents Tail, 1997).
Blincoe, Nicholas, *Acid Casuals* (London: Serpent's Tail, 1998).
Blincoe, Nicholas, *Manchester Slingback* (London: Pan, 1998).
Brook, Jonathan, 'Sangria', in Sarah Champion (ed.), *Disco Biscuits: New Fiction from the Chemical Generation* (London: Sceptre, 1997).
Butts, Colin, *Is Harry on the Boat?* (London: Orion, 1997).
Champion, Sarah, ed., *Disco Biscuits: New Fiction from the Chemical Generation* (London: Sceptre, 1997).
Champion, Sarah, ed., *Disco 2000* (London: Hodder & Stoughton, 1998).
Davidson, Toni, ed., *Intoxication: An Anthology of Stimulant-Based Writing* (London: Serpent's Tail, 1998).
De Abaitua, Matthew, 'Inbetween', in Sarah Champion (ed.), *Disco Biscuits: New Fiction from the Chemical Generation* (London: Sceptre, 1997).
De la Mer, Nina, *4 a.m.* (Oxford: Myriad, 2011).
Dyer, Geoff, *Paris Trance: A Romance* (Edinburgh: Canongate, 1998).
Fingers, Two, *Bass Instinct* (London: Boxtree, 1996).
Fingers, Two and James T. Kirk, *Junglist* (London: Boxtree, 1995).
Fingers, Two and James T. Kirk, 'Puff', in Sarah Champion (ed.), *Disco Biscuits: New Fiction from the Chemical Generation* (London: Sceptre, 1997).
Fletcher, Tony, *Hedonism* (London: Omnibus, 2003).
Fowler, Christopher, *Disturbia* (London: Sphere, 1998).
Gallin, D. C., *Kiss the Sky* (n.p.: Telemachus Press, 2012).
Garland, Alex, 'Blink and You Miss It', in Sarah Champion (ed.), *Disco Biscuits: New Fiction from the Chemical Generation* (London: Sceptre, 1997).

Garland, Alex, *The Beach* (London: Penguin, 1997).
Geraghty, Geraldine, *Raise Your Hands* (London: Boxtree, 1996).
Graham, Ben, 'Weekday Service', in Sarah Champion (ed.), *Disco Biscuits: New Fiction from the Chemical Generation* (London: Sceptre, 1997).
Greenpike, Ryan, *One Day in the Promised Land* (London: RG Publishing, 2015).
Hall, Charlie, 'The Box', in Sarah Champion (ed.), *Disco Biscuits: New Fiction from the Chemical Generation* (London: Sceptre, 1997).
Hendersen, Pat. W., *Decade* (London: Phoenix Publishing, 2009).
Hendersen, Pat. W., 'Club' (Unpublished manuscript).
Hewitt, Paolo, *Heaven's Promise* (London: Heavenly, n.d.).
Holleran, Andrew, *Dancer from the Dance* (New York: Perennial, 2001).
Hornby, Nick, *How to Be Good to Be Good* (London: Penguin, 2001).
King, Daren, *Boxy an Star* (London: Abacus, 2000).
Kureshi, Hanif, *The Black Album* (London: Faber & Faber, 1995).
McInerney, Lisa, *The Glorious Heresies* (London: John Murray, 2015).
McInnes, Colin, *Absolute Beginners* (London: Allison & Busby, 2011).
Millar, Martin, 'How Sunshine Star-Traveller Lost His Girlfriend', in Sarah Champion (ed.), *Disco Biscuits: New Fiction from the Chemical Generation* (London: Sceptre, 1997).
Miller, Trevor, *Trip City* (London: Avernus, 1989).
Monaghan, Nicola, *Starfishing* (London: Vintage, 2009).
Morrison, Simon A., *Discombobulated – Dispatches from the Wrong Side* (London: Headpress, 2010).
Noon, Jeff, *Vurt* (London: Pan, 1994).
Noon, Jeff, 'DJNA', in Sarah Champion (ed.), *Disco Biscuits: New Fiction from the Chemical Generation* (London: Sceptre, 1997).
Noon, Jeff, *Pixel Juice* (London: Anchor, 2000).
Noon, Jeff, *Needle in the Groove* (London: Black Swan, 2001).
Owen, Frank, *Clubland Confidential* (London: Ebury Press, 2004).
Random, Bert, *Spannered* (Bristol: Silverwood Books, 2011).
River, Michael, 'Electrovoodoo', in Sarah Champion (ed.), *Disco Biscuits: New Fiction from the Chemical Generation* (London: Sceptre, 1997).
Rushkoff, Douglas, *The Ecstasy Club* (London: Sceptre, 1997).
St. James, James, *Disco Bloodbath* (London: Sceptre, 1999).
Warner, Alan, *Morvern Callar* (London: Vintage, 1996).
Warner, Alan, 'Bitter Salvage', in Sarah Champion (ed.), *Disco Biscuits: New Fiction from the Chemical Generation* (London: Sceptre, 1997).
Welsh, Irvine, *Trainspotting* (London: Minerva, 1994).
Welsh, Irvine, *The Acid House* (London: Vintage, 1995).
Welsh, Irvine, *Ecstasy: Three Tales of Chemical Romance* (London: Jonathan Cape, 1996).
Welsh, Irvine, 'The State of the Party', in Sarah Champion (ed.), *Disco Biscuits: New Fiction from the Chemical Generation* (London: Sceptre, 1997).
Welsh, Irvine, *Glue* (London: Vintage, 2002).

Index

Note: Page numbers followed by "n" refer to notes.

Abbott, Sara   207 n.19
abject, the   87
Absolute Beginners (MacInnes)   75
Acid Casuals (Blincoe)   6–7, 63, 133, 134, 139–43, 145–8, 150, 151, 153, 212 n.5
acid delirium   146–8
acid house   184 n.26
Acid House, The (Welsh)   6, 63, 89
Acid House [parties] Bill   36
Acid House Squad   36
'Acid Tracks' (Phuture)   23
'Acperience 1' (Hardfloor)   23
Adorno, Theodor   19, 21, 25, 101, 102, 105, 131, 153, 171, 185 n.5
Aesthetic Theory (Adorno)   105
Afrika Bambaataa   23
Allen, Steve   120
All Hail the New Puritans (Blincoe)   132, 134
Almond, Mark   44
American Psycho (Ellis)   92
Amis, Martin   164
Amram, David   120
Anderton, James   36–7
And the Beat Goes On (Mistry)   191 n.17
'Ardwick Green' (Blincoe)   67, 134, 137–9
Armies of the Night (Mailer)   60
'Around the World in 80 Clubs' (Morrison)   3
Arthrob   69, 75, 83, 201 n.28
Arthur   27
Atari's ST computers   23
Atkins, A. D.   65, 161, 162
Attali, Jacques   19, 22, 24
Attias, Bernard   23
Auden, W. H.   91
audience penetration   105

authenticity   43, 45, 46, 50, 55, 73, 74, 102, 134, 136, 139, 145, 164, 192 n.48, 194 n.108
and cultural formation   148
historical-cultural   69
subcultural   151
subterranean   95
'Authenticity as Authentication' (Moore)   45
Automated Alice (Noon)   109
avant-garde   107, 112, 116, 121, 123, 124, 128, 135, 136
experimentalism   139
laboratory   129–32
Average White Band   149

'Baby Wants to Ride' (Knuckles)   186 n.37
Back to Basics   83
Badham, John   20
Bakhtin, Mikhail   80, 85, 189 n.132
carnival and marketplace   86–7
on club as carnival   37
and counterpoint   117
on cultural elevation   106
lower bodily stratum   96, 101, 102, 105, 121, 171
and polyphony   97, 98, 112, 117
sense of the carnivalesque   19
Bangs, Lester   16
Barnes, Julian   164
Barthes, Roland   31, 74, 148, 164, 187 n.49, 188 n.82
on cultural code   56
on myths   58, 101
on structural linguistics   140
on structural similarities of narratives   43
Bate, Jonathan   75
Baudrillard, Jean   76, 109, 168

Index

BBC Radio 1   194 n.94
Beach, The (Garland)   6, 190 n.139
Beastie Boys   35, 136
Beat Generation   2, 16, 27, 56, 62, 63, 70, 100, 110–12, 128, 147, 156
Beats   166
Beat This   104
bebop   16, 22, 62, 69, 70, 73, 75, 76, 83, 84, 96, 116, 169, 201 n.29
The Bee Gees   187 n.66
Beeler, Stan   42, 80, 90, 96, 99, 104, 137, 138
   first function   41
   on phenomenon–artistic representations dialectic relationship   40
   second function   41, 45, 46, 52, 55, 59
belonging   55
Benjamin, Walter   25, 77, 165
Bennett, Andy   12–13, 19, 26, 27
   and 'MADchester'   30
   and subculture theory   26
Benson, Mike   67
Benson, Stephen   73, 117
Bentham, Jeremy   19
Berezan, David   211 n.155
Berger, John   164
Bernhart, Walter   7
Berthke, Bruce   111
Bey, Hakim   1, 39, 100
Birmingham School. *See* Centre for Contemporary Cultural Studies (CCCS)
'Bitter Salvage' (Warner)   67
Black Album, The (Kureshi)   6
Blatter, Klaus   83
Blincoe, Nicholas   8, 28, 30, 68, 82, 86, 105, 115, 159–61, 171, 212 nn.2, 7, 213 n.17, 214 nn.50, 63, 73, 215 n.102, 216 n.120, 217 n.153
   Acid Casuals   6–7, 63, 133, 134, 139–43, 145–8, 150, 151, 153, 212 n.5
   aesthetic ambitions   121
   All Hail the New Puritans   132, 134
   'Ardwick Green'   67, 134, 137–9
   as 'British noir'   153
   casual style aesthetic   146–8
   on crime genre   52
   developmental influences   108
   on ghosts   131
   Jello Salad   7, 134, 148–53
   Manchester Slingback   7, 37, 133, 134, 146, 148–55, 212 n.5
   marks of present-day   164
   New Puritan Generation, The   135
   New Puritan Manifesto   132, 134–5, 146, 157
   writing, literary diegesis in   133–57
Blind Date   138
Bloom, Harold   135
'Blue Monday'   70
Blur   95
'Boogie Nights' (Robinson)   27
Boon, Marcus   21, 82, 89, 105, 170, 221 n.24
bop prosody   117
Bourdieu, Pierre   12, 30, 92, 93, 170
   hierarchies of taste   156
   vertical taste hierarchy   171
Bowie, David   125, 210 n.132
'The Box' (Hall)   67
Boy's Own   67
BPI. *See* British Phonographic Industry (BPI)
Bradbury, Malcolm   161
Brady, Ian   217 n.153
Brewster, Bill   127
bricks-and-mortar pointillism   143–5
Brinkley, Douglas   56
British Phonographic Industry (BPI)   186 n.37
Broe, Dennis   153
Brook, Jonathan   66
Broughton, Frank   127
Brown, Adam   100
Brown, Calvin S.   7, 159
Buddha of Suburbia, The (Kureshi)   145–6
Bugged Out!   83
Bukem, LTJ   69
Bukowski, Charles   65
Burr (Vidal)   60
Burroughs, William S.   27, 65, 82, 121, 147, 210 n.122, 215 n.105
   on cutups   107, 112, 118, 124

Index

on lower body functions 101
on sonic landscapes 120
Butts, Colin 191 n.17

Caballé, Montserrat 189 n.98
Calarco, Matthew 165
Calcutt, Andrew 72, 81, 89, 105, 156, 162, 170, 171
Capote, Truman 147
'Cardigan' 42, 44
'Carino' (T-Coy) 30
carnival 86-7
  club as 37-8
Carroll, Lewis 123
Carroll, Rachel 83
Cartland, Barbara 89
'Car Wash' 72
Cassady, Neal 108
Cassette Store Day 25
casual style aesthetic 146-8
Cavern Club 164, 218 n.24
Centre for Contemporary Cultural Studies (CCCS) 11, 12, 39, 53, 82, 163, 167
Champion, Sarah 3, 6, 9, 53, 54, 56-9, 61, 63-9, 79, 90, 97, 102, 107, 109, 110, 133, 134, 161, 199 n.79, 212 nn.2, 5
Channel SK1N (Noon) 130
'Charly' (Prodigy) 23
Cheeseman, Matthew 12
Cheetah 27
Chemical Generation 47, 63, 75, 79, 108, 133, 135, 147, 181 n.4
Chicago White Sox 28
Chtcheglov, Ivan 29, 31
cinema, re/presentation of EDMC in 45-53
'Clear' (Cybotron) 23
Clink Street raves 67
Closed Romantic Realism 48
Club (Hendersen) 5
club, as carnival 37-8
Club-A-Vision 3, 191 n.17
clubbers 55
club culture 1, 4. *See also individual entries*
  communication 56

fiction 137
journalism 53-9
subterranean club cultures, global roots of 19-38
Club & Drug Literature 3, 109
Club Kids 6
Clubland Confidential (Owen) 6
Cobbing, Bob 120
Cobralingus (Noon) 108, 118, 143
Cohen, Sara 19
Cohen, Stanley 53
Cohn, Nik 20, 27
Coleman, Ornette 73
Coleridge, Samuel Taylor 82
Collin, Matthew 44, 149
Collins, Karen 111
Colston-Hayter, Tony 35
'Conjecture' (Fisher) 142
contemporaneous enculturation 161-2
Coombs, Sean 208 n.77
Coronation Street 150
counterpoint 87, 88, 98, 117, 123, 132, 136, 137, 142
Cousins, Mark 48
Creem (Bangs) 16
Cremona, Vicky-Ann 24
Criminal Justice and Disorder Act of 1994, Section 63 (1b) 65
Criminal Justice and Public Order Act of November 1994 36
CR model 23
Crosby Homes 188 n.82, 218 n.26
Crosthwaite, Paul 164
CSI 51
cult
  club fictions 104-6
  elevation of 170-3
  fiction 3, 105, 134, 156, 160, 163, 170, 171, 176
cultural elevation 104-6
cultural musicology 17, 83
cultural relevance 67, 83, 104
Cummins, Kevin 184 n.29, 221 n.25
cutups 107, 112, 118
cyberfiction 107, 110-12, 115
cyberpunks 110, 111, 113, 123

Index

cyborg machines 121–4
Cybotron 23

Dahl, Steve 28
Dance, Drugs and Escape (Beeler) 41, 137
Dancecult 45, 62, 196 n.135
dance culture 34, 36, 62, 125
dancefloor. *See also individual entries*
   definition of 1
   as psychogeographic locus 26–7
   as tabula rasa 146
   as Temporary Autonomous Zone 1, 19, 27, 32
Dancefloor-Driven Literature. *See also individual entries*
   defining 61–77
   shelves of, delineating 5–7
   taxonomy of uses of music in 8–9
Dancer from the Dance (Holleran) 1, 14, 35
dance tourism 32
Datacide 161
Davidson, Toni 65
Davies, Claire 189 n.106
Davis, James 'Disco' 57
Dayan, Peter 73
de Abaitua, Matthew 67
Dead Men's Trousers (Welsh) 98
'The Death of the Author' (Barthes) 145, 164
Debord, Guy 31
Defoe, Daniel 171
de la Mer, Nina 65
Deleuze, Gilles 31, 123
Deller, Jeremy 165, 166
Departures (N-SIGN) 100
De Quincey, Thomas 82
Derrida, Jacques 96, 134, 140–2, 156, 163, 210 n.128
   on automatic and machine writing 123
   on ghosts 131
   on hauntology 26, 31, 73, 125
dialogics 79, 106, 169
Dick, Duncan 57
Dickens, Charles 87
diegetic music 49–51
Digweed, Jon 95

Disco Biscuits (Champion) 6, 9, 61, 63–9, 75, 76, 107, 109, 121, 125, 131–4, 172, 212 n.2, 214 n.50
   'Ardwick Green' 67, 137–9
   Blincoe's biography in 135, 206 n.15
   'DJNA' 107, 109, 112–14
   'State of the Party, The' 80, 87–9
Disco Bloodbath (James) 6
Discographies (Pearson and Gilbert) 23
Discombobulated (Morrison) 3, 68, 196 nn.135, 141, 202 n.54, 218 n.14
Disco Music Club (DMC) 54
'Disco Sucks' movement 28
Dispatches from the Wrong Side 3
Distiller's Company 202 n.80
Distinction (Bourdieu) 30
DJ 3, 34, 40, 53, 54, 58, 59, 64, 68, 96, 103, 218 n.14
DMC. *See* Disco Music Club (DMC)
D-Mob 83
Drabble, Margaret 136
drift (dérive) 31, 32
dub
   fiction 123, 125, 128
   Pixel Juice 126–7
Duffett, Mark 84, 90, 163
Durutti Column, The 188 n.83
dying of the light 165–7
dysco-pia 72, 111, 122

Eagleton, Terry 220 n.69
Eco, Umberto 122
Ecstasy (Welsh) 6, 40, 46, 48–52, 80, 83, 104, 139, 160
   music as signifier of taste in 89–97
The Ecstasy Club (Rushkoff) 6, 89
Edison, Thomas 24
EDMC. *See* Electronic Dance Music Culture (EDMC)
1876 (Vidal) 60
808 State 24, 25, 199 n.79
Electric Circus 115
Electric Kool Aid Acid Test (Wolfe) 66
electronic dance music 22, 26, 34, 51, 62, 79, 82, 105, 107, 114, 140, 148, 159, 160, 162, 163, 165, 176

Electronic Dance Music Culture
    (EDMC)   3, 14, 16, 17, 19, 26,
    99, 133, 143, 155, 157, 162–5,
    168–70
  evolution of   33
  in popular culture media,
    re/presentations of   39–60
  scholarship   1, 2
electronic technology   21–6
'Electrovoodoo' (de Abaitua)   67
Ellis, Brett Easton   92
Ellroy, James   153
Empire   208 n.77
EMU   22
Emulator Sampler   22
enculturation   5, 9, 28, 40–2, 45, 52,
    59–61, 105, 156, 160
  contemporaneous   161–2
Energy Flash (Reynolds)   72, 184 n.20
Entertainments (Increased Penalties) Act
    of 1990   36
Eshun, Kodwo   23, 163
Essays on Literature and Music (Scher)   7
'Essentials of Spontaneous Prose'
    (Kerouac)   107
Evening Standard   70
*Everybody in the Place: An Incomplete
    History of Britain 1984–1992*
    (Deller)   165
'Everybody Needs a 303' (Fatboy
    Slim)   23
'Express Yourself' (Morrison)   189 n.103

Fabio   67
The Face   40, 54, 59, 62, 161, 162
fact and fiction, friction between   59–60
Factory   31, 188 nn.82, 83, 208 n.73
  cataloguing system   29, 164, 188 n.71,
    215 n.79
  Records   31, 82, 136, 164, 184 n.22,
    188 n.77, 200 n.114, 214 n.73,
    215 n.84
Falling Out of Cars (Noon)   112
Family Guy   41
Farm   199 n.79
Farren, Mick   60
Farrugia, Rebekah   122
Fatal Strategies (Baudrillard)   76, 168

Fatboy Slim   23
Faulkner, William   60
Fear and Loathing in America
    (Thompson)   56
Fear and Loathing in Las Vegas
    (Thompson)   55
Fearless, Richard   69
Fernández, José Francisco   86, 87, 135,
    161
fictional ethnography   148
fiction and fact, friction between   59–60
54   46
figurative use of music, in Welsh's
    work   79–106
  beats, rhythms and literary remix   82–5
  carnival and marketplace   86–7
  cultural elevation and cult club
    fictions   104–6
  Ecstasy, music as signifier of taste
    in   89–97
  'The State of the Party'   87–9
Filth (Welsh)   102
Final Scratch   25
Finitribe   88
Finn, Mickey   67
First Summer of Love   37
Fisher, Mark   26, 39, 142, 164
flat folk culture   171
Fleming, Ian   153
folk culture   90, 106, 170, 171
Fontaine, Seb   25
Forde, Eamonn   58
'Formulary for a New Urbanism'
    (Chtcheglov)   29
Forrest, David   12
Forster, E. M.   91
'Fortune's Always Hiding' (Welsh)   89
Foucault, Michel   19
Frankfurt School   101
Freedom to Party   36, 113
'French Kiss' (Lil Louis)   189 n.105
Frith, Simon   21, 25, 68
Full Circle   67
Full Moon Parties   76
Future Publishing   54

Gallin, D. C.   5, 65
Garage Band   23

Gargani, Adam 220 n.2
Garland, Alex 6, 134, 190 n.139
Gaye, Marvin 23, 95
Gay Village 32, 37, 148, 150, 151, 216 nn.109, 126
generational illiteracy 54–5
Generation Ecstasy (Reynolds) 72, 82, 184 n.20
genre
  barriers 86
  melding 153–7
  music 13, 28, 49, 52, 53, 67–9, 72, 73, 83, 94, 107, 111, 138, 141, 142, 148, 151, 160, 161, 169, 171, 175, 176, 184 n.20, 206 n.3, 207 n.36, 210 n.128, 213 n.25, 220 n.70
Geraghty, Geraldine 65, 161
Gibson, William 111, 113, 123
Gilbert, Jeremy 21, 23
'Gimme Love' (N-SIGN) 103
Ginsberg, Allen 16, 65, 66, 69, 120
Glam Damage 114, 115–16
Glas (Derrida) 73
glitch, *Pixel Juice* 128–9
Glue (Welsh) 6, 80, 83, 85, 97–104, 151
Godard, Jean-Luc 57
'God's Cop' (The Happy Mondays) 150
gonzo journalism 3, 53, 55–8, 60, 66
Gorbman, Claudia 49, 51
Graham, Ben 67
Gramsci, Antonio 14, 209 n.100
Granada Studios 31
Granta 218 n.31
Grasso, Francis 127
Gray, Alasdair 85
Gray, Spalding 75
Greenberg, Clement 172
Gretton, Rob 29
Grim, William E. 8
Gristle, Throbbing 209 n.88
'Groovy Train' (The Farm) 199 n.79
grotesque realism 86, 87, 202 n.54
the *Guardian* 20, 107, 132, 135, 165
Guattari, Félix 31
Guest, Katy 153
GUNchester 32, 137
Gysin, Brion 112, 124

Haden, Uva 28–9
Haden-Guest, Anthony 27, 28, 33
Hall, Charlie 67
Hall, Stuart 11, 39, 163
Hallé, Sir Charles 219 n.57
'Hands of the DJ' (Noon) 122, 123, 129
Hannett, Martin 29
Happy Mondays, The 30, 150, 221 n.25
Haraway, Donna 123
Hardfloor 23
Haslam, Dave 46, 97
hauntology 26–7, 31, 73, 125, 131, 142, 145–6, 164, 210 n.128
Hebdige, Dick 11, 47, 49, 66, 80, 100, 102, 103, 149, 150, 166
hegemonic culture 14, 15, 91, 171
Hellhound Sample, The (Murray) 116
Hellman, John 40, 53, 58
Hendersen, Pat W. 5, 162
Henderson, Sheila 33, 35, 38, 96
Hertz, Eric 7, 84, 92
Hesmondhalgh, David 12, 13, 15
heteroglossia 98, 180, 204 n.140
Heydon, Rob 46–53, 192 n.52, 193 n.54
'Higher State of Consciousness' (Josh Wink) 23
Hindley, Myra 217 n.153
'History of Bop, The' (Kerouac) 128
Hitchcock, Alfred 45
Hitman Records 73
HMV 69, 93, 139
Hodkinson, Paul 13, 14
'Holiday' 30
Holleran, Andrew 1, 2, 14–15, 24, 35, 61, 77
Hollowell, John 40, 53, 56–7, 60
Holmes, David 67
Hornby, Nick 5–6
Howl (Ginsberg) 66
'How Sunshine Star-Traveller Lost His Girlfriend' (Millar) 76
How to Be Good (Hornby) 5–6
Huffington Post, The 71
Hughes, Langston 120
Humphries, Tony 95
Huq, Rupa 19, 35, 38, 55, 81
Hussey, Nick 50, 193 n.76
Hütter, Ralf 23, 122, 129

Huxley, Aldous   21, 82, 98
Hynes, Jessica   44

Ibiza, subterranean club cultures in
    (1990s)   32–3
Ibiza: The Silent Movie (Temple)   191 n.17
Ibiza Uncovered   191 n.17
i-D   54, 59
identity   145–6
i-DJ   54
'Inbetween' (De Abaitua)   67
incidental music   49, 51
'In Defence of Subculture: Young People,
    Leisure and Social Divisions'
    (Shildrick and MacDonald)   13
the *Independent*   57, 68, 153
Inspector Morse   40, 42
Inssomniak   104
intermediality   7–8, 107, 111, 172
    interstellar   200 n.123
    musico-literary   7, 9, 17, 41, 62, 68,
        70, 114, 134, 173, 177
    partial   8
    systematic theory of   167
    total   8
International Association for the Study of
    Popular Music   39
International Publishing
    Corporation   195 n.111
interstellar intermediality   200 n.123
intertextuality   7–8, 76
IPC   54
Irvine Welsh's Ecstasy (Heydon)   40,
    46–8, 80
Is Harry on the Boat? (Butts)   191 n.17
It's All Gone Pete Tong   41

James, James St.   5
Jargon of Authenticity, The (Adorno)   102
Jay, Mike   22
Jefferson, Marshall   69
'Jeff Noon's Literary Manifesto'   107
Jello Salad (Blincoe)   7, 134, 148–53
Jim Giraffe (King)   212 n.9
Jockey Slut   54
Jocks   54
Johnson, Robert   116
Jones, Grace   189 n.98

Joy Division   67, 164, 215 n.105
Junior, Sammy Davis   149

Kakehashi, Ikutaro   186 n.20
'Keep Music Live' campaign   23
Kelly, Ben   29, 146
Ken, Kenny   67
Kerouac, Jack   57, 62, 65, 69, 74, 76, 82,
    96–7, 117, 118, 120, 123, 125,
    147, 169, 170, 204 n.134
    bebop prosody   75, 96
    constructed dialogue   85
    'Essentials of Spontaneous Prose'   107
    'The History of Bop'   128
    and Noon   107, 108, 112
    On the Road   16, 30, 66, 70
    The Subterraneans   16
Kevin & Perry Go Large   41, 59
Kid Creole   72
King, Daren   134
Kiss 102 Radio   194 n.94
Kiss Radio   3, 68, 188 n.70, 218 n.25
Kiss the Sky (Gallin)   5
Kittler, Friedrich   164
knowing field   141
Knowledge   54
Knuckles, Frankie   24, 28, 186 n.37, 187
    n.60
Konspiracy   217 n.144
Kraftwerk   23
Kramer, Lawrence   17
Kristeva, Julia   15, 87, 144
Krivit, Danny   27, 28, 187 n.65
Kureshi, Hanif   6, 145–6

Lacan, Jacques   15, 210 n.113
Lanark (Gray)   85
Lancaster, Sophie   13
'Language of the Marketplace'
    (Bakhtin)   88
Last, James   149
Last Party, The (Haden-Guest)   33
Leal, Ernesto   201 n.28
Leavis, F. R.   77, 135, 171
Lecercle, Jean-Jacques   134, 140, 143, 145
Le Club   27
Leighton, Clare   30, 144
Leonard, Elmore   153

Lettrist International 186 n.38
licensing laws 37
Lincoln 60
literary diegesis, in Blincoe's
    writing 133–57
  acid delirium and casual style
      aesthetic 146–8
  bricks-and-mortar pointillism 143–5
  Disco Biscuits: 'Ardwick Green' 137–9
  genre melding 153–7
  hauntology 145–6
  Jello Salad 148–53
  Manchester Slingback 148–53
  New Puritan generation 134–7
literary remix 82–5
'Literature and Music' 8
LitPop (Carroll) 83, 91
Litt, Toby 134
'Living the Dream' (Welsh) 100
Loben, Carl 83
locations 26–7
Logic Audio 23
London Review of Books 135
'Loose Fit' (Happy Mondays) 30
'Lorraine Goes to Livingston' (Welsh) 89
Louis, Lil 189 n.105
Love Can't Turn Around 104
Lyotard, Jean-François 31

MacDonald, Robert 12, 13, 167
machining the voice 123
McInerney, Lisa 65
MacInnes, Colin 75
McKay, Andy 32, 33
McKay, Mike 32, 189 n.106
McLeod, Kembrew 44, 52
McRobbie, Angela 11
MADchester 30, 32, 137, 164, 181 n.9
magic realism 202 n.62
Mailer, Norman 60
Malbon, Ben 100
Malone, Anthony 35
Manchester, subterranean club cultures in
    (1980s) 29–32
Manchester City Council 30
Manchester Institute of Popular Culture
    (MIPC) 11, 12, 37, 163, 167,
    182 n.12, 189 n.92, 213 n.17

Manchester Slingback (Blincoe) 7, 37,
    133, 134, 146, 148–55, 212 n.5
Manning, Bernard 30
Manson, Scott 57, 195 n.112
Manumission 32, 33, 83, 216 n.109
marketing 47–9, 52, 68, 69, 89, 105, 109,
    137, 167, 179
marketplace 86–7, 88, 90, 102, 106
Massey, Graham 24, 25, 186 n.36
May, Derrick 69
MDMA. *See* methylen-
    edioxymethamphetamine
    (MDMA)
media squared 122
M8 54
Mellor, Chris 54, 58
Melly, George 130
Men Behaving Badly 40, 42, 44, 59
'Mentasm' (Second Phase) 23
Mercury, Freddie 189 n.98
'Metaphorazine' (Noon) 122
metaphorical escape, music as 97–104
methylenedioxymethamphetamine
    (MDMA) 22, 34, 52, 90
Metropolitan University of
    Manchester 11
Middleton, Richard 17, 47, 105, 111,
    129, 162, 164, 169
MIDI. *See* Musical Instrument Digital
    Interface (MIDI)
Millar, Martin 76
Miller, Trevor 6, 43, 85, 198 n.74
  Trip City 7, 9, 61, 69–76, 117–18,
      139, 160, 161, 194–5 n.108
Mingus, Charles 120
Ministry 53, 54
Ministry in Ibiza 54, 56
Ministry of Sound 54
Minogue, Kylie 72
MIPC. *See* Manchester Institute of Popular
    Culture (MIPC)
miscegenation 4
Mistry, Jimi 191 n.17
Mitchell, Julian 42
Mitchell, Tony 124
Mixcloud 198 n.77
Mixmag 3, 40, 48, 53, 54, 56, 57, 59, 64, 68,
    81, 96, 103, 189 n.91, 204 n.143

Monaghan, Nicola 65
Morrison, Van 149
Morse 44, 45, 59
Morvan Callar (Warner) 6
Muggleton, David 81
multivocality 98
Murray, Charles Shaar 116
music, as drug 116–17
Musical Instrument Digital Interface (MIDI) 23
Musicalization of Fiction: A Study in the Theory and History of Intermediality, The (Wolf) 7, 9
musical mechanics, in Noon's fiction 107–32
   avant-garde laboratory 129–32
   cyberfiction and Beat Generation 110–12
   Disco Biscuits: 'DJNA' 112–14
   Needle in the Groove 114–21
   Pixel Juice 121–9
Music and Literature: A Comparison of the Arts (Brown) 7
Musicians' Union 23
Music in Contemporary British Fiction: Listening to the Novel (Smyth) 82
musico-intoxication 116
musico-literary intermediality 7, 9, 17, 41, 62, 68, 70, 114, 134, 173, 177
Music Week 28
Muzik 3, 29, 54, 81, 187 n.67
Mythologies (Barthes) 58

Narrative Arc 43, 44, 47, 98, 138
'The Narrative Nightclub' (Cheeseman and Forrest) 12
narrative pointillism 134, 144, 145, 155
naturalism 5, 6, 134, 138, 139, 144, 145, 149, 155, 213 n.25
   acid 144, 148, 157
   characteristics of 136
Nedeljkov, Nikolina 80, 84, 85, 94, 109, 115, 128, 163
Needle in the Groove (Noon) 6, 74, 107, 126, 131
   genealogy, technology and metaphorphiction 114–18

musico-literary collaboration 118–21
New Journalism 53, 57, 62, 66
New musicology 17
New Order 29
New Puritan Generation 134–7
New Puritan Generation, The (Blincoe) 135
New Puritan Manifesto 132, 134–5, 146
   Clause Seven 139–40
   Clause Six 135
   Point 7 213 n.39
New Society 24
New Statesman 14–15, 166
New York, subterranean club cultures in (1970s) 27–9
New York Times 135
NME 215 n.105
Noise (Attali) 22, 24
non-diegetic music 49, 199 n.90
Noon, Jeff 6–8, 25, 38, 43, 66, 82–4, 86, 94, 105, 135–7, 141, 150, 159, 160, 164, 206 n.15, 208 n.71, 212 n.2
   Automated Alice 109
   Channel SK1N 130
   Cobralingus 108, 118, 143
   combative stance against Blincoe's New Puritan Project 133
   Falling Out of Cars 112
   fiction, musical mechanics in 107–32
   Needle in the Groove 6, 74, 107, 114–21, 126, 131
   Nymphomation 110
   'Pixel Dub Juice' 108
   Pixel Juice 6, 107, 114, 121–9, 131
   Pollen 68–9, 109
   'Scorched Out for Love' 114, 121
   Vurt 109
northern noir 153–7
'Not Forgotten' (Leftfield) 199 n.79
Nothing Here Now but the Recordings 118
N-SIGN 98–100, 102, 103
Nye, Sean 45
Nymphomation (Noon) 110

Oakenfold, Paul 25, 209 n.88
Oasis 95

the *Observer* 153
Ondine 27
One Week to Live 54
'On the B-Side' (Noon) 107
On the Road (Kerouac) 16, 30, 66, 70
Orb, the 95
organic technology 21–6
'Orgmentations' (Noon) 122, 127
Orwell, George 87
Owen, David 135
Owen, Frank 6

'Pacific State' (808 State) 199 n.79
panopticon 19
Park, Christopher 190 n.123
Park, Graeme 28, 31, 46, 52, 58, 192 nn.46, 48
Pater, Walter 124, 159
Pay Party 36
Pearson, Ewan 21, 23
Pearson, Lawrence 111
Pegg, Simon 44, 45
Penman, Ian 142
Perfume Sword 122–3
Perry, Lee Scratch 21
pharmaceutical technology 21–6
Phillips, Dom 37, 44
philology
  definition of 75
  subcultural 156
  subterranean 75–7, 163
Philosophy through the Looking Glass: Language, Nonsense, Desire (Lecercle) 134, 140
Phuture 23, 72
Pickering, Mike 30, 46, 192 n.48
'Piece of Clay' (Gaye) 95
'Pixel Dub Juice' (Noon) 108
Pixel Juice (Noon) 6, 107, 114, 131
  cyborg machines and mechanics of music 121–4
  DJ techniques in 124–9
  dub 126–7
  glitch 128–9
  remix 125–6
  scratching 127
  segueway 127–8
'Planet Rock' (Bambaataa) 23

pointillism 157
  bricks-and-mortar 143–5
  narrative 134, 144, 145, 155
politics of dancing 33–7
The Politics of Dancing 190 nn.118, 128
Pollen (Noon) 68–9, 109
polyphony 97, 98, 112, 117
Popular Music 8, 111
post-rave fragment 31
post-subcultural theory 14
  scenes, tribes and 12–13
Powell, Steve 109
Pride and Prejudice and Zombies (Steers) 206 n.3
Priest, Hannah 111
Primal Scream 95
Prince, Dan 55
Prince, Tony 54, 55
print media, re/presentation of EDMC in 53–9
Problems of Dostoyevsky's Poetics (Bakhtin) 117
Prodigy 23
PSV 142, 214 n.73
psychic nomadism 31
psychogeographic locus, dancefloor as 26–7
psychogeography 26, 108
Pubic Lice 83
Puff Daddy. *See* Coombs, Sean
pulp fiction 134, 140, 153–7, 257 n.154
The Pure 95
Pynchon, Thomas 43

Rabelais, François 86, 101, 106
Rabelais and His World (Bakhtin) 86
Raise Your Hands (Geraghty) 65
Rajan, Amol 57
Rapture TV 3
readership communities 90
Reading Pop (Middleton) 17, 62, 162
'Rebel Energy: The Return of Rave Culture' 166
record library 27
Record Store Day 25

Redhead, Steve   12, 66, 86–7, 89, 90, 103, 145, 147, 163, 166, 167, 172–3, 181 n.4, 182 n.12, 197 n.5, 213 n.17
   conversation with Noon   108–9, 122
   death of   11
   on friction between fact and fiction, 60
   literary remix   83, 85
   and repetitive beat literature   162
   Repetitive Beat Generation   6, 40, 65, 80, 81, 106–9, 171
   on re/presentation of EDMC   47, 53, 55
   and subcultural chain   15
   Subculture to Clubcultures   161
Reed, Lou   217 n.160
Regine's   27
Relevance Theory   55–6
remix   7, 107, 115–17, 128
   cyberfiction   111, 112
   literary   82–5
   'Pixel Dub Juice'   108
   Pixel Juice   125–6
   Trip City   71
Repetitive Beat Generation (Redhead)   6, 40, 65, 80, 81, 106–9, 171
repetitive beat literature   162
Representation: Cultural Representations and Signifying Practice (Hall)   39
re/presentation of EDMC   39–60
   cinema   45–53
   fact and fiction, friction between   59–60
   print media   53–9
   TV   42–5
retro-participant observation   3
Revolt into Style (Melly)   130
Revox B77, 26
Reynolds, Simon   19, 31, 35, 36, 72, 81, 87, 100, 173
Rhythim Is Rhythim   199 n.79
"Rhythm of Life" (Junior)   149
Rich, Richie   30
Rietveld, Hillegonda   100
Road of Excess: A History of Writers on Drugs, The (Boon)   82, 105
Robinson, Lisa   27

Rock around the Clock   45
Rock's Backpages   196 n.147
Roessner, Jeffrey   7, 84, 92
Roland   23, 24, 186 n.20
Rolling Stone (Bangs)   16, 55, 64
rootless cosmopolitanism   31
Roussel, Raymond   144
Royal Northern College of Music   169, 219 n.57
Royle, Freddy   89
Rubell, Steve   28, 33
Rushkoff, Douglas   6, 89, 161
Russell Club   214 n.73
Ryder, Shaun   184 n.29, 221 n.25

'Salsa House' (Rich)   30
Sanchez, Roger   95
Sandvoss, Cornel   141
'Sangria' (Brook)   66, 67
Sankeys Soap   83
Sartre, Jean-Paul   82
Saturday Night Fever (Badham)   20, 34, 187 n.66
Saussure, Ferdinand de   47, 55, 141
Savage, Jon   23
saved night, archival function of   162–5
Savile, Jimmy   89
scene theory   14, 15, 26, 27
Scher, Steven Paul   7, 8, 114, 159
'Scorched Out for Love' (Noon)   114, 121
scratching, *Pixel Juice*   127
secondary artistic phenomena   162
Second Phase   23
Second Summer of Love   3, 4, 9, 16, 35, 74, 160, 181 n.5
segueway, *Pixel Juice*   127–8
Serato   25, 26
7   54
'Sexual Healing' (Gaye)   23
Shapiro, Harry   35, 81, 170, 221 n.24
Shephard, Richard   72, 81, 89, 105, 156, 162, 170, 171
Shepheard's   27
Shildrick, Tracy   12, 13, 167
Shoom   67
Shrager, Ian   28, 33
Shulgin, Alexander   22
Simpson, Gerald   71

Sinclair, Adam 51
Sisters of Transistors 25
Situationist International Manifesto 29
Situationists 31, 164, 208 n.62
Skinvader 122
Skrufff, Jonty 57
Sleaze Nation 54, 117
Smash Hits 41
Smith, Andreas Whittam 57
Smith, Craig 95
Smyth, Gerry 8, 70–1, 82, 83, 85, 91, 94, 125, 141, 148, 150–2, 155, 171–2
social realism 5, 86, 136, 139, 213 n.25
Sontag, Susan 100
Sound Effects 68
Spaced 40, 44
spectacular subculture 11–12, 165–7
Spectes of Marx (Derrida) 210 n.128
Spectrum 67
Spiral Tribe 38
Stairway 13 83
'Starman' (Bowie) 125
'State of the Party, The' (Welsh) 80, 87–9
Steers, Burr 206 n.3
Steinberg's Cubase Audio 23
Sterling, Bruce 111
Stonewall Inn 190 n.123
Straw, Will 13, 19
Street, John 8
Stringer, Graham 30
'Strings of Life' (Rhythim is Rhythim) 199 n.79
Studio 54 27, 28, 30, 32, 33, 46, 189 n.98
subcultural capital 29, 47, 68, 83, 89, 92, 95, 98, 99, 151, 152, 162, 175
subcultural chain 15
'Subcultures, Scenes or Tribes? None of the above' (Hesmondhalgh) 13
Subcultures Network 13
Subculture: The Meaning of Style (Hebdige) 100
subculture theory 12, 26
Subculture to Clubcultures (Redhead) 161
subterranean club cultures, global roots of 19–38

1970s New York 27–9
1980s Manchester 29–32
1990s Ibiza 32–3
club, as carnival 37–8
locations 26–7
organic, electronic, pharmaceutical technologies 21–6
politics of dancing 33–7
subterranean continuum 15–17
subterranean culture 13–15. *See also* subterranean club cultures, global roots of
subterranean lifecycle model 15–17
subterranean philology 75–7, 163
The Subterraneans (Kerouac) 16
subterranean systems theory 167–70
the *Sun* 54
Sunday Social 213 n.34
Sunrise 67
'Superfly Guy' 72
Super Nature 67
Superstar DJs, Here We Go (Phillips) 44
'Superstition' 72
surrealism/surreality 87, 91, 110
Sutherland, Andrew 35
Sweet Harmony: Rave Today exhibition, London Saatchi Gallery (2019) 166

tabloid newspapers 30
Take That 95
Tarrantino, Quentin 154
Taste 67
taxonomy, of music uses in Dancefloor-Driven Literature 8–9
Taylor, Steven 120
TAZ. *See* Temporary Autonomous Zone (TAZ)
TB model 23
T-Coy 30
Technics 24–5, 127, 159
Temple, Julien 191 n.17
'Temple of the Sun' 31
Temporary Autonomous Zone (TAZ) 1, 19, 27, 32, 37, 59, 96, 135
textual determinism 84
thalidomide 89, 202 n.80

Index

Thompson, Hunter S.   16, 55, 57, 60, 62, 75, 76, 82, 108, 117, 123, 147, 163, 170, 204 n.134
Thorn, Tracey   14
Thorne, Matt   134
Thornton, Sarah   12, 20, 47, 54, 80, 92, 98, 151, 162, 168, 171
the *Times*   68
Todd, Neil   34
Tony Wilson Place   31
Toop, David   118, 119, 121
'Tower of Power'   185 n.4
Trainspotting (Welsh)   47, 48, 66, 75, 80, 84, 87, 98, 101, 109
Traktor   25, 26
Transformer (Reed)   217 n.160
Transpontine, Neil   161
Travolta, John   20
'Tribal Rites of the New Saturday Night' (Cohn)   20
Tricky   142
Trip City (Miller)   7, 9, 61, 69–76, 117–18, 139, 160, 161, 194–5 n.108
TR model   23
Truffaut, François   57
TV, re/presentation of EDMC in   42–5
24 Hour Party People (Winterbottom)   31, 41, 46
Twisted Wheel   138
'Two Fingers' (Puff)   68

'The Undefeated' (Welsh)   52, 80, 89, 90, 92, 95–7
Unholy Trinity   16–17, 22, 116, 117, 164, 168, 169
University of Birmingham   11
University of Chester   2

Vanity Fair (Robinson)   27
verisimilitude   6, 52, 95, 109, 114, 136, 140, 144, 150, 152, 157
    architectural   46
    discursive analysis of   134
    naturalistic   67
Vidal, Gore   60
the *Village Voice* (Bangs)   16
Visit to Cambodia (Gray)   75

Vurt (Noon)   109
vurtuality   109

Waiting for the Man (Shapiro)   81
Walton, Stuart   36, 37
Warhol, Andy   29
Warner, Alan   6, 60, 67, 163
Waterstones bookstore   3, 109, 139
Wax   54
Weatherall, Andrew   67, 69, 95, 121, 201 n.28
Webster Hall, New York   187 n.46
We Call It Acieed (D-Mob)   83, 104
Weekender   47
Weingarten, Marc   40, 53
Welsh, Irvine   8, 23, 107, 108, 113, 117, 120, 125, 131, 135–7, 139, 145, 155, 159, 160, 162, 164, 170, 172, 182 n.25, 192 n.52, 194 n.108, 201 n.28, 204 n.143
    The Acid House   6, 63, 89
    Dead Men's Trousers   98
    Filth   102
    Glue   6, 80, 83, 85, 97–104, 151
    'Living the Dream'   100
    'Lorraine Goes to Livingston'   89
    on politics of dancing   35
    on re/presentation of EDMC   57, 58
    'The State of the Party'   80, 87–9
    Trainspotting   47, 48, 66, 75, 80, 84, 87, 98, 101, 109
    work, figurative use of music in   79–106
Wenaus, Andrew   112, 130, 131
West, Geoffrey   220 n.58
Whiteley, Sheila   87, 169
Wigan Casino   138
Wilde, Oscar   76, 154, 156, 168
Wilson, Anthony H.   29, 31, 145, 164, 215 n.89
Wilson, Greg   25–6
Wilson, Tony   75
Wink, Josh   23
Winterbottom, Michael   31, 46
Withers, Bill   72
Wolf, Werner   7, 9, 39, 76, 97, 124, 159, 164, 167, 172

Wolfe, Tom 66, 101, 114, 168
Womack, Bobby 95
Woman's Own (Thatcher) 35
'Word and Music Studies' 7
Worley, Matthew 13
Woundings (Noon) 109

Write in Tune (Hertz and Roessner) 7, 92, 94–5
Wynne, Derek 11

Yu, Jonathan 123

Zuum 115

www.ingramcontent.com/pod-product-compliance
Lightning Source LLC
Chambersburg PA
CBHW072138290426
44111CB00012B/1910